—

TENZING

ALSO BY ED DOUGLAS

Chomolungma Sings the Blues

Regions of the Heart:
The Triumph and Tragedy of Alison Hargreaves
with David Rose

Hero of Everest

TENZING

A BIOGRAPHY OF TENZING NORGAY

Ed Douglas

NATIONAL GEOGRAPHIC

WASHINGTON, D.C.

For Andy

Published by the National Geographic Society

Copyright © 2003 Ed Douglas
First Printing, March 2003
Softcover edition, March 2004

Printed in U.S.A.
Design by Melissa Farris

Library of Congress Cataloging-in-Publication Data

Douglas, Ed.
   Tenzing: hero of Everest. a biography of Tenzing Norgay / Ed Douglas.
   p. cm.
   Includes bibliographical references.
   ISBN 0-7922-6983-7, Softcover ISBN 0-7922-6557-2
   1. Tenzing Norkey, 1914- 2. Mountaineers--India--Biography. 3.
Mountaineers--Nepal--Biography. 4. Sherpa (Nepalese people)--Biography. 5. Everest,
Mount (China and Nepal) I. Title.

GV199.92.T46D68 2003
795.51'092--dc21
   [B]

                                                                        2002033802

One of the world's largest nonprofit scientific and educational organizations, the National Geographic Society
was founded in 1888 "for the increase and diffusion of geographic knowledge." Fulfilling this mission, the Society
educates and inspires millions every day through its magazines, books, television programs, videos, maps and
atlases, research grants, the National Geographic Bee, teacher workshops, and innovative classroom materials.
The Society is supported through membership dues, charitable gifts, and income from the sale of its educational
products. This support is vital to National Geographic's mission to increase global understanding and promote
conservation of our planet through exploration, research, and education.

For more information, please call 1-800-NGS LINE (647-5463) or write to the following address:

National Geographic Society
1145 17th Street N.W.
Washington, D.C. 20036-4688 U.S.A.

Visit the Society's Web site at www.nationalgeographic.com.

CONTENTS

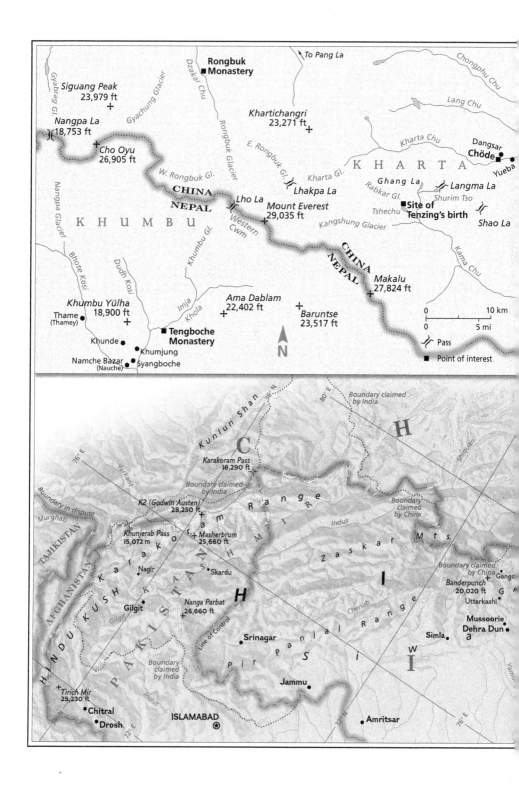

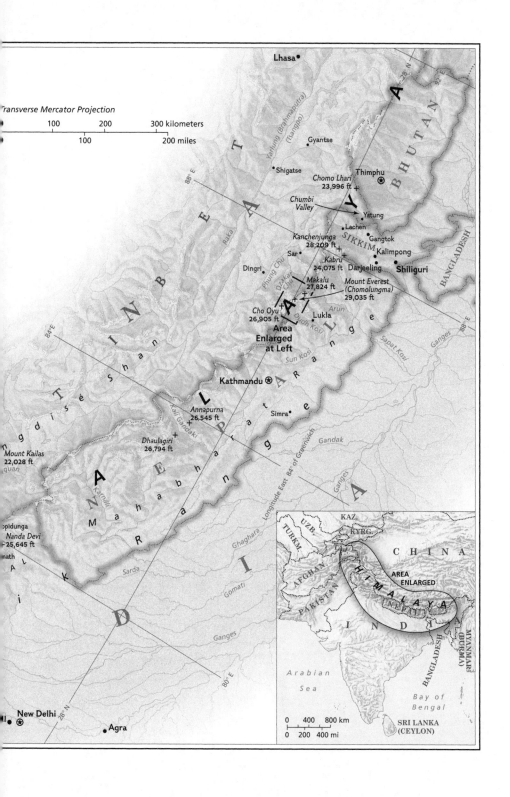

Lhasa●

Transverse Mercator Projection

| 100 | 200 | 300 kilometers |
| 100 | | 200 miles |

Yarlung (Brahmaputra) (Tsangpo)

T I B E T

Gyantse●

●Shigatse

Raka

Chomo Lhari
23,996 ft

Thimphu ⊛

Chumbi
Valley

B H U T A N

●Yatung

L A Y

Kanchenjunga
28,209 ft

●Lachen
Gangtok●

S I K K I M

Kalimpong●

88 E

Sar●

Dzakar

Phung Chu

Dingri●

Kabru
24,075 ft

Darjeeling●
Shiliguri

B H U T A N I N

Makalu
27,824 ft

Mount Everest
(Chomolungma)
29,035 ft

Cho Oyu
26,905 ft

Dudh Kosi

Lukla●

Arun

BANGLADESH

Area
Enlarged
at Left

A

88 E

g

e

Sapat Kosi

Sun Kosi

Kathmandu ⊛

R A N G E

Ganges

Gangdisê Shan

84 E

L

Annapurna
26,545 ft

Simra●

Bharat

Pata

Gandak

Dhaulagiri
26,794 ft

Karnali

Mount Kailas
22,028 ft
quan

N

M

A

E

Mahabhan

R

Ghaghara

I

Gandak

Ganges

opidunga
Nanda Devi
25,645 ft

nath

A L

Sarda

Sarda

Gomati

K

i

D

Ganges

80 E

Longitude East 84° of Greenwich

26 N

New Delhi ⊛

●Agra

Arabian
Sea

UZB.

KAZ.

TURKM.

KYRG.

C H I N A

AFGHAN.

T

HIMALAYA

AREA
ENLARGED

PAKISTAN

NEPAL

I N D I A

Bay of
Bengal

BANGLADESH

MYANMAR
(BURMA)

| 0 | 400 | 800 km |
| 0 | 200 | 400 mi |

SRI LANKA
(CEYLON)

INTRODUCTION

T ENZING NORGAY was one of the first two men to stand upon the summit of the world—with New Zealander Edmund Hillary he reached the top of Mount Everest on May 29, 1953, and became for a few years one of the most famous humans alive.

Hillary took a photograph of him standing on the summit, holding high his flag-bedecked ice ax against a dark blue sky, and this became an icon of the time, familiar around the world. But as Ed Douglas observes in this book, it hardly showed Tenzing at all, so muffled and burdened was his figure in anorak, heavy gloves, snowballs, and oxygen cylinders, and so entirely invisible was his face behind its oxygen mask. It might have been a robot, or a character in space fiction. More to our point, it might have been anybody.

For it seems to me that Tenzing possessed to a remarkable degree the quality of allegory. He always *meant* more than he *was*. He was not exactly larger than life, as so many public heroes are said to be—if anything it might be said that he was smaller, being a light-footed man of exceptional neatness, more like a Puck than an Ajax. He seemed to me, when I first met him in the prime of his young manhood, more like life itself: springy, darting, always eager, never apparently tired.

I did not know then just how symbolic he was. Now I discern for the first time, reading Mr. Douglas's revelatory book, three great allegorical themes to the story of Tenzing—or perhaps four.

WHEN I FIRST MET HIM he was already the most distinguished of all the Sherpas, the people living in the mountain valleys around Everest who had become celebrated as the high-altitude porters of Himalayan climbing expeditions—more than porters, indeed, rather closer to mountain guides of the European kind, and the aristocrats of their calling. Tenzing was already a celebrity, and was not only the sirdar or majordomo, so to speak, of the 1953 Everest expedition, but had proved himself as capable as any European of reaching the ultimate summits. It was significant that he did not climb simply for the money, like most of his compatriots: He was impelled by the authentic mountaineering urge to reach the top of a hill because it was there.

This book makes it clear what an achievement that was in itself. Tenzing was born underprivileged, in a material sense, to a degree almost unimaginable in today's Western societies. He was the son of an itinerant yak herder in the southeastern valleys of Tibet and was probably born in a tent. And if this almost mythologically demanding origin were not enough, even when as a young man he had moved to the marginally more comfortable Sherpa country, he was a second-class citizen as a Tibetan immigrant from the north—not quite the real thing among the intensely clan-conscious Sherpas.

Yet already, when I first met him 50 years ago, he had become a prince among the Sherpas, a star and a cynosure. He had reached this eminence by force of personality, by extreme professionalism, and by an exceptional responsiveness to the world at large. He had mixed easily with foreigners—Britons, Swiss, Frenchmen, and Americans—made friends with many, and readily adopted some of their ways. Although when I first knew him he had never been out of the Indian subcontinent and had never seen the sea, he was already a true cosmopolitan.

ALL THIS, I SEE NOW, was the first allegory of Tenzing—this fable-like emergence from the snowy wastes of Tibet, where the yak herds roamed, to a status of honor among his own people, and among the foreigners who met him. The second allegory is, of course, the arrival of glory. A kind of apotheosis attended Tenzing when he reached the top of Mount Everest in 1953. It was as though a halo had settled on him. He was not merely the most celebrated of all mountaineers, one of the most famous of all adventurers, up there with the great explorers of the past: He was a man out of another world, the new world of a renascent Asia. He rode above the petty jealousies, personal, political, and national, which fell upon upon him the minute he returned from Everest, and seemed to face the world at large with a grand serenity. Nobody had known anyone quite like him before. Wherever he went in those years of his blazing celebrity, he was treated as a being fabulous in himself—like some marvelous unicorn, perhaps, or an elegant creature of the snows.

I dare say there will never be quite such a phenomenon again. Brilliant people out of Asia are commonplace now, and Himalayan valleys do not seem so remote as they did half a century ago. Then Tenzing seemed to most people sui generis, and I always remember the old English gentleman who, observing Tenzing in the full flush of his splendor at an official banquet in London, remarked to me how good it was to see that Mr. Tenzing knew a decent claret when he had one.

YET IN ALLEGORY AS IN ALL ELSE, pride really does precede a fall. Tenzing never did fall from grace, or perhaps from pride either, but the last part of his life was a story of decline. Perhaps it was inevitable. Age crept in, of course, weakening the feline grace of the man, and with it came ill health. His family affairs grew complex. His fame began to fade, and with it his confidence. In his last years, Douglas tells us, he was plagued by depression—the very last condition I would ever have associated with Tenzing when I saw him bounding down the mountain at his moment of triumph.

But here perhaps is that fourth, last allegory. In all his years, of hardship and success, of fame and obscurity, of magnificent strength and debilitating old age, Tenzing seems to have remained essentially himself. He seldom let himself down. He looked fortune (and history) in the eye, and remained a man for a' that.

Kipling, then, would have been a better person than I am to write an introduction to this book, or perhaps Robbie Burns; but nobody could have written its text with more perception and sensitivity than Ed Douglas, a distinguished mountaineer himself, to give the old champion a worthy and permanent literary memorial.

–JAN MORRIS
NOVEMBER 2002

BEHIND THE MASK

I have never regarded myself as much of a hero
but Tenzing, I believe, undoubtedly was.
From humble beginnings
he had achieved the summit of the world.
— SIR EDMUND HILLARY, JUNE 1997

ON MAY 29, 1953, at around half past eleven in the morning, two men climbed to the summit of Everest for the first time in history. Only one of them, however, would be photographed standing on it. Before reaching for his camera, Edmund Hillary, relieved that the "long grind" of the ascent was over, had extended his hand to Tenzing Norgay "in good Anglo-Saxon fashion." Tenzing was more effusive, putting an arm around Hillary's shoulders and thumping him on the back with infectious delight. Hillary joined in and soon, Tenzing recalled, the two men were out of breath, despite their oxygen sets. In Tenzing's account of their climb, the two men then spent time looking about them, at the other huge mountains—Lhotse, Makalu, Kanchenjunga—now all below them, as well as the valleys where Tenzing had grown up. "It was such a sight as I had never seen before," he said, "and would never see again—wild, wonderful, and terrible. But terror was not what I felt. I loved the mountains too well for that. I loved Everest too well. At that great moment for which I had waited all my life my mountain did not seem to me a lifeless thing of rock and ice, but warm and friendly and living."

Hillary, on the other hand, was preoccupied by more practical matters. Of the moments following their embrace, he wrote: "But we had no time to waste!" Slipping off his oxygen set and breathing hard on what thin air there is at the summit of the world, Hillary took his camera out of his windproof pocket, clipped on its lens hood and an ultraviolet filter, and shuffled a few steps back down the ridge they had recently climbed. Tenzing unfurled four flags that had been wrapped around his ice ax, those of the United Nations, Britain, Nepal, and India, and then lifted the ax above his head. Hillary took three shots, one of which would soon be on the front page of newspapers and magazines around the world.

Tenzing said that he motioned to Hillary to give him the camera so he could take a picture of him as well in their shared moment of triumph, but Hillary shook his head. "I didn't worry about getting Tenzing to take a photograph of me—as far as I knew, he had never taken a photograph before and the summit of Everest was hardly the place to show him how." Some climbers might have taken a chance on Tenzing's getting lucky. Instead Hillary returned to the summit and started making a photographic record of its panorama.

And so the only image we have of this unique event is of Tenzing Norgay. Hillary knew it was a good shot. "Clad in all his bulky equipment and with the flags flapping furiously in the wind, he made a dramatic picture, and the thought drifted through my mind that this photograph should be a good one if it came out at all." The choice of the word *drifted* seems curious, but without his bottled oxygen, Hillary had entered a dream state induced by severe hypoxia. When he came to put his camera away a few minutes later, he found his fingers had become "doubly clumsy," and he realized with a start that he was losing control and should turn his oxygen set back on. The famous photograph he took captures his sense of unreality, an altered state of consciousness, of being somehow of another world. The sky above the summit darkens quickly into near blackness, giving the false impression that the edge of space lies just above Tenzing's head. The flags whip around his raised ice ax in the strong wind, and he grips the thin cord he had used to secure them in his left hand to prevent that from flailing around as well. His left leg is planted on the uphill slope, close to the very apex of the mountain, giving the figure a dynamic appeal, his legs sturdier in their thick layers of clothing.

This photograph records the triumph of human achievement on the limits of the possible. Somewhere below them on the North Ridge, Hillary and Tenzing both knew, were the bodies of George Mallory and Andrew Irvine, who had disappeared in 1924. Thirteen men had died on 11 previous expeditions of one form or another. It's not surprising that this photograph quickly became one of the iconic images of the 20th century. More so than any photograph from the expeditions to the Poles, the picture of Tenzing expresses the instinct in all of us to explore, to test boundaries, to reach goals. It might be a modern activity, but climbing mountains matches some ancient impulse in those who pursue it, the metaphorical summit realized by an actual summit.

Everest has always been, to Western climbers especially, nothing so much as a gigantic mirror. In recent years it has reflected the West's consumeristic and competitive nature, the wealthy seeking a physical challenge to illustrate their success elsewhere or professional adventurers following their own version of the rat race. It was a different world on May 29, 1953, more innocent in some ways than our own, in others vastly more experienced. Memories of the horrors of World War II, and the triumph against fascism, were fresh. Dwight D. Eisenhower had just moved into the White House. The Korean War was drawing to an uneasy close, Stalin had died in March, and both the Americans and the Russians were rushing to perfect their hydrogen bombs. *Time* magazine's Man of the Year for 1953 was Konrad Adenauer, the chancellor of West Germany, for his role in returning self-respect and confidence to his countrymen, while in East Berlin students armed with stones took on Soviet army tanks. Postwar excitement was congealing into Cold War certainties.

On the other hand, discovery and exploration were everywhere. Shortly before Tenzing and Hillary's historic climb, Francis Crick and James Watson announced their discovery of the structure of deoxyribonucleic acid, or DNA, the blueprint of life. That summer Chuck Yeager smashed the world airspeed record by flying his Bell X-1A aircraft at two and a half times the speed of sound. Of the Everest ascent itself, *Time* magazine concluded: "In this feat of the New Zealand beekeeper, Edmund Hillary, and the sinewy Sherpa tribesman, Tenzing, millions down in the mundane valleys felt a vicarious exhilaration—the reminder that by valour and dedication man may surmount his Everests."

The optimism and triumph encapsulated in Hillary's photograph was felt nowhere more strongly than in Britain. It was, after all, a British expedition that had put men of, as the *News Chronicle* phrased it, "British blood and breed" on the summit. This great success coincided with the coronation of a new monarch, Elizabeth II, adding to the sense of renewal, a fresh era in a weary nation's long history. It was, as the *News Chronicle* suggested in its headline, "The Crowning Glory."

India, where Tenzing had lived for the previous quarter of a century, was also remaking itself under the leadership of Jawaharlal Nehru, released from its recent colonial history, and Tenzing's success was another brick in the process of nation building.

The one jarring feature of Hillary's photograph is the masked face of Tenzing. His raised right arm has twisted his windproof hood so that at first glance it appears as though Tenzing is looking down to his left. In fact his goggled eyes and oxygen mask are directed squarely at the lens. Hillary wrote that despite these encumbrances, "there was no disguising his infectious grin of pure delight as he looked all around him." But in the photograph Tenzing's face is completely hidden and the figure is anonymous. There is none of the Sherpa's joy or sensitivity in this photograph. Perhaps this has made it easier for the image itself to be adopted as an icon of the triumph of the human spirit, precisely because the figure standing on the summit could be any of us.

Of course, there are plenty of pictures of Tenzing without an oxygen mask on, and in many of them he is smiling. He had a dazzling smile, warm and open, promising integrity. He was unfailingly polite, when he became famous, to the unceasing demands of the public. And if he was famous in the West, then in Asia, where Tenzing was worshipped by some as an incarnation of Shiva, the pressure of fame was even more intense. Tenzing's origins were poor and obscure, and yet he achieved global stature. His self-confident pose on top of Everest held a particular message for other Asians: Their moment had come.

For the Sherpas who had migrated to Darjeeling to work with climbing expeditions, smiling and being good-natured were part of the job. European and American climbers forged a remarkable partnership with them in exploring the Himalaya before the war. The "sahibs" provided the ambition, resources, and skill; the Sherpas provided local knowledge and skilled labor. Yet it was their character that quickly made them indispensable.

Sherpas, in most accounts of Western climbers, are usually described in these terms: good-humored, prepared to put up with difficult conditions, loyal. They are also often described as having simple lives. Sherpas have no written form of their language and were, in Tenzing's youth, almost entirely illiterate. Working as farmers and traders and ruled by the seasons rather than the clock, compared with their Western employers Sherpas did seem less sophisticated. But behind the willingness to please was a society as full of jealousies, ambition, and rivalries as our own but made harsher by the threat of sudden illness or disaster. That Tenzing, from the most difficult start imaginable, fought his way to the position where he could even begin climbing Everest was remarkable in itself. His origins were more limiting than any Westerner climbing with him on Everest could guess. Behind the mask of the cheerful conqueror of Everest is another, even greater story, less neat, at times more equivocal and unhappy, but one that only deepens Tenzing's achievement.

CHAPTER ONE

THE SHERPAS OF DARJEELING

On his back a fifty-pound load,
His spine bent double,
Six miles of steepness in the snows of Magh,
Naked bones,
There is two rupees of life in his body
To challenge the mountain.
—LAKSMIPRASAD DEVKOTA, "Sleeping Porter"[1]

I N 1950 THE *Himalayan Journal,* the annual publication of the
Himalayan Club, ran an article about porters and guides available for
hire at Darjeeling.[2] It was intended as an aid for prospective mountaineering
expeditions to choose staff as activity resumed in the Himalaya after the
war and its chaotic aftermath in South Asia. At first glance, it seems a bland
document, but its pages trace the unique story of the Sherpas and their
role in the birth of Himalayan mountaineering. In the history of exploration or adventure, before or since, there has been nothing like it.

The men were needed because of the remoteness of the mountains
being attempted and the weight of high-altitude equipment then in use.
When Tenzing came to Darjeeling in 1932, there were few roads in the
eastern Himalaya and no aircraft flying into remote strips to ferry supplies. Early Everest expeditions were modeled on the attempts to reach
the South Pole, a series of camps and equipment dumps building toward
a final launching pad from which the summit could be reached in a day.

There were six camps on the north side of Everest before the war, and each one required tents, stoves, sleeping bags, food, and so forth. In the 1920s this equipment was made from heavy natural fabrics. In the 1950s oxygen sets weighed 30 pounds. (Now a titanium oxygen bottle weighs 6 pounds and a tent even less.) On lower peaks, many climbers now prefer not to use Sherpas or high-altitude porters at all, partly from not wishing to risk their lives, but more because the ethic of Himalayan climbing more closely matches that in the Alps. The one exception, still, is on Everest where the Sherpas remain crucial in carrying loads and supporting often weaker climbs. At the start of Himalayan climbing, Western climbers needed lots of porters to get their supplies to Base Camp, and then a further few to carry loads on the mountain itself. The latter became semiskilled climbers, used to carrying heavy loads of tents, supplies, and oxygen to high camps. These were the men listed in the *Himalayan Journal.*

The author was Ludwig Krenek, the Himalayan Club's local secretary. Krenek presented the information as a table, listing each porter's number, name, date of birth, and expedition experience. All 175 porters included in the Himalayan Club's records before the outbreak of World War II and from the few expeditions in the late 1940s appear on the list. All of the men were either Sherpas from Solu Khumbu or Bhotias—Tibetans—who had also migrated to Darjeeling. Krenek writes, "Of the 175 porters mentioned 51 have died and 24 were killed in the mountains. Twenty-nine, still fit for mountaineering, are at present available in Darjeeling."[3] Most of these men who perished were in their 20s and 30s. Life as a porter, on or off the mountain, was fragile and uncertain.

Krenek added a comment after each entry about the man's experience, or how he died if known, or where he was. Behind the cool brevity of these notes is the life story of an individual. The entry for No. 18, Ila Kitar, lacks a date of birth but records that he worked on the German attempts on Kanchenjunga beginning in 1929, and also on the British expeditions to Everest in 1935 and 1936. He spent a lifetime roaming the Himalaya with barely enough to eat and hardly any money in his pocket. In Darjeeling he would have lived in a shack, maybe pulled a rickshaw or cut wood when there were no expeditions to go on. Krenek records, "Now at Sola Khumbu," and the waters of history close above Ila Kitar's head.

Nukku (No. 70) was born in 1910. In 1937 he went to the Shaksgam in the northern Karakoram, then largely unexplored, with Eric Shipton and Bill Tilman. Michael Spender, the poet Stephen's brother, was surveyor; J. B. Auden, brother of W. H. Auden, the expedition's geologist. They crossed Francis Younghusband's Aghil Pass and roamed across the Surukwat Basin, filling in blanks on the map as they went. Nukku died in the Assam Himalaya of cerebral malaria in 1939 while exploring with Tilman.

Pasang Phutar (No. 79), Krenek tells us, "lost seven fingers on Masherbrum [in the Karakoram], now has heart trouble. No longer fit." He received compensation of 10 rupees per finger, 70 in all, and had to fight even for that. Another Sherpa became a policeman in Calcutta, a third had a business in Lhasa, a fourth was working as a "rickshaw coolie." Often the only comment is: "Died, date unknown." A few of the men have prospered, and their lives are better known. Ang Tharkay (No. 19) is described as "very likely the best and most experienced Sherpa now working. Highly praised." (Tilman described Ang Tharkay as "a sort of Jeeves, Admirable Crichton, and Napoleon rolled into one," adding that "his stews and curries have always been masterpieces.") Dawa Thondup,[4] a friend of Tenzing's from his days in Nepal, is also singled out: "Though rather old [he was 43 at the time and would climb into his 60s], he is still really excellent. He reached the summit of Abi Gamin in 1950. Order of German Red Cross." By then Dawa Thondup had climbed on Everest twice, and on K2, the world's second highest mountain, in 1939. He was on Masherbrum with the British when Pasang Phutar lost his fingers, had been to the Garhwal in India three times, to Nanga Parbat for the bitter tragedy of 1934, and on and on—it is a climbing record of epic proportions. An asterisk appears against the names of both Ang Tharkay and Dawa Thondup, indicating that the Himalayan Club considered them to be among the best men still available. Only 8 of these names out of 175 are marked. Tenzing's is one of them.

The story of the Sherpas is extraordinary but even now hardly known. Like the early bluesmen of New Orleans, or European fishermen on the Grand Banks off Newfoundland in the 15th century, these men were a close-knit group breaking new ground. They didn't become wealthy, and few became well known, even within the world of mountaineering. How did this tiny group of a few dozen men come to be chosen in the first place? Why Darjeeling? And how did they become so quickly praised and valued by the early mountain explorers and climbers? The reasons are intertwined with the history of the British Raj and the influence of a handful of mostly British mountaineers.

At the start of the 19th century, Darjeeling—or Dorje Ling in Tibetan, the place of thunderbolts—was a little-known part of Sikkim. When the British defeated the Gorkhali Shah dynasty in Nepal in 1816, a large part of Sikkim was ceded to the East India Company. As early as 1828, an army report[5] identified Darjeeling, on a heavily wooded hill, as an excellent location for a sanatorium, high above the heat and malaria of the Terai, and tea plantations were established in the early 1840s, although not until the mid-1860s did the hill station's development begin to accelerate.

Located between Bhutan and Nepal to the east and west, Jalpaiguri and Calcutta to the south, and Sikkim and Tibet to the north, Darjeeling quickly became an important trading center, filled with different tribes from all over the eastern Himalaya. The indefatigable L. S. S. O'Malley of the Indian Civil Service, who wrote the 1907 gazetteer to Darjeeling, recorded the town's cosmopolitan excitement in his description of the bazaar:

" … ugly enough in itself with its closely packed huts and shops, but of interest on account of the medley of races found in it. Here may be seen sleek, black-bearded Marwaris, sitting in their cloth shops and perpetually conning mysterious account-books, before a little wooden door concealing the shrine of their favourite god Ganesh; specious smooth-tongued Kashmiri and Punjabi merchants; petty Hindustani shop-keepers from the plains; and a crowd of hill people of various nationalities, such as the brawny Sikkimese Bhotias, the placid Lepchas, and the active and alert Nepalese."[6]

As the forests were cleared and the tea plantations grew, Nepalese were drawn in their thousands by the need for labor, and the population of Darjeeling doubled every decade between the censuses of 1871 and 1901 and continued to grow strongly thereafter.[7] For the British, it was a place for exhausted workers from Calcutta to recuperate and for their families to spend the summer months, in the cooler air at 7,000 feet above sea level.

Amusements, typically of an improving nature, were built: the Botanic Gardens, the Gymkhana Club, the Natural History Museum. The town also developed a reputation as a center for education. St. Paul's School transferred to Darjeeling from Calcutta in 1864, taking an impressive position above the town at Jalapahar, and St. Joseph's College, run by the Jesuits, opened in 1888, moving to the northern part of the station in 1891. There were two girls' schools, the Diocesean was Protestant, whereas the Loreto Convent School was Catholic. (It was at the Loreto Convent that Mother Teresa began her life as a nun in India.) Even before the modern age crushed the town's aesthetic hopes under tons of concrete and a film of smog, Darjeeling was hardly distinguished by its architecture. O'Malley reported drily that "the buildings are all modern and of little interest."[8] One Everest Sherpa, visiting the suburbs of England for the first time, suddenly understood what his hometown was modeled on. Because the town overlooks the Teesta Valley to the east, and to the northwest rises the vast, shimmering bulk of Kanchenjunga, the world's third highest mountain, it became known as the "Queen of the Hills," the most attractive of all the Raj's hill stations.

Trevor Braham, later a distinguished honorary secretary of the Himalayan Club, remembers spending his summers in Darjeeling as a boy. His father was in business in Calcutta, and the family would take a house for the hottest months. They would hire a "coolie" for the whole season to pull their rickshaw. This was the kind of work favored by the Sherpas and Bhotias living in the shantytowns that grew up on the lower slopes of Darjeeling, or in Toong Soong Busti, near the broad square of Chowrasta, just below the Windamere Hotel—one fragment of the empire that has survived into the modern era. "You can't imagine the slums these men lived in during those days," Braham recalled. "Busti means a slum, a shantytown, just ramshackle things put up with bamboo poles and sheets of corrugated iron. They lived under very primitive conditions." Tenzing, nostalgic for his youth, said: "Except for a handful of merchants and traders—most of whom had moved away— we were all dirt poor.... We lived in wooden shacks with tin roofs, with usually a whole family in a single room. Our food was rice and potatoes. Our earnings, even when we were working, were very small, and the only blessing was that our wants were small."[9]

Bhotias—literally people of Bhot, the Sanskrit transliteration of Bod, the Tibetan word for Tibet—had been migrating to Darjeeling for half a century before they started mountaineering work, taking casual jobs as porters and "rickshaw-wallahs," according to historian Kenneth Mason. The 1901 census split them into four categories: Sikkimese Bhotias, descendants of the original Lepchas and Tibetan immigrants; the Sherpas from eastern Nepal; the Drukpas from Bhutan, who were largely confined to the nearby town of Kalimpong; and Tibetans who had migrated down the Chumbi Valley to the north. The 1901 census reported 3,450 Sherpas in Darjeeling district, the most numerous of the four classes but a tiny minority compared with the more than 130,000 Nepalese who were by then living in and around Darjeeling. O'Malley, reporting in Darjeeling's gazetteer, wrote in 1907:

"As a race, the Bhotias have been described as rude, turbulent and quarrelsome, but this seems an unfair estimate of their character. On the whole, they are a merry, cheerful people, quick to enjoy a joke, and most willing workers, not so pushing as the Nepalese, not so law-abiding as the Lepcha. Powerfully built and of great natural strength, they are capable of carrying the heaviest burdens—there is a story current that in the days before the railway a single Bhotia carried a grand piano up the hills to Darjeeling, 50 miles distant and 7,000 feet in elevation. But their natural love of display and an inordinate love of gambling soon dissipate the sums which they can easily earn by labour."[10]

They could drink, too, as Trevor Braham recalls: "During the winter when there was no work they'd drink a lot and I remember as a little boy watching two of these men stone drunk having a fight, slashing at each other, throwing bricks at each other." This kind of behavior, well documented elsewhere, would often be attributed to a lack of "civilization." But then again, Maj. Edward Felix Norton, who climbed to within a few hundred feet of the summit of Everest in 1924, saw the Sherpas as "a childish edition of the British soldier" who is "perpetually a nuisance when drink and the attractions of civilization tempt him astray," but who "often comes out the strongest when 'up against it' in circumstances where the milder man fails." H. W. Tilman, hiring Sherpas for Everest in 1938, said that Rinzing Bhotia, who won a Tiger's Badge for his contribution that year, was a "grand chap once he gets above, not the snow-line, but the beer-line."

Climbers and explorers often projected onto the Sherpas those aspects of character they admired in Europeans, and sometimes robbed them of qualities unfairly to prove European superiority. Bentley Beetham, who was on Everest with Norton in 1924, dismissed the idea that the Sherpas could climb Everest because they lacked the "right mentality." Sir Francis Younghusband, explorer, soldier, and chairman of the Mount Everest Committee, observed that while they had the necessary physical qualities to "reach the summit of Everest any year they liked," they did not do so because they "have not the right spirit," presumably an English sort of spirit. Tenzing himself would subvert Younghusband's view by becoming one of the first two men to climb the mountain. But it wasn't a question of "spirit"—it's obvious that the Sherpas were tough enough mentally—just a question of motivation. For the sahibs, the advantages in reaching the summit of Everest were obvious: fame, prestige, honor, even wealth. Tenzing was the first porter to realize this, and after his climb the summit became a worthwhile objective for Sherpas as well.

What of the men who hired them, the sahibs, or "masters," who put them into such mortal danger? Sherpas now have long experience of climbing in the Himalaya and understand the risks, but in the 1920s glaciers were known purely as a threat. They had no knowledge of climbing on snow and ice and relied heavily on the experience of the European climbers who hired them. Who were these men who believed risking the lives of their porters was worth standing on the summit of a mountain? It's too facile to classify them as upper-class twits. They were certainly privileged and, in the case of the British, almost exclusively part of a social elite, members of the Alpine Club who reacted in horror to the idea of someone "in trade" becoming a member. But just as there were all kinds of Sherpas, the sahibs reflected every political hue from fascism to Marxism, and every social outlook. Some of the climbers were army officers who had absorbed the attitudes of the empire; a few displayed attitudes that today are termed racist. Younghusband, for instance, when he heard that seven Sherpas had died in an avalanche on Everest, wrote to his wife, "Thank goodness no European life was lost." Nor was the issue defined by political views. Charles Howard-Bury, George Mallory's leader on the first Everest expedition in 1921 and politically far more conservative, showed constant interest and admiration for the Tibetans.

Mallory, despite his liberal credentials, thought Tibet "a hateful country inhabited by a hateful people."

Howard Somervell, whose experiences as a surgeon on the Somme in 1916 turned him into a pacifist, accompanied Mallory on Everest in 1924, interrupting his work as a medical missionary in southern India. After the expedition he wrote of his pleasure at arriving back in Darjeeling from the dry plateau of Tibet too early for an official reception by the town's band, "so the official welcome was appropriately enough given to the coolies, who are the chaps who really deserve it."[11] Somervell had strong views on racial tolerance: "East is East and West is West, and the twain *can* and *do* meet; but only on terms of friendship, mutual trust, and mutual understanding."[12] Problems, Somervell believed, arose because the "West usually refuses to take the trouble to get to know the language, thought and life of the East."

H. W. Tilman, leader of the 1938 Everest expedition, would refer to the Sherpas as "blokes" in his diaries, but like his friend Eric Shipton, he developed a lasting devotion to the men he hired. Tilman instituted the system of awarding "Tigers" a badge, a practical advantage in getting work. In 1935, after his expedition to the Nanda Devi Sanctuary, he wrote: "For nearly five months we had lived and climbed together, and the more we saw of them, the more we liked and respected them. That they can climb and carry loads is now taken for granted; but even more valuable assets to our small self-contained party were their cheerful grins, their willing work in camp and on the march, their complete lack of selfishness, their devotion to our service. To be their companion was a delight; to lead them, an honour."[13] And yet, although some of the Sherpas liked and admired Tilman for carrying heavier loads than they did and for mucking in around camp—he would bake them cakes—other Sherpas disliked him. Pasang Phutar, who lost his fingers on Masherbrum, thought him dangerous and irresponsible, and held him responsible for the death of a Sherpa on Nanda Devi in 1936.

A few of the sahibs did see climbing Everest as an expression of the values that built the empire, but others saw it as an escape from those same values, even a subversion of them. The kinds of expedition were widely divergent as well. If the first attempts on Everest were quasi-militaristic affairs conducted by a group of men from a particular social class and with the backing of the establishment, men such as Alexander Kellas were merely dedicated enthusiasts. Kellas, a Scottish doctor working as a chemistry lecturer at the Middlesex Hospital in London, had an interest in the effects of high altitude and a passion for the Himalaya. John Noel would visit Kellas in his laboratory at the Middlesex and later wrote about Kellas's exploratory zeal and good humor. George Mallory told his wife, "I love him already,"[14] when they met at the start of the 1921 Everest Reconnaissance. Kellas died only weeks later after a bout of dysentery left his heart exhausted. His obituary in the *Alpine Journal* described him as having a "most retiring disposition."[15]

Kellas was a great champion of the Sherpas. He had hired Swiss guides in 1907 for his first exploration in Sikkim, but found the experiment a failure, much preferring the Sherpas who came with him as local porters. In an article about his fourth expedition in 1912 he acknowledged their "little foibles"—several Sherpas had disappeared with his money box for a few days—but he could not have praised them more highly:

"Except for the trivial incidents recorded, their behaviour was excellent. By the end of the trip we were all working together most harmoniously. Really they are the most splendid fellows. Of the different types of coolie, the writer has found the Nepalese Sherpas superior to all others. They are strong, good natured if fairly treated, and since they are Buddhists there is no difficulty about special food for them—a point surely in their favour at high altitudes."

The Sherpas had other advocates. Two Norwegian climbers, Carl Wilhelm Rubenson and Monrad Aas, who had reached the summit plateau of the 24,000-foot peak Kabru in the Sikkim Himalaya in 1907,[16] singled them out in the *Alpine Journal* as the best porters available. But it was Kellas more than anyone else who sang their praises. He trusted them so completely that before the Great War he hired Sherpas to return to Nepal, then off-limits to Europeans, and travel up the Arun River into Tibet to photograph Everest from its eastern side.

The Sherpas' ascent was by no means assured at first. The Hon. Charles Granville Bruce was a rambunctious Gurkha officer nicknamed "Bruiser," who liked to wrestle half a dozen of his men at a time and was described by one of his friends as having the energy of "a steam engine plus goods train." Bruce's first Himalayan expedition was in 1892, and almost from then on, for the next 30 years, he was one of the key players in pushing for an expedition to Everest. Bruce used Gurkhas, the troops he knew and admired, on his early expeditions, but they lacked the adaptation of the Bhotias and couldn't tolerate harsh mountain conditions so readily. Two Gurkhas whom Bruce took as leader in 1924, a cobbler called Manbahadur and an NCO called Shamsher, died horribly, the latter of a brain hemorrhage. Manbahadur suffered horrific frostbite and rotted to death with gangrene after his legs thawed.

If Bruce had to admit that the Gurkhas weren't the men for the job, he didn't discriminate between Sherpas and Tibetans, writing all Bhotias were worth hiring because of their strength at altitude. Kenneth Mason, who worked for the Survey of India and was a founder of the Himalayan Club in 1928, explained the differentiation very clearly in *Abode of Snow,* his history of Himalayan climbing, while describing Howard-Bury's preparations for departure to Tibet in 1921:

"He engaged about forty Sherpas and Bhotias at Darjeeling to act as porters for the expedition. Sherpas are of Tibetan stock, born and bred in the uppermost reaches of the Dudh Kosi tributaries, the best of them from villages, such as Namche Bazar, within a few miles of Everest and are accustomed from birth to high altitudes and cold. Bhotias are Tibetans who for much the same reasons come to Sikkim; the best of them also make good porters, and are hardy and reliable if looked after properly."

Charles Howard-Bury also believed Tibetans to be just as good. After hiring Sherpas at Darjeeling in 1921 before leaving on the reconnaissance of Everest, Howard-Bury offered this assessment:

"[The Sherpas] were an especially hardy type of coolie, accustomed to living in a cold climate and at great heights. They proved at times quarrelsome and rather fond of strong drink; they turned out, however, to be a useful and capable kind of man, easily trained in snow and ice work and not afraid of the snow. We later on picked up a few Tibetan coolies in the Chumbi valley and these proved to be as good as the best of the Sherpas."[17]

Howard-Bury's opinion would not count for much. He was a stopgap leader, a nonclimber drafted in to hold the position open for Bruce when a full attempt on the mountain could be made in 1922. He wasn't liked, especially by Mallory, and any opinion held by Howard-Bury would be viewed prejudicially by the next expedition. Mallory, who quickly gave up bothering to learn even rudimentary Tibetan, was often exasperated by the "coolies" but had a clear preference for the Sherpas, viewing the local Tibetans as "notably less strong than our Sherpas."[18] Eventually, in the 1930s, even those porters used just to take loads up the East Rongbuk Glacier would include Sherpas, hired in Khumbu by Darjeeling Sherpas and sent over the Nangpa La in advance of the expedition. Local Tibetan porters were used less and less. In 1921 they were ordered to serve the British by their local dzongpens, or governors, and dared not refuse. By contrast, Sherpa society was freer. They had no obligations to landlords to hold them back. If they came on an expedition, they came of their own free will and for wages. In the long run, this freedom to work and earn as they chose was a crucial advantage.

As Himalayan climbing grew, so did the reputation of the Sherpas, at the expense of other Bhotias. Climbers became familiar with the names of Sherpa villages—Namche Bazar, Khumjung, and Khunde—and believed that Sherpas from Khumbu—as opposed to the lower altitudes of Solu—were the best.

The value of the Sherpa "brand name" wasn't lost on Tibetans. "Many Bhotias would claim to be Sherpas," Dorje Lhatoo said. Lhatoo married Tenzing's niece, and was one of the foremost climbing Sherpas in Darjeeling. "The Sherpas were timid as far as the Tibetans were concerned. The Tibetans could be bullies. They would say that from now on they were Sherpas, and if anyone said otherwise they would kill them." Not literally, of course, but Lhatoo also recalled a saying among Tibetans that roughly translates as "Sherpas are to mankind what lungs are to meat." For their part, the Sherpas have a saying that every Tibetan has two knives, one in his boot, which he can draw quickly to stab you in the stomach, and another in his waistband to stab you in the back when you embrace him. It's a question of perspective. To some, the Tibetans were charismatic and robust; they stood up for themselves whereas the Sherpas did as they were told. To others, the Sherpas were honest and agreeable whereas the Tibetans were aggressive and recalcitrant. Tenzing himself thought this. In one of the few passages cut from the manuscript of his autobiography *Tiger of the Snows*, he says, "Tibetans or Bhotias would often pretend that they were Sherpas so as to get jobs. Bhotias are very quarrelsome and often draw their knives."

"There was that feeling, that competitive element between the two," Trevor Braham recalled. It was a competition that the Sherpas were always likely to win. They had more experience of dealing with Hindus and were more amenable, especially when things went wrong. "A Sherpa will be annoyed but will accept it if you offer him less than he expects," Lhatoo said. "Whereas if you offer a Tibetan less, he will take out his knife." Trevor Braham agreed: "The Sherpas were a superior crew, which is not to say that they didn't have the normal vices of drunkenness and gambling which they all had in Darjeeling." Tenzing sometimes fell between the two communities, according to Lhatoo: "He was the subject of a tug of war. He was pulled from all directions." When Tenzing adopted the name Sherpa after climbing Everest, "the Darjeeling Tibetans were very angry. They said: 'Yesterday he was a Bhotia, now he's a Sherpa.' They called him a traitor."

The Sherpas built their professional reputation deliberately, taking on the high-altitude work on Everest in 1922 to prove themselves tougher and worth more financially than the Tibetan porters. From then on most expedition leaders preferred the Sherpas as porters high on the mountain. Although there were many cases of intermarriage with Tibetans, the Sherpas worked hard to retain their identity and so protect their reputation. As more Sherpas arrived in Darjeeling in the late 1920s and 1930s, inspired by the success of their older cousins and brothers, the percentage of Sherpas working as porters went up too. They became fiercely protective of their name and showed remarkable ingenuity in keeping a closed shop. Over the course of the three attempts on Kanchenjunga beginning in 1929, the Sherpas vigorously defended their position, actually bringing legal action against the paymaster of the 1930 expedition and demanding of Paul Bauer, leader of the 1931 German attempt, that he hire only Sherpas or face their withdrawal.[19] This was the mercantile tradition of the Sherpas shining through; they were friendly, enthusiastic, upbeat, and financially shrewd.

Tenzing, who was born in Tibet, was known in Darjeeling most usually as Tensing Bhotia, and occasionally as Tensing Khumjung, the village in Khumbu where he had worked before leaving for Darjeeling. The Himalayan Club, which held his employment records, used the name Tensing Bhotia, and that is how Trevor Braham remembers him: "He always called himself Tensing Bhotia; he never concealed the fact." Edwin Kempson, a schoolmaster from Marlborough College, was one of the climbers on the 1935 Everest reconnaissance, Tenzing's first expedition. He kept a record of all the porters' names in his diary, along with their village. Tenzing's appears as "Tensing, Bhotiya [sic], Kharta Shikar." Kharta Shikar was the local ruler's house in Kharta, across the river from Tenzing's childhood home in Tibet. Of the 15 porters taken to Everest that year, 7 of them were born in Tibet, but Tenzing related that they were all Sherpas even though he specifies that the expedition took many more "non-climbing porters, mostly Tibetans." By the time Tenzing came to give his life story in the 1950s, evolution of the name Sherpa, begun in the 1920s, was complete. If you wanted prestigious, well-paid high-altitude work, being a Tibetan wasn't enough. You had to be a Sherpa.

As they became famous for their strength at high altitude, Sherpas and Bhotias used their higher status to escape the drudgery of carrying loads at low altitude and move up a rung on the social ladder. By the 1930s, climbers had to accept that the Sherpas could be used to carry loads only on the mountain, above the snow line—or face strike action.[20] The Sherpas took great pride in this kind of social advancement. Their pay was better too and the equipment they received from Western climbers a symbol as well as a reward for their skill and bravery. Mountain climbing was a trade or craft like any other, and the Sherpas were developing a monopoly on it.

While the Sherpas were busy cementing their reputation, the sahibs were developing systems for exploration in the Himalaya. They learned how Bhotia societies worked, and good expedition leaders became sensitive to the way porters were hired and organized. This process was accelerated by the formation of the Himalayan Club in 1928. Its founding members were an elite group: leading geographers, soldiers, senior civil servants. Its inaugural meeting was held in the rooms of Field Marshal Sir William Birdwood—commander of the Anzac forces at Gallipoli—at Army Headquarters in Delhi. The club's purpose was ambitious: "To encourage and assist Himalayan travel and exploration, and to extend knowledge of the Himalaya and adjoining mountain ranges through science, art, literature and sport."

It had the expertise and contacts to assist the increasing numbers of expeditions both from Britain and elsewhere in Europe and North America.

Advice on logistics, purchasing stores, traveling through the country, and hiring porters could now be managed systematically. This extended to the management of porters at Darjeeling. It became the responsibility of the honorary secretary of the Darjeeling branch of the Himalayan Club to manage the porters and hold lists of who was available for hire. Sherpas and Tibetans were issued a number and a book in which was kept a record of all the expeditions they had worked on along with a comment from the leader. None of them could read these comments, but the books were prized as passports to regular employment. Working conditions were regularized, pay schedules drawn up, and compensation levels set. Because payments increased above the snow line, this was defined as 12,000 feet. Sherpas were to travel third class on the train, but were given two rupees a day for food. Porter loads were limited by weight and advice given on baksheesh, now generally referred to as a tip. Equipment was always a potential area of conflict, since it was worth a great deal to Sherpas both financially and as an expression of prestige. Small expeditions could rely on finding men who would hire their own equipment, garnered from other expeditions, for 20 rupees a month. The club held detailed records of who had done what on which mountain, and a kind of career structure developed. After 1924, those who had carried loads high on Everest were called "Tigers," a source of pride among Sherpas as well as a boost to their employment prospects. Most prized of all was becoming a sirdar, an Indian term meaning leader. The sirdar chose the porters and kept them disciplined, presented their grievances, and organized work on the mountain. The job carried benefits and status that only increased as more expeditions arrived and interest in Himalayan climbing grew. Some sirdars would take baksheesh from Sherpas desperate to work, and others would expect a cut of their wages.

Darjeeling became a kind of home port for the Sherpas, where men were hired and sent all over the Himalaya. These teams were close-knit, like a ship's crew, working for a wage but in it for the adventure too. They were, in Joseph Conrad's phrase, "a fragment detached from the earth." And just as a ship's crew might not be interested in the importance of their master's trade, mountaineering itself was of little consequence to them. "They couldn't conceive that you could become famous climbing a mountain," said Dorje Lhatoo.

The Sherpas had their own code, a sense of camaraderie and a strong sense of honor. In "port" they might drink and gamble, and they might occasionally mutiny when working conditions weren't acceptable, but climbing made their lives exciting and it was better, in most ways, to pulling a rickshaw. "Anyone who knows what we have done cannot believe that it is only for a few rupees that we go to the mountains," Tenzing said.[21] The risk of injury or death existed, but as the Himalayan Club's list shows, injury and premature death were a commonplace for Sherpas who didn't climb.

Ang Tsering, whose first cousin married Tenzing, climbed with Mallory and Irvine in 1924. He had no interest in climbing mountains and couldn't understand why anyone would. "We went on expeditions to earn money. No one had any ambition to climb Everest." He shared the view of many Sherpas that the monks at Rongbuk were right when they said there was a lion made of pure gold on the summit and that's what the British were after. Ang Tsering didn't reach the summit of a mountain until 1960, when he was in his 50s. I asked him how much he earned on the expedition in 1924. "Twelve annas a day; that's three-quarters of a rupee." In 1924 a rupee could buy 32 pounds of rice. Ang Tsering had also worked as a woodcutter and I asked him how the pay compared. "I made ten rupees a week as a woodcutter."

"So why did you go to Everest for less money?"

There was a wheezy chuckle. "Because the work was easier."

Ang Tsering carried loads to above 26,000 feet earning himself the accolade of "Tiger," and there is a haunting photograph of him with five of his workmates, leaning on their ice axes, their snow goggles pushed back on their foreheads, grinning at someone or something out of frame. Ang Tsering brushed his hand across the photograph and said, "*Chaina*— They're all gone." Working conditions were inevitably harsh, and to begin with, the British did not take sufficient care of their porters. Ang Tsering recalls how their clothing on Everest was too thin in 1924 and how badly they suffered with the cold. But that gradually changed and Ang Tsering had few complaints. "The British were very fair," he said. "They looked after us. If someone was killed in the mountains, then the families would get compensation. The Sherpas couldn't do the paperwork and the Himalayan Club looked after that." Not all Sherpas shared this point of view. Tenzing himself campaigned hard for an improvement in working conditions.

Ang Tsering suffered his worst experience during a German attempt on Nanga Parbat in 1934. Just as the British returned again and again to Everest, in the 1930s the Germans developed a long-standing and even more tragic relationship with Nanga Parbat, at 26,661 feet the ninth highest mountain in the world, towering over the Indus Valley. An expedition in 1932 led by Willy Merkl had reconnoitered the Rakhiot face, but the Germans relied on local Hunza porters, who weren't interested in working hard and stole supplies from their loads. When Merkl returned in 1934, he made sure he had Sherpas, 35 of them in all, and thanks to them the expedition ran smoothly. The Germans made good progress, despite the sudden death from edema of Alfred Drexel, and on July 1 the lead climbers started out for the summit, fixing ropes on the northeast wall of Nanga Parbat's Rakhiot Peak. On July 4, the Sherpas followed with the team's equipment and supplies, climbing ropes on ground that was steeper than anything most of them had experienced before. The expedition gained height and some Sherpas dropped out and went down so that on July 6, 11, including Ang Tsering, set out with 5 of the German sahibs and reached the Silver Saddle, just 2,300 feet below the summit beyond a flat white glacial expanse called the Silver Plateau at over 24,000 feet. Two of the climbers, the Austrians Peter Aschenbrenner and Erwin Schneider, crossed this and got to within 900 feet of the top that afternoon, but returned to find their companions had established Camp VIII early. Still, the Germans were confident that the next day they would climb Nanga Parbat.

During the night a storm broke. The wind was savage, snapping tent poles and driving snow inside to soak their sleeping bags. The stoves refused to light, making it impossible for the climbers to melt snow for drinks. Ang Tsering recalled that the thirst was the worst part: "*Nau din dekhi hume him khayo*—For nine days I ate only ice." All through July 7 the storm raged, the tents enveloped in blank fog, the men struggling to breathe the thin air in the confines of their tents.

The next morning the storm continued, but the 16 men abandoned the camp anyway. The two Austrians broke trail with three of the Sherpas, while Merkl and two others, the great Willo Welzenbach and Uli Wieland, took care of the rest. In the evening of July 8, Aschenbrenner and Schneider reached the safety of a lower camp. Their porters, Pasang Norbu, Nima Dorje, and Pintso Norbu, they said, were somewhere behind them. In fact, they had stopped at a higher camp, too nervous to go on alone after the Austrians had untied from them and skied down. This act of cowardice went unrecorded in the official accounts, but the older Sherpas knew all about it and Ang Tsering took my arm as he told me, the outrage still sharp in his mind.

The rest of the expedition didn't make it off the Silver Saddle, bivouacking in the snow. A porter called Nima Norbu died in the night, and in the morning two more, Gaylay and Dakshi, were snow-blind and too ill to move. Ang Tsering stayed with them as the others descended. Wieland collapsed in the snow and died a hundred feet from the tents as climbers at Base Camp watched through a break in the clouds. The situation was now completely out of control. Merkl and Welzenbach had reached the next camp, too exhausted to continue. Instead they opted to send their four remaining porters—Kitar, Tenzing's old friend Dawa Thondup, Nima Tashi, and Pasang Kikuli—farther down the ridge to the camp after that, Camp VI. They didn't make it, bivouacking again, close to where the three Sherpas who had been left behind by Aschenbrenner and Schneider had reached that day. On July 10 these two groups of Sherpas finally joined together and the seven started descending the ropes they had climbed up six days before. Nima Tashi and Nima Dorje collapsed on the wall and died of exhaustion. Pintso Norbu died just before Camp V. The other four made it back to the tents more dead than alive.

The agony above them continued. On the Silver Saddle, Dakshi died during the night of July 11, and Ang Tsering and Gaylay descended to where Welzenbach and Merkl were slumped in their tents. Merkl was now incoherent with exhaustion and cold, but Welzenbach was suffering the most, writhing in agony on the tent floor. Neither man had a sleeping bag. Welzenbach died first, during the early hours of July 13. When morning came, the survivors, Merkl, Gaylay, and Ang Tsering, dragged themselves out of Camp VII and struggled down the ridge below toward safety. Merkl was exhausted and soon collapsed. The two Sherpas scraped out a shelter from the snow, and Gaylay stayed with the sahib Merkl while Ang Tsering ploughed through deep snow down the ridge toward Rakhiot Peak and the safety of the lower camps. He came across the body of Nima Dorje hanging from the fixed ropes, a sheen of ice frozen like a mask across his face, his head thrown back and his right leg extended.

Ang Tsering survived, but just barely. He spent a year convalescing. At Srinagar they cut his toes off, and by the time he reached Darjeeling the wounds were filled with maggots. They probably did him good, saving him from infection on the long train journey home. Afterward he couldn't face going back to the mountains. The horror of what had happened was too much. Krenek's list of porters for the Himalayan Club noted that Ang Tsering "works on trek below the snowline." But in the end he did go back, reaching 24,000 feet again on an expedition in 1950 and becoming sirdar in 1954 on a yeti-hunting expedition. Ang Tsering was awarded the Medal of Honor of the German Red Cross. Gaylay was found years later, sitting next to Merkl in the snow. He had tried to get his sahib farther down the mountain and then stayed with him as he died, too weak to move himself.[22]

The Nanga Parbat disaster in 1934 was the worst climbing accident since 1870. In all, six Sherpas and four climbers had died. An inquiry, of sorts, was conducted. Adolf Hitler's Reichssportführer, Hans von Tschammer und Osten, concluded that the Austrians Aschenbrenner and Schneider were "without honour," not for abandoning the Sherpas, who actually needed their help even as the Austrians were untying from them and disappearing down the mountain, but for abandoning the three Germans, Welzenbach, Merkl, and Wieland.

A German expedition went back to Nanga Parbat in 1937, to avenge the deaths of 1934. Shortly after midnight on June 14, an avalanche struck the expedition's Camp IV under Rakhiot Peak. Most of the expedition's climbers, seven in all, and nine Sherpas were sleeping inside the tents. They were buried so completely that when Uli Luft, the expedition doctor, arrived two days later to join his comrades, he could see no sign whatsoever of their camp. Sixteen more men were dead, among them nine of the strongest Sherpas of Darjeeling.

After the two accidents on Nanga Parbat in 1934 and 1937, the Sherpas judged those hiring them with a much more critical eye. Tenzing had been out of Darjeeling during the summer of 1934, but arrived back more determined than ever to break into expedition work. All the talk among the Sherpas was what had happened that summer: "And it was not happy talk, because there had been a terrible disaster ... As a result, there was mourning and grief in many homes in Toong Soong Busti, but there was also a certain deep pride in what our men had borne and accomplished." Tenzing had not actually been on a mountain yet, but far from dissuading him, "such a story made me, too, proud to be a Sherpa."[23]

How Sherpas accept death has intrigued Western climbers from the outset of Himalayan mountaineering. Most believed that a cultural gulf separated the two worlds, East and West. In 1922, when seven climbers were swept away by an avalanche below Everest's North Col, the expedition leader, General Bruce, took the fatalistic view: "If it was written they should die on Everest, they should die on Everest. If it was written they would not die on Everest, they would not, and that was all there was to be said in the matter."[24] John Noel, the expedition's cinematographer, describes how the surviving porters, "mostly blood relations, brothers and cousins of those who had vanished," were demoralized and listless, unwilling to aid in the search. "The spirits had struck at them. Survivors would only be braving the spirits' wrath by going to help him."[25] Afterward, local Tibetans, on a mission to recover supplies abandoned by the British, reported that they saw seven bears emerging from a cleft in the mountain, the spirits of the seven porters come back to haunt the place of their deaths.

This mixture of fatalism and superstition was a common European interpretation, but there was sympathy too. Howard Somervell, who also assisted in the rescue, was distraught: "Only Bhotias and Sherpas killed— why, oh why could not one of us Britishers have shared their fate? I would gladly at that moment have been lying there dead in the snow, if only to give those fine chaps who had survived the feeling that we had shared their loss." Dzatrul Rinpoche, the lama at Rongbuk who had given Tenzing his name, made the most incisive comment about the accident: "I was filled with compassion for their lot who underwent such suffering on unnecessary work. I organised very important dedications for the dead."[26] The sahibs had their own myths, although they would not have thought of them as such. When Mallory and Irvine died in 1924, Somervell wrote, "The loss of these splendid men is part of the price that has been paid to keep alive the spirit of adventure. Without this spirit life would be a poor thing, and progress impossible."[27]

Tibetan Buddhism teaches its adherents to avoid the stress that strong emotions bring. In a world filled with uncertainty, the ability to let go of even the closest personal relationships is a defense mechanism, a way of going on. If you are bringing up children who rely on you, this has obvious advantages. But it would be wrong to imagine that Sherpas are immune from grief; resisting the dangers of attachment is a lot easier in a monastery. The wife of Da Tenzing, one of the greatest pre-war Sherpas, was so distraught at hearing of her son's and husband's deaths on separate expeditions that she drowned herself. "She was inconsolable," wrote Tashi and Judy Tenzing, "but in the typical reserved and stoic Sherpa manner kept her grief to herself. A few nights later however, after dark, she went out into the biting cold of a Khumbu night and threw herself into a river."[28] Tragically, the report of Da Tenzing's death was wrong. He returned home safely, to discover he had lost his wife and son.

Although death could summon up images of demons or angry gods, there are also more prosaic examples of the fear of death among Sherpas, the kind of horror that Westerners would more easily understand. An example of this was the fate of Pasang Bhotia, who suffered a stroke on the North Col of Everest during the expedition of 1938, led by H. W. Tilman. Ang Tharkay was the sirdar and Tenzing one of the porters, still a young man of almost 24. Pasang Bhotia lay stricken in his tent when Tilman arrived in camp. At first the sahibs thought Pasang "off his head" but they quickly established that his right side was paralyzed and he was completely helpless. Pasang was a cousin of Ang Tharkay, and friends with the other Sherpas at the North Col that day, but despite this they wouldn't help him. After a halfhearted attempt to build a stretcher out of tent poles, they suggested that they just leave Pasang where he lay. Tilman was furious, although that anger didn't emerge in his account of the incident: "[The Sherpas] regarded his misfortune as a judgement, either on him or the whole party, for supplicating too perfunctorily the gods of the mountain.... As they saw it, the mountain claimed a victim, and if we cheated it of Pasang then some other member of the party would be taken; for choice one of those who had taken pains to bilk the mountain of its due."[29] Finally they tied a rope onto him and lowered and then dragged him down the mountain.

This became a much discussed incident, an illustration of Sherpa superstition about Chomolungma and the goddess who lived there. But behind the myth was a more mundane explanation, according to Ang Tharkay: "Tilman asked me to do something for Pasang. I asked Nukku and Norbu to give me a hand carrying him down to a lower camp. But the idea completely disgusted them, because of Pasang's dirty condition, and they turned a deaf ear."[30] Because Pasang Bhotia had soiled himself and stank, the Sherpas would not touch him. They were hiding their instinctive fear of a stricken man behind their myths of angry spirits and deities. Ang Tharkay, who was widely recognized as a man of outstanding qualities, overcame his revulsion and stepped forward to help Pasang, who survived but whose climbing career was over. He died in 1948.[31]

An element missing from more academic studies of the unique relationship between climbers and Sherpas is the fun and the close friendships they often shared. The devotion they felt for each other went far beyond professional courtesy. After a surveying expedition to the Kurumtoli Glacier with Eric Shipton in 1936, Ang Tharkay and Sen Tensing—nicknamed the "Professional Sportsman" by Tilman—went on a trip with Shipton and his lover, Pamela Freston, seeing the Taj Mahal at Agra and having a short vacation at Bombay. Peter Steele, Shipton's biographer, describes how "the Sherpas slept on the floor outside the memsahib's hotel bedroom, and spent the morning going up and down in the lift. They all went sailing in a yacht on the Indian Ocean, went to 'the flicks'; and finally the captain showed them, from the bridge to the engine room, the boat on which Pamela and Shipton were returning to England." Freston described in her diary how Sen Tensing and Ang Tharkay waved good-bye until they were just two dots on the quay: "The last sound we heard from India was Angtharkay's [sic] piercing whistle echoing over the water as we had heard it so often on the trek echoing across the hills."

Often for the sahibs, their best memories were of the enthralling days they spent tramping through the mountains in a world that seemed limitless. The Sherpas were part of those memories, and inevitably nostalgia colors the written recollections of those days. Yet Himalayan climbers in the 1920s and 1930s really were discovering a new world.

The Sherpas also shared the excitement of the enterprise and welcomed the chance to travel and see new things, to become men of the world rather than farmers from an obscure valley in Nepal. Eric Shipton could hold a reasoned, unsentimental view of Sherpas, pointing out that unrealistic expectations by Europeans had killed several inexperienced men, particularly on Nanga Parbat.[32] But he also wrote that "the best of them are unbeatable" and he loved Ang Tharkay, in his way: "He was a most loveable person: modest, unselfish and completely sincere, with an infectious gaiety of spirit."[33] Trevor Braham, in his obituary for Ang Tharkay in the *Himalayan Journal*, wrote, "I learnt much about human relationships by watching the way in which he treated his men, and witnessing their respect and affection for him. He was a man of the highest integrity."

In the early 1920s, Sherpa pioneers such as Ang Tsering, with no real mountaineering experience at all, quickly learned the requirements of living and working at high altitudes. The second generation, men such as Tenzing and Ang Tharkay, arrived in Darjeeling in the late 1920s. Within two decades, the Sherpas, with no previous understanding of why anyone would climb a mountain, had developed into trustworthy and capable high-altitude porters. After Nepal opened its borders in 1949, the focus for climbing and trekking in the eastern Himalaya shifted from Darjeeling to Kathmandu, but the Sherpas moved on as well, always attuned to the next development. In the modern era, they are strong high-altitude climbers in their own right, routinely setting records on Everest, and the commercial expeditions now running in the Himalaya could not function without them. At the beginning, however, those that survived the early years of Himalayan exploration had little to show for it. Few Sherpas saved money, and they faced an old age of poverty and in some cases dereliction. Lhakpa Chedi, who carried loads for the 1924 expedition alongside George Mallory, wound up a doorman for a Calcutta department store. Other Sherpas subsided into alcoholism or were left crippled by frostbite injuries. The foundation of the Sherpas' present-day success was laid by men earning less than a rupee a day for carrying loads up the most dangerous mountains on Earth.

In 1938, on the last Everest expedition before the war, the Sherpas performed heroically again, and Tilman had his idea to present an award to the best of them, the Tiger's Badge. Walt Unsworth, the Everest historian, wrote:

"They were not yet climbers, in the European sense, but the men who were with Tilman in 1938—Angtharkay, Tenzing, Pasang and the rest—were very different from the 'coolies' who had traveled with Howard-Bury. Once the value of the Sherpas had been proved on the first three Everest expeditions, they were in demand by expeditions throughout the Himalaya: German, French, American, Dutch, Italian, Japanese, and many British expeditions had used the natives of Sola Khumbu, and the Sherpas had learnt from all of them. The best of them, though lacking in technique, had been infected with the spirit of the game: 'Previously,' wrote Shipton, 'it has always been rather a question of driving these men to extreme altitudes; now the position was almost reversed.'"[34]

The new town of Darjeeling had become a crucible for the Sherpas and Bhotias migrating there to gamble their lives by signing up for climbing expeditions. It was the world where Tenzing would make his mark, the world that shaped his future and eventual triumph. But the land that formed him was far more remote and his origins more obscure than the bustle of modern colonial Darjeeling. Like the other mountain porters, Tenzing had been transplanted from another, more ancient world that had grown up on the slopes of Everest itself. Half hidden, half forgotten, it is that world that holds the key to Tenzing's life.

CHAPTER TWO

THE LAP OF HIS MOTHER

So much is made of politics, of nationality. Not on a mountain itself:
there life is too real and death too close for such things, and a man is a man,
a human being, and that is all. But later it begins—politics and more politics,
argument and bad feeling—and no sooner was I down from Everest than it began
for me. For the first thirty-eight years of my life no one cared what nationality
I was. Indian, Nepali, or even Tibetan: what difference does it make?
—TENZING NORGAY [1]

F ROM THE EDGE OF SPACE, the world's mountain ranges flatten from
three dimensions into two, appearing simply as geometric stars and
whorls on the surface of the Earth, white glaciers curling between black
mountain ridges. All mountain ranges, that is, except the Himalaya. From
the cockpit window of the space shuttle, the collision of India with
Central Asia is clearly visible, the crumpled hood of a geological car wreck
soaring within a few miles from an altitude of a hundred feet to the summit of Everest itself, five and a half miles high. [2] Forty million years ago
the region was flat, submerged by the shallow waters of the Tethys Sea,
but as India separated and drifted north from the mass of Gondwanaland
toward the coast of what is now Tibet, the ocean bed began to lift and
buckle. Fossils from this ancient sea are found on the limestone
summit of Everest and throughout the region. Ammonites, holding the
symbolic pattern of the Buddhist mandala, are highly prized and sold to
pilgrims as talismans.

Geographical superlatives abound in the Himalaya. At 1,550 miles it is far from being the longest mountain range, but it is comfortably the highest. All 14 of the world's 8,000-meter peaks are there, and the deepest gorges too, such as the Kali Gandaki, buried four miles deep between the gigantic peaks of Annapurna and Dhaulagiri. This is landscape on a scale that is hard for the mind to comprehend, mountains so high that they block the monsoon rains from reaching the arid brown plateau of Tibet. The process of uplift is far from finished, as India continues to plunge beneath Tibet at an average rate of two inches a year, driving the Himalaya still higher. It is a place of earthquakes and tremors, of landslides and avalanches, of floods released from glacial lakes.

Himalayan geography has shaped every aspect of the lives of the people who live there, from the biological adaptations among Tibetans for living at high altitude to the gods people worship and the food they eat. Human history here is very long. Dravidians built great cities in the Indus Valley of modern Pakistan in the third millennium B.C. Aryans invading from Persia in 1500 B.C. crossed the Hindu Kush and conquered this region, a meeting of cultures that generated its major ancient religions, Hinduism, and ultimately Buddhism. The sense of the sacred in South Asia is intimately connected to the mountains, even for those who have never seen one. White, ethereal summits floating above the dusty plains and green jungles make an irresistible appeal to the soul. Where else would gods choose to live? The Skanda Purana, an ancient Hindu text, advises: "In a hundred ages of the gods I could not tell thee of the glories of Himachal, where Shiva lived and where the Ganges falls from the foot of Vishnu like the slender thread of the Lotus flower.... As the dew is dried up by the morning sun, so are the sins of mankind by the sight of Himachal."

The relationship between landscape and religion is much closer in the Himalayan region than in the Christian tradition. In parts of rural Tibet, for example, the more structured systems of Buddhism and the older Bön religion were layered over a more deeply rooted animist relationship with the forests and cliffs, the animals and birds, a tradition that persists today in the remote valley, close to Everest and the border with modern Nepal, where Tenzing Norgay was born in 1914.

The Tibetan plateau has been occupied by humans for more than 50,000 years, probably much more. People there are more closely related to Korean, Mongolian, and Siberian populations than the modern Han Chinese and other Southeast Asian populations, although the Tibetan language is part of the Tibeto-Burmese group, suggesting a period of isolation from the original source. But if the Tibetan Himalaya was populated by people migrating from the north, its dominant religion, Buddhism, was founded south of the chain, in a princely kingdom at the foot of the Nepalese Himalaya. In 500 B.C., Siddhartha Gautama, drawing on early Hindu traditions and abandoning his wealthy inheritance, taught his followers the path to nirvana, or enlightenment, and was called Buddha, the enlightened one. His teachings spread rapidly over South Asia, to be subsumed eventually in India by Hinduism, and eventually crossed the Himalaya into Tibet. Although the mountain range is thought of as a sacred, peaceful region, it is the crossroads of conflicting cultures that have frequently been at war. This ebb and flow of Himalayan history is reflected in the story of the *béyüls*, sacred hidden valleys like the one in which Tenzing began his life.

"It has often been said that I was born in the village of Thamey, but that is not quite right. My family lived in Thamey, and I grew up there, but I was born in a place called Tsa-chu, near the great mountain Makalu. And only a day's march from Everest. Tsa-chu, which means "hot springs," is a holy place of many stories and legends, and my mother had gone there on a pilgrimage to the monastery of Ghang La, that being also our clan or family name. Near it is a great rock, shaped like the head of the Lord Buddha, out of which water is said to flow if a pious person touches it and prays."[3]

Tenzing's account of his birth reads like a myth or family legend, but it reveals a great deal about his background. He is describing border country, remote valleys on either side of the Himalayan chain. Thamey, usually transcribed now as Thame, is miles to the west of Everest, just inside Nepal. "Tsa-chu," more accurately Tshechu, is miles to the east, across the border in Tibet. If Tenzing's life as a famous man was plagued with questions about his nationality, then these remote valleys on either side of the great mountain are where those questions began. As for the Buddha-shaped rock and the water that springs from it at the touch of a pious person, these were the important strands of the story, because Tenzing was born in the heart of a sacred landscape, a place of religious stories and ideas overlaid on the mountains and lakes.

Geomancy, the art of divination from the shape or relationship of geographical features, is a current in Tibetan Buddhism. Béyüls, or hidden valleys, are places of deep spirituality, drawing faithful pilgrims. As fragments of heaven on Earth, they are intimately connected to the idea of nirvana. Some of these are known, some remain undiscovered, waiting for the appropriate master to "open" them. A century after Songtsen Gampo died, Tibet's second great Buddhist king, Trisong Detsen, ascended the throne. At the age of 21, he invited several Buddhist masters to help extend the influence of Buddhism in Tibet, founding the first of the country's monasteries, institutions that would dominate Tibetan life until the Chinese Cultural Revolution of the 1960s. One of these teachers was Padmasambhava, known in Tibet as Guru Rinpoche. He revealed to Trisong Detsen the existence of a béyül called Khenbalung[4] that had formed when a lotus flower fell to Earth, a gift from the king of the gods that went astray. It would be, Guru Rinpoche prophesied, a heavenly refuge during times of war and catastrophe in Tibet, when the dharma was under threat. This was the sacred Kama Valley where Tenzing was born.

Here the Bhong Chu, a river older than the mountains it pierces, turns sharply south, dropping steeply toward the Gangetic plain in Nepal, where it becomes the Arun. The gorge is so deep that the monsoon penetrates along its course into the Himalaya, almost to the foot of the east face of Everest, at the head of the Kama Valley. Consequently the valley is fertile and verdant, one of the most beautiful places on Earth, surrounded by gigantic mountains, their fluted ridges pinned against a crystalline sky or looming out through gaps in heavy gray clouds. The lower hillsides are blanketed with impressive stands of juniper and silver firs, mountain ash and birches, willow and vast rhododendrons. Plants and flowers, many of them used in Tibetan medicine, are spread across the higher, treeless slopes in summer, chief among them the red and blue poppies of the genus *Meconopsis*—*upa mendog* in Tibetan— the very lotus flower that the king of the gods had let fall to Earth.

The first European to explore the valley, Col. Charles Howard-Bury, leader of the 1921 Everest reconnaissance expedition, described it thus: "We had explored many of these Himalayan valleys, but none seemed to me to be comparable with this, either for the beauty of its Alpine scenery, or for its wonderful vegetation. We shall not easily forget the smiling pastures carpeted with gentians and every variety of Alpine flower that rise to the very verge of icebound and snow-covered tracks, where mighty glaciers descend among the forests which clothe the lower slope."[5]

The Kama Valley lies at the heart of Béyül Khenbalung, and it is used by the people of the Kharta Valley living to the northeast as summer pasturage for their yaks, a source of medicinal and other plants for food and fuel, and a place of pilgrimage. Each béyül has a guide-text, or *neyig*, and Khenbalung is no exception. It was "opened" in the 14th century by Rindzin Godem, who discovered its guide-text near the monastery of Sangsang Lhabrag, in a rocky peak shaped like a heap of poisonous snakes. Since then, mystics from beyond Kharta have traveled to these remote places, living at altitudes of 17,000 feet through the long, bitter winters, abandoning society and its conventions to experience a simple but harsh relationship with nature. And so local traditions, centered on the cycle of farming and nomadism that sustain the villages in the Kharta Valley, have blended with Buddhism to create a rich cultural mix. In this place myth and fact lose their polarity. Even among Tibetans, the mountains mean different things.

Among the most sacred locations for meditation and pilgrimage in Béyül Khenbalung is Tshechu, the spring of life water. Above the Kangshung Valley, which leads to the east face of Everest, is a lake a kilometer in length and roughly pear-shaped; its stalk, where a stream drains it to the south, points toward the Kama Valley and Nepal. Makalu, the fifth highest mountain in the world, dominates the skyline, appearing abruptly above the lake to the southwest. A steep path leads north to the lake, flanked by small cairns wreathed with juniper. It continues along the lake's eastern shore to a steep scree slope that leads to a huge red cliff that is shaped, to an imaginative eye, like the Buddha's head. At the base of the cliff is a deep cave where a few stone huts offered shelter to the hermits who used to meditate here before the 1959 uprising against the Chinese and now contain a number of holy objects removed from nearby monasteries destroyed during the same period. To the east of the cave, and a little below, is a small shrine. Prayer flags have been strung up to frame a few wrinkles in the cliff from which, improbably, a trickle of water emerges, apparently from the rock itself. This is the life water that is drunk to purge sins, heal the sick, and give *tsewang*, or life power. At the bottom of the scree slope that leads to the lake, on whose surface the pure in spirit can see prophetic visions, are stone shelters for pilgrims and, in summer, the tents of yak herders. It was in such a tent, by this remote lake in Tibet, that Tenzing Norgay was born in the late spring.

TENZING'S OWN ACCOUNT OF HIS BIRTH acknowledges that many people believed he was born in the village of "Thamey," a small Sherpa village on the trail to the Nangpa La, a high glacial pass leading from Khumbu on the Nepalese border into Tibet. The Sherpas of Khumbu are the Tibetan tribe or group with which Tenzing is most closely associated, and many of his European climbing companions assumed he was born among them. In his obituary of Tenzing for the *Alpine Journal*, John Hunt, leader of the 1953 British expedition to Everest, described Tenzing as having been born in Thame.[6] Ed Hillary also believed that. "I remember many times talking with Tenzing casually about his birth and he always said he came from Thame." But Tenzing was not born into a family living in Khumbu. He was born in the Kharta region of Tibet and spent the first years of his life there.

Why would Tenzing not openly state this? Part of the problem lies in our own Western ideas of a border. They are concrete entities, sometimes literally, and you often need a passport to cross them. In the Himalaya, a line on a map means little to hill people trading and farming in patterns that are far older than the national boundaries they cross. Loyalties are not to the idea of nation, but to family and community and religion. Nepal's border with Tibet has shifted over the centuries. The two countries fought a brutal war at the end of the 18th century during which Nepalese troops reached Shigatse, far to the north of Kharta. The impact of the war, fortifications, and depopulation, was still visible to Charles Howard-Bury in 1921.[7] There was still a Nepalese headman in the Tibetan town of Dingri, the ancient entrepôt for trade between Lhasa and Kathmandu, where the first Everest climbers based themselves. "We were remote from the rest of our country," Tenzing said of his years in Nepal. "What went on there did not seem to affect us; we had our own customs and ways of life, and knew almost nothing about the nation of which we were politically a part."

The Sherpas are ethnic Tibetans whose forebears most probably crossed the Nangpa La into Khumbu in the mid-16th century. Anthropologist Michael Oppitz has argued that Sherpas originated in the eastern Tibetan province of Kham—Sherpa, or Shar-wa, means "easterner"—and migrated first to Lhasa and later to the Dingri region looking for new land. From there the earliest settlers made their journey over the Himalaya into Khumbu where they could practice their brand of nomadic pastoralism and where there were few existing inhabitants. From Khumbu they moved deeper into Nepal; there are far more Sherpas in the lower and more hospitable district of Solu and elsewhere in Nepal.

Khumbu comprises three valleys: the most westerly leading south from the Nangpa La following the river called Bhote Kosi; the central valley of the Dudh Kosi, or milk river; and the third valley to the east that leads from the Khumbu Glacier below Everest itself. Above the confluence of the Bhote Kosi and Dudh Kosi is the sacred peak of Khumbu Yülha, Khumbu's most important mountain deity. The biggest villages and most extensive fields are found on the mountain's lower slopes.

Sherpas are Tibetan Buddhists, followers of the Nyingmapa or "Red Hat" sect, and their language is a dialect of Tibetan. Most Tibetans can more or less understand the Sherpa language. Even so, Sherpas in Khumbu and other regions of Nepal regard themselves as a distinct tribe from other Tibetan groups near Everest, with their own religious festivals and their own local deities. They have different farming practices, and their architecture and dress is also distinctive.

In Khumbu, Tibetan newcomers were called Khambas and were absorbed into the Sherpa community over a relatively short period of time. But in Tenzing's youth they were looked down on, and even excluded. As anthropologist Stanley F. Stevens explains, "Sherpas have long drawn a distinction between the older clans, the descendants of older settlers, and those who came more recently and have drawn a far sharper line between Sherpas and Khambas." Tenzing's childhood was colored by his family's move to Khumbu, where he was regarded as a Khamba, a Tibetan immigrant who worked as a servant.

The root of any tension between Tenzing and more established Sherpas was wealth and position. In his early years, when he lived in extreme poverty, Tenzing found acceptance harder. His path was that of immigrants everywhere, burning with ambition for a new and better life, knowing that the door back to the life of his ancestors was closed forever. "In a way," he recalled, "Tibet is the home of my spirit, but as a living man I am a stranger there."[8] In the villages of Kharta, where his family originated and where he spent his first years, his remaining family and other local people revere Tenzing as a great man. And they all call him Tenzing Sherpa. The more interesting question is why he and at least some of his family chose to leave Tibet in the first place.

Tenzing told James Ramsey Ullman, the writer who turned his memories and opinions into prose for his first autobiography, *Tiger of the Snows*, that his mother had been on a pilgrimage to Tshechu when she gave birth to Tenzing. Many of the farming population in Kharta make pilgrimages to Tshechu in the late summer, before the start of the harvest. After the harvest, the first winter snows close the high passes leading into the béyül. But Tenzing was clear in his own mind that he had been born earlier in the year. "It could be fixed by the weather and the crops, and it was in the later part of May. This has always seemed a good sign to me, for the end of May has been an important time throughout my life. The time of birth to begin with. The time of great expeditions and best mountain weather. It was on the 28th May that I almost climbed to the top of Everest with Lambert, and on the 29th, a year and a day later, that I reached it with Hillary."[9] The year of his birth, 1914, was fixed by correlating Tibetan and Western calendars. Each year in the Tibetan 12-year cycle is given a name, and the name of Tenzing's year was *yoa*, or hare. This meant he was born in 1902, 1914, or 1926. "I hope I am not so old as the first and am afraid I am not so young as the second."

Tenzing's mother, Kinzom, came from a village outside the Kharta Valley, either Pharing or a hamlet just before it called Chongda. When she was born is difficult to verify, but in his second autobiography, *After Everest*, Tenzing says she was 84 in 1954, meaning she was born in 1870. That would have made her 44 when she gave birth to Tenzing, who was her 11th child out of 14. Dolka Marpa, who was a servant in the great house at Tsawa where Kinzom and Tenzing's father later lived, remembers her as a tough but kindly woman, devoted to her faith. The head lama at Thar-baling, the only religious institution still functioning in Kharta, remembers her as having led a difficult life, but recalled that she found strength in her religion and was always prepared to help those in difficulty.

Although her family was not of the powerful land-owning aristoc-racy, they were noteworthy for their piety; Kinzom's first cousin, Trulshik Rinpoche,[10] became the second head lama at Rongbuk, on the north side of Everest. He was an incarnation of the great Dzatrul Rinpoche's own "heart lama," and appointed by Dzatrul as his successor at the monastery when he was just 19. After the exile of the Dalai Lama in 1959, he fled Tibet, living with Tenzing and his family for a while in Darjeeling. Trulshik Rinpoche is now in exile at the monastery of Thupten Choeling, near Junbesi, in the Sherpa district of Solu.

Eight of Kinzom's 14 children died in infancy or childhood. Living conditions in the Kharta region are harsh, and although Tenzing's family could rely on traditional medicines, infections and accidents regularly have afflicted children and young adults. Obstetrics was also unknown, and women helped each other through childbirth. Tshechu is at an altitude of 14,500 feet, and most fit, nonpregnant Western women would feel a sense of achievement in just reaching it. Tibetan women are adapted to live at high altitudes, and uterine blood supply is more generous than in women who live at sea level, allowing babies to achieve a higher birth weight. Even so, it is hard to believe that a heavily pregnant woman would choose to go to Tshechu on a pilgrimage. So is the story of Tenzing's birth more fable than truth?

Although Tenzing said his mother was on a pilgrimage when he was born, another reason could explain her presence there in early summer. Kinzom married a man from Kharta called Mingma—it translates as Tuesday[11]—who spent most of his life as a yak herder, or *drokpa*. Like Kinzom, Mingma has left a deep impression on the communities of the Kharta Valley. Some of his descendants still live in Kharta near the house Mingma occupied around the time of Tenzing's birth. It is a fertile valley, greener and more sheltered than the Bhong Chu to the east, dot-ted with small hamlets where it broadens, the largest village being Yueba on the south bank of the Kharta Chu. The houses here differ from the villages to the north of Everest. They are left unpainted, fringed with a wooden ledge the color of ocher. The roofs are flat, but the larger houses have a square step on each corner, like turrets, making the larger houses seem like small forts. Juniper is stacked on top of the walls on all four sides. Each house has a main living area on the first floor, with benches around the walls for sitting and sleeping and a hearth. The animals are stabled below.

MINGMA WAS KNOWN AS GHANG LA MINGMA — Ghang La, Tenzing explained, being his family or clan name.[12] In fact, Ghang La is not a clan name, but it did meant a great deal to Tenzing, who in later years named his house in Darjeeling Ghang La, as a way of cementing his connection with his dead father. The Tibetan word *gang* means snow, and *la* is a pass. It is also the name of a short valley, not far from Tshechu, poised above the glacial sweep of the Rabkar Chu, another of the holiest sites in Béyül Khenbalung. At Ghang La was located the monastery of Namdag Lhe Phodang, the "perfectly pure god's palace,"[13] which, according to legend, is built over the palace of Khyikharathö, a mythical child born illegitimately to the wife of the great Tibetan king Trisong Detsen. This child had the face of a dog and the horns of a goat and is, according to anthropologist Hildegard Diemberger, a central figure in the myth of Béyül Khenbalung. Feeling ashamed of his wife's child, Trisong Detsen had Khyikharathö placed on a flying wooden cart which landed at Ghang La, where the child founded a great kingdom. In more recent history, Ghang La has been a place of retreat and meditation, like the cave at Tshechu. During Tenzing's childhood, a number of skilled women tantrists occupied the site, before the monastery was destroyed after the Lhasa uprising of 1959.

Ghang La is part of a huge expanse of pastureland that lies at the foot of the Langma La, one of the inner gateways from the Kharta Valley into the béyül. It lies high above the Rabkar Chu on an undulating terrace of several square miles, studded by turquoise lakes, all of which have legends of their own. Generations of yak herders have spent the summer here. Even today everything in a yak herder's tent seems to be either wooden or made from yaks, including the tent itself, which is yak hair.

Despite the looseness of its weave, to allow wood smoke out, it is surprisingly waterproof fabric. The tents are uniform in style, being ten feet square, with a fire in the center and a small altar just behind it. Stones are used to ring the base of the tent, and these are left in place when the herder moves on. Thus the same sites come to be occupied year after year. Inside the tent is a yak-leather barrel of fermenting milk, outside a press for making *churpi* or yak cheese. Tea is always available, brewed on the fire and then mixed in a tall wooden churn with yak butter and salt to give a highly calorific drink. The herders eat *tsampa,* or parched barley, which is ground up and mixed with tea to form a kind of thick dough, but they will eat meat too if an animal dies accidentally.

Juniper wood, which has deep religious significance to Tibetan peoples, crackles on the fire's embers, releasing thick smoke, which from a distance has an aromatic intensity that breeds nostalgia, but up close is choking, at least to the uninitiated. Tibetans seem oblivious, but lung infection and cancer rates among rural Tibetans testify to the smoke's long-term effects. Yak dung is also collected, dried, and burned. Herders will often keep a dog to guard the encampment from wolves or other trouble. Cultural rules about the slaughter of animals are strict. One yak herder said that a butcher has to be fetched to kill a wounded beast, a long knife driven through the yak's armpit into its heart. In summer the living is good, with plenty to eat and a more relaxed lifestyle than the farmers working in their fields of barley, although there is still plenty to do, which is why herders like to have their families with them. The children of herders work from a young age. Beasts must be milked, butter churned, and wood collected. In winter it is a cruel business, bitterly cold and harsh, and families stay at home. One herder told me of bleeding a yak for a meal, a practice that Tenzing describes in *Tiger of the Snows.*[14] Done in the autumn, herders believe it pacifies animals that are difficult to handle after a summer's rich grazing. Herders have a score of songs to coax their beasts along, and they judge the condition and mood of their animals with precision. This was the world of Ghang La Mingma, and the world into which Tenzing Norgay was born.

Mingma's yaks did not belong to him. In Tibet, before the Chinese occupation, almost all political and economic control was exercised by the monasteries and landowners. The laity usually worked for one or the other as serfs or monks. A monastery established in the 1600s called Sangnak Choeling, north of the Kharta Valley, held the grazing rights to Ghang La. This was the monastery that Mingma worked for, tending their yaks in the summer months there, and in the winter on grazing land near the Pang La, several days' march away, where the winter snowfall was lighter. How Mingma came to hold this position is unclear, but it was not the job held by his father or grandfather, according to some older villagers in the Kharta Valley.

Mingma's family had a long-standing connection with the powerful *dingpon* or landowner at Tsawa, 20 miles north of Kharta. This house was destroyed by Red Guards and its lands divided after the 1959 uprising, and most of the family fled Tibet, living with Tenzing in Darjeeling before moving to Kathmandu. Tenzing's family had a small homestead in Dangsar, and the men worked for the landlord at Tsawa as yak herders. Some of the women in Mingma's family worked there too as servants.

The house at Tsawa is now much reduced, its top floor with the traditional prayer room ripped away and much of its east wing collapsed. But it had clearly been one of the most substantial houses in the Kharta district. This was an important family. An impressive gateway and substantial wooden doors remain. Cracked, weathered frames that once housed prayer wheels run around a courtyard on the first floor. Low doorways lead off into a number of rooms. The house and the village occupy a pretty emerald crescent of flat land beside the river, with stands of willow and birch, nestled against the stark brown hills. It was here that Tenzing's father would spend his last years.

Mingma, the youngest of three sons, could not expect to inherit the job his father held, and although how Mingma came to work for Sangnak Choeling isn't known, the monastery is not far from Tsawa, and landowning families were the natural sponsors of religious institutions. It seems unlikely that Mingma could have gotten this position without some cooperation from the landowner at Tsawa. It was, in effect, a type of serfdom. Charles Howard-Bury provides a glimpse of Tenzing's childhood world in *Mount Everest: The Reconnaissance, 1921.* "Shepherds in this country are but poorly paid, getting only thirty *trangkas* per annum. But house servants are still worse off, getting only eight *trangkas* per annum. However, they seem to thrive under those wages and there is no discontent or trades unionism among them."[15] A trangka was only three old pence, perhaps 50 cents in modern terms, but yak herders gained more prestige from the size and quality of their herd than from any monetary wealth—there still isn't much to buy in Kharta—and they viewed themselves as freer than farmers and occupying a higher position in the social order. It was better to be managing a large herd of yaks at Ghang La than working in the fields of the Kharta Valley.

Monasteries would put money into local communities and then expect a return on their investment: "food, barley, milk, eggs and fuel," according to Howard-Bury. Local officials were also entitled to a cut of what each village produced. People were at the mercy of their local administrative leader, for better or worse, and the *dzongpen* at Kharta during Tenzing's childhood was not a magnanimous ruler. Stories about the cruel punishments he inflicted on his people—beatings, burying victims up to their neck, exposure—still circulate.

When Kinzom married Mingma, she took the title *dokmo*—a female herder, equivalent to the masculine, drokpa. During the summer she would accompany her husband with their growing family to the summer pasturage. Although the terrace below the Langma La is the biggest expanse of grassland in the Kama Valley, it often gets more snowfall in winter than other pasturage close by. Early in the summer, the grass can still be buried under several feet of snow, and herders start the summer grazing elsewhere. Tenzing believed he was born in the early summer, and so Mingma and Kinzom could have been with their yaks at Tshechu, waiting to move to the grazing around Ghang La. Kinzom had a sister, Tenzing Kundol, and one villager in Kharta recalls that she had been an *ani la,* or nun, at Ghang La. Nomad women would help each other when their time to give birth came, and so it is possible that Kinzom's sister was at Tshechu for Tenzing's birth. The lamas living in the hermitage at Tshechu considered his place of birth highly propitious: "According to my parents, the holy men told them to take especially good care of me for at least three years, for if I was still alive then I would grow up to be a great man."

Tenzing's genetic inheritance is worth examining, since it gave him such an advantage in his work as a Sherpa porter.[16] While the lamas divined great things for the boy, his biology was already adjusting in ways that were impossible for them to fathom but were the consequence of tens of thousands of years of natural selection. Unadapted babies from the lowlands suffer from reduced oxygen saturation in their blood if born at altitude, whereas Tibetan infants don't. Nor do they suffer a further fall over subsequent weeks, as unadapted babies do. Fetal cardiovascular patterns, particularly high blood pressure, persist in unadapted babies, whereas Tibetan infants adjust quickly, saving them from the risk of hypertension and the failure of the right side of the heart, complications that kill Han Chinese babies in Lhasa. The infant Tenzing had a greater lung capacity than children born at sea level—some would later joke that Tenzing had a third lung—although smoky fires at home could undermine this advantage. His heart would work harder on Everest than that of a European, his blood pressure would be lower, and, for biochemical reasons not yet fully understood, his muscles would work more efficiently. During exercise, the delivery of blood to the brain is more efficient in Tibetan peoples, an advantage in decision-making and performance when climbing a mountain. Put together with the resourcefulness that managing a herd of yaks, often alone, engendered and the physical toughness of life in a country with no modern amenities, Tenzing's genetic advantage made him well suited for high-altitude climbing before he'd ever set foot on a mountain.

DURING THE AUTUMN, before the first winter snows closed the high passes, the yaks were driven for several days to the winter pasturage at Pang La, where the beasts could find a little grass to nourish them until the spring. Then the family remained in the house at Dangsar. The Kharta Valley is broad and open, with fields of barley greening in the spring, the yaks dragging a wooden plough through them after the harvest in September. Men and women work in the fields together, the children in the fields too, babies sleeping in wooden boxes covered with blankets, older kids carrying younger. Everyone's face is grimy from the smoke of fires and the reluctance to wash and strip the face of valuable oils that protect the skin from the sun and wind of high altitude. In the monsoon the hillsides are smothered in flowers, in the fall the trees turn gold and orange. It is a fertile, textured place, damp and green compared with the valleys to the north. The bells tied round the necks of the yaks mean that you can always hear a dull clanking from the fields, the houses cluster together creating narrow lanes offering shelter from the bitter cold of winter. Among the fields, on prominent trees or boulders, there are prayer flags and bundles of bamboo signaling the spiritual connection of the farmers with their land. Houses have yak horns nailed over the doorways—the doors are low so you have to duck—to keep bad spirits out. Dung is stuck to the walls, drying in the sun to be used for fuel. This was the family's other world, for more than six months of each year.

Tenzing had two surviving older brothers, Kesang and Chingdu, whose son Topgay would join him on Everest in the 1950s. Then came two sisters, Kipa and Thakchey. Tenzing also had a younger sister, Sonam Doma, who would remain in Khumbu until the later 1950s. Tenzing's memories of his early life were fragmentary but very poignant:

"There are, of course, many things from that time that I have forgotten, but a few I remember well. One is riding round on the back of one of my older brothers, who is now long ago dead. Another is the animals in winter. When they were crowded into the lower storey of our house, and how they steamed and smelled as they came in out of the cold. Still another is the rest of us, the family, almost as crowded in the upper storey: all of us packed together in no space at all, with the noise and the stenches and the smoke from cooking, but happy and contented because we did not know there was any other way to live."[17]

Tenzing was given the name Namgyal Wangdi by his parents, but the chronic ill health that affects so many children in rural Tibet left him weak, and so Kinzom and Mingma turned to the old Tibetan practice of renaming a child to give it a new start, a new direction to improve its fortunes. They took Tenzing to see Nawang Tenzing Norbu, more commonly known as Dzatrul Rinpoche, the great religious leader. Born in 1866, he was the catalyst for religious reform in the area, raising funds among the rich traders at Dingri for new institutions. In 1902 he founded the current *gompa* at Rongbuk, and after World War I he was the guiding hand behind the exquisite monastery at Tengboche on the southern approach to Everest. Dzatrul was also the lama whose blessing the

Everest expeditions of the 1920s and 1930s sought. He told Tenzing's parents that their son was the reincarnation of a wealthy man who had died recently. Because of this his name should be changed to Tenzing—or "supporter of religion"—Norgay, meaning "wealthy." Tenzing was Dzatrul's own name, a common one for monks, and it was commonplace for monks to give children brought to them their own name.

As the third son, Tenzing was placed in a monastery by his parents with the long-term intention of his becoming a lama. Which monastery they put him in is unclear, because there have been seismic upheavals in religious practice since the Chinese occupied Tibet. Tenzing's nephew Gombu studied at Rongbuk, but he remembers this was not his uncle's gompa. In Tenzing's youth, the great monastery in the Kharta Valley was Chöde, of which only a ruin now remains. Howard-Bury refers to it as Gandenchöfel, because Ganden, the great institution near Lhasa, was its parent monastery:

"This was a curious building, square in shape, and surmounted by a cupola. It was very solidly built of stone and was, [the monks] told us, about 500 years old. It was founded by a saint called Jetsun-Nga-Wang-Chhöfel, who after a great flood which swept down the valley, destroying all the houses in it, had taken a large frog (which animal is believed to represent the Water God) and buried it under the centre pillar of the temple. With great reverence they showed us the spot under which this unfortunate frog had been immured in the centre of the shrine."[18]

As a young monk, Tenzing would have had his head shaved and put on the heavy woollen maroon robes of Tibetan Buddhist monks. Young monks don't take vows immediately, but after a year promise not to kill, not to steal, not to lie, and not to have sex, but there's no evidence that Tenzing got that far. His days would have been filled by prayers, doing chores, and taking the first steps of a religious education. He would have spent hours each day learning mantras by rote in the gloomy prayer room, the smell of butter lamps in his nostrils, shivering in winter and watching stray shafts of sunlight filtering into the darkness in the spring. The monastery was an entire community. Some monks concentrated on the religious life while others dealt with more practical matters, such as collecting rents. None of it appealed to Tenzing.

One lama lost his temper with the boy and struck him on the head with a stick. He ran away to his parents, who allowed him to stay with them. Tenzing speculated on what might have happened if his father had forced him to go back—perhaps he would have remained a lama—but the practical consequence of his escape from monastic life was losing the one real chance he had of learning how to read and write. In the West it is now almost impossible to meet a highly intelligent person who is totally illiterate and to comprehend how they see the world and themselves. Tenzing was driven by the idea of education, and perhaps his greatest source of pride was seeing all his six surviving children go through school. "I climbed Everest so that you wouldn't have to," he told his son Jamling when he came seeking permission to join an Indian expedition to Everest in 1983. "You can't see the entire world from the top of Everest, Jamling. The view from there only reminds you how big the world is and how much more there is to see and learn."[19]

Tenzing may never have gone to school, but he was a lifelong learner, acutely aware of how people carried themselves, of their ideas and what they could offer him intellectually. Rabindrinath Mitra, a young Bengali tea planter and publisher who befriended Tenzing a couple of years before he climbed Everest, recalls how the Sherpa would spit into a handkerchief, even walking down the street in Darjeeling, while others would just hawk into the dust at their feet, much as they do now. In microcosm, the anecdote shows how Tenzing was conscious of other habits, ideas, cultures in the world, and that he could benefit from learning about them. Although he would never achieve total fluency in English, he was very expressive and also spoke a number of Asian languages, Nepali—the eastern Himalaya's lingua franca—among them, and all this without the benefit of a classroom. But his illiteracy was a cause of frustration, especially for a proud man who felt quite rightly that he was the intellectual equal of many of the Europeans and Indians for whom he worked.

As for religion, Tenzing maintained a skeptical distance from the world of monasteries and monks while keeping his faith in the dharma. "True religion is one thing," he said. "Its outward forms and practices, unfortunately, can be another."[20] While admiring great lamas, he suspected that many of them couldn't look after "a herd of yaks, let alone human souls" and was sure that many monks were interested only in the best living they could get with the least effort. When he climbed Everest, a local Darjeeling monastery asked for a donation, but Tenzing preferred to give money to a hostel for impoverished travelers or pilgrims rather than rewarding "a group of monks who would use it only for themselves." The pragmatism Tenzing showed in the mountains applied to his soul as well.

Another of his early childhood memories focuses on literacy and also shows how Tenzing considered himself to be different from his peers, an echo of which is picked up in Mitra's story about him not spitting in the street: "As a grown man I have come to realize that in some ways I am a little different from most of my people. And I think the difference had already begun at this time. I remember I was very shy and stayed much by myself, and while the other boys chased one another and played games with mud and stones I would sit alone and dream of far places and great journeys. I would pretend I was writing a letter to an important man in Lhasa who would come and get me. Or that I was leading an army there. And sometimes I would make my father laugh by asking him for a horse, so that I could go."[21] The urge to leave and explore what life outside his valley had to offer was already strong. Many climbers of whatever cultural background would recognize this feeling in their own motivation. Tenzing clearly had a good relationship with his father, for whom Tenzing would perform tasks "even when I didn't have to." His sister Lhamu Kipa would tell him he was their parents' favorite. The circumstances of his birth, the place, and the lamas' predictions had been propitious, and the family had done well in the years afterward.

The anthropologist Sherry B. Ortner sees another revealing aspect to these memories of his childhood, particularly in Tenzing's daydream about writing a letter to an "important man" in Lhasa. This accords with the Tibetan idea of a *zhindak*,[22] a patron or sponsor who helps a lesser man succeed and in doing so draws strength himself. Ortner adds that this idea characterizes human relationships with the gods who inhabit the world around Everest. They also grow stronger when "lesser" beings seek their intercession. Sherpa society is much more egalitarian than the Hindu caste system in Nepal and India. Outside the family, Sherpa men consider themselves as good as anyone else, no matter how rich or poor they are. The zhindak is not part of a hierarchy, more a device to help even up the odds. As Ortner explains: "The junior party is not positioned as a child or a social inferior, but rather something more like a talented but disadvantaged protégé. In folktales, for example, the junior party is usually a bright young man who is down through no fault of his own, but who needs some extra help and power to come back strongly and defeat those who are illegitimately besting him."[23]

Most small boys have heroes, whether they are football players or great lamas, and early experiences of such figures can leave deep impressions. Some believe that as a small boy Tenzing met George Mallory, who was a member of all three expeditions to Everest in the 1920s, disappearing with Andrew Irvine on the north side of the mountain in 1924 and prompting speculation on whether he reached the summit 29 years before Tenzing and Ed Hillary. In 1921 Mallory and the rest of the expedition spent a considerable amount of time exploring the Kharta region and the eastern approaches to Everest. Mallory's diary reveals how he came to be lost near Tenzing's home in the village of Dangsar. Another possibility for an encounter could have taken place much closer to Everest, below the Langma La. Mallory crossed this pass on August 3, 1921, in bad weather, and camped at its foot. The next day he traversed the grassy terrace and descended to the Kama Chu Valley, crossing the rickety wooden bridge at the bottom and then climbing up the Kangshung Valley and onto the true left bank of the glacier that flows from the east face of Everest. At this point in the summer, Tenzing and his family would have been at Ghang La, herding their yaks. Mallory did camp alongside some yak herders, frustrated by the continuing thick cloud blanketing the mountains. "At least," he wrote in his diary, "we should have the advantage here of good butter and cream from this dairy farm."

Howard-Bury followed Mallory two days later, crossing the Langma La in clearer conditions, taking his usual delight in the incomparable view: "We now descended through grassy uplands for nearly 3,000 feet, past another beautiful lake called Shurim-tso, and came to a curious long and narrow terrace about 1,000 feet above the bottom of the valley. Here there was a tent belonging to some yak herds; and as wood and water were plentiful I determined to stop and spend the night with them."[24]

The first Europeans in Kama Valley would have generated huge excitement among the local population of yak herders. But even if

Tenzing did encounter George Mallory, he didn't dream of climbing Everest because of a chance meeting with one of the *chilina-nga*, the pale foreigners whose eccentricity was beyond comprehension. The worldliness and success of the expedition porters were what impressed him. He says in *Tiger of the Snows* that everyone knew all about them and that Sherpas and Tibetans living in Darjeeling had worked for them. "They came back with all sorts of stories abut the *chilinanga*, and about climbing almost to the sky; and most of them wore big boots and strange clothes such as we had not seen before. I was so fascinated that one day I paid money to use a pair of the boots, but they were so big and heavy for me that I could not walk at all."[25] Dorje Lhatoo said that Tenzing would sometimes recall these early experiences of mountaineering: "He remembered expeditions coming to the Kharta Valley when he was small. When we worked together and we'd be sitting round the campfire he would tell stories about his childhood in Tibet. He talked about how he would look up to these Sherpas and Bhotias who seemed to have a very good life, wealthy, with fancy clothes and heavy boots. He aspired to be one of them."

Whether or not Tenzing met Mallory or any of the other climbers from the 1920s, their true importance was the opportunity they offered the poor young Sherpas and Tibetans with few other options to take their first steps up the ladder of advancement. Later, when Tenzing found himself derided for his impoverished background, climbing mountains would offer him the chance to prove that he was as good as anyone.

ONE MORE EARLY RELATIONSHIP HELPED form the direction of Tenzing's life, and that was with Everest itself. "I have dedicated my story to Chomolungma," he said in *Tiger of the Snows*, "for it has given me everything. To whom else should I make my dedication?"[26] As a boy, in the pastures around Ghang La, Tenzing would have seen Chomolungma whenever the weather was clear, floating above his head, perfect and sharp against the blue sky. The mountains seeped into his consciousness in the same way that the streets and buildings of our childhood neighborhoods do. What seemed an everyday thing becomes much later a reminder of the security and love of our parents and our home. Later, when he and his family migrated to Khumbu, the mountain would change character again, more elusive behind the wall of Nuptse, and black instead of white, the shark's fin of its upper southwest face spearing out from lesser peaks as he watched the yaks from high pastures. And then, before he was 21, camped with the British in the Rongbuk Valley with the huge mass of the north face filling the end of it, he would see the mountain at its most impressive.

Chomolungma, the Tibetan and Sherpa name for Everest, is usually and erroneously translated as "Mother Goddess of the Earth" and less frequently as "Mother Goddess of the Wind." Tenzing himself offered an alternative he took from his mother, "The Mountain So High No Bird Can Fly Over It," which has more of a ring of truth. Edwin Bernbaum, in *Sacred Mountains of the World** argues that it should be transcribed Jomolangma, or "The Lady Langma," *jomo* meaning "lady" and Langma being a compressed version of the goddess Miyolangsangma,[27] who inhabits the mountain, according to Tibetan Buddhism. Sir Basil Gould, the Tibetologist and diplomat, argued that the name means "Land of Hen Birds," an interpretation of the Lhasa spelling of the name. Perhaps most credible is Trulshik Rinpoche's translation "Unshakable Good Elephant Woman." Others have suggested it means simply "The Peak Above the Valley" since *chomo* often refers to a peak, and *lung*—to rhyme with "put"—can mean a broad valley. For what it's worth, a yak herder in the Kama Valley recently offered me this answer:

"What does Chomolungma mean?"

"Hen."

"Hen?"

"Yeah, but a big hen, with all its feathers puffed out. So it looks fat."

"Big fat hen?"

"Yeah, big fat hen."

Most important, Tibetans below Everest see the mountains as one massif rather than individual peaks; there is no Sherpa word for "summit." Mountain climbers were the ones who valued the top of a peak, not the villagers who lived in its shadow. Tibetans in Kharta still call Makalu, which is an obviously distinct mountain, Chomolungma, something George Mallory first discovered in 1921. When the expedition reached the Kangshung Glacier below the east face of Everest, Charles Howard-Bury wrote, "Everest from here is seen to fill up the head of the valley with a most formidable circle of cliffs overhung by hanging glaciers, but it is not nearly such a beautiful or striking mountain as Makalu or Chomolönzo. The shepherds would insist that Makalu was the higher of the two mountains, and would not believe us when we said that Mount Everest was the higher."[28]

The Sherpas view the mountain in a different, and much more complete, way. Climbing is of course about reaching the top, and ambition and a need for achievement are among the primary motives. Sherpas have woven myths into their relationship with Everest. Ideas of pollution—everything from repugnant smells from burning garbage to extramarital sex—are offensive to the mountain goddess and likely to lead to disaster. Miyolangsangma is angered by emotions such as lust, greed, or pride. Of course, the more rational explanation behind the stories is that these emotions are bad for anyone on a mountain, where the struggle to stay alive requires all your concentration.

Tenzing lived far from Everest for most of his life, but he could, from the hills above Darjeeling, just see its summit appearing on the horizon on a clear winter morning. It was a link with Kharta, a reconnection to those first simple days in his parents' tent, or in the house at Dangsar, listening to the animals shifting downstairs in their stables and to the laughter of his family around the fire. After he climbed Everest, he said: "Seven times I have tried, I have come back and tried again; not with pride and force, not as a soldier to an enemy, but with love, as a child climbs onto the lap of its mother."[29] For Tenzing Norgay, Chomolungma meant home.

CHAPTER THREE

LIFE AS A KHAMBA

Tenzing of Mount Everest fame is an outstanding example
of a landless Khamba, who owes his fortune solely to mountaineering success.
He was born in Tibet, came to Khumbu as a young boy,
and worked for several years for one of the rich families of Khumjung.
—CHRISTOPH VON FÜRER-HAIMENDORF, *Himalayan Traders*[1]

O VER 40 MILES TO THE WEST of the Kharta Valley is a high glacial pass in the shadow of Cho Oyu, sixth highest mountain in the world, that crosses from Tibet into Khumbu, the Sherpa homeland across the border in Nepal. Sherpas call it the Nangpa La; people in Kharta refer to it as Khumbu La, or Khumbu Kang La—the "Snowy Pass Into Khumbu." In recent years the Nangpa La has become known as one of the favored routes for refugees leaving Tibet to escape the Chinese occupation. At over 18,753 feet, the route is treacherous in bad weather, and many suffer frostbite or snow blindness on the long trek to freedom. But long before Tibetans started fleeing their homeland, the Nangpa La was a trade route, the conduit by which Khumbu Sherpas achieved their wealth as the ultimate high-altitude middlemen.

In 1828 the Rana government in Kathmandu forbade Tibetans crossing the Nangpa La from approaching nearer than Nauche, the Sherpa market town. It also decreed that Sherpas from Solu could not trade directly with Tibetans. The 1,500 Sherpas in Khumbu found themselves with a monopoly on trade, and they quickly exploited it, carrying grain and butter, paper from Solu, buffalo hides for boot making, sugar, and other commodities, even iron, into Tibet. On the return trip they brought back highly prized Tibetan salt and wool. "Big men" trading across the Himalaya concentrated on commodities. Poorer "small men" exploited the discrepancy in value between salt and grain, because a measure of salt was worth several measures of rice or corn in Nepal while the converse was true in Tibet. The Sherpas in Khumbu prospered, buying property in Dingri and elsewhere in Tibet. They also gained experience of the world, a few traveling widely to Lhasa and Indian cities such as Calcutta. Slowly, they began to look outward from their little valleys at the foot of Everest.

Agriculture, the other branch of their prosperity, also began to change. Less than one percent of land is arable in Khumbu, and the shortage of food restricted population growth for the first 300 years of Sherpa settlement. That changed with the introduction of the potato in the mid-19th century. It had three times the calorific value of the barley grown on the stony fields carved out of the hillsides below the shimmering white peaks. With this one new food and the development of trade, Khumbu could support many more people, sparking a social revolution. New monasteries such as Tengboche were built, allowing the Sherpas to reinvigorate their Tibetan heritage, halting the spreading influence of Nepal's Hindu culture.[2] Khumbu's economic progress also drew a wave of poor Tibetan migrants across the Nangpa La to take advantage of easier living conditions, leaving behind the oppression of a feudal society. This migration, continuing into the 20th century, was the historical tide that swept Tenzing and members of his family into Khumbu in the 1920s. It was not, however, the immediate cause.

Tenzing's family history is difficult to pin down. None of them could read or write, and they had no photographs and few heirlooms. More important, the Tibetan peoples have scant interest in recalling their own personal histories or for seeking out those of their parents or grandparents, perhaps because of the Buddhist practice of letting go attachment to dead relatives, releasing them for their next reincarnation. Nor is there the same fascination in examining their own personalities as there is in the West. Ang Rita, a highly respected Sherpa working for the Himalayan Trust, said, "Sherpa parents are just not very good at telling their children about their families." Pem Pem, Tenzing's eldest daughter, says the family knew little about his early life. She discovered she had relatives in Kharta only after the Everest veteran George Band visited the region in 1998. She had questions about her father's roots, but he died before she could bring them up: "I never expected that my father would pass away so suddenly. I never asked him about some of these things."

In 1914 Tenzing's father, Mingma, seems to have been prosperous. Tenzing said that in the year following his birth a hundred young yaks were born, "and after that we had as many as three or four hundred at a time."[3] Even allowing for exaggeration, Mingma must have managed a considerable number of beasts, and even though they belonged to the monastery, his success must have improved their lives and prestige. "We ate only the simplest food," Tenzing said, "but there was always enough of it—I do not remember ever being hungry—and from the yak wool and hides—we would take the hides if they died a natural death—we made clothing to keep us warm during the long, cold winters."

One theory suggests that Mingma and his family were forced to leave Khumbu after falling out with the landowner at Tsawa. Lhamu Kipa, Tenzing's big sister, to whom he was devoted, worked as a servant girl there and fell in love with the landowner's younger son, Nawang—a monk— and became pregnant by him. The two migrated to Khumbu when their son Gombu, born in 1936, was five. It was not the disgrace of leaving his monastery that forced Nawang and Lhamu Kipa to leave Tibet. That happened regularly enough and was accepted. A relationship between a member of the aristocracy and a serf, on the other hand, was not. Later, perhaps because Nawang's father was dead, Nawang and Lhamu Kipa returned to Tibet, because Tenzing met Lhamu Kipa at Rongbuk monastery in 1947.

In such a scenario, Mingma and Kinzom's own situation would also become difficult, their lives made unbearable by a vindictive landlord. Yet the evidence points in another direction. In the first place, Tenzing left Tibet as a boy in the early or mid-1920s, years before Gombu was born. Furthermore, although Lhamu Kipa and Nawang fell from favor, Mingma and Kinzom were still living at Tsawa in the 1940s and the two families remained on good terms. Tsering Bhuti Dingsta, now a nun in Kathmandu, was the daughter of a family of doctors from Sakya who married Nawang's eldest brother, Kasang, the man who eventually inherited Tsawa. She remembers Mingma and Kinzom were living at the house during this period, albeit after the old landowner died and was succeeded by his son. When she and her family were forced to abandon the house in 1959 and flee to India, Tsering Bhuti Dingsta and her family stayed with Tenzing, an unlikely event if the families were so bitterly divided over an inappropriate love match that one of them had been forced into exile.

That Tenzing's father suffered some kind of setback is clear from *Tiger of the Snows*. After he had been living in Darjeeling for 18 months, Tenzing heard in 1934 that his parents believed him dead and were performing funeral rites for him. In his account, he returned to Khumbu, although it may well have been Kharta, to reassure them he was still alive. While there, his father persuaded him to carry salt over the Nangpa La from Tibet to Nepal. Tenzing doesn't say if it was for his father or for a trader in Khumbu, but whoever it was for, this was a tough way to make a living. The salt would have been bartered for rice or grain and only those with no other means at their disposal would resort to this kind of work, humping 80-pound loads over the Nangpa La, as often as a dozen times a season. Why would the herder of several hundred yaks, a substantial number even in the days when trade with Nepal was straightforward, resort to sending his son across the Nangpa La with salt?

The explanation is that sometime in the 1920s, Mingma and his family suffered a catastrophe. One autumn, as he always did, Mingma took the yaks from the pasturage at Ghang La on the long trek to the north side of Everest and Sangnak Choeling's winter pasturage at the Pang La, *pang* meaning "grass." The Pang La is an inhospitable and bleak place in comparison and at a similar high altitude to Ghang La, but there were good reasons to take yaks there in the winter, as Charles Howard-Bury discovered in 1921. "It is curious," he wrote, "that even in the winter-time [herders] can find grazing places, but the secret lies in the fact that the slopes face the south in the regions where the wind blows strongest, so that the surface is usually bare. [The] herds obtain sufficient nourishment from such scattered patches of frozen grass or lichens as they are able to find."[4] Howard-Bury's description doesn't remotely do justice to the harshness of yak herding in winter. Mingma would have been without his family, perhaps taking one of his older sons

to help him in the brutal cold. They would have faced a constant struggle just to stay warm and healthy, anxious if snow fell that it would leave
their animals starving, working in temperatures far below freezing. And
at some point during this particular winter, all his nightmares came true.
The yaks started dying, all of them, until Mingma was left with nothing.

The event is still remembered in the Kharta Valley. Dolka Marpa,
who worked at Tsawa and nursed Mingma in his final years, remembers
it clearly. Kinzom's sister Tenzing Kundol also passed the story down to
her family. And Tenzing himself told his ghostwriter, James Ramsey
Ullman, about the disaster during interviews for *Tiger of the Snows*. A
comment left out of the final manuscript reads: "It was very difficult with
yaks because sometimes a disease would break out and most of them
would die."[5] This is what happened to Tenzing's father.

What caused the animals to die in such numbers is unclear, but Dolka
Marpa talked about a disease that left lesions on the skin, something infectious that spread quickly through the yaks, already weakened by cold and
wind. This sudden reversal left Tenzing's parents in a desperate situation. After years of successful breeding, Mingma's herd was gone and his
job with it. The summers of plentiful food were over. While the family
had the small property in the Kharta Valley, there were six surviving
children, and some of them already had their own children to support.
Making a living in Kharta was difficult, and plenty of Tibetans took the
opportunity to trade across the Nangpa La or work as a servant or a
farmhand in Khumbu, either year-round or seasonally. Tenzing's older
brothers, Kesang and Chingdu, carried loads over the Nangpa La for
wealthy trading families in Khumjung. They might have done this
anyway, even if Mingma hadn't lost his job, but such a large herd would
have offered a lot of work for his children.

Although they worked in Khumbu, neither brother seems to have settled there. In 1953 the anthropologist Christoph von Fürer-Haimendorf
found Chingdu's widow, Kinsum, living in a small house in Khumjung
working as a daily laborer.[6] She had only recently arrived from Tibet after
the death of her husband; her one son, Topgay, had by then gone to
Darjeeling to live with her brother-in-law Tenzing.

Half of the families in Khumjung were newcomers like Kinsum—
or, as the Sherpas called them, "Khambas." Some of the Khambas were

of Nepalese origin, but most were Tibetan migrants who, from the late spring onward, would trek across the glacial wastes of the Nangpa La, some coming to work for the summer, others coming for good. They were considered inferior socially. Sherpas would say they arrived with nothing but "a basket and a stick." If necessary, they would beg for a few potatoes, and sleep in the unused ground-floor rooms of Sherpa houses in return for laboring in the fields or collecting wood. Those migrants who already had family in Khumbu could rely on them for help, and presumably, as Tenzing's family members came one by one over the Nangpa La, they smoothed the way for each other.

During harvest, work was plentiful, and the Khambas had practical skills that the Sherpas often lacked. Without the need to do unpaid labor required by dzongpens and other officials within Tibet, and with food more plentiful, some Tibetans flourished in Khumbu and quickly became subsumed into Sherpa culture within a couple of generations. Others would stay for the summer and return home, or even migrate to Darjeeling and seek work there, as Tenzing did. Khumbu relied on this influx of manual labor as poorer Sherpas moved out of Khumbu in their own migration.

Resentment against Khambas, especially those first-generation Tibetans whose position in Sherpa society was not yet secure, was never far below the surface. Anthropologist Christoph von Fürer-Haimendorf, whose fieldwork was done in the mid 1950s, wrote:

"There is the widespread feeling that Khambas are basically inferior to Sherpas, and this sentiment finds expression in many a loose generalisation on Khamba character and behaviour. As most Khambas arrive in Khumbu as paupers their standards of honesty are as a rule much lower than those of settled Sherpas. Such petty thefts as occur in Khumbu are usually committed by Khambas, and Sherpas are no doubt justified in doubting the trustworthiness of seasonal workers and new arrivals who live from hand to mouth and have very little to lose."[7]

Although Sherpas are a sexually tolerant people, they viewed Khambas as overly promiscuous and prone to live together without bothering to go through any marriage ceremony. The reason for not doing so was reasonable enough—weddings cost money, which the migrants lacked—but it gave another reason for established Sherpa families to feel morally superior to recent arrivals from Tibet. Marriage between Sherpas and Khambas was certainly possible, and for those Khambas that put down roots in Khumbu it was the easiest way to advance socially. But wealthy Sherpa families were more cautious in allowing Khambas to be absorbed in this way. Von Fürer-Haimendorf records that over the course of two generations among six prominent families in the village of Khumjung, there were 34 marriages, 28 of them within Sherpa clans and only 6 between Khambas and Sherpas. Even then, the Khamba families involved were established and economically successful.[8]

Mingma was far from that level. Many in the family believe he had fallen into serious debt and may have resorted to "mortgaging" the teenage Tenzing to one of the prominent Khumjung families or clans—the Thaktua—as a yak herder. In return for a pittance, the servant would work an agreed period of time or until the father of the child repaid the debt. Tenzing never spoke about this, and the account of these years in *Tiger of the Snows* is deliberately hazy; the past was painful for him. Mingma would have needed to go to the local administrator and tax collector, the *pembu,* who was almost certainly related to the family Tenzing worked for in Khumjung or may have been the pembu himself, since this hereditary position was held by established Sherpa clans. No Khamba could settle in Khumbu and scratch out new fields on uncultivated land without permission from the pembu.

Tenzing would have known his place in Sherpa society and that his chances of progressing were slight. He was not a wealthy Khamba who could expect to marry a Sherpa from an established family; his children might advance in this way, but the most he could have expected was to help free his father's debts and acquire his own house and a little land. At a party or a festival, after *chang*—the local beer—had blunted Sherpa politeness, Tenzing's bearing, intelligence, and charisma would have irritated weaker but better-born men. He was taller than most Sherpas at five feet eight inches, and less stocky. He would have spoken the Sherpa dialect less than fluently when he first arrived, and his Tibetan was always marked by a Kharta accent. As Dorje Lhatoo explained, "We have a name for them: Kharta-wa, people from Kharta." Although Tenzing would have been tolerated, he was not on the inside. The irony is that if he had settled in Khumbu permanently, his children and their children would have integrated over the years completely as Sherpas, but Tenzing himself would never have become famous, scratching out a life as a subsistence farmer.

When Tenzing arrived in Khumbu is not certain. Norbu Tenzing, his eldest surviving son, and others in the family believe Tenzing was around seven, perhaps even younger. But Dolka Marpa, the servant at Tsawa, remembers that he was an adolescent, perhaps 14. He may have gone to Khumbu seasonally to begin with and later, when his father put him into service in Khumjung, settled there for good. Some clues in *Tiger of the Snows* show that Dolka Marpa's memory is correct. In the account of Tenzing's childhood, many events that apparently took place in the Khumbu actually occurred in Tibet, because Tenzing wanted to underplay his Tibetan roots. For instance, when his curiosity about the outside world prompted him as a 13-year-old to run away from home, he said, "I went to Kathmandu roundabout, by way of Makalu, at first alone and then with some other travellers whom I met on the way; and it took a little more than two weeks to get there."[9] Yet if he started from Thame, traveling to Kathmandu via Makalu is an odd choice, since Makalu lies to the east and the city to the west. From Kharta, however, the quickest way to Kathmandu is down the Arun Valley, and the mountain that dominates this more easterly route is Makalu.

Tenzing spent a fortnight in Kathmandu, the first city he had ever seen. He found free lodging in a Buddhist monastery and explored the city's temples and bazaars, being particularly struck by the Nepalese army parading in Durbar Square. In the 1920s Nepal was still controlled by the Rana prime minsters, the Shah dynasty of kings mere figureheads. The country itself was effectively the private treasury of the Ranas, who lived in astonishing luxury, ruling a people whose lives were locked in poverty without education or prospects. Kathmandu was a city crammed with the most exquisite art whose citizens were condemned to live in squalor. Few foreigners visited Nepal in the 19th and early 20th centuries. Kathmandu itself was isolated with no road linking its valley with the outside world, just a ropeway carrying in supplies. There were no newspapers until after the war. The British in India were content to let the Ranas behave as they chose as long as Nepal's chief export—its people—continued to swell the ranks of the Gurkha regiments. More than a hundred thousand of them had fought for the empire in the Great War.

But even as the 13-year-old Tenzing watched the strange faces going to the temples in the morning or filling the bazaars at dusk, the world was on the verge of turmoil. Inspired by Gandhi and the independence movement in India, Nepalese democrats were agitating for a political revolution. The British era was drawing to a close and Europe's fortunes would soon turn again, and for the very worst. In the Himalaya, the 1930s were the last gasp of an old order that would soon collapse as the pace of change accelerated in Asia.

Tenzing knew none of this. He soon became homesick in the big city. He describes meeting pilgrims and travelers from Solu Khumbu returning home and went with them: "This time we took a more direct route, along the same way I was to go many years later with the Swiss and British to Everest."

Exactly when Tenzing left Tibet behind doesn't really matter; the impetus for going was the same. Tibetans migrated for economic reasons, sometimes to escape punishment, and Tenzing's family was no exception. His ambition to be among the Bhotias working on Everest, his ambition to be someone of consequence was already set, but until he found the opportunity to strike out on his own, he had for the meantime to take whatever living he could find. All three of Tenzing's sisters would eventually migrate into Khumbu, and his mother may have done so too, at least for a time. She was in Khumbu in the early 1950s, but most probably came from the house at Tsawa to see her one surviving son during his climbing expeditions to Everest. Perhaps during the bad years following the loss of Mingma's yaks she worked in Khumbu, which would explain how Tenzing may have come with her as a young boy if stories about his being a teenager when he migrated are not correct. His father may never have left Kharta at all, except to trade or visit relatives and to do seasonal work. A Kharta man called Tashi who died in 2000 claimed to be Mingma's son, by a woman from Moyü called Tseten. If true, Mingma's relationship with Tseten might have coincided with one of Kinzom's absences in Khumbu. By the late 1930s he had resumed working for the house at Tsawa as a yak herder. Kinzom was living there then as well, according to Tsering Bhuti Dingsta, who arrived from Sakya to marry Kasang, and they were certainly both living there in the 1940s when Dolka Marpa came to take up her duties as a house servant. Both of

Mingma's sons stayed on in Tibet. The elder, Kesang, was the progenitor of Tenzing's relatives who still live at Dangsar.

TENZING COULD HAVE SPENT HIS LIFE as a herder or farmer, perhaps occasionally working as a porter on expeditions like scores of others from Khumbu and Tibet. But like Ang Tharkay and Dawa Thondup and other adventurous, ambitious young Sherpas, the excitement of the outside world enthralled him. He would prosper only if he left Khumbu, and in 1932 there was talk of another expedition to Everest the following year, the first for some time. There had been attempts on other mountains since 1924, notably Kanchenjunga, and the prestige and excitement that surrounded the Sherpas and Tibetans who returned from these expeditions was impossible to ignore. Tenzing was now 18 and too impatient to wait any longer for his chance to join them.

Ang Tharkay was, until 1953, even more famous as a Sherpa than Tenzing himself, largely because of his contribution as *sirdar* to the 1950 French expedition to Annapurna, the first of the fourteen 8,000-meter giants to be climbed. But as his autobiography reveals, he too sprang from the humblest origins to a position literally and metaphorically on top of the world. The family had some land, but Ang Tharkay's uncle inherited most of it. His father fell into debt, and Ang Tharkay was forced to scratch out a living as a laborer, cutting wood or tending yaks, much as Tenzing did. With limited land and the nature of inheritance in Sherpa society, there would always be disaffected but talented young men looking for alternatives. Like Tenzing, Ang Tharkay saw opportunity in following the example of those who had gone to Everest in the early 1920s. Ang Tharkay actually mentions seeing one of his childhood friends parading around the village in the equipment he'd been given as a Sherpa on Everest. It wasn't success in the conventional sense, but it fired Ang Tharkay's imagination and gave him hope of something better. Nor were Tenzing and Ang Tharkay isolated cases. A large number of young men and women, tough, resourceful, outward-looking, hampered by circumstance but not trapped by Hindu notions of caste, would leave the tiny valley of Khumbu behind, dreaming of a better life in the hill station of

Darjeeling. The cash that mountaineering provided allowed them the kind of social mobility they could not have achieved remaining in their home villages. By risking their lives climbing mountains like Everest, they could buy the land and animals that their more well-born neighbors took for granted. Climbing mountains was the start of a tourism-based social revolution. As von Fürer-Haimendorf explains: "The sudden affluence of successful porters brought to the fore men of a class which used to live in the shadow of the rich families of inherited wealth. Several well-known high-altitude porters were Khambas of humble origin. Tenzing Norgay is an outstanding example of landless men who owe their fortunes solely to mountaineering prowess."[10]

Tenzing had another reason for escaping the small, confining valleys of Khumbu. In Thame Og, or Lower Thame, lived a girl, Dawa Phuti, the daughter of a prosperous Sherpa called Sepa Phurba, a trader who owned yaks and land and lived in a house below the Thame monastery. He had three daughters, Nimi and Choeki were the others, but no sons. Dawa Phuti was beautiful and very strong-willed, and she fell in love with Tenzing.

Sherpas are in many ways very relaxed about relationships between the sexes, certainly compared with the Hindu population to the south. They love flirting, have a robust sexual sense of humor—women included—and aren't fazed by issues such as premarital sex, premarital childbirth, divorce, and occasional adultery. Despite this, Sherpas are not particularly promiscuous. In Tenzing's youth, Sherpas all slept in the same room, worked in the same fields, went to the same festivals and dances, and any kind of liaison, sexual or otherwise, was played out in front of the others. Tenzing was tall, very handsome, had a beautiful smile, clear skin, and a confidence beyond his years. That Dawa Phuti even contemplated marrying him says a great deal about Tenzing's charisma, because he had nothing else to offer her. Although Sherpa parents were content for their children to follow their hearts, it was well understood that this could happen only between those of equal social standing.

The process of marriage for Sherpas is long and drawn-out and characteristically features a number of celebrations.[11] Sherpas do like a party. The first step, *sodene,* or in Tibet *dri-chang,* meaning "asking beer," involves a visit on behalf of the suitor to ask for the girl's hand. Who takes that role depends on how welcome the prospective match will be. If it is acceptable, the boy's father goes, often with other male relatives. If the match is not certain, another male relative or even a friend makes the offer of chang instead. If parents can anticipate an unwelcome betrothal coming, they can try to forestall it by making another, more suitable match. This is what Sepa Phurba did. Recognizing that Dawa Phuti and Tenzing were in love, he arranged a marriage to the son of a more established Sherpa family. "If Tenzing had arrived with lots of money," Dorje Lhatoo reflected wryly, "then it would have been a very different story. But a poor Tibetan boy coming across the border could only work as a farmhand or a domestic servant. He wasn't worthy of a Sherpani's hand." If they were going to find a way to stay together, then a drastic solution was required.

Christoph von Fürer-Haimendorf understood the problem very well. "A rapid departure to Darjeeling," he wrote, "became recognized as an easy way out of disputes and marital tangles."[12] That was the choice the two lovers faced: Accept Sepa Phurba's decision or run away to Darjeeling and start a new life together. They chose the latter. "There were twelve of us who left home together—both boys and girls—and we had been planning it for a month, holding secret meetings and collecting food and supplies. All I had been able to get for myself, though, was one blanket, which I took from our house. I had no money, nor did any of the others. In fact, that was the reason why most of us were going: to earn money. And also to see the world."[13]

Even for a well-equipped and -funded party, trekking to Darjeeling from Khumbu in 1932 would have been a daunting prospect, taking several weeks across hard ground. The young Sherpas and Sherpanis had to rely on the kindness of those they met along the way, sleeping where they could at night and by day slogging over steep ridges and through thick forests. Included in the little band of adventurers was Dawa Thondup, who filled Tenzing's head with ideas about how they would both get jobs on the expedition to Everest the following year. Their lives would be interwoven over the years, on various expeditions the length of the Himalaya. In the lists of porters held by the Himalayan Club in Darjeeling, Tenzing would hold the number 48; Dawa Thondup, 49. But Dawa Thondup, the elder by seven years, would be the first to find work.

When they got close to the border with India, Tenzing was for some unexplained reason left behind. "There was some sort of mix-up," he related, "and the others went on without me, taking all the food." That is all the explanation he offered. Soon afterward, at a town near a *simana,* "border crossing," he met a wealthy man who took him in. He gave him lighter Nepalese clothing to wear, and work to earn his keep—cutting firewood and doing jobs around the house. The man was a Tibetan trader, called Ringa Lama, who agreed, after a few weeks, to take Tenzing with him to Darjeeling, where he had business. Ringa Lama got Tenzing a job with a cousin, Pouri, whose cows Tenzing tended. Pouri lived at Alubari, which translates as "potato field," a small hamlet above Darjeeling that has a gompa where Sherpas are still cremated.

Tenzing described himself as a "lonely outsider" during 1933. While he was stuck in Alubari, the Sherpas who had traveled from Khumbu with him were living more than a mile away in Toong Soong Busti, the Sherpa shantytown clinging to the steep southeastern slopes of Darjeeling's hilltop. Marrying Dawa Phuti without a place of their own to live and any kind of income was impossible. Mixed with the excitement of all the new things he was experiencing in Darjeeling—cars and steam trains, hundreds of chilina-nga and their grand houses, a movie theater and glass-fronted stores, tea shops where the English women spent the afternoons—was the frustration of knowing that all of it was beyond his reach. Worst of all, his chance of joining an Everest expedition evaporated.

In late February the first expedition to Everest in nine years began assembling in Darjeeling. "The town," Tenzing recalled, "was upside down with the preparations." The expedition leader was Hugh Ruttledge, kindly, good-natured, and rather surprised to be leading an expedition to Everest at all. He wasn't a mountaineer, and he limped—improbably— from a pig-sticking accident. Yet as a former commissioner in the Indian Civil Service, he possessed good local knowledge and had traveled extensively in the Himalaya. He and the rest of his team set up in the Planters' Club, the social focus for Europeans in the town, and began hiring Sherpas. Those who would carry the sahibs' loads relied on family, tribe, and previous experience to secure employment. Tenzing had none of these. He went to Dawa Thondup, already hired by the expedition, but his friend would not intervene on his behalf because, he said, Tenzing was too young, a drawback echoed by other Sherpas in Toong Soong Busti. "They would do nothing for me," Tenzing said bitterly, "and I have never been more angry in my life."[14] Given that Sherpas made sure their relatives were looked after first, the Tibetan-born Tenzing, without any relatives of his own, felt his status as a Khamba was held against him. Ang Tsering, one of the great names among the Sherpas, had gone to Everest in 1924 with George Mallory and Andrew Irvine and was taken by Hugh Ruttledge in 1933. He was also Dawa Phuti's first cousin, as good as a brother for Sherpas, and would soon become related by marriage to Tenzing. But Tenzing was still unacceptable to the family in 1933 because, Ang Tsering recalled, he was poor and Tibetan.

Not willing to give up his chance, Tenzing approached the expedition directly, but he must have cut an unconvincing figure. Still only 18, he wore Nepalese clothes, hardly an authentic touch, and his hair was cut short. He didn't look like a Sherpa. He once had worn his hair long and braided with cotton, a fashion still prevalent in Kharta, where it is called *tapshu*. Arriving in Darjeeling, though, he had been told he looked like a girl, so he cut it in a Western style. His lack of any relative or friend to recommend him meant his chances were negligible. Still, he made the long climb up the steps to the Planters' Club, normally off limits for someone like Tenzing, to face the sahibs' cool indifference as they lounged on the verandah, and then was casually dismissed. "And you go away," he said, "wondering if you will never get a job in your life, because you have not had one already."[15]

As the expedition marched off up the Chumbi Valley to the border with Tibet, Tenzing was left behind to carry on miserably with his work as a cow herder in Alubari. Throughout the summer and fall of 1933 he continued as before, herding Pouri's cows and cutting fodder. Then, on January 15, 1934, one of the worst earthquakes in India's history struck the border area between the state of Bihar and Nepal. An area of 120,000 square miles was rocked, and more than 10,700 people died (unofficial estimates place the number as high as 30,000). Kathmandu was badly damaged and even Darjeeling suffered. In Khumbu, the new monastery at Tengboche was destroyed and Tenzing's family home was damaged. Tenzing recounts that his parents, who had heard nothing from their son for more than a year, believed him to be dead. He heard from travelers recently arrived from Khumbu that they were performing funeral rites, and he immediately made plans to return home. Some in Tenzing's family believe that Dawa Phuti went with him to see her family and plead their case once more. Ang Tsering recalls that Sepa Phurba had sent Dawa Phuti's brothers to Darjeeling to bring her home to Thame but that she ran away again, back to Tenzing. Nima Tenzing Galang, the couple's second daughter, says that Sepa Phurba himself came to take her home.

Tenzing had family problems of his own. He describes his parents' relief at finding him well, and he immediately set about helping them rebuild their house. In the summer of 1934 he was back working in the fields and with the yaks, and later he journeyed across the Nangpa La into Tibet to fetch salt to trade. At this juncture, Tenzing faced a choice: to turn his back on the excitement of Darjeeling, Dawa Phuti, and the possibility of a better life, or to return to help his parents through their last years at a time when their fortunes were low. He was devoted to his family, and it seems he considered the possibility, but in the autumn of 1934, when his father asked him to cross the Nangpa La again, he said no. "By now I knew for certain that I could never be happy in this life, and that I must return to the outside world."[16]

Tenzing would see his father twice more, in 1935 and 1938, when he was with expeditions on Everest. His knowledge of the Kharta Valley was useful in buying supplies and smoothing their passage. He was reunited with his brothers and their children as well. As for his mother, she and Mingma were living at Tsawa by the late 1930s. Tenzing wouldn't see her again until 1952 and 1953, and according to Dolka Marpa, Tenzing came to collect her at Tsawa in 1955 to take her to Darjeeling. She would eventually outlive 12 of her 14 children.

Mingma's final years were tragic. Old and with his health broken, the yak herder deteriorated badly in the late 1940s. Like most rural Tibetans, he washed his body only once a year and rarely removed his clothes. He was infested with lice and his skin became infected. None of the servants in the house would touch him until Dolka Marpa washed his wounds with hot water to ease his discomfort. He died in 1949. Perhaps because he was the youngest son, and one with such a propitious birth, Tenzing remembered Mingma as a generous and loving father.

Leaving his parents behind in Tibet grieved him. When he returned to Darjeeling, he knew he was hurting them:

"Again I went without telling my parents. And this was a sadness, because they had been kind to me and I loved them. They were very simple and pious people, especially my mother, who through all her life has never worn good clothes or eaten good food, but has given them instead, whenever she has had them, to the lamas and nuns of the monasteries. Then and always she has been a true mother, my *ama la*. And I know that her devoutness, her faith, her blessings and prayers, have had much to do with the success I have been granted."[17]

CHAPTER FOUR

TO EVEREST

It has been said that these men could easily reach the top
if they themselves really wished to do so.
I do not believe it for one moment ...
they have acclimatized bodies,
but lack the right mentality.
— BENTLEY BEETHAM, EVEREST, 1924

IN 1935 TENZING STILL HAD NO CLIMBING EXPERIENCE. He had spent the winter helping repair the chapel at St. Paul's School in Darjeeling, damaged in the earthquake of 1934. The wages were good enough,[1] but Tenzing's ambition to go to the mountains was stronger than ever. Although the German expedition to Nanga Parbat had been a disaster, the stories of Sherpa heroism had inspired him. Furthermore, his landlord, Ang Tharkay, had worked on a successful exploratory expedition that summer into the Nanda Devi Sanctuary in the Garhwal Himal with Eric Shipton and Bill Tilman. These were two of the British going to Everest that summer. If Ang Tharkay could rise so quickly from a poor country boy to a respected and trusted lead Sherpa, then so could he.

When he had gotten back to Darjeeling, instead of returning to his job as a dairyman at Alubari, he moved into the Sherpa district of Bhotia Busti, renting a room in Ang Tharkay's house. Other Sherpas lived in Toong Soong Busti, much nearer the center of town, such as Dawa Thondup and Ang Tsering, both now veterans of numerous expeditions.

They had both been porters on the tragic German expedition that summer. Tenzing now was at the heart of things, surrounded by the men he had admired so much as a boy.

In early 1935 he married Dawa Phuti. This was the point at which Tenzing began to be accepted by the Sherpa community, but if he and Dawa Phuti had hoped her father would come around, they were disappointed. "She was totally disowned," Nima Tenzing Galang recalled. "She never received her inheritance." Instead, her sister Nimi's husband was brought into the family to inherit Sepa Phurba's wealth. Also, a rift would open between Ang Tsering and Tenzing that would never be completely healed.

Dawa Phuti's name means a "wife who brings children," and she lived up to it, quickly becoming pregnant. Tenzing wanted to make his mark, to provide for his wife and to show her family that she had chosen well. The problem, however, remained the same. He didn't have a book from the Himalayan Club; his name did not appear on any register. Those holding the keys to his future were unknown to him: Eric Shipton, the expedition leader; W. J. Kydd, the Darjeeling secretary of the Himalayan Club; and Karma Paul, the Tibetan businessman and interpreter who acted as a linchpin in identifying and hiring porters for expedition work. Educated in Darjeeling, Paul spoke several languages well, and as Charles Bruce recalled, was "always good company, and always cheerful." His position as interpreter was pivotal, partly because Shipton believed a native should pick the crew. "If one can find a Sherpa whose judgement can be relied upon absolutely, it is a good plan to entrust him with the task of choosing his own companions, for no one can know the Sherpas as well as they know themselves."

Before Shipton arrived in Darjeeling, Karma Paul and Bill Tilman sorted out 14 porters, men who had worked for Shipton on previous trips, such as Ang Tharkay, Kusang Namgyal, and Pasang Bhotia. Tenzing was bitterly disappointed, but then he had a stroke of luck. When Shipton arrived, he decided the expedition needed two more. Slipping on a brand-new khaki bush jacket, Tenzing hurried to the Planters' Club and mingled with 20 other hopefuls as the sahibs made their decision. A photograph taken by Charles Warren captures this moment: Tenzing stands somewhat awkwardly on the club's veranda, looking intently at a group of sahibs sitting at a table in front of him. Tenzing recalled that Shipton and Kydd lined the men up and then checked each candidate in turn, so it seems that Tenzing is waiting for the chance to present his case. Other men in front of him had experience, and if Nanga Parbat hadn't robbed the Sherpa community of several porters, Tenzing probably would not have gotten that far. When he presented himself to Kydd and Shipton, he couldn't yet speak a word of English and had to gesture that he had no certificate from the Himalayan Club. The sahibs asked him to step out of line, and Tenzing thought his chance was lost. But Shipton had been taken by the young Bhotia, and Tenzing was hired. (The last boy taken was another Ang Tsering,[2] who had already been to Everest in 1933. He would die in the avalanche on Nanga Parbat in 1937.) Shipton wrote: "From a hundred applicants, we chose fifteen[3] Sherpas to accompany the expedition from Darjeeling. Nearly all of them were old friends, including, of course, Angtarkay, Pasang and Kusang; but there was one Tibetan lad of nineteen, a newcomer, chosen largely because of his attractive grin. His name was Tensing Norkay—or Tensing Bhotia as he was generally called."[4]

It wouldn't be the last time that Tenzing's radiant smile won him friends among the sahibs. He went away delighted, even though some of the "older men were annoyed because I was a novice and had been taken in."[5] He not only had several weeks of work at 12 annas a day, rising to a whole rupee a day above the snow line, but also he now possessed papers from the Himalayan Club—as good as a promise of future work. He was on the threshold of joining the ranks of the Sherpas and Tibetans who had left such a deep impression on him as a boy. Leaving his pregnant wife in their room in Bhotia Busti, he marched north with the expedition through Sikkim and into Tibet.

BRITAIN SENT SEVEN EXPEDITIONS TO EVEREST between the wars, three in the 1920s and four in the 1930s. Two of these were reconnaissance expeditions, and of the remaining five, three were hamstrung by the early arrival of the monsoon. The climbers were working at altitudes on the limit of human survival, with equipment that was rudimentary and too heavy, dressed in clothing that worked well in moderate conditions but which offered insufficient protection in bad weather. Knowledge of just about every aspect of high-altitude physiology was either slight or nonexistent. No European had been within 60 miles of Everest before 1921, so no one knew the best route of ascent. It was a huge unknown, a whole new voyage of discovery.

That voyage would be made by the British, and the British alone. Mountaineering historians have often said that had other nations— Germany, Italy, and the United States, for example—been allowed by the British to approach the Tibetan government for a permit, Everest would have been climbed long before 1953. British mountaineers, who had dominated the first decades of the sport in the Alps, had fallen behind the Germans, Italians, and French, at least in terms of technical ability, and wouldn't catch up until well after the war. These men, even in the 1920s, seemed from a bygone era, dressed in their Chamonix caps and tweeds, appearing in George Bernard Shaw's phrase "like a picnic in Connemara surprised by a snowstorm."

Despite these drawbacks, the British possessed other qualities. For a start, the technical difficulties on Everest weren't great. The climbing required determination and stamina rather than dazzling skill. They also would prove their strength in logistics. George Mallory put his finger on the problem as early as 1921 in his assessment of what it would take to climb the mountain: "Anything like a breakdown of the transport will be fatal."[6] Climbing Everest required putting two fit and healthy men at a well-supplied camp close to the summit with sufficient good weather to complete the task.

Yet they overlooked the central issue in supply, the use of bottled oxygen. The British were confused and divided over the use of oxygen. Most in the organizing committee saw it as unsporting. The secretary of the Mount Everest Committee, Arthur Hinks, declared that only "rotters" would use oxygen. George Mallory saw it as "damnable heresy," although that didn't stop him from setting off to the summit in 1924 carrying the stuff and taking Andrew Irvine with him because he knew how to fix the contraption when it broke down. There is a level of machismo in such attitudes, but those who didn't see climbing Everest as a matter of national or personal prestige genuinely felt that making the outcome a certainty defeated the object. Tilman, part of the 1935 expedition, warned that if it was climbed with bottled oxygen, "there would be for mountaineers an instinctive urge to climb it again without" and on that basis they might as well start from the premise that oxygen was a waste of time. As it turned out, Tilman was right. Ascents of Everest with oxygen are now considered routine, whereas those climbing without are thought of as stronger climbers making a purer ascent. What Tilman and Shipton really hated were big expeditions, something that the use of oxygen necessitated. In the 1950s these huge, well-supplied national events were considered imperative as competing nations rushed to climb the fourteen 8,000-meter peaks. No one could afford to gamble on failure. By the late 1970s, the lightweight philosophy became accepted again as climbers realized that since anything could be climbed with sufficient resources, where was the challenge?

Vacillation in the Mount Everest Committee extended to the choice of expedition leaders and personnel. Those with a military background, the imperial explorers of the Royal Geographical Society, clashed with the more talented but less disciplined climbers. After the 1933 attempt, Hugh Ruttledge, who had the leadership of the expedition "thrust upon him,"[7] was urged by his younger climbers to get rid of the fossils on the Mount Everest Committee, especially Sir Percy Cox, president of the RGS, whom Jack Longland described as "a deeply deceitful diplomatic old soldier." Nothing came of it, and the tradition of compromise continued into the 1950s. A good example is the 1933 climb, the best opportunity to climb Everest before the war. The selection of the climbers themselves was pleasingly eccentric. Tom Brocklebank, distinguished more for his rowing than any climbing experience, got his place after a chat with one of the old guard at their London club. Even those climbers with the necessary experience and skill were drawn from the very highest social echelons. As it turned out, the most talented climbers yet to attempt the mountain enjoyed reasonable weather, but they were poorly led, and hesitation at a critical point by two of their less capable members undermined their chances.[8]

Tenzing was unwittingly caught up in the consequences of all this politicking. The 1935 reconnaissance was in itself the best of a bad job. With an unexpected permit granted by the Tibetan government beginning in the summer of 1935 and running into 1936, the Mount Everest Committee decided to send a lightweight expedition as a precursor for another, big effort the following year. Eric Shipton, whose "dislike of massive mountaineering expeditions had become something of an obsession,"[9] leaped at the chance to lead a small party. Out went the hampers from Fortnum and Mason's; in came local mutton and Tilman's homemade bread. The prospect of roaming across unknown mountain ranges was enchanting.

Shipton had begun perhaps the most successful partnership in the history of mountain exploration with H. W. Tilman. Both men had been planters in Kenya, and their exploration of Nanda Devi was a classic illustration of their philosophy, which had less to do with the celebrity of mountaineering and more to do with a sort of nomadic instinct. Other members were Charles Warren, a distinguished physician as well as a good climber; the schoolmaster Edwin Kempson; and a medical student, Edmund Wigram. The team was completed by the surveyor Michael Spender and a New Zealand mountaineer, Dan Bryant. An outstanding ice climber, Bryant was tough, and with his background of tramping in the Southern Alps, he relished the opportunity to join Shipton in roaming across southern Tibet. His place on the team was almost a fluke. He had dropped an application off at the Royal Geographical Society the year before and expected to hear nothing more about it. It was typical of a Shipton expedition to take a chance on the unknown. Because of this, a New Zealand connection was made that would ultimately lead to Ed Hillary's joining another British team in 1953.

Shipton hardly rushed to Everest. First the expedition explored the unknown ranges bordering the eastern side of the Arun Gorge, the Nyonno Ri, and Ama Drime, which reach more than 21,000 feet. From the top of these mountains Everest could be clearly seen due to the good weather. In fact, the monsoon would reach the Himalaya only on June 26, the day the party left the Nyonno Ri for the north side of Everest, arriving at Rongbuk on July 4. By then conditions had changed on the mountain, and the monsoon snows hampered progress.

Tenzing, meanwhile, was getting a crash course in expedition management. Early in the expedition, at the start of June, resentment among the porters about their treatment and working conditions boiled over.

"There was a hellish row outside the bungalow while we were break-fasting," Dan Bryant wrote in his diary. "The muleteers arguing among themselves, our own porters threatening to return if they had to carry heavy loads—in fact loads of any description to Tangu [the next village on their trek]. They even went and collected their own private gear from the mule-loads as a gesture of their intention. The Everest tradi-tion seems to be that the porters should not carry anything. Our party swears at this damned tradition. Warren tells of how when their porters refused to go on with such loads two years ago one of the sahibs put a porters load on top of his and strode on up the hill. The remainder of the porters were shamed into carrying their loads on!"

Bryant couldn't know it, but he was witnessing what would be called in the British trade-union movement "demarcation." The Sherpas saw load carrying as a sign of status, designating their place in their own soci-ety. Only the lowest had to carry loads for others; it was a matter of pride. Ang Tharkay recalled: "We got the order for each of us to carry a load of 70 pounds from Gangtok to Lachen. Since in principle carrying loads wasn't something Sherpas did before base camp, we protested, deciding unanimously to strike and go home."[10] Next morning, while they were packing up to leave, Shipton invited Ang Tharkay into his tent to broker a compromise. The Sherpa told Shipton, more or less, that it was a ques-tion of one out, all out. Shipton then effectively capitulated, asking that the Sherpas carry for one more day—a face-saving measure only—and then they would be excused. By 1938, when Tilman led his expedition to Everest, the process was complete. "It is wise to discount the Sherpas as a carrying force so long as any other transport is available. They either put their loads on the already sufficiently laden animals or hire animals on their own account and present you with the bill."[11]

With the situation resolved, the expedition moved on. Ang Tharkay and Tenzing shared a double sleeping bag for warmth on the approach to Everest in 1935. "I've treasured the sleeping bag ever since," Ang Tharkay recalled, "as a souvenir which Tenzing let me keep at the end of this memorable expedition."[12] It's likely that as the senior man, Ang Tharkay would have kept the sleeping bag anyway, since equipment was almost as important as pay. Also, the two still found themselves on opposite sides of the line when drunken arguments arose between the Sherpas and Tibetans. When the expedition stopped at the Tibetan village of Sar, Tenzing and Ang Tharkay were drinking chang amicably in a house with the rest of the Sherpas when they were driven apart:

"A young hothead, the son of the village headman, took offence at our conversation with a young girl, accusing us in the most offensive way of having designs on her. My friends, Tenzing included, carried on without saying anything, leaving me to reply to the smear. I approached the boy and asked him why he wanted to insult us with no justification. I told him that Sherpas were honourable and that our conversation with the girl was perfectly innocent. But when he carried on with the insults, I suddenly lost control and thumped him in the face. This caused uproar and the boy's father soon arrived and asked me why I'd hit the boy, his only son. I couldn't answer him and left, ashamed."[13]

Next day, the father, the boy, and his mother all went to see Shipton and the interpreter, Karma Paul, to complain. When Ang Tharkay arrived, he knew he was in deep trouble. Karma Paul told him to give the headman a *kata*—the honorific Tibetan silk scarf—and compensation of five rupees, more than five days' pay. Ang Tharkay told him he didn't have a kata or the money and defended himself. "I told them I'd go to Gyantse or Shigatse where there was a Gorkhali [Nepalese] representative who would judge the case with more fairness. Mr Shipton explained that because we were in a part of Tibetan territory for which we didn't actually have authorization, the incident was potentially compromising to the future of the expedition."[14] Shipton gave Ang Tharkay a kata and Ang Tharkay offered one rupee; the incident was closed, more or less. Afterward, the other Sherpas told Ang Tharkay he'd been unfairly blamed and held a collection to compensate him for his loss.

The expedition moved on to Rongbuk and Everest Base Camp. A more serious confrontation arose on July 10 as the climbers tried to establish a camp on the North Col, gateway to the mountain's Northeast Ridge. With monsoon conditions now covering the mountain in fresh snow, the risk of avalanches, especially on the slopes leading up to the North Col, where seven Sherpas had died in 1922, was very real. Shipton, Kempson, and Wigram were taking turns to kick steps through the soft new snow to hard ice with the Sherpas following behind when the snow began to fall again. Unnerved by the conditions, they put down their loads and refused to go on—they were "rude and tiresome" according to Kempson—to a flat spot on the climb where they could leave their loads in safety and return when the weather improved. "They just dumped their loads and laughed at us," Charles Warren wrote in his diary. Seeing that they would not be persuaded to go on, Shipton ordered everyone back to the camp below. There he gave the Sherpas a lecture on their attitude. Kempson wrote in his diary, "On arrival we had a great confab and agreed that we should do entirely without porters, doing all our own carrying. Happily however the clouds of dissipation disappeared and they were all immensely contrite after Eric's talk."

Tenzing makes no mention of these confrontations in *Tiger of the Snows*. He was often discreet in this way and anyway, they were hardly rare occurrences. He himself was highly praised on the expedition. Because it was small, it was much easier for Tenzing's qualities to stand out. If his first trip to Everest had been on the gigantic expeditions of 1933 or 1936, he might not have made such a good impression so quickly. Dan Bryant, in his account of New Zealand's climbers on Everest, wrote:

"It is interesting to record that of our porters Tenzing, the Sherpa who finally reached the summit of Everest with Hillary, was the youngest and least experienced. My own diary reference to him gives some indication, however, of things to come. I wrote in 1935: 'He was with Warren and me on the Rapui La and again on the 22,740ft unnamed peak we climbed. Most obliging, willing and helpful in camp, he is a delightful chap with a keen sense of humour. He is one of the first porters I would take were I going on another expedition. He will make an excellent climber with a little more experience.'"[15]

Tenzing was already showing all the qualities that would mark him out first as a porter and then as a sirdar: his strength at altitude, his willingness to work hard for his employers, his cheerfulness. "I watched the others carefully," he said later. "No one taught me to climb. I learned from experience on every expedition. I learned what to do, and what not to do. I soon knew which climbers to watch."[16] The appearance of a smiling porter at the tent door first thing in the morning, offering a cup of tea, is the common experience of everyone who has climbed or trekked with Sherpas in the Himalaya and it creates an almost overwhelming sense of gratitude. They have certainly set the standards by which others are now judged. According to anthropologist and climber Mike Thompson, "their individualistic, exuberant, risk-taking, reward-enjoying trade has formed the basis for a cheerful, convivial, easy-going, open and hospitable life-style that has endeared them to generations of Western mountaineers."[17]

The Sherpa desire to serve without being servile was well understood by Eric Shipton, but the British didn't always read their signals correctly. Sherpas become anxious and upset just by watching confrontation or strong negative emotions like anger or aggression. They are regarded as a kind of pollution, an emotional sickness, which was why Ang Tharkay had felt such shame in his confrontation with the Tibetan boy. So disagreements and resentments are concealed, especially from outsiders, although chang can quickly bring them to the surface.

The Sherpas climbing up toward the North Col were anxious and unhappy for several reasons: the bad weather and heavy snow, the difficult terrain, and a feeling of discontent with the sahibs. But there was another reason. The day before they set out for Camp IV and the North Col, an event took place which disturbed them deeply, even though the English climbers thought their reaction the exact opposite.

On July 9, above Camp III, the expedition came across the body of Maurice Wilson, a self-fantasist who, without any prior mountaineering experience, believed he could climb Everest alone. Wilson was the third son of a wealthy, self-made family from the Yorkshire mill town of Bradford who had been scarred, mentally and physically, by his experiences in the Great War. After demobilization, he immigrated to America and then New Zealand before returning to Britain on the verge of a nervous breakdown. Racked with illness and doubt, he launched into a program of fasting and prayer, which eventually cured him. Wanting to share his message with the rest of the world, he hit on the idea of climbing Everest as a demonstration of what his ideas could accomplish. He learned to fly, and bought a Gypsy Moth in which, despite the best efforts of the Air Ministry in London, he flew to India. While the authorities considered ways of getting rid of him, the papers followed him everywhere, and his mixture of eccentricity and determination made him a celebrity. In early 1934, with three porters, all Tibetans who had been with Ruttledge on Everest in 1933, Tewang Bhotia,[18] Rinzing Bhotia, and

Tsering Tharkay—he set out for Everest. Apart from a few weeks' walking and scrambling in the Lake District, he had no climbing experience whatsoever. He did not get far.

Shipton's party found Wilson's body curled up on the East Rongbuk Glacier below the climb to the North Col, where he had lain for over a year. Charles Warren saw him first, thinking that he'd found an equipment dump from the 1933 trip. "I say, it's this fellow Wilson!" he shouted to the others, and they crowded around to look. "The body was lying on its left side with the knees drawn up, in an attitude of flexion," Warren wrote in his diary. "He was wearing a mauve pull-over and grey flannel trousers with woollen vest and pants underneath." In a telling observation, Warren had this to report about the Sherpas: "We wondered whether to tell the porters but by this time they had come up to us and had seen what we had discovered. For the most part, they took the matter very casually." This cool reaction was noted by several of the climbers, including Tilman: "Blokes [Tilman always called the porters 'blokes'] seemed quite unmoved by W's body. One took his boots."

Western mountaineers have often remarked on the Sherpas' indifference in the face of death, not realizing the Buddhist injunction to control strong emotions. In fact, Ang Tharkay gives a detailed description of the body, and Tenzing certainly didn't view Wilson's death casually. While the mountaineering historian Walt Unsworth absolved Wilson's porters of any responsibility,[19] Tenzing was outraged. "I was angry and ashamed of them, because back in Darjeeling I saw that they had a lot of money, which must have been Wilson's. And, besides, they should have gone out to look for him or at least waited longer for him to come back."

What Tenzing doesn't say is that the porters hired by Wilson were experienced, had been high on Everest in 1933, and were hired by Shipton in 1935. Ang Tharkay reports that Rinzing was there with them, looking at Wilson's pathetic remains, curled up on the stones and ice. He offered his explanation for what had happened, that they had tried to persuade Wilson to abandon his attempt. It's very unlikely the other porters took the matter "casually" any more than Tenzing did. Tsering died in 1936—of a broken heart according to Ang Tharkay[20]—but he, Rinzing, and Tewang all worked on Everest that year with Tenzing, and Rinzing in particular shared a number of expeditions with Tenzing elsewhere in the

Himalaya. Tewang, who had been on Everest with Mallory and worked with Frank Smythe in 1937, went mad during the war and died, perhaps from alcoholism. Rinzing died in 1947. After they were dead, Tenzing wrote of his shame at their actions and of their alleged theft of their client's money. Yet for years he maintained a working relationship with them.

That night in 1935, below the North Col, the Sherpas and Bhotias gathered in their tents at Camp III to eat and talk away from the sahibs. Given Tenzing's sharp criticism 20 years later, the young porter must have overheard a heated exchange between the older men. No wonder they were out of sorts the next day. Wilson's lonely death was an early example of the strangeness that Everest still engenders, but it also offers an insight into the unspoken stresses and grudges that underpinned the outward cheerfulness of the Sherpas.[21] If Tenzing felt resentment toward Rinzing, no sahib they worked for together ever noticed it. He suppressed his real views in the interests of the job at hand. There was a whole world of emotions and allegiances among the Sherpas and Bhotias that their employers rarely if ever penetrated.

DESPITE THE LIMITED ATTEMPT ON EVEREST IN 1935 and the discovery of Wilson's body, Tenzing was exhilarated. He was issued high-altitude clothing, good boots, and snow goggles, the physical symbols of his new status. He ate food out of cans, the first time he done this in his life, and slept in a sleeping bag. He had crossed glaciers and snowfields before, but now he cut his first steps with an ice ax and held a climbing rope. It was as though he had stepped through a door into a previously forbidden world. The work was hard, shouldering loads of up to 90 pounds to the camp below the North Col, and 50 pounds above it, but he had no complaints. Although the older Sherpas were happy to dump their loads and hurry down to the shelter of a lower camp, Tenzing was already dreaming of going higher: "When I am on Everest I can think of nothing else. I want only to go on, farther and farther. It is a dream, a need, a fever in the blood."[22]

To cap it all, his father visited him at Base Camp, staying "quite a while" and sleeping at camps on the East Rongbuk Glacier, probably carrying loads for the expedition as a way of earning a little extra money. It was here, at Camp I, that Mingma saw a yeti. He had seen one before, near Makalu, and described it as a gray, hairy, four-foot apelike creature with a pointy head, a female with heavy breasts that she carried as she ran away up the mountainside to get away from him. The yeti's proximity on that occasion had left Mingma ill for a year—he considered himself lucky to survive the encounter. On Everest in 1935 he watched the yeti from a distance traveling down the glacier until it was out of sight, and there were no ill effects. Afterward he rushed up to Camp II, where his son was waiting: "I come all this way to see my son. And instead what I see is a *yeti.*"[23] None of the sahibs mentioned this occurrence in their diaries, though a photograph was recently discovered of "yeti footprints" taken by Eric Shipton in 1935, presumably those of whatever Mingma saw.[24] Tenzing certainly believed that his father had seen something, but he was, for a Bhotia brought up with tales of fabulous monsters, a total rationalist. In *Tiger of the Snows* he quotes the biologist Sir Julian Huxley, whom Tenzing met in Darjeeling, speculating that the yeti was a bear. Tenzing believed that it was more likely an ape that lived on berries and small mammals.

On July 16 the expedition withdrew from their attempt on Everest, thwarted by heavy monsoon snows blanketing the mountain. "There then commenced," Walt Unsworth wrote, "what can only be described as an orgy of mountain exploration and climbing."[25] Over the next six weeks Shipton and his team roamed over the Everest region, surveying, exploring, and climbing mountains wherever they went, including Khartaphu, overlooking Everest's Northeast Ridge, and Kharta Changri to its north, both in excess of 23,000 feet. They explored the Lingtren peaks, where Bryant almost perished stepping through a cornice. On the border with Nepal, they photographed the Western Cwm from the col between Lingtren and Pumori, the first men to look up the long valley that would eventually lead the way to the summit 18 years later. ("I should very much like to have the opportunity one day of exploring it," Shipton wrote in the *Alpine Journal,* and he did.) In all, the expedition climbed 26 peaks over 20,000 feet, more than had been climbed to that point in the whole history of Himalayan climbing. "We had a delicious time," Shipton said afterward.

Tension between porters and sahibs flared again as the expedition headed eastward and then south, moving through villages with distractions such as chang and better food. Tenzing, however, continued to earn praise. Before the war, each sahib had been assigned a porter as a kind of personal servant. The job didn't carry a bigger salary—they could expect a bigger tip—but the extra prestige and a good reference was useful for future jobs. Edmund Wigram's porter, Kusang Bhotia, left the expedition as the climbers marched out of Tibet when he learned of his mother's death, and Wigram chose Tenzing as a replacement.

Back in Darjeeling, Tenzing stayed for a few weeks with Dawa Phuti in Toong Soong Busti. She gave birth to their first child, a son, much to Tenzing's delight, whom they called Nima Dorje. Later, in old age, Tenzing would recall these early years in Darjeeling as a kind of age of innocence when life was harder but simpler. Dawa Phuti's daughter Pem Pem recalled: "He was always telling me, 'Your mother was a wonderful person, she was such a good wife. We were really in love.' Sometimes he would talk about their life together and I could tell he missed her, to the end of his life. Two days before he died, we talked about her. He wanted me to go with him to visit her grave in Chitral."

In November Tenzing had another job, portering an 80-pound sack of rice to the base camp of Kabru, within sight of Darjeeling on the western end of the Kanchenjunga massif. He wasn't wanted on the expedition itself. Those jobs were reserved for such men as Ang Tharkay and Pasang Kikuli, the Sherpa who would become famous for his repeated attempts to save a stricken American climber, Dudley Wolfe, who was stranded in a tent high on K2. As Tenzing turned for home he must have reflected that despite his success on Everest that year, he hadn't yet broken into such illustrious company. He had at least performed strongly, and got to know Pasang Phutar, the Sherpa who would lose his fingers on Masherbrum in 1938.

Over the years they became great friends. Pasang was born at Namche Bazar in 1910 and came to Darjeeling a couple of years before Tenzing. He'd worked as a grass cutter for two years before getting a job on Paul Bauer's 1931 expedition to Kanchenjunga. Two years later he carried a load to almost 26,248 feet with the British on Everest, earning himself the title "Tiger" and securing his chances of work. Although his injuries on Masherbrum could have ended his portering career for good, after the war he went back to the mountains, carrying high on Everest with Tenzing as sirdar and becoming a sirdar himself for the Japanese on Manaslu.[26]

Tenzing spent the winter with Dawa Phuti and Nima Dorje, happy in his family life and doing odd jobs in Darjeeling, but also anxious to get back to Everest. Because Shipton's expedition had been only a reconnaissance, there hadn't been an opportunity to go high on the mountain and earn himself the accolade of "Tiger." At least when the British returned in the spring he had no trouble getting hired to go back to Everest. It was a vast enterprise in comparison with Shipton's trip, and plenty of jobs were available. In fact, the transport officer, John Morris, asked Ang Tharkay and Ang Tsering to go to Khumbu to round up some more porters because there weren't enough in Darjeeling. More than 60 porters would leave with the expedition in 1936, and another hundred went directly from Khumbu to meet the expedition at Base Camp. Having made his mark the year before, Tenzing was an obvious choice, although the leader, Hugh Ruttledge, accepted all those with previous experience of Everest.

Ruttledge had been put back in charge largely because no one else on the Everest Committee's wish list was prepared to take the job. The tension between the younger climbers and the old guard at the RGS and Alpine Club simmered on, and Ruttledge, a kindly and well-liked man, found himself caught in the middle. It was not a very propitious start. Shipton[27] was chosen as one of the lead climbers, along with Frank Smythe, but there was no place for Bill Tilman, who had not acclimatized well in 1935, or for Noel Odell, the 1924 veteran who was considered too old. Both men would reach the summit of Nanda Devi that summer, at 7,817 meters the highest mountain climbed before the war. Dan Bryant was left out for the same reason as Tilman, and a young army officer named John Hunt was selected but failed the medical test. Still, Ruttledge could draw on a strong complement of climbers, and the British had every right to be optimistic. Tenzing was assigned to Charles Warren, the doctor who had discovered Maurice Wilson's remains the year before. The idea of a "personal Sherpa" seems strange now and was a largely British habit even then. When Charles Houston joined Bill Tilman on

Nanda Devi, he was taken aback by the scheme: "For us Americans the idea of a 'personal' Sherpa was a new and at first an embarrassing experience. We were accustomed to carrying and doing everything ourselves." Warren was a kindly man and an outstanding doctor, going on to develop the use of ultraviolet light in treating jaundiced infants. He became very fond of Tenzing: "I can remember how once I was called into medical consultation by the Dzongpen of Shekar and went along to see him, with Tenzing carrying the medical case. While I was in consultation Tenzing was given a meal and a tip. After that I rose considerably in reputation with him as the Doctor Sahib." After Tenzing climbed Everest and came to Britain to share in the celebrations, he stayed with Warren at his home in Felsted. "In those days we couldn't talk to each other easily because of the language difficulties. But usually a laugh, a smile and a gesture were enough for both of us to know what was wanted. I used dearly to love seeing Tenzing's cheerful face at the entrance to my tent nearly every morning. By 1938, when he did so well above the North Col with Tilman, he could converse in English quite well."[28]

The huge expedition split into two parts as they left Darjeeling to make it more manageable, and then the whole vast caravan rumbled across the Tibetan plateau. Ruttledge and his team reached Rongbuk monastery on April 25, where he and the other sahibs received the blessing of Dzatrul Rinpoche. Tenzing saw his cousin Trulshik Rinpoche again, who as a 12-year-old lama was thrilled by the excitement being generated. "People came from all over," he recalled, "from Khumbu, from Dingri, from Kharta, even Darjeeling." Among the porters arriving from Kharta would have been more of Tenzing's relatives. The expedition set up Base Camp and once again started the laborious process of stocking the three camps to the foot of the North Col. On May 9, Shipton, Smythe, and Warren reached the col, and after two days' bad weather, the porters set off to carry loads to Camp IV. Ruttledge had told Smythe to save himself for the upper reaches of the mountain, so he handed the lead to Rinzing Bhotia, who cut steps, in the words of one sahib, "in the tireless manner of the first-class guide." It was the first time a porter led the route on Everest.[29] On May 14 and 15, 46 and 50 porters carried loads to establish Camp IV on the North Col. Tenzing recalled, "We found ourselves in drifts up to our chests." Deep snow blanketed the mountains, and on May 18 it snowed again, forcing Smythe to evacuate the North Col. Avalanches were threatening to wipe out anyone who continued to risk climbing the slopes leading up to it, and he didn't want anyone to be cut off at Camp IV. In any case, the upper slopes of the mountain, still extending more than 6,500 feet above the North Col, were deeply covered in snow as well.

The news got worse. For the first time all the camps were linked by primitive radios, and Base Camp learned that the monsoon had formed early off the coast of Ceylon, so they could expect it to arrive in the eastern Himalaya in just two weeks. Instead, it sprinted north, reaching Darjeeling in only four days. The climbing season was effectively over, and the expedition thwarted before either had properly begun. The monsoon had broken a month and a day earlier than it had in 1935. Fifty porters were sent halfway up the snow-laden slopes to the North Col on June 4, but it was clearly foolish to continue and the expedition retreated soon afterward. On the way out of the Rongbuk Valley, Hugh Ruttledge went to pay his respects to Dzatrul Rinpoche:

"I will never forget his last words to me. He now believed that our motives were not materialistic, and that we underwent a spiritual experience on Mount Everest. He gave me a little silver cup, a pamphlet printed at the monastery for the use of pilgrims, and a cordial invitation to visit him again. On my saying that I was too old to climb again but would like to sit at his feet and learn wisdom, he laughed happily and gave me his blessing. He was a great and a good man."[30]

Hugh Ruttledge would meet Tenzing again after his successful climb in 1953. "He grasped my hand and said, 'Son, you have done a wonderful job. Now I am old. I tried and failed on Everest, but it makes no difference, because now you have succeeded.'" Ruttledge died in 1961, age 77. "He had been a father to us all," Tenzing said.

Back in Darjeeling, Shipton met Gordon Osmaston of the Survey of India, who was planning a surveying expedition up the Rishi Gorge into the Nanda Devi basin. Osmaston, then in his late 30s, was a distinguished soldier and geographer who had traveled the length of the Himalayan chain, mapping the Garhwal and Almora districts. He'd spent the first part of 1936 on the Gangotri and Chaturangi Glaciers, trekking under the beautiful peaks of Shivling and the Bhagirathis, coming to

Darjeeling when the monsoon interrupted work. He asked Shipton, who with Tilman had first penetrated the Rishi Gorge in 1934, to guide him to the foot of Nanda Devi. Shipton gathered a few porters together, Tenzing among them. It was the first of several expeditions with Osmaston that Tenzing would work on, although this trek up the Rishi Gorge was almost his last.

Three days out from Joshimath, the expedition met the ragged figure of Peter Lloyd, one of the climbers on the expedition to Nanda Devi, who gave Shipton the news that Tilman and American climber Charles Houston had reached the summit. Tenzing meanwhile came down with a fever. He had never before traveled across the plains of India, had never been on a train or visited a big city like Delhi, and somewhere among all these new experiences he had picked up a bug. On the expedition's sixth day Tenzing fell seriously ill. The terrain was rugged and tough going. Osmaston wrote:

"At one point we had to climb down the trunk of a small tree which leant against a steep rock face; then across a huge rock which formed a natural bridge over the river. We camped under overhanging cliffs close to the water. A climb of 1,500ft up steep slopes brought us to a rocky cliff about 50 ft high. This was climbed by a series of cracks and ledges rather like a moderate climb in the Lake District, but the loads [which included a live sheep] had to be pulled up on ropes."[31]

By this time Tenzing was stumbling along at the back of the group with Osmaston carrying his rucksack and even occasionally Tenzing himself. Finally they crested the last ridge and found themselves inside the sanctuary.

The next morning, Osmaston went over to Tenzing's tent and took his temperature. It registered 108°F. "I am afraid Tenzing is dying," he told Shipton,[32] who examined the thermometer and discovered a hole in the end. Fortunately, by this stage Tenzing had recovered a little. He recounted the incident with typically effusive generosity: "No one has ever been kinder to me than Major Osmaston, and I promised myself that some day I would be of real service to him, as he now was to me."[33] He was told he had a "bilious fever," probably some kind of food poisoning, and the expedition's local porters told him to make a soup from a particular kind of moss growing on the stones of the sanctuary.

"I vomited so much that I thought all my insides were coming out. But the fever went away."[34]

Tenzing was still too weak to leave Base Camp, however, and the rest of the expedition got on without him. Osmaston would reach altitudes of more than 20,000 feet, establishing surveying stations and making a photogrammetric record of the region. Shipton, always itching to go somewhere new, explored the peaks at the head of the Changabang Glacier before taking Ang Tharkay and Sen Tensing and retracing the route down the Rishi Gorge to Dibrughita. From there he attempted to climb the Southwest Ridge of Dunagiri, a beautiful peak of more than 22,967 feet, coming within a thousand feet of the top. Tenzing was "not at all pleased" that he had been "of so little use." His fate could have been much worse. Near the base camp in the Nanda Devi Sanctuary was the grave of Kitar, a veteran of several Everest expeditions and one of the porters Tenzing had worked with on Kabru the autumn before. He and all the other Sherpas with Tilman on Nanda Devi had contracted dysentery, and Kitar hadn't recovered. "Anyhow," Tenzing recounted, "I am luckier than he."

Osmaston took Tenzing with him twice more to the Garhwal. In the spring of 1937 he was surveying above the Dhauliganga River in bad weather when he fell ill at their highest camp with a fever. This time it was Tenzing who helped Osmaston down to a lower altitude, where he recovered. In 1938, soon after that year's Everest expedition, Osmaston hired Tenzing to trek through the Almora district, east of Nanda Devi and close to the border with Tibet. With them went Rinzing. Osmaston and his team trekked up to the Milam Glacier,[35] north of Nanda Devi, before crossing the Anta Dura Pass at 17,600 feet where they looked north across a bleak landscape of stark red mountains with wildly twisted strata before dropping down to Topidunga. Osmaston became increasingly concerned about Tenzing's health, undermined by his weeks on Everest earlier that year. He was suffering from dysentery, but after a few days he seemed to rally, and Osmaston set out to return to Milam. Crossing the Anta Dura again was agony for Tenzing, and by the evening he collapsed into his tent. By now he hadn't eaten for three days. The next day Osmaston found him almost crawling down the trail, stopping every 50 yards. Eventually, despite Osmaston's help, he stopped for good. "We were still about five miles from

Milam, so I packed him up in his sleeping bag and made him as comfortable as possible on a rocky shelf," Osmaston wrote.[36] "I then lit a fire and heated water as a hot drink." By chance, a traveler passed their bivouac and Osmaston sent a message with him down to his camp at Milam. A pony returned for them with two men who propped Tenzing on the saddle and carried him. On one rough stretch he toppled off. In the morning he started to recover, and soon he was back at his duties.

Even so, the expedition ground to a halt days later attempting to cross high terrain to the east of the Milam Glacier. The existing maps were incomplete, and the weather was poor. Their path was blocked by a broken icefall, and one of the porters was hit by a falling stone. Retreating back down the valley to camp, Osmaston asked his two Sherpas, Tenzing and Rinzing, what they thought he should do. Their respective answers were revealing. Rinzing replied automatically: "*Ap ke kushi, sahib*—As you please." Tenzing, by contrast, took control and formulated a plan. "First the local coolies would take the wounded man back home," Osmaston wrote, "and bring back the extra rations we needed because of the delay. Meanwhile the four of us would remain and, in two separate parties, try to find the pass. Surely shades of Tenzing becoming a famous leader later."[37]

Osmaston put Tenzing's plan into effect, and the next day the two men found the elusive pass. They took two more days to cross it in heavy snow and low temperatures, and then, descending the far side, they were forced to climb down a complex icefall. Tenzing led the way but was caught in an avalanche and buried completely. Osmaston and the other porters quickly pulled him out, and they all continued down, weaving their way among the labyrinthine crevasses, overlooked by huge tottering ice cliffs. At least the sun remained hidden, leaving the glacier securely frozen.

Tenzing was learning on the job, relying on his instinctive affinity for the mountains. He had a talent, a practical common sense in moving across harsh terrain. More than 30 years later, on a rafting trip down the John Day River in Oregon, guide Bob Peirce appreciated Tenzing's self-assurance at a moment of crisis in a new and alien environment: "When someone stupidly got one of the wood boats hung up in the middle of big rapids, he waded in with me and seemed to know just what to do to get it out. I remember thinking this guy has really had big-water experience. Turns out I was dead wrong. It's just that he was a Sherpa and had an instinct for knowing what to do in difficult situations."

Tenzing crossed the glacier, allowed for the first time to take charge. In one day the group descended 5,500 feet to camp just beyond the snout of the glacier. Two of the local porters were snow-blind, the party was exhausted, but Tenzing and Rinzing immediately cooked their first hot meal in several days.

Tenzing climbed no summits on these journeys with Osmaston, but they were good training for him. On the third trip in the autumn of 1938 they spent more than two months in the mountains, relying on each other and learning all the time. Mountaineering often involves coping with discomfort and awkward, loose ground rather than technical brilliance, and in an era before antibiotics or any sort of rescue the consequences of a mistake or sudden illness could be disastrous. The environment called for a mixture of caution and decisiveness, depending on whether you were looking at trouble or were already in the middle of it. Tenzing's initiative under these circumstances was prized by Osmaston and, like Dan Bryant, he recommended Tenzing to others interested in exploring the Garhwal.

One of those was Jack Gibson, a newly arrived schoolmaster at the recently founded Doon School in Dehra Dun. Gibson was a charismatic geography and English teacher remembered fondly by students at both the Doon School and later at Mayo, where he was the headmaster. Gibson was also an enthusiastic mountaineer and a great believer in its educational value. One of his pupils was Nandu Jayal, later the first head of the Himalayan Mountaineering Institute. Gibson's headmaster, Arthur Foot, was a member of the Alpine Club, and John Martyn, who had left England with Foot in 1935 to found the Doon School, was a rock climber and a tough mountain traveler. In 1940, Roy Holdsworth, another Himalayan pioneer, arrived, as well as Gurdial Singh, who joined the staff after the war and would climb Everest with India's first successful expedition. Tenzing would get to know them all over the course of three expeditions to a comparatively modest peak called Bandarpunch—"the monkey's tail"—in the Garhwal, which he nicknamed the Doon School mountain.

In 1937 Gibson and Martyn organized the first of these "expeditions," which were focused more on spending time in the mountains than rushing to the summit. They sought Osmaston's advice as the Survey of India's expert on the region: "Osmaston has helped us enormously. He knows the area we are going to, having been on the survey that covered it, and has lent us tents, and made copious notes on what to do, what to take, and how many porters are needed. He is now on leave in England, but has left his two Sherpa porters, 'tigers' who have been on Everest expeditions, behind at Mussoorie for us to take over. They are Rinsing and Tenzing, and it is taking us time to recognise one from the other. They are great fun, and splendid men."[38]

In the 1930s, this area of the Indian Himalaya was still undeveloped and pristine, with few roads and far fewer people. Gibson and Martyn with their small band of Sherpas and porters trekked over the rising hills to Uttarkashi and then climbed to Dodi Tal, a beautiful lake set among rhododendrons and deodars. The weather was bad, and they were held up waiting for a permit, but the journey had other pleasures. They discussed yoga with holy men at an ashram above the town. They ate stewed apricots bought from villagers on their way to market and foraged for wild raspberries "as good as any you can buy." The lake was full of trout, though they had nothing to catch them with. Instead, they contented themselves exploring the approaches to Bandarpunch, walking through banks of kingcups, primulas, lilies, and blue poppies.

Through early July they advanced across the Darwa Pass toward the mountain, placing a little base camp south of the Hanuman Ganga, which flowed from the mountain's glacier. Next day they crossed the river—finding shallots on the far bank, which they ate—and trekked up to a camp at 14,400 feet. The day after, they ascended to 17,300 feet, on the ridge leading to Bandarpunch's summit at over 20,000 feet. "We sent the porters back to the Hanuman Ganga as they were not much good on snow, but the Sherpas have been wonderful," Gibson wrote. "The event of the day has been John's fall. He slipped on a steep snow slope and fell about 400 feet, head over heels and in all directions, losing his rucksack and bedding."[39] Martyn managed to perform an ice ax arrest before falling over an ice cliff, and Rinzing went down to help him back up while Tenzing dug out platforms in the snow for their tents. The next day they tried for the summit but weren't fit or experienced enough to reach the top in a day. "The rock scrambling was easy," Gibson wrote, "but we had to cut steps all the way up the snow ridge. The Sherpas did most of the hard work as I was not up to it and John had no experience."[40]

On the way down, the mist closed around them, and Tenzing and Martyn became separated while looking for the local porters. "Rinsing and I have both sat yodelling from time to time, and looking at each other. It does not make it any easier that neither can speak the other's language." Tenzing and Martyn attempted to climb back to the camp, where Gibson had lit a lantern, but they were forced to bivouac. "We wandered about, shouting," Tenzing recalled, "but in the mist we could not see where we were going, and then it rained so hard that we couldn't hear our own voices. We found a cave and had to spend two days in it."[41] The Sherpas were more used to this kind of physical privation and didn't suffer from the altitude as Martyn and Gibson did. They were also more experienced and relaxed in the high mountains. As they neared camp that night, all of them could smell meat cooking. The porters had caught a mountain sheep and were roasting it whole, inside its skin. They spent the next three days eating it. "The kidneys for supper were the best I have ever tasted," Gibson wrote.[42]

They spent another month exploring the western Garhwal, trekking to Gaumukh, the source of the Ganges above Gangotri, and crossing into the Arwa Valley. In all, they covered 400 miles. Tenzing recalled that they were often hungry and resorted to living off the land. Struggling down the trail to Harsil, Gibson writes that they were pleased to find wild strawberries and walnuts, and that a sheep they bought and had killed left some of them ill. At Harsil, Gibson tells that he picked up food belonging to two Brahmin shopkeepers—Tenzing says at his sugges-tion—which had become polluted, according to Brahmin custom, and thus inedible. Tenzing says the sahibs offered to pay 20 rupees for it, considerably more than its value since an entire sheep could be bought for 5 rupees, but that the shopkeepers rushed off to complain to the village headman.[43] Gibson makes no reference to this, suggesting that the Brahmins were happy with the money, so perhaps the story grew with the telling. "There were three pints of jolly good milk in the pot. We haven't had any fresh milk for a long time, and I told the Sherpas to use it for soup and cocoa. They misunderstood and cooked up a mixture of all three which proved smooth and delicious."[44]

Gibson proved a good friend to Tenzing over the next decade. In 1946, during the hardest times Darjeeling's Sherpas experienced, he gave Tenzing some badly needed work, and soon after recommended him for another job, this time as an instructor with the Indian Army. But Bandarpunch was not Everest, and through the winter months of 1937 and 1938 Tenzing could think about little else than returning to the Rongbuk. Nima Dorje was now two, and according to his father "a very handsome boy" who won first prize in a baby show. Dawa Phuti was pregnant with their second child. After three years of working in the mountains Tenzing felt on the verge of something altogether greater.

CHAPTER FIVE

TRIUMPH, WAR, AND LOSS

Man, unlike any other thing organic or inorganic in the universe,
grows beyond his work, walks up the stairs of his concepts,
emerges ahead of his accomplishments.
—JOHN STEINBECK, *The Grapes of Wrath*

THE GREAT DEPRESSION touched most of the world in the early 1930s. John Steinbeck recorded the suffering of migrant families escaping the Oklahoma Dust Bowl in *The Grapes of Wrath*. In *The Road to Wigan Pier*, George Orwell described how in Britain jobless men and women would risk their lives scrabbling in slag heaps for chips of coal to heat their homes. Hardship was a constant in the lives of the Sherpas, who were among Darjeeling's poorest inhabitants, yet the Great Depression had an impact even in this small corner. Since the 1936 expedition to Everest had gotten nowhere at a cost of £10,000—£500,000 or $700,000 in modern values—the feeling grew that there was something morally doubtful about money being spent on something as frivolous as climbing Everest when ordinary people were going hungry. Even some of the climbers thought so. Raymond Greene, brother of the novelist Graham Greene, who had been on Everest in 1933, said: "I think a lot too much has been said in the past about the spiritual and mystical significance of climbing Everest and about its possible effects on British prestige. However true that may be, the fact remains that we go to Everest not for those reasons at all, but either simply because it is fun or in order to satisfy some purely personal and selfish psychological urge. I do not think we are any longer justified in spending large sums of public money in satisfying these private urges."[1]

What's more, the Mount Everest Committee was broke, so things had to be done more cheaply. In 1937 Freddie Spencer Chapman's successful "expedition" to Chomo Lhari, a peak of almost 24,000 feet, comprised two climbers and three Sherpas and cost £39 5s 0d. Couldn't that kind of parsimony be applied to Everest?

Bill Tilman was determined to prove that hundreds of porters weren't needed to climb a big Himalayan mountain, and believed that mountaineers should do without anyway, as a matter of principle. With the purse strings tightened in London, he got his chance. The Mount Everest Committee invited Tilman to lead a much lighter expedition to Everest, underwritten not by public funds but by a private individual, Tom Longstaff, one of the early pioneers of Himalayan climbing. Included in the team were Eric Shipton and Frank Smythe—most likely contenders for the summit—Charles Warren, the 1924 veteran Noel Odell, Peter Oliver from the 1936 "show," and one newcomer, Peter Lloyd. It was a good team, and with better weather Tilman might have succeeded.

The 1938 expedition cost a quarter of the 1936 trip, and for the Sherpas that difference was critically important. The money expeditions brought in had prompted an exodus in Khumbu. Sherpas left their homes just on the off chance of work. "It was a much smaller party than the one in 1936," is all Tenzing has to say, but the consequences were obvious: There was more competition for jobs and the standard of porters was higher and their responsibilities greater. The opportunities would be greater too. Tilman chose only 12 Sherpas in Darjeeling, men who were tried and trusted, in contrast to the 60 that Ruttledge took in 1936. Sen Tensing was sent home to Khumbu to make arrangements for 30 porters to trek over the Nangpa La to Base Camp at Rongbuk. These men and women would bring food supplies and carry loads up the glacier to the foot of the North Col.

Ang Tharkay, whom Tilman and Shipton rated so highly, was appointed sirdar, and others from their previous expedition were also hired: Kusang Namgyal, Pasang Bhotia, and Rinzing Bhotia among them. To improve rations at Base Camp, Ang Tharkay and Kusang were sent on a two-month cookery course by Shipton in advance of the expedition, given by Shipton's friend Bunty Odling. "I was terrified she would find me a bad student," Ang Tharkay recalled.[2] "But she was so kind and put me at my ease straightaway." That the climbers still complained about the food stemmed more from their leader's belief in iron rations than Ang Tharkay's shortcomings.

Before leaving Darjeeling, the Sherpas were packed off to the infirmary. ("Don't forget to worm your porters!" General Bruce had whispered to Frank Smythe, seeing him off at Victoria Station on an earlier expedition.[3]) Then, in early March and for the seventh time since 1921, the Everest caravan left Sikkim for Tibet. "The whole organization creaks and groans like your own joints," Tilman wrote. He was coolly exact in describing the Sherpas he had hired. Nukku was "bovine but tireless," and Lhakpa Tsering had "the manner and the appearance of an Apache." Tenzing he described as "young, keen, strong and very likeable,"[4] but was not yet among the Sherpas identified as good mountaineers. In the three years since he was first selected to work on Everest with Eric Shipton, he had carried one load to Kabru, returned to Everest with Ruttledge and got no higher than he had in 1935, and traveled to the Garhwal twice. He had a long way to go before he could be ranked alongside Ang Tharkay.

Tilman got his own thumbnail sketch from Tenzing himself. "[He] was a very fine quiet man, and all the Sherpas liked him. He had such shaggy looks and big eyebrows that we nicknamed him Balu—the bear."[5] Tilman was for some the quintessential British explorer: tough, unsentimental, and reserved, qualities that Tenzing exhibited himself, but which he found off-putting in the British. In *Tiger of the Snows* he took some care to explain why he preferred the Swiss: "The English in general are more reserved and formal than the men of most other countries whom I have known; and especially is this so, I think, with people not of their own race."[6] Tenzing certainly liked the Swiss more, and they responded more positively to the Sherpas, but in this assessment is mixed in some of James Ramsey Ullman's typically American distaste for colonialism; how much it reflected Tenzing's true opinion is difficult to judge.

Tilman was reserved with everyone, including his own "race." In his relationship with the Sherpas, he never praised them wildly or imagined them to be free from the faults of any other group of people. He also understood how adept the Sherpas were at improving their working conditions. While Tilman accepted that Sherpas wouldn't carry loads before Base Camp, he thought it "an unfortunate tradition" and couldn't see how carrying 25 pounds or so on the approach across Tibet would harm them. He had little tolerance for the niceties of social distinction when there was a job to be done. Tilman hired a mule on which to carry the Sherpas' supplies of rice and lentils and their cooking gear, expecting them at least to carry their own kit. When the Sherpas offered to carry the sahibs' day packs as well, Tilman thought it "praiseworthy keenness" until he realized that they had secreted their own packs on the expedition mules and weren't carrying anything.

He was also good-humored, and he shared the Sherpa zest for practical jokes. When a mule carrying fodder stepped over a cliff and fell 200 feet to its death, he persuaded Tenzing, who was again acting as Charles Warren's personal servant, to tell his master that his personal gear had gone over with the mule. "Wretchedly bad actor though he was, Tensing managed to convince his master that the worst had happened; but we were disappointed of our jest because Warren, instead of acting in the expected fashion, beating his head against a stone or tearing his hair, expressed no more concern than he might have done at the loss of a pocket handkerchief."[7] The Sherpas had a good joke at Noel Odell's expense. The 47-year-old, always vague, got lost as the expedition approached Khampa Dzong, and the Sherpas found him wandering near a nunnery. They nicknamed him "Gompa La Sahib—Mr. Nunnery."

Arriving at Rongbuk in early April, the climbers found the mountain still cold and battered by spring storms. At the monastery, Dzatrul Rinpoche blessed the expedition—"he seemed pleased to see us all again"— warning Tilman that an Earth tremor had been felt in February and this had put the mountain in a strange mood. Tenzing, meanwhile, was reunited with his father, possibly the last time they met. Unlike 1935, when Tenzing had last seen his father, there is no mention of Mingma going up the East Rongbuk Glacier, so either there was no work for him, or he was working at Tsawa, because the visit was a fleeting one.

The expedition started well, establishing depots along the East Rongbuk Glacier before stocking Camp III below the North Col. No one was in a hurry to start climbing in such low temperatures. Tilman decided to send most Khumbu Sherpas home as they weren't needed. Only afterward did he realize that some of them had taken pairs of boots needed for the Sherpas at high altitude. One of the Darjeeling Sherpas, Ang Karma, had come down with laryngitis, and Tilman had to send him home. Because of the boot shortage, Tilman asked for Ang Karma to hand his back, since they were now "of far more importance than he was." Ang Tharkay asked Shipton if Ang Karma could keep his high-altitude gear for the journey home, but Shipton said no, and Ang Tharkay appealed to Tilman. "The business was taking on a bad direction," the sirdar recalled, and although none of the other Sherpas would come out openly in support of Ang Karma, they muttered privately that they would quit the expedition if he wasn't treated fairly.[8] Tilman, who happened to be reading *Don Quixote* at the time, offered to buy the boots from Ang Karma, but the Sherpa whispered in his hoarse voice such an extravagant price that Tilman gave up and let him keep them, telling Sen Tensing that he would have to give up his instead, since it was his fault for hiring thieves.

To quell any further rebellion from the Sherpas and to give the climbers, most of whom were ill, a chance to recover their strength, the expedition crossed the Lhakpa La and descended the Kharta Glacier to lower altitudes and abundant vegetation where they could buy fresh food and relax. For Tenzing the detour meant much more; he was back in his childhood valley. The climbers quickly got fed up sitting around— "What a vile waste of time this expedition is," Shipton wrote in a letter home—and the weather refused to improve. The mountain was sunk in deep, avalanche-prone snow. When they returned to the Rongbuk, where the interpreter Karma Paul had been waiting for them, they discovered that it had snowed hard for a week since May 5, and the mountain was now even more out of condition. Could the monsoon have broken already? Setting out from Camp III on May 18 for the slopes leading to the North Col, they discovered that conditions were better than expected. Still, 300 feet from the top, Peter Oliver, leading the route with Tenzing and Wangdi Norbu, was forced to traverse under a line of ice cliffs while Tilman, waiting with two more Sherpas, paid out the rope they were fixing as a handrail for the porters. Here the snow was softer, and Oliver slowed as he cleared a track. Tenzing and Wangdi Norbu bunched behind him, and their concentration of weight started a small avalanche. There is a graphic account of Tenzing being dragged down the slope:

"The snow was very steep, and also deep—as high as our waists—and we are moving slowly and with difficulty, when suddenly there is a sort of cracking sound all around us, and the snow begins to move too. The next minute we are all sliding down with it. I am off my feet, turning over and over. My head is under the snow, and it is dark. I remember, of course, what happened here in 1922, and I think, It is the same thing again. It is the end."[9]

In Tenzing's account, he managed to stop himself with his ice ax. Tilman writes that they stopped him on the rope—it hardly matters. The avalanche showed what a risk they were taking sending porters up the heavily laden slopes. Shipton thought the slopes below the North Col "a death trap," and said he and Smythe would have nothing more to do with them. But Tilman didn't want to give up on Everest that easily. Despite the logistical difficulties, the team decided to try to move around to the Rongbuk Glacier itself and attempt to reach the North Col from the west. Then the weather improved and Tilman changed plans again, sending loads up to the North Col from the east side. Their agony of indecision continued as May slipped away and the uncertain weather continued. It seemed that the monsoon really had started three weeks earlier than 1936, but the climbers didn't give up just yet. On May 28, with Smythe and Shipton back at Rongbuk, the other four climbers took 13 porters back to the North Col in fierce heat: "A stifling mist hung over the snow slopes from which the sun beat up in our faces as though from a desert of sand," Tilman wrote.[10] The porters were plagued by thirst, and their lives hung in the balance, threatened by tons of loose snow. Reaching the North Col, they stayed in bed the next day as more snow fell, but the following morning Tilman walked over to the Sherpas' tent and woke them before cooking everyone scrambled eggs, a dish that the Sherpas called "rumble-tumble."

Tilman and Tenzing pressed on a little farther, exploring the upper reaches of the mountain for the first time since 1933. It was almost June, and it must have seemed like a waste of time with the monsoon already upon them. Reaching 24,500 feet, "the tireless Tenzing" broke trail for much of the time, eager to be leaving the North Col below him, before Tilman decided enough was enough. The snow was just too deep and heavy for any real progress. "Tensing complained his feet were cold—they had probably got wet. But it was a pleasant day and though most of the country below was hidden by a veil of clouds, they themselves formed a wonderful and constantly changing picture."[11]

Because of the buildup of snow on the eastern slopes of the North Col, Tilman finally committed the expedition to the west side of the North Col. The climbers put in new camps and reoccupied Camp IV. "It was a bloody place," Shipton wrote of the slopes on the west side, "OK for a climbing party; but long, continuously exposed and very steep. A slip by one of the heavily laden porters would have been almost impossible to hold." But they got there, and the weather improved a little. The climbers sorted out enough tents and food for two more camps and three more days. It was vital that all the loads make it to Camp V at 25,800 feet. Any breakdown in logistics would ruin what slight chance they had.

Their prospects did not look hopeful. "Tensing was going very strong," Tilman wrote, "but none of the others at all happy."[12] Only Peter Lloyd was using oxygen; few of the others thought it worth the bother. Tenzing claimed he hadn't seen oxygen before—no one had got high enough in 1936 to use it—and he was bemused by the contraption. The other Sherpas laughed and told him it was "English air." "It was a big, heavy apparatus, not at all like that we used on Everest many years later, and seemed much more trouble than it was worth."[13]

Two of the porters dropped out and dumped their loads 700 or 800 feet below Camp V, a significant distance in the thin air of almost 26,000 feet. The remaining 13 porters made good progress, for the snowbank leading up from the North Col was solid, yet on the rocks above conditions deteriorated and then a snowstorm began. The weaker Sherpas wanted to give up, but Shipton and Tilman brought the stragglers into Camp V. Seven of the porters, including Tenzing, would stay with Shipton and Smythe while Lloyd and Tilman started back down toward the North Col at around four o'clock with the other six. As they passed the abandoned loads, the Sherpas above called down for them to bring them up, since one of them contained a tent needed for that evening. Tilman couldn't blame the Sherpas for telling their friends to forget it. "The only possible reply to this was the Sherpa equivalent for 'Sez you'; for I do not think that any of our party, had they been willing, were capable of doing it."[14] It was now that Tenzing came into his own, the critical moment when his strength at altitude shone through. "There was a discussion about what to do," he said. "The other Sherpas at Camp Five said that if they were sent down they wanted to stay down, but I said I would go down and get the things and come back again. So I went alone. I found the tents and fuel about halfway down to the [North Col], where the two Sherpas had left them before turning round, and, slinging them on my back, started up."[15] On the way back he nearly fell, his hobnailed boots slipping on the loose stones as he struggled with his load. He barely stopped himself with his ice ax, and he resumed climbing on a wave of adrenaline to Camp V, where Smythe and Shipton were waiting to congratulate him.

Tenzing's account isn't quite right. He hadn't gone alone. Pasang Bhotia had descended with him to share the loads, but it was still a powerful effort. Tilman, slogging down the soft snow, encouraging the exhausted porters down to the North Col, could only watch and applaud their enthusiasm. "To descend and ascend with loads another seven hundred feet, on top of the toil they had already endured, was a remarkable example of unwearying strength and vitality gallantly and unselfishly applied."[16] After the expedition, Tenzing received a bonus of 20 rupees for his trouble. Much more important than that, his performance had fixed in the sahibs' mind that he was the strongest porter on the mountain. He had taken the initiative and proved himself.

The next day, June 7, an easterly wind pinned the climbers and porters down at Camp V. But the following morning was clear. Shipton hoped that the fine weather in the previous week and colder temperatures had left the upper ridge as consolidated as the snowbank leading from the North Col. Instead they had to wade through a heavy, wet mass of snow above Camp V. Hours slipped by as they struggled across the Northeast Face. What had been easy ground to cover in 1933 had turned into a trial of will. Finally, they reached their site for Camp VI at 4:15, just below the Yellow Band at 27,200 feet. Tilman wrote, "I have never seen the blokes so completely corpsed as when we got there. One is like a sick man climbing in a dream, too doped and sub-normal to appreciate anything on the upper part of Everest."[17]

Tenzing, Pasang, and the other Sherpas had nowhere to sleep at Camp VI, so they had to turn around immediately and descend, despite their exhaustion. "They must have had a hard struggle to get back to Camp V before dark," Shipton wrote.[18] He and Smythe spent a restless night and started for the summit at daybreak. Finding it was too cold, they retreated to the warmth of the tent until the sun struck the Yellow Band. Even then conditions were hostile. They sank to their hips in snow, the summit hovering 1,500 feet above them like a vision of the grail. Shipton thought the ridge with its three steps looked too hard, especially in the conditions, but a lower traverse line was too full of snow. It was hopeless, and they turned back.

While Tilman and Lloyd moved up the mountain for their attempt, they passed Tenzing and the others on their way down. They looked exhausted, and Pasang was ill, perhaps showing the first symptoms of the stroke that would leave him paralyzed a few days later. Tilman and Lloyd made their attempt, more out of curiosity about the route ahead and the notorious Second Step than any hope of success, and then retreated. Pasang's condition sealed the attempt. It was already the second week of June, all the climbers were exhausted and now they had a dangerously ill man on their hands, which would require a long and awkward evacuation. Tenzing too was feeling the effects of carrying a 30-pound load over 27,000 feet. His voice failed completely on the way down to Base Camp, his throat desiccated by the thin, dry air.

The final chapter of the early Everest expeditions had reached its end, although plans were still being laid a few months before the invasion of Poland for attempts in 1940, 1941, and 1942. Just as the world was swept into war, the Mount Everest Committee became focused. Not everyone was happy about it. "I wish to God the Tibetans would prohibit any further attempts," Eric Shipton wrote in a letter to his former lover Pamela Freston. "They seem, like war, to bring out the worst in people—because they have become a pure stunt and nothing else, on no higher plain than dancing non-stop for a week."[19]

Shipton's attitude might have been in tune with more thoughtful climbers who saw through the mythology that had grown up around Everest, its symbolism of success and the prestige it brought, but too much was now invested in reaching its summit. In the 1920s the

Sherpas and Bhotias were bewildered by the foreigners wanting to climb a mountain. By the end of the 1930s, Tenzing was thinking about going "all the way." He understood the point very clearly. If Shipton was bored and disillusioned, Tenzing was aching for another chance to go back.

It was Tilman's last expedition to Everest. When they returned to Darjeeling, he organized a big dinner for the Sherpas both to celebrate their safe return and as a mark of gratitude for their efforts. Tenzing and Pasang got their 20-rupee bonus for their double carry to Camp V, and all the porters who carried to Camp VI were given Tiger Badges. This was Tilman's idea. Always the pragmatist, he understood the value of such an honor to the Sherpas in securing future work. "I shall never forget Mr Tilman," Ang Tharkay recalled after the war. "The last letter I got from him was dated 1951. He told me that he was getting old and had given up climbing. Mr Tilman always showed himself to be, in my eyes, a man of great courage and a higher spirit."[20]

Soon after Everest, Tenzing went back to the Garhwal with Osmaston. His success on Everest showed in the confidence and maturity he displayed in keeping Osmaston's surveying mission on track: "Sometimes we could look across the border of Tibet and see Mount Kailas, which, though only about 22,000ft high, is the most holy of all the peaks in the Himalayas, both to Buddhists and Hindus."[21] The money he earned was as welcome as a glimpse of the sacred mountain. That winter Dawa Phuti gave birth to their second child, a girl they called Pem Pem. Nima Dorje was now three, and his father was devoted to him. "Sometimes I would look at him and say to myself, 'When you are too old to climb he will begin and take your place. And he will be the best of all Tigers.'"[22] In the winter of 1938 Tenzing was not yet 25. In just three years his situation had changed utterly, mostly because he had taken his fate into his own hands. He felt confident about the future, even though there was to be no Everest expedition in the following year.

Instead, Tenzing was hired by a young Englishwoman for an attempt on a mountain called Tirich Mir, far to the west in the Hindu Kush. Tenzing called Beryl Smeeton a Canadian, and ultimately she would be, becoming a Canadian citizen in 1955, but she was born at Tolpuddle in Dorset, the daughter of an infantry officer killed in the Great War. Beryl was a tough, resourceful, attractive, independent, and adventurous woman whose travels took her all over the world. Francis Chichester said of her, "One is filled with wonder and admiration and a kind of exaltation that such women should exist in our time." At the age of 21 Beryl married a war hero called Tom Peddie. The marriage soon foundered and she began an affair with one of her husband's junior officers, Miles Smeeton. Eventually she inspired him to resist a conventional military career and embark instead on a life of adventure. During the 1930s, however, he was more often with his regiment while Beryl made a series of remarkable journeys, the culmination of which was a solo ride through Patagonia. Afterward, she married Miles in Yorkshire, and they returned to India to rejoin his regiment, stationed at Loralai, close to the Northwest Frontier in modern Pakistan's Balochistan Province.

Both the Smeetons had experience in climbing and, although not expert, enjoyed it immensely. So when two Canadian friends based in Quetta invited Miles to join an expedition attempting Tirich Mir, he leaped at the chance. It seemed Beryl would have to stay behind, because the mountain was located in Chitral, a Muslim state that refused access to Western women. She wasn't kept out of the picture for long. When one of the Canadians dropped out, she and Miles decided to try anyway, and just left her name and gender off the application for permission. In the meantime, Beryl drove to Calcutta—a round trip of 3,500 miles—to engage porters and borrow equipment from the Himalayan Club. The club promised to send her two experienced men—Tenzing and Ang Tenzing—and two newcomers. They also gave Beryl the equipment she needed, which she loaded into the back of her Austin van. As for nutrition, her ideas were drawn heavily from the books of Bill Tilman, who had cycled across Africa "practically living on dried bananas."[23] Now for the first time an expedition would resent Tilman's ideas on diet without his giving the orders.

Beryl and Miles, together with Hugh Millar, the remaining Canadian, traveled to Lahore in May 1939 to collect Tenzing and the other porters, but they weren't on the right train. "We felt like parents whose children had failed to appear on the train bringing them back for the holidays," Miles Smeeton wrote, "and clucked about the station like old hens until news came that they were on another platform. We found them looking like children home for the holidays too, with beaming faces, as out of place in Lahore as Eskimos in Egypt. Tenzing was the leader of the four, and talked in a patois of mixed English and Urdu. Both he and Ang Tenzing were experienced porters, both Tigers from Everest, but not the other two. Angwa, whose laughter bubbled irrepressibly at almost everything that he saw, was only sixteen."[24]

Dressed for the hills in old expedition sweaters or woollen hats, the Smeetons led the four porters through the sweltering streets of Lahore to the cinema, keeping them amused while they waited for their train north. "It was a hot jazzy leg-show, and Beryl and I felt quite ashamed that they would see it, but they laughed uproariously at the sob-stuff and were solemn when the film was supposed to be funny in a way that would have astonished the producer."[25] The next day they traveled to Nowshera and then hired a bus to take them to Dir at the foot of the Lohari Pass. At the frontier post on the border of Chitral, they realized that Beryl's arrival had been anticipated. The police would not allow her through. While Millar, Tenzing, and the other porters continued into Chitral, Miles and Beryl detoured to Nathiagall for an interview with the governor of the province. Not for the last time, red tape was jeopardizing a Himalayan expedition. When the governor reminded them that no ordinary woman was allowed into Chitral, Miles protested, "My wife's no ordinary woman." That did the trick. Soon they were on a bus, bumping toward Chitral with a guard of black-turbaned levies on the roof.

At Drosh they discovered that Millar had gone on toward the mountain. Waiting for them was Richard Orgill, a late addition to the climbing party who Miles described as having a sparkling sense of humor and "the consistency of a golf-ball." The Smeetons unpacked tuxedo and evening dress for dinner in the officers' mess. Beryl was the first European woman the Jat Regiment had seen for some time, and she caused quite a stir. In the morning they continued on to the barracks of the Chitral Scouts a few miles beyond Drosh, where Ang Tenzing was waiting with Mingwa, left behind by Millar to help them catch up. Trekking to Tirich Mir would take four days, and the Smeetons decided to carry 40-pound loads to toughen themselves up for the mountain. The Sherpas, on the other hand, would carry nothing. With a few rupees' advance pay, they had hired a local porter to carry their kit and "were strolling along like lords with a stick in their hands and nothing on their backs."[26] At the tiny villages on the approach they stopped for ice-cold water and mulberries provided by villagers, who offered to massage their legs as well. One headman chastised Miles for allowing his wife to carry a load when even the Sherpas were unladen and offered to hire one for her.

The Smeetons were not really equipped for a peak of over 25,000 feet—Tirich Mir is the highest mountain in the Hindu Kush—and they picked an awkward approach up the southern Owir Glacier and then up the South Ridge. Although the climbing was straightforward, no one had attempted Tirich Mir before, and they discovered their chosen line wasn't practical for such a small party with limited equipment. For two weeks they carried loads up the Owir Glacier, placing their third camp at its head. From here they followed old avalanche runnels to the ridge at 19,000 feet, placing their fourth camp just below its crest.

Beryl decided that instead of slogging back down, she, Miles, and Ang Tenzing should instead glissade, sliding down on the soles of their boots. Quickly losing control, they sped off down the mountain, and Miles found himself dragged after them on the rope. As Beryl and Ang Tenzing steadied each other, he swept them off their feet and they shot off toward the gaping *bergschrund* (the gap between a snowfield and a glacier at the bottom of a slope). Beryl and Ang Tenzing cleared it completely, but Miles was left with his behind stuck through the snow bridge spanning its black depths before being hauled out and brushing himself down. Tenzing had been watching all this as he walked up from Camp III to meet them. Miles wrote: "We were always struck by the grace with which he moved, but now he seemed to be bent double and rolling awkwardly up the hill; when he arrived he was shaking with uncontrollable laughter, and tears ran down his cheeks as he put us on our feet again."[27]

In his travelogue of life in India with Beryl, *A Taste of the Hills*, Miles wrote a great deal about Tenzing. The book was published in 1961, by which time Tenzing was famous, and the childlike simplicity of the porters is rather overplayed. Still, Smeeton was a bright writer and gives a sharp impression of the 25-year-old Tenzing: "[He] was tall for a Sherpa, and his open face had such charm and friendliness that he inspired a quick affection. He was uncomplicated and loyal. I couldn't imagine him capable of a mean action, nor of a selfish thought, and his character shone clearly in his oval brown eyes."[28] In his broken English, Tenzing regaled the sahibs with stories of climbing on Everest with the famous Eric Shipton and Frank Smythe. No longer was he the junior porter keeping a low profile. Although in *Tiger of the Snows* he makes a point of resisting the title sirdar, Tenzing was effectively fulfilling that role, organizing the local porters and leading the Sherpas on the mountain. "Tenzing had something special about him," Miles Smeeton continued. "He was a thoroughbred. He was more than that; a hill peasant, a carrier of burdens, but we felt that he had been touched by some divine spirit which made him a little different from ordinary men."[29]

As the climbers moved slowly up the South Ridge, their perspective on the mountain changed. Slowly the magnitude of their undertaking hardened into disappointment. The ridge reached a fore-peak, quickly nicknamed "The Deceiver," at about 23,000 feet before plunging down steeply to a saddle 800 feet below. They would need at least another week and two more camps to reach the summit of Tirich Mir this way, and they had neither the experience nor the equipment to extend themselves that far. "'What would Shipton or Tilman do?' we asked Tenzing. He shook his head and smiled: 'They'd go another way,' he said."[30]

Tenzing explained that they had been "climbing for pleasure," but Miles Smeeton noticed how disappointed Tenzing was at not reaching the summit. Like most Sherpas he felt a strong sense of competition. While Tenzing was climbing on an amateurish excursion to Tirich Mir, the sirdar Pasang Kikuli was leading a group of porters on an American expedition to K2. One of those Sherpas, Pasang Dawa Lama, almost reached the summit with Fritz Wiessner before they retreated just 250 meters from the top, an outstanding achievement for the 1930s on the toughest big mountain of them all. Pasang Kikuli and two of his friends would die that summer coming to the assistance of Dudley Wolfe, marooned high on the mountain in controversial circumstances. Even so, these men were heroes in Darjeeling. The status and recognition Tenzing desired were theirs already.

Ambition was one thing, providing for his family quite another. There would be no more big expeditions that year, and Tenzing needed to earn some money to keep Dawa Phuti and the children going through the winter. At Drosh, during the approach to Tirich Mir, he had met Maj. E. H. White, an Irishman[31] in the 9th Gurkhas commanding the Chitral

Scouts. Jack Gibson of the Doon School and White were friends, so White probably knew all about Tenzing from Gibson's climbing trips before the war. When the Smeetons returned to Drosh, White offered Tenzing and Ang Tenzing jobs as personal orderlies, and both men decided to stay for a few weeks even though Miles Smeeton was reluctant to leave them behind: "They were so far from their homes and their families and we had been responsible for getting them there, but they were anxious to stay, and were well looked after."[32] Angwa and Mingwa were put back on the train at Lahore, and Miles returned to Britain. Later, on a troopship bound for India, he listened to Neville Chamberlain's radio broadcast declaring war on Germany. By this time his wife was thousands of miles away, walking by herself through Siam.

Tenzing was happy in Chitral. Jack Gibson, who stayed with Tenzing and White in 1940, gives an impression of how attractive the country was: "Drosh is a delightful place. Outside the fort they have made themselves a swimming pool and tennis court. The garden is full of singing birds and the temperature that of an English summer."[33] The weeks turned into months, and with the outbreak of war in September, Tenzing reasoned that there was little purpose in rushing back to Darjeeling. There would be no more climbing expeditions now. The Chitral Scouts were charged with maintaining defensive positions along the Northwest Frontier in case any Afghans tried to take advantage of the war by raiding across the border.

At the end of 1939 Tenzing heard from his family in Darjeeling. It was the very worst kind of news. Nima Dorje, his beloved son, had died. The four-year-old had drunk polluted water and died of dysentery, a common cause of child mortality even now. Tenzing left Chitral and traveled across India to Darjeeling and was reunited with Dawa Phuti after an absence of more than six months. She soon after gave birth to their third child, a little girl whom they also named Nima. "I stayed only a short while in Darjeeling," he explained in his autobiography. "I had been very happy in Chitral, and, besides, there was now war in Europe, and there would certainly be no big expeditions for a long time. So I took my wife and two daughters with me, and went back to Chitral."

At first Tenzing returned to working as White's personal orderly. Later he took a job in the officers' mess, which was based in the town of

Chitral itself, but in 1942, after a reorganization of the regiment, was moved to the walled fortifications at Drosh. While working in the mess Tenzing became an expert cook; "he really was first class," Trevor Braham recalled. The regiment moved around their corner of the Northwest Frontier, and Tenzing and the family followed. "I still remember the Khyber Pass," Pem Pem said. When White was able to take time off, he took Tenzing on small expeditions, such as skiing in Kashmir, where the Ski Club of India had an annual event, or trekking in the Hindu Kush. In July and August 1940, Jack Gibson arrived in Chitral to play polo and do some exploring. With him came Rinzing. White had asked Gibson to bring another Sherpa to work at Chitral, so Gibson inevitably chose a man he knew. Sir Charles Frossard, then a captain in the Indian Army, recalled that the officers in the mess gave the three Bhotias nicknames: Ang Tenzing was Huntin', Tenzing was Shootin', and Rinzing was Fishin'. He too found the country beautiful. There were fresh apricots, plums, apples, and mulberries in summer, trout in the rivers, and curd from the flocks of sheep grazing in the mountains. The fields were irrigated with *zhoi*, channels carved into cliffs or constructed to cross gaps as aqueducts, feeding water to the barren valleys. "It was lovely country," Frossard said, "a sort of Shangri La. But it was very remote and you had to be able to put up with the loneliness. There was an airstrip for supplies but in winter everything came in on the backs of coolies."

Rinzing and Tenzing found themselves working together again in the mountains. While White checked on positions and recruited local villagers for the Scouts, Gibson tagged along, playing polo by moonlight and chatting with the Mehtar of Chitral's brother. ("He has a story-teller who tells him stories in Persian every night until and after he has gone to sleep."[34]) When White's duties were over, they trekked into the Hindu Kush with Tenzing and Rinzing, climbing up to the Kotgaz Pass. Gibson took a photograph of Tenzing and Rinzing at Rosh Gol, sitting by the side of a lake, the mountains behind reflected in its waters. On the frontier between Afghanistan and Chitral, they looked along the course of the Oxus Valley to the Pamirs and Russia and down long ice fields into Afghanistan itself before retreating the way they had come for a rest day. Then they climbed up the valley of Tirich Gol, attempting a peak of around 18,000 feet above it. Their climb was thwarted by lack of daylight, but they were still rewarded by the vast stretch of mountains around them. The whole of Chitral appeared at their feet, mountain ridges interlocking like fingers and the valleys between lost in gradations of blue shadow. To the north Gibson described Tirich Mir towering white above their heads against the indigo sky.

Frossard recalls that Rinzing wasn't happy in Chitral and returned home before the end of the war to Darjeeling, where he died in 1947. Tenzing and his family, meanwhile, remained trapped at Drosh by economic need. At least he had steady work and in the winters there were skiing trips to relieve the monotony. "I enjoyed skiing as much as anything I had ever done, and Major White suggested that some day I might find it useful in my mountaineering," Tenzing recalled. "Once I had a bad fall, in which I broke some ribs and sprained my knees, but that did not stop me, and I went at it again as soon as I could."[35]

Then tragedy struck. Dawa Phuti had not adjusted well to life in Chitral and was often in poor health. After Nima was born in early 1940, she had no more children. Tenzing had struck up a friendship with the local Indian Medical Service doctor, Nugent Jekyll,[36] but despite his best efforts Dawa Phuti grew weaker. In the autumn of 1944, she died.

It was a bitter blow for Tenzing. His life with Dawa Phuti, which had started with such excitement in Darjeeling ten years before, had ended. His little family was isolated, thousands of miles from home. The link with their old way of life was broken forever. "I do not even have my own mother's photograph," Pem Pem said.

For a while Tenzing struggled on, hiring a tall Pashtun called Bulbul Khan to care for Pem Pem and Nima, but the arrangement didn't last long. Tenzing needed to return home, where he could make more lasting arrangements for their care. In early 1945 Tenzing set out for Darjeeling. Popping each daughter into a bag and loading them on either side of a pony, he trekked down the valley of Chitral to Dir, where he hoped to get a train. With the war, resources were stretched thin, and for days he couldn't get a berth. Finally, he put on an old uniform White had given him, and climbed aboard the first-class section of the first military train he saw. His impersonation, a typically self-confident solution, went unchallenged, and the family traveled home across the breadth of India in style for no cost at all. When they reached Siliguri, only a day's journey from Darjeeling, Tenzing become anxious about being recognized still wearing the uniform of a Chitrali Scout, and he changed back into his civilian clothes.

He had to face the future. His wife and son were dead, he no longer had a job, and he had two young daughters to protect. During the years in Chitral, Tenzing's youthful enthusiasm ebbed away, replaced by a toughness and wisdom. The world had changed utterly in the years of war. And Tenzing had no idea of what would happen next.

CHAPTER SIX

RETURN TO DARJEELING

I have been able to give my family
a much nicer home and a much better start in life
than I had foreseen before the great climb.
This is what gives me the greatest satisfaction;
my family is my first concern and my greatest pleasure.
—TENZING NORGAY, *After Everest*

IN THE SPRING OF 1945 Tenzing moved into the Sherpa district of Toong Soong Busti, where his dead wife's relatives were living, with Pem Pem and Nima. He was almost 31, and after five years working for the Chitral Scouts, he had around 1,500 rupees to his name. With the war well into its fifth year, there was no possibility of any expeditions arriving in Darjeeling. Tenzing wasn't employed, and there was no prospect of any employment in the foreseeable future. He had no family around him, apart from his daughters. His three sisters were still living either in Khumbu or Tibet, and his mother and father were at Tsawa. Tenzing couldn't be certain they were even still alive. It is difficult to imagine a man more alone and further from achieving his ambition. Seven years had passed since Tenzing had been to Everest with Bill Tilman's lightweight expedition. Almost six years had gone by since he had last climbed on a big mountain with the Smeetons. The interruption to his climbing career was now longer than the career itself.

His plight was shared by most of the Sherpas and Bhotias of Darjeeling, and Tenzing at least had earned some money to keep his family fed. Krenek's 1950 list of the whereabouts of porters approved by the Himalayan Club shows how their community had dispersed, forced by the turmoil of war into making a living wherever and however they could. One dramatic example was Ang Tsering, who spent some of the war in Assam, working for a British Army officer until he witnessed a Japanese bombing raid and fled back to Darjeeling—without his pay.

Many of Tenzing's old friends were dead. Sixteen of the porters Tilman used on Everest in 1938 were listed by Krenek, and what had happened to them in the meantime shows how tenuous the lives of Sherpas and Bhotias were. In 1950 only three of them were still working: Ang Tharkay, Gyalgen Mikchen, and Tenzing himself. Of the other thirteen, three had returned to Khumbu or Tibet, going back to their home villages to live by farming or herding.[1] One, the famous sirdar Wangdi Norbu, was still living in Darjeeling, his working life over. The other nine were dead. These were men of Tenzing's generation, still in their 20s and 30s.

Tenzing knew he couldn't even begin to think about going back to Everest or any other mountain until he sorted out a home for his daughters. Their lives were uncertain enough without the hazards of a climbing expedition. What would happen to them if he died? Plus, a single father in Sherpa society was very uncommon. The girls needed a mother.

When Tenzing had married Dawa Phuti, he was a 20-year-old deeply in love. Ten years later, he had two young daughters and no work. When in 1945 he picked up his Tiger's Badge from the Himalayan Club, earned on Everest in 1938, it must have seemed a hollow triumph. To his old friends he was almost a stranger. They called him "Pathan," a reference to the Pashtun tribe on the Northwest Frontier, and mocked his military-style dress. He couldn't go back to Khumbu. He had no land or house there. Nor could a man who had traveled the breadth of India, living with motor cars and trains, Indian food and customs, tolerate becoming someone's servant again for a pittance. His parents-in-law were still there—he had told them of Dawa Phuti's death—but to throw himself on their charity would be an admission of failure. His home in Tibet had been left even farther behind.

Tenzing's choice of a second wife marked the start of the upswing in his fortunes. He met a woman he had known from his first year in

Darjeeling, a Sherpani called Ang Lhamu, with whom he used to hag-
gle over the price of the milk he sold in town. Tenzing described their
exchanges: "'If I buy from you you must give me an extra measure,' she
would say. 'No, I cannot,' I would tell her. 'You are cheap and stingy,' she
would say. 'And you are a hard bargainer,' I would answer."[2]

For Pem Pem and Nima the overriding memory of Ang Lhamu is
one of love. "She looked after us so well," Pem Pem recalled, "like we
were her own children. She was a wonderful mother. My father was having
a very hard time. There were very few expeditions and when there was
no work it was hard. She shared my father's burden and when he couldn't
find work she worked as well." Nima said: "To the two of us, she was kind
and loving. We grew up calling her 'Mummy.'" Ang Lhamu was older
than Tenzing by four years, and although her family hailed from the village of Thamo in Khumbu, she had been born in Darjeeling. A distant
cousin of Dawa Phuti, Ang Lhamu had also been married before, and
widowed, but she discovered during her marriage she couldn't have children. Instead, she earned her living working as an *ayah,* or nanny, for
British families living in Darjeeling. She had even gone to London with
one of them in 1938, living for a while at a hotel near Hyde Park. She
could remember lying ill in hospital, being taught how to use a gas mask
in the days before the outbreak of war, and suffering terribly from sea-
sickness on the voyage from India. Her English was considerably better
than her new husband's, and she had a broader view of the world than
people sometimes assumed. Everyone who knew her well speaks of her
incisive intelligence. She was also very modest. The British she worked
for had no idea her husband was the famous Tenzing Norgay.

Trulshik Rinpoche, who took over Rongbuk monastery after
Dzatrul's death, recognized Ang Lhamu as an incarnation of
Miyolangsangma, the deity living on Everest. He remembered coming
to Calcutta before Tenzing climbed Everest.[3] Tenzing sent Ang Lhamu
to act as an interpreter for his cousin, who spoke only Tibetan. He
recognized in her the generous character of the goddess but never told
Tenzing about this. Trulshik's implication is that her spiritual connection with Chomolungma gave Tenzing an advantage in climbing the
mountain. Although Tenzing joked about their arguments in *Tiger of
the Snows*, casting Ang Lhamu as resolute and sometimes obstinate, she

was the soothing influence on Tenzing's family life. "She took life as it came," Pem Pem said, "with a smile. I never heard her lose her temper. Daddy would. At that time he had a terrible temper, but not Ang Lhamu."

Though she was the daughter of a pious couple who were committed followers of Dzatrul Rinpoche at Rongbuk, Ang Lhamu did not make a great show of her religion. "If you talk about religion in terms of mourning rituals, then she was not all that religious," Nima recalled. "But she was a good person who practiced what the scriptures taught. She was generous of heart and self-effacing. She knew how to give, how to welcome and how to love." Ang Lhamu had what the Sherpas call *nyingje*, selfless, devoted compassion, the kind of love a mother has for her child.

On the surface, she and Tenzing appeared to be an unlikely couple. Physically, Tenzing was coming into his prime, a tall, lithe, and extremely handsome man. Ang Lhamu was a solid, coarse-featured woman whom one friend described as "five foot square." The British climber George Band said she had a "formidable" exterior. Yet she was warm and popular. "She was full of jokes," Nima said. "She liked a drink, but always chang or *rakshi* [rice spirit]. Daddy would bring her wine sometimes, but she'd just give it away." She also smoked *bidis,* the strong hand-rolled cigarettes favored by poorer Indians. "He'd bring her foreign cigarettes, but she'd give them away to her friends. They were like air to her. She liked her *paan* [beetelnut] too. She'd go to the movies once a week, to see the latest Hindi pictures. She would take us sometimes, but my father didn't like that. He was quite strict; he didn't want us to be spoiled."

Not everyone was delighted by the prospect of marriage. Ang Tsering, Dawa Phuti's first cousin, objected, wishing to defend his family's interest in Pem Pem and Nima. "They had every right," Pem Pem recalled. "People in our community can be very fussy." Tenzing solved the issue neatly by sitting on his doorstep, sharpening a formidable *khukri*, the curved Nepalese blade carried into battle by Gurkha regiments. The message was clear: Anyone who wanted to object to the wedding would have to answer to him. The wedding went ahead, but the tension between Tenzing and his first wife's family remained.

Though not a love match, Pem Pem believes it was a strong marriage. "They were good friends. There was never any problem." Tenzing found stability and a mother for his children. Ang Lhamu found an outlet for her instinct to love, and she defended her husband's interests diligently. Trulshik Rinpoche told Jamling Tenzing Norgay, Tenzing's second son by Daku, his third wife: "She was a protectress, a grantor of good fortune. She was the one who guided your father up the mountain. She provided him with the home life, the stability, the sense that he needed in order to climb it safely—through her blessings."[4]

After the marriage, when the fortunes of the Sherpas in Darjeeling reached their lowest ebb, Ang Lhamu carried on as an ayah to help make ends meet. Later she worked as an assistant for Smith Brothers, an American dentistry practice in Darjeeling. Inflation was eating into Tenzing's savings; prices had increased five times since before the war. "For a while ... there seemed to be no ups—only downs," Tenzing recalled. "My wife kept us going, and for myself there was only a day's work here, another day's there, all of them menial and dreary, and in between them nothing."[5] Through the long months in Darjeeling with nothing to do but wait, Ang Lhamu helped Tenzing find his direction once again. "I could never forget what she did for us all during those hard and bitter days."[6]

Tenzing spent some of his savings on a couple of horses, which he would lead to the square at Chowrasta in the morning and hire out to carry loads or the American tourists (mostly military men left over from the war) who arrived in Darjeeling in 1945 and 1946. Several Sherpas did this, including Dawa Thondup and Ang Tsering, who developed quite a stable. The horses would race at the Lebong racecourse outside town, sometimes with Tenzing riding, and both Ang Tsering and Tenzing had winners. They also picked up business guiding what tourists there were to the top of Tiger Hill above Darjeeling, where the sahibs would watch the morning sun strike the summit of Kanchenjunga. In the mid 1940s it was a small clearing in the forest. Tenzing would diligently point out the insignificant triangle of Everest, barely cresting the intervening ridge and apparently lower than the summit of Makalu, which less scrupulous guides would identify as Everest to please their clients. Tenzing didn't allow himself self-pity, but his situation, pointing out distant mountains to ignorant tourists when he felt he should be climbing them, rankled at times. He made short treks to other tourist spots, such as the high mountain ridge at Sandakphu, staying in *dak* bungalows, keeping the *burra sahibs*—the great masters—happy. A fortnight after he married Ang

Lhamu in 1945, he even took an American colonel on a two-month trip through Sikkim and across the border into Tibet, riding ponies as far as Gyantse with its spectacular Newari stupa and its imposing fortress.

In early 1946 Tenzing got word that Jack Gibson was planning another attempt on Bandarpunch and wanted to take Tenzing with him. "I was as excited as if I were not a grown man, but a boy. 'You are going back to the mountains!' That was all I could think, and it was like a great shout inside of me. 'You are going back to the mountains where you belong!'"[7] Gibson was limited to school vacations, and that meant the monsoon. Although they were hampered by heavy snow, they managed to ascend a thousand feet higher up the summit ridge that had thwarted them in 1937. This time Gibson was joined by a Royal Artillery officer called John Munro, and Roy Holdsworth, who had been on Kamet with Frank Smythe in 1931. Also included was Nandu Jayal, Gibson's former pupil, who was now a lieutenant in the Indian Army.

If the weather was bad, at least the mountains were carpeted in flowers—yellow potentillas, purple asters, and primulas—and the team could relax in their tents playing bridge during the prolonged storms. As the old climbing star, Holdsworth took over the leadership of the expedition, but his equipment was ancient. His boots fell apart and he had to borrow Gibson's spare pair. They were stopped at 18,000 feet by steep, hard ice plastered with a thin coating of snow. Combined with the bad weather, Holdsworth announced that the difficulties were greater than anything they'd experienced on Kamet. "The Sherpas are marvellous," Gibson wrote, "and without them we shouldn't be here. I got a real mountaineering thrill watching them move back through the mist to bring up our supplies."[8] There's no record of who the other two Sherpas were—Gibson refers to Dawa, which may have been Dawa Thondup. He had a special affection for Tenzing, describing him as "the hero of this trip." He was dynamic, eager to work and bursting with optimism. They climbed a small, subsidiary peak of 18,000 feet, but gave up on a second attempt on Bandarpunch when several of the porters came down with malaria and Gibson contracted a stomach illness. Instead they descended to Dodi Tal, where they spent several days fishing, pulling a hundred trout out of the lake and smoking them over the campfire. A few days later, as the expedition trekked back to the roadhead, Gibson and Tenzing offered to catch a wild boar that had been destroying a local farmer's crops. Gibson had a rifle, Tenzing his khukri. The boar never showed up, though, and both men slept in the fields undisturbed until sunrise.

In June 1953, when Gibson heard of Tenzing's success on Everest, he dropped him a short congratulatory note that reminded Tenzing of this expedition. "Do you remember," he wrote, "the dispute I had with Nandu Jayal when he wanted you to become his batman, and I told him I would never speak to him again if he interfered with what I expected to be a great climbing career. Well, now you've done it, and all of us here send you our very warmest congratulations."[9]

Jayal's offer to Tenzing of a job as his batman must have been tempting. Gibson's expedition took only a month, and Tenzing had no other expedition work in 1946. Travel and currency restrictions in Europe meant that not even resourceful and thrifty climbers like Bill Tilman could escape to the Himalaya, and Tenzing had no idea when things might pick up. He took what climbing work he could. Soon after he got back to Darjeeling, he made a couple of trips to the Kanchenjunga area, guiding an Indian Army officer around the Zemu and Yarlung Glaciers. The American widow of an Indian businessman had asked them to look out for any sign of her husband. He had disappeared trekking near Kanchenjunga during the war, and she wanted some proof of what had happened to him. They found the businessman's partially cremated remains near Green Lake[10] close to the Zemu Glacier at 16,500 feet, and took his wristwatch and a fragment of wrist bone to give to his widow. At Green Lake they also discovered the remains of a Sherpa who had disappeared with three others on an attempt to climb a peak called Sugarloaf, just to the northeast of Kanchenjunga. When Tenzing got back to Darjeeling, he was hired by another young Gurkha, Jim Thornley, to return to the Green Lake region to look for the others in the party.

In the spring of 1947, an even stranger opportunity arose, one that would take Tenzing back to Everest for the first time in nine years. It would also reconnect him in a very personal way to the miserable and lonely death of Maurice Wilson in 1934. Earl Denman, a Canadian-born electrical engineer, was an introverted and serious man whose childhood had been dominated by the illness that paralyzed his father and forced his mother to bring them all to England, where their savings dwindled to nothing.

Poverty haunted his life like an accusing ghost, and he escaped the drudgery of his life by dreaming of adventure. Denman was fascinated by the heroes of African exploration—Livingstone, Speke, and Burton—and after serving his apprenticeship he started applying for jobs in Africa. He dreamed of the Belgian Congo, drawn by Stanley's descriptions of the Ruwenzori, called by Ptolemy the "Mountains of the Moon." Instead, he had to settle for the Sudan, which bored him and left little time for exploring until he was released by the outbreak of war. Denman was not a natural soldier—"the petty restrictions of Service life irked me"[11]—but at least he was able to build up £650 in savings. With this sum set aside, he set off to climb the eight volcanoes of the Virunga Mountains, which reach about 15,000 feet on the border between Congo and Rwanda. These are not difficult mountains, little more than a hard walk, but Denman was clearly a determined man prepared to make long and difficult journeys on his own: "During my early days on mountains the opportunity of climbing with more experienced men never came my way, and so I made my own trips with none but native Africans as guides and porters, and these I came to look upon also as friends and companions."[12] He eschewed boots, preferring to trek barefoot—even, he claimed, above the snow line. And having dispatched the Virunga, he decided he was ready for Everest.

Denman was a contrary character, at one moment awkward and self-derogatory, the next almost arrogant. "I grew up with an ambition and determination without which I would have been a good deal happier."[13] He doesn't seem to have taken much pleasure in his travels, and he was prone to making sanctimonious boasts. One notable one concerned Tenzing. "It was not," he wrote after their expedition, "until some years later that Tenzing, due to his outstanding qualities, came to be given a real chance on Everest. I was, as a matter of fact, the first to grant a measure of equality to any Sherpa."[14] This was as much an underestimate of Tenzing as Younghusband's belief that Sherpas and Bhotias lacked the right spirit to climb Everest. Tenzing didn't need Denman's "opportunity" to get ahead. In fact, Tenzing seems to have taken a cool, intelligent look at Earl Denman and decided for all sorts of reasons that he had much to gain from the self-conscious, cash-strapped but determined traveler.

Arriving in Darjeeling in mid-March, Denman wandered around town and saw the name "Paul" on a shop sign. Figuring that the owner must be a relative of Karma Paul, the Tibetan sirdar and interpreter on the pre-war Everest expeditions, he went inside and discovered that in fact the shop belonged to Karma Paul himself. When Denman explained what he wanted to do and that he didn't have a permit, Paul gave him "a strange incredulous"[15] look and said: "Impossible!" Paul must have thought he was seeing the ghost of Maurice Wilson walking through the door. Denman rushed to explain that unlike Wilson, he was in command of his mental faculties and was an experienced mountaineer. The former at least was more or less true. After some persuasion, Paul said he knew a man who might be able to help and arranged a meeting for the next day.

Why Paul introduced Denman to Tenzing is interesting in itself. He had been to Everest three times before from Darjeeling, but then so had many other porters. It seems that Paul knew as well as Tenzing that Denman would get nowhere on Everest and wanted to make sure he didn't get into too much trouble while failing, as Wilson had with Rinzing and the other Bhotias in 1934. Tenzing was vastly more experienced as a climber than Denman. He had, after all, worked alongside men such as Frank Smythe, who were genuinely talented mountaineers. He must have known that he would be going for an extended trek. Denman might have thought it was his trip, but Tenzing would be making the real decisions.

At their first meeting. Denman stressed his poverty and his guilt at paying the men so little. He thought it fortuitous that Tenzing saw his shoddy room in Darjeeling. It offered proof he wasn't being stingy. In *Alone to Everest* and a number of earlier newspaper articles, the entire enterprise has the air of a desperate gamble that Denman clearly believed would come off. Here is Tenzing's account in *Tiger of the Snows:*

"What there was to think about I don't know, because nothing made sense about it. First: we would probably not even get into Tibet. Second: if we did get in we would probably be caught, and, as his guides, we, as well as Denman, would be in serious trouble. Third: I did not for a moment believe that, even if we reached the mountain, a party such as this would be able to climb it. Fourth: the attempt would be highly dangerous. Fifth: Denman had neither the money to pay us well nor to guarantee a decent sum to our dependents in case something happened to us. And so on and so on. Any man in his right mind would have said no. But I couldn't say no. For in my heart I needed to go, and the pull of Everest was stronger for me than any force on earth."[16]

On the other hand, there were several good reasons why Tenzing would want to go to Everest. The first was the money. Tenzing chose another Sherpa to go with him, Ang Dawa, who was roughly his age and had climbed on Everest before the war. Ang Dawa was from Thame, and Tenzing knew him well. (Denman uncharitably describes him as "stronger, but less intelligent in appearance.") Tenzing opened negotiations on their behalf. Both men wanted a down payment of 600 rupees each, roughly £50. "It was made plain that I could offer no more than Rs300 as an advance payment," Denman wrote. "This would become their property on proceeding beyond Rongbuk, the monastery within sight of Everest. After this they would be paid Rs5 for each day spent on the mountain and on the return to Darjeeling."[17] If they got turned back at the Tibetan border, a lower rate would apply, although Tenzing knew perfectly well how porous the Tibetan border was. He took the terms.

The next day Tenzing arrived at Denman's apartment with Ang Lhamu.[18] "She did not have much to say, but her calm composure and reassuring smile made me feel that she had confidence in me and would trust her husband to my care."[19] Denman sealed two envelopes each containing 300 rupees, and the "expedition" was under way.

Denman might have thought he was paying his guides too little, but the truth is that Tenzing and Ang Dawa were paid very well indeed. According to Krenek of the Himalayan Club, a sirdar in 1950 on a big expedition—a far more complex job than what Tenzing was planning— could expect to get between Rs150 and Rs175 per month. He adds: "It should be noted that members resident in India often complain that foreign expeditions tend to spoil porters by paying enhanced rates, e.g. Rs210 per month was paid in 1950 to a sirdar."[20] Even allowing for the rigorous thrift of the Himalayan Club, Denman's two guides clearly made a good deal. They needed only 17 days to reach Rongbuk, at which point Tenzing and Ang Dawa qualified for 300 rupees each. From that point they were making 5 rupees a day. As it turned out, the expedition spent another 20 days attempting the mountain *and* returning to Darjeeling— the quickest Everest expedition in history—meaning Tenzing and Ang Dawa earned another 100 rupees. In total, Tenzing worked for a month and six days and made 400 rupees. This came at a time when work in Darjeeling was almost nonexistent.

There was nothing dishonest about what Tenzing did. Denman was a fantasist with something to prove. While he didn't share Maurice Wilson's belief that fasting and prayer would get him up the mountain, his need to transcend his own brittle character by an outrageous adventure was potentially dangerous not just to him but to Tenzing and Ang Dawa. Tenzing had seen Wilson's body, his face desiccated by the cold and wind and pecked at by choughs. He understood the perils of the situation perfectly. Athough they were paid very well, Denman couldn't afford to pay compensation in the case of a fatal accident, so Tenzing would have felt justified in charging a premium.

Getting Denman even to Rongbuk proved awkward. Across the border near the village of Tarnak, they were overtaken by six officials, Denman says, and ordered to go no farther. Tenzing took a considerable risk going on, at least at first. Later he was on home ground, close to his childhood home in the Kharta Valley, and he knew many of the places they visited and people they met.

Going home might also have been part of Tenzing's motivation in taking Denman into Tibet. It gave him a chance to see relatives who, because of the war, he had not seen in almost a decade. Denman, sometimes unwittingly, offers proof of this. After crossing the Bhong Chu with some difficulty, Tenzing led Denman along the Dzakar Chu, which flows past the village of Tsa, where his parents, Mingma and Kinzom, were now living. He tells us that Tenzing asked to slip off for the night "to see a friend." He certainly called there on the way back, because Denman gives a full account of it.

"Tsa seemed to be deserted by everyone but extraordinarily vicious dogs, but at length we chanced upon the fine house of Kasang Chola La, who was obviously the most wealthy Tibetan we came across."[21] There was no chance about it, of course, but Denman didn't know that. Kasang was the new landowner, part of the family that had employed Tenzing's family as servants for several generations. This was the great house where Tenzing's father, Mingma, would die in 1949 and where Tenzing would come to fetch his mother, Kinzom, to Darjeeling in early 1955. Denman offers no clue as to their whereabouts, but he describes Kasang—"he was not unhandsome, except when he smiled and showed his uneven teeth"[22]—and two of his children, whom Denman photographed. Tenzing hired three horses from Kasang, telling Denman to part with Rs105 for them for the week's trip to Lachen. Giving their master business was indirectly a favor to his parents.

Denman met Tenzing's sister Kipa in person, when they reached the monastery at Rongbuk. He was encouraged to discover Tenzing had contacts at Rongbuk, making their sojourn there more straightforward. "She was rather handsome, like her brother, and was married to a monk. The news came as a complete surprise to me, and I was pleased to know that Tenzing would be able to renew acquaintances after an interval of several years."[23] Lhamu Kipa was entrusted with Denman's will and his remaining funds. He also describes meeting the "regent" of the seven-year-old reincarnation of Dzatrul, who may have been Tenzing's cousin Trulshik Rinpoche.

For much of his time in Tibet, Denman seems to have experienced a waking nightmare. He liked his porters and enjoyed their company, but Tenzing's English was rudimentary and Denman felt disoriented and lonely. He recoiled from the squalor of ordinary Tibetan lives, was in a constant state of nervous panic over Tibetan guard dogs, and suffered, much as the pre-war climbers had, from poor health. He didn't like the landscape much, and he certainly didn't like the food. He deserves credit for sticking it out as long as he did. They set off for the mountain on April 10 with little fuel, two thin tents, and only meager supplies. "We were all porters and we were all climbers," Denman wrote, although Tenzing and Ang Dawa were in fact carrying far heavier loads than he was. "Beyond that we were just three men striving to give some meaning to a life which otherwise remains meaningless. What *were* we striving for if not for immortality? It is only deeds which satisfy, and men and women are only remembered for their deeds, whether they be good or bad."[24] With a philosophy like that—one that plenty of Everest climbers have shared—it's not surprising that Denman's rapid failure on Everest hit him hard, not least because he still had no idea of the scale of his under-taking even as he trekked up the Rongbuk Valley. They camped four times, the final night spent below the slopes of the North Col, which was as clear of snow as Tenzing had ever seen it. He knew, as he had all along, that this was as far as they were going. Denman was suffering horribly from the cold and had moved into the Sherpa tent after the first night. Now, with the decision made, he turned around and descended as fast as he could, sparing Tenzing and Ang Dawa the awkward difficulty Maurice Wilson's porters had faced of talking their employer into retreat. Denman described himself as "humiliated" by his experience. "I thought I saw in the vision of success a wonderful meaning to life—my triumph over the gross of materialism into which our civilisation as I knew it had been plunged."[25] All he saw looking at Everest was a vision of himself. Denman believed that Tenzing shared his dreams, especially of climbing Everest in a small party, but Tenzing had more pragmatic concerns: housing, an education for his children, and enough to eat.

At Rongbuk, Denman's physical deterioration and mental exhaustion frightened him into imagining he had scurvy. His skin was falling off his face from sunburn, giving him a sickly pallor, and he was close to collapse. More than anything he wanted to return to India. Tenzing, with the horses he had hired from Kasang, obliged as quickly as he could, and two weeks later they arrived back in Darjeeling.

Denman would come again to attempt Everest in 1948—this time with more money and more equipment—but without a permit, Tenzing refused to accompany him and so did everyone else. It wouldn't do to displease the Himalayan Club again and jeopardize future chances of work. Denman gave up and returned to South Africa, leaving all his equipment with Tenzing, and in 1953 the Sherpa would wear Denman's balaclava to the summit. Despite this irony, Tenzing was generous to Denman in *Tiger of the Snows*.[26] Perhaps he recognized in Denman some of his own determination.

Within a day of arriving back in Darjeeling, in late April 1947, Tenzing signed on for another expedition. "That was my father's job," Nima Galang said. Tenzing's second daughter was then barely seven years old. "If he didn't go then there was no food. Like all Sherpa wives, Ang Lhamu was used to it." This time, however, there would be no subterfuge or desperate rush to the mountain. The man recruiting porters was a Swiss, André Roch, who had been to the Himalaya several times before and was well known in Darjeeling. He had chosen as sirdar the Bhotia Wangdi Norbu, an Everest veteran, a survivor of the catastrophe on Nanga Parbat in 1934, and an old friend of Frank Smythe's. "He is a little fellow, all bone and wiriness, who does not carry an ounce of superfluous flesh and has one of the hardest countenances I have seen; he looks a 'tough,' but in point of fact he is sober and law abiding. He is quick and jerky in action and in speech; it is as though some fire burns within him which can never properly find a vent."[27]

Tenzing and Wangdi were both Bhotias, old friends who had survived a great deal together, not least the avalanche below the North Col on Everest in 1938. Wangdi was older, more experienced, and just as tough as Tenzing. In 1929 he had fallen into a crevasse and was not discovered for three hours but came through all right. On Everest in 1933, when Tenzing was left behind in Darjeeling, Wangdi had contracted pneumonia and was not expected to live. But within a month of evacuation he was back at Base Camp, requesting a load to carry.

Smythe had done some hard rock climbing with Wangdi Norbu on a 19,000-foot rock spire in the Indian Himalaya. In certain sections Smythe couldn't find anywhere to place a piton or secure himself to the rock and had relied on Wangdi to get over awkward, steep ground, climbing up cracks and over an overhang, without falling and pulling them both off. Descending the mountain, Smythe had to rely on Wangdi even more. The Tibetan cut nicks in the ice "just large enough for the extreme toe of his boots" to cross a steep slope to easier ground. "He was skill and caution personified: a Knubel or a Lochmatter could not have descended more confidently,"[28] he wrote, referring to two of the greatest Swiss guides, Josef Knubel and Franz Lochmatter.[29]

Roch, himself a mountain guide and glaciologist, wanted porters for an expedition to the Garhwal. At 40 years old, Roch had been one of Europe's top climbers before the war and had already explored the Garhwal, making the important first ascent of Dunagiri in 1939. He hired a team of eight Sherpas that included many of the strongest men then available, not just Tenzing and Wangdi Norbu, but Dawa Thondup, Ajiba, and Ang Dawa, who had climbed with Roch before. Partly the strong crew was due to the lack of work, but the Swiss also had a good reputation as well-funded and well-equipped employers.

The idea for the expedition had come from Annelies Lohner, a vivacious young Swiss woman who in the last winter of the war took a mountaineering vacation with her guide Alexandre Graven. Discussing their plans for the next summer, she asked, "Well, what about going to the Himalaya one day?" (Graven was a top climber, but hardly loquacious. Asked for a biography of himself, he replied, "The ice axe is not a pen.") When Roch brought his team of Sherpas to Mussoorie to meet the rest of the team, Tenzing was assigned to Lohner as her personal Sherpa on the 165-mile trek to the mountains: "Tenzing, my man, was an absolute gem. Neat and full of initiative, he spoilt me dreadfully. Hardly had we arrived than I found my bedding roll and washing water laid out ready, and my box transformed into an elegant washstand. He was the only Sherpa who could speak English and he had a wife and two daughters whose photos he always carried on him in a small frame."

The group took four days to reach Uttarkashi and then followed the pilgrims' trail to Gaumukh, on the snout of the Gangotri Glacier, venerated as one of the sources of the Ganges. The expedition was small, at least by Everest standards, and at once Tenzing felt appreciated, especially by Lohner, who enjoyed a teasing, flirtatious relationship with her Sherpa. "I had liked the Swiss tremendously," Tenzing said. "Even though there was much language difficulty, I had felt truly close to them and thought of them not as sahibs or employers, but as friends. And that is how it has been ever since."[30] Alfred Sutter, a wealthy businessman and keen amateur climber, and the good-natured Genèvois translator René Dittert completed the Swiss contingent, while Trevor Braham answered a general invitation by the Swiss to the Himalayan Club to send a representative.

Dittert was popular with the Sherpas and would talk with them around the campfire at night. Sutter was also a game hunter and supplemented the expedition's diet on the trek to Gangotri with pigeon and deer. For Tenzing it offered a marked contrast to the privations of the Doon School's trip to Bandarpunch the year before. Now the Sherpas had full stomachs as they trekked toward the mountains. The plan was not to limit themselves to one particular peak but, as on an Alpine vacation, choose a number of objectives, all around 22,000 feet, which they would climb quickly with the minimum of equipment. Their first objective was Kedarnath, and on June 25 a team of climbers set out from their top camp. Tenzing was not among them; he had stayed at Base Camp with his *memsahib*, Annelies Lohner, who was not considered strong enough to join the men. Roch and Dittert, who as the team's French speakers became a close partnership, tied in together with Ang Norbu, while Alex Graven shared a rope with Ang Dawa. Alfred Sutter, who was also one of Graven's regular clients, joined Wangdi Norbu.

By ten o'clock the teams had reached a fore-summit at more than 22,000 feet and they judged the main summit almost within reach, but distances are deceptive in the Himalaya, and for several hours it seemed to retreat before them as they climbed a long ridge. The Swiss had brought the latest equipment, Vibram-soled boots, which, unlike the nailed boots the Sherpas knew, required crampons. None of the Sherpas had worn crampons before, and as Graven led the others toward the summit, Wangdi Norbu caught one of the sharp metal points against his other leg and fell, shouting "Sahib!" as he did. Sutter attempted to stop his fall, driving his ice ax into the snow and whipping the rope around it. Wangdi swung across the ice slope below as the rope came taut, burning through Sutter's gloves and into the flesh of his hands. For a moment it seemed the fall had been arrested. Then Sutter's ice ax popped out of the snow, and both men accelerated away down the steep, icy slope. At its base, 800 feet below the ridge, was a cliff with a shallower snow slope beneath it. Graven turned his head away to avoid watching Sutter and Wangdi shoot into space over the cliff, but Roch was transfixed as the two men ricocheted into the air and hit the slope below. As they stood on the ridge, watching the bodies of their friends, Sutter recovered, stood up and waved. He was bruised but unhurt. Wangdi, however, was motionless.

It was impossible to descend where they were, so those on the ridge continued for another hour and a half until they reached ground they could descend safely. Sutter's hands were cut, his face bruised and he was in shock, but otherwise unharmed. Wangdi, however, had a head injury, his left ankle was broken, and a crampon point—most probably Sutter's—had punctured his right knee. Roch took one of the Sherpa's rucksacks, and Dittert, Graven, and Ang Dawa began dragging Wangdi Norbu across and down the slope, pausing every 20 yards to catch their breath, because they were above 20,000 feet. Already exhausted by the climb, they made painfully slow progress. Graven cursed himself for not being tied into his client, thus leaving Sutter to hold Wangdi's fall alone.

By evening, as the sun left the snow slope, the temperature plummeted to -20°C (-4°F). The exhausted climbers began to look with increasing desperation for somewhere to spend the night. Just inside the shelter of a crevasse, they laid Wangdi down on a snow bridge and then chopped seats for themselves to wait for dawn. All night they rubbed themselves to beat off the cold. At first light, plagued by thirst and exhausted by 24 hours of continuous effort, they decided to go down and get help from fresh men. Telling Wangdi they would be back, Roch and the others began the long descent at four o'clock.

Three Sherpas, Ajiba, Thondup, and Pasang Urgen, came to meet them as they reached the talus at the foot of the slope. Graven, Dittert, and Roch gave them some of their equipment to make the climb up to the crevasse where Wangdi was stranded. The Sherpas had the tracks of the others to follow, but when Roch woke at lunchtime, he discovered them already back. The snow had melted badly in the sun, which made Ajiba and the others unnerved by the crevasses they needed to cross. It was by now too late to reach Wangdi Norbu that day, so Roch and Dittert made plans to go back up early next morning.

Graven, who had not acclimatized well, brought the shocked Sutter down to Base Camp. When Tenzing heard about the accident, he left immediately with Braham to climb up to Camp I. That evening it snowed a little, raising the temperature and allowing the climbers some optimism that Wangdi would survive his night out alone.

Early the next morning, Dittert and Roch took two amphetamine pills each to boost their energy for the long day ahead. All were desperate to reach Wangdi, terrified at what they might find. "Dittert, Tenzing and Ang Norbu led like men possessed," Roch wrote.[31] In three hours they reached the fallen Sherpa—and discovered a horrific sight. Wangdi had cut his throat with his knife—which, covered with blood, lay in the snow by his side. "He told us later that he had seen three men coming to fetch him, but that, seeing them turn back, he had thought himself abandoned. He also heard his wife's voice and thought he was dying of thirst. He decided to end his life as quickly as possible so tried to pierce his heart. Being unsuccessful he tried to cut his throat. His neck and chest were covered with dried blood when we found him, but fortunately he had missed the artery and had only succeeded in making a large gash like a second gaping mouth in the middle of his throat."

Wangdi was tied up like a parcel and lowered slowly over the steep ground below the crevasse and then dragged and carried back to the valley. The gaping wound in his throat was sewn up, and his leg was set in plaster. One of the Sherpas grasped Wangdi's heavily infected right knee and squeezed it to draw off the pus. For ten days the climbers and sherpas looked after him, and as soon as he was fit enough to travel, Wangdi was evacuated to a hospital in Dehra Dun, more than 500 miles away. "When I saw him later in Darjeeling," Tenzing said, "it was obvious that what he had suffered had had a lasting effect, not only on his body but on his mind. Old Tiger Wangdi never climbed again, and he died in his home a few years later."[32]

Tenzing was the inevitable choice as the new sirdar. Roch referred to him as "our best man" and the Swiss acknowledged the difference he had made in bringing down the injured Wangdi. He was popular with the other expedition members too. Alfred Sutter, for one, recognized his ambition and determination to succeed. These qualities came to the fore when, in early July, the climbers returned for a second attempt on Kedarnath. Sutter noticed that the other Sherpas, particularly Ang Dawa and Ang Norbu, were "rather anxious about making the final assault with us, for superstitious fear made them hesitate to return to the scene of the accident but there was a gleam of determination in Tenzing's eyes."

The other Sherpas descended with Trevor Braham, but hardly because of superstitious fear. Seeing a man with his throat cut would color the mood of most mountain climbers, and the Sherpas had no interest in reaching a summit. Sutter himself went weak at the knees as he crossed the spot where Wangdi had fallen. "Some internal impulse threatened to shake me off my balance, and I had to force my trembling legs to tread firmly in the steps."[33]

Clouds swirled around the summit of Kedarnath as they climbed higher. The sun filtered through to melt snowflakes as they fell, wetting the climbers' clothes even as their throats were cured like leather in the thin air. Graven led at first, chopping steps with his ice ax and leading his client Sutter with steady momentum. Then, after abseiling a short way down a gap in the ridge, the rope of Dittert, Roch, and Tenzing moved into the lead. Now at over 22,000 feet, it was Tenzing who attacked the final slope of deep, soft snow that stretched for more than 500 feet to the summit. "I wondered where the man drew his strength from," Sutter wrote, "and tried to catch up with him, but he still kept well ahead. Finally, Dittert's voice, which even here had not lost its strength, announced that we had only 150 feet to go."[34] Tenzing's group paused just below the summit to wait for Sutter and Graven, then they continued all together, hugging and shouting with excitement and joy.

Climbing with the Swiss changed Tenzing's outlook. He had known top climbers before the war, particularly Frank Smythe, but his experience in the Gangotri was more like the joyful mountaineering practiced in the Alps, not the tough grind of an Everest expedition. The climbers were back at Base Camp by 9:15 that evening and spent the rest of the evening drinking and talking. Tenzing shared in this celebration, and the experience was a revelation. "That evening, when we all came back to base camp," Trevor Braham recalled, "and we all sat down, he sat down with us and drank a glass of wine. This was something unheard of. Shipton and Tilman wouldn't have thought this odd but I can think of plenty of English climbers who would have done."

Tenzing's ambition to reach the summit pushed him across a kind of threshold in the eyes of the Swiss. Here at last was a Sherpa who appreciated what drove the sahibs in their endeavors. For his part, sitting around a campfire laughing and talking with his well-traveled and wealthy companions about their shared success opened a door in Tenzing's mind. It also bred a deep loyalty for his new friends. The expedition enjoyed more successes over the next six weeks, although Tenzing missed out on another first ascent, contracting a stomach illness the night before the climb to the summit of Satopanth. "But all the rest had been good—the best it had ever been on a mountain trip—not only in the success of our climbs, but in the enjoyment we had from them," Tenzing said.[35]

Trevor Braham left the expedition before its conclusion, forced to return to work at the end of his leave. He crossed the Kalindi Khal above the Chaturangi Glacier and then trekked down the Arwa Glacier toward Joshimath. So it was that Braham found himself on his own on the stroke of midnight as August 14 became August 15 and India achieved independence. While Tenzing settled into his tent in the Garhwal after another long day in the mountains with his new Swiss friends, Jawaharlal Nehru was addressing India's Constituent Assembly: "Long years ago we made a tryst with destiny, and now the time comes when we shall redeem our pledge, not wholly or in full measure, but very substantially. At the stroke of midnight hour, when the world sleeps, India will awake to life and freedom. A moment comes which comes but rarely in history, when we step out from the old to the new, then an age ends, and when the soul of a nation, long suppressed, finds utterance."

Independence and Nehru's ideal of a modern, progressive India would sweep Tenzing up after Everest, but the savagery of Partition was his first experience of this brave new world. India's transport system was in chaos as Muslims and Hindus attempted to cross the new border created between India and Pakistan. After the Swiss were put on an army truck back to Delhi, Tenzing and the other Sherpas spent two weeks at Joshimath before Tenzing could arrange their own ride out of the mountains. A truck took them to Dehra Dun, where Jack Gibson was helping organize refugee camps for local Muslims too frightened to stay in their homes; he even sheltered refugee children in his own home. The Doon School remained an oasis of calm amid the rioting and killings. The Sherpas were able to stay there under Gibson's aegis until the situation stabilized and he could arrange transport to take them home to Darjeeling.

Because of the delay, Tenzing spent all his earnings from the Swiss on the difficult journey home, and the winter of 1947 proved the toughest period since the war. Political upheaval across the region prompted another hiatus in climbers and travelers visiting the Himalaya, so once again Tenzing was reduced to relying on Ang Lhamu's earnings as an ayah. Her mother was in her last illness, and caring for her added to the family's burden. "Just before the end," he remembered, "she put out her hand from her bed and blessed me, saying that I had been good to her and that God would reward me and make things better. And what she said came true. Soon after her death our fortunes began to improve, and they have never been so bad again."[36]

Salvation came in an unlikely form. Giuseppe Tucci was an Italian academic in his mid-50s, an eccentric and awkward man. "Idiosyncratic" was how his traveling companion Fosco Maraini remembered him.

Maraini described the scholar-explorer as he settled in after embarking at Naples for India. "By rights he should dress in a style more reminiscent of the late nineteenth century, but he doesn't take much interest in his appearance. Under his arm he has the inevitable book. I am prepared to swear that within five minutes he will be curled up in some corner, reading it. Reading it? That's not the right word. To describe the process properly you'd need some such expression as 'ploughing' through it."[37]

Tucci was a man driven along a path of his own making. He had an encyclopedic memory for Tibetan and Nepalese history and an intimate understanding of Japanese culture, which he had studied exclusively after 1937 and the last of his pre-war visits to Tibet.

He despised politics and more particularly those in it. "To the vanity, inconsistency and double-dealing of politicians," he wrote, "I have opposed the saints and the heroes, the poets and scientists, in a word those few whose wisdom and industry, imagination and hard work conjure up or create the things which the course of events and the fury of fools never quite succeed in destroying."[38] Tucci's concern was not the here and now but the eternal, and modern politics were a distraction to an understanding of true human nature. It explains why he came to praise Mussolini in the prefaces of several books published before the war—Tibetan Buddhism held a fascination for fascists in the 1930s, and Tucci capitalized on this—or why while staying in Lhasa he could argue with Heinrich Harrer that the world was flat, simply to humor his Tibetan hosts. As long as he got what he wanted, such compromises meant nothing.

In 1948 Tucci made his eighth journey to Tibet, and Maraini, an anthropologist who had been interned in Japan during the war, came along to take photographs. They hired Sherpas in Darjeeling to help them on their journey through Tibet, but Tucci's inconsistent behavior and sudden bursts of temper meant he and his staff had fallen out before they reached Gangtok. Karma Paul, still acting as an agent for Sherpas and Bhotias after almost 30 years, called Tenzing to his office and said that Tucci wanted a new man to manage his travel arrangements. After a brief interview, Tucci gave him the job and thereafter left all arrangements to Tenzing, handing over the keys to his money chest and allowing Tenzing to run his affairs however he saw fit.

The expedition traveled north from Gangtok to the Chumbi Valley and the small village of Ya-tung, where Dorje Lhatoo, then an impressionable seven-year-old, met his future wife's uncle for the first time. Just as the older Bhotias and Sherpas had affected the young Tenzing, Lhatoo was mesmerized by the handsome mountain climber, in his riding breeches and boots, his long black hair pushed back from his forehead and his broad smile winning the confidence of all he met. From Ya-tung, Tucci moved on to Gyantse, where he made an important study of its history and architecture, particularly of the elegant stupa at its heart, before continuing to Lhasa.

Perhaps the greatest disappointment that stems from Tenzing's illiteracy is not the lack of a diary from his days on Everest—Tenzing's role was keenly observed by all sorts of people—but the absence of an account of these travels through Tibet with Tucci and Maraini in 1948. A chapter of his autobiography is given over to the expedition, but much of it is concerned with explaining to Western readers basic details about Buddhism; there is little of the actual journey. Tenzing was a close observer of people, and his practical intelligence would have added greatly to the picture of the Italian scholar, who knew far more about Tibetan history and culture than almost all the Tibetans they met. Tucci spoke Tibetan fluently, and so Tenzing and he could converse about everything from obscure Tibetan saints to Nehru, whom Tucci knew and to whom he promised Tenzing an introduction. Maraini and Tucci both wrote books about this nine-month expedition, and Maraini's in particular is rewarding and full of insight and compassion, though he wrote nothing about Tenzing.

At Lhasa, the expedition met the Austrian mountaineers Heinrich Harrer, author of *Seven Years in Tibet,* and Peter Aufschnaiter, who had escaped together from a British internment camp in northern India and crossed the Himalaya into Tibet. Harrer recalled meeting Tenzing and Tucci, and in his later book *Return to Tibet* he wrote about his friendship with Tenzing, with whom he stayed in the 1950s and whom he met again in Lhasa in 1982, when they were part of the same tour group. In 1948 they talked half seriously about going off to do a climb together, and Harrer says that he had a plan to include Tenzing on an attempt to climb Kanchenjunga. Harrer also noted that Tenzing's mother was present in Lhasa in 1948. He described her, erroneously, as a Lhasa woman and his father a man from Rongbuk. By contrast, Tenzing says explicitly in *Tiger of the Snows* that neither Kinzom nor Mingma ever went to Lhasa, but certain events in Ullman's account of his life have been contradicted by the facts. It may be that Kinzom, a pious woman who, like every Tibetan, dreamed of making a pilgrimage to Lhasa, realized that dream.

One encounter about which Tenzing's own words would be most valuable was his first meeting with the Dalai Lama, Tenzing Gyatso, then a 13-year-old boy. "As an old friend," he recalled, "Professor Tucci was privileged not only to pay his respects, but to have long talks with him, and while they spoke I was lucky enough to be allowed to stand by, watching and listening." They would meet again several times, and despite his pragmatism in religious matters, Tenzing never wavered in his devotion to the Dalai Lama. If the connection was personal, it was also a way of honoring his mother and his mother-in-law, who had been a devoted follower of Dzatrul Rinpoche.

Like his expedition to Nepal with Bill Tilman the following year, Tenzing's journey with Giuseppe Tucci in 1948 harked back to an earlier, simpler world of Himalayan travel, the twenties and thirties, than to the new postcolonial era that was sweeping away the old certainties of Asia. As the shadows of war in Europe lifted, the advances in mountaineering made in the Alps in the 1930s would soon be used to conquer the highest mountains on Earth. A new world of Himalayan climbing was dawning, but there was no certainty at all that Tenzing would be at the heart of it.

CHAPTER SEVEN
THE BRINK OF FAME

Men like him, I didn't know they existed.
—LOUIS DUBOST, *Himalaya: Passion Cruelle,* 1955

O N JUNE 2, 1950, AT 24,600 FEET on the northeastern face of
Annapurna, a group of four men, heads thumping from lack of
oxygen, their feet freezing solid inside their boots, leveled a platform
in the snow, drove two pitons into some nearby rocks, and pitched their
tent. Two of them were Frenchmen, Maurice Herzog and Louis
Lachenal, and the following day they reached the summit of Annapurna,
the first peak over the mythical barrier of 8,000 meters to be climbed,
earning themselves the status of heroes in their native France. Within
10 years, 13 of the 14 mountains over this height would be climbed, a
sort of Klondike in mountaineering sparked by the realization that anyone who wanted to stake a claim had better get on with it before the
mine was exhausted.

The other two men high on Annapurna that afternoon were Sherpas,
the famous Ang Tharkay, sirdar of the expedition, and Sarki, a tough man,
30 years old but on one of his first expeditions. All four of these men
were capable of reaching the summit, and the French had declared that
they wanted to take a Sherpa with them. Ang Tharkay was the obvious
candidate for the role. On the eve of the final push, Herzog, leader of
the expedition, panting with exhaustion and lack of oxygen, attempted
to persuade Ang Tharkay to come with them to the summit:

"'Tomorrow morning Lachenal Sahib and Bara Sahib go to the summit of Annapurna.'

"'Yes sir.'

"'You are the Sirdar and the most experienced of all the Sherpas. I should be very glad if you will come with us?'

"'Thank you, sir.'

"'We must share the victory! Will you come?'

"At that moment I felt it my duty to take into consideration the Sherpas' very understandable feelings. After a pause Angtharkay replied. He was grateful for the choice of action I had given him, but he held back:

"'Thank you very much, Bara Sahib, but my feet are beginning to freeze ... '

"'I see.'

"' ... and I prefer to go down to Camp IV.'

"'Of course, Angtharkay, it's as you like. In that case go down at once because it is late.'

"'Thank you, sir.'"[1]

The two Sherpas quickly packed their equipment and hurried down the steep snow slopes back to the security of Camp IV. "How oddly their minds worked," Herzog wrote from his hospital bed in Neuilly, where he was being treated following the amputation of all his frostbitten toes and fingers. "Here were these men, proverbial for their trustworthiness and devotion, who quite certainly enjoyed going high on the mountains; and yet, when on the point of reaping the fruits of their labours, they prudently held back. But I don't doubt that our mentality struck them as even odder."[2]

In his own autobiography, Ang Tharkay acknowledged the honor that was being done him and claimed that the idea of retreat for this, *l'épreuve suprême*—the ultimate test"—is "odious to me."[3] But, he continued, his feet were beginning to make him suffer, and he had a "terrible, obsessive fear" of seeing them frozen. Ang Tharkay knew what frostbite could do. He'd seen it plenty of times in his career, affecting or ending the careers of such men as Ang Tsering and Pasang Phutar. The stench of rotting meat, maggots pulled from healing wounds: These would be the price paid by Herzog and Lachenal. "Annapurna, to which we had gone empty-handed, was a treasure on which we should live the rest of our days," Herzog concluded in his account of the climb.[4] But while he could earn a living without his fingers and toes—he would have a long political career—the potential sacrifice Ang Tharkay faced was, in his judgment, too great.

If anyone understood Ang Tharkay's choice, it was Louis Lachenal, Herzog's partner on the summit of Annapurna. A Chamonix mountain guide whose life *was* the mountains, he suffered terrible frostbite injuries himself. "For me," he wrote, "this climb was only a climb like others, higher than in the Alps but no more important. If I was going to lose my feet, I didn't give a damn about Annapurna. I didn't owe my feet to the Youth of France."[5] But Lachenal continued with the climb anyway, despite knowing how driven Herzog had become. He could not leave his climbing partner to what he felt would be certain death. "That march to the summit," he concluded, "was not a matter of national glory. It was *une affaire de cordée.*"[6]

Had Tenzing and not Ang Tharkay been at Camp V on Annapurna on June 2, 1950, he would—almost certainly—have agreed to go with Herzog and Lachenal to the top. After the French returned home heroes, Ang Tharkay was given the Légion d'Honneur by France, but he is now largely unknown outside mountaineering circles. After Everest, Tenzing would become famous. Perhaps it was better that way. According to Trevor Braham, Ang Tharkay never resented Tenzing's success. Later, in the 1960s, he bought a farm in Nepal and returned to his native country. His final years were calm and happy.

These two men, along with Pasang Dawa Lama, were the great sirdars of the early 1950s. Ang Tharkay was seven years older than Tenzing and vastly more experienced. Throughout the 1930s, when Tenzing had been one of a number of faces, Ang Tharkay had become celebrated, especially in Britain, for his role in a series of groundbreaking expeditions, mostly with Eric Shipton and Bill Tilman. He had explored the remote Rishi Gorge with them in 1934; he had been sirdar on Tenzing's first expedition to Everest in 1935; he had shared a bold assault on the summit of Dunagiri with Shipton while Tenzing was ill with fever in the Nanda Devi Sanctuary in 1936. On Everest in the same year, Hugh Ruttledge had described him as probably the best of all the Sherpas. Ed Hillary thought Ang Tharkay the better sirdar: "Ang Tharkay had a greater sense of responsibility to the foreign climbers. Tenzing was very good as a sirdar but it was rather easy for his family to persuade him to give them jobs and all the rest of it." Trevor Braham, who was a friend of Tenzing's, had no doubt who he would pick: "I would say, if I'd been given a choice in the 1950s, I would choose Ang Tharkay every time, rather than Tenzing. I was very fond of Tenzing, but his was a touchy, sensitive character." Wilfrid Noyce, a member of the successful 1953 team, whose book on the expedition, *South Col,* is a mountaineering classic, shared the widely held view of Ang Tharkay as the preeminent sirdar, but recognized that Tenzing's ambition would take him further. "Angtharkay might have a firmer grip on his troops, stand less nonsense from anyone, and be a first-class organiser. But his own duty and aim as sirdar is to give his sahibs satisfaction. That given, his work is done.... With Tenzing it was different."[7]

If Tenzing's pride broke to the surface more readily than Ang Tharkay's, his sensitivity was also part of the reason he would stand on the summit of Everest. This charge of hypersensitivity, of being too readily offended, has been made against Edmund Hillary too, particularly as a young man. Both men had something to prove and hated being patronized. Both men disliked the cool aloofness they experienced among the English. Always in the back of Tenzing's mind was the idea that this aloofness was superiority. From his days as a servant in Khumjung, he could not tolerate the idea that people looked down on him. This force of personality was a character trait everyone who climbed with Tenzing observed. And this was Tenzing's advantage over Ang Tharkay; he wanted it more.

Partly it was the difference between a Bhotia and a Sherpa. Ang Tharkay could feel by turns offended if he wasn't treated fairly, and embarrassed by the naïveté of his fellow Sherpas, but was never as forthright in fighting for his rights as Tenzing was. In 1953 Ang Tharkay was brought to Paris to be reunited with his French teammates from Annapurna. When the plane arrived in Paris, the flight attendant asked Ang Tharkay to remain in his seat. With little English and no French, the Sherpa found himself unable to protest what he thought was a slight. He imagined that because of his appearance he was being treated with suspicion.[8] Only after he was invited to leave the plane did he realize that a crowd of reporters, photographers, and cameramen had gathered outside to meet him. He was a celebrity, not a suspect.

Herzog may have spoken of equality between his team and the Sherpas, but he could still write how thrilled he was "to see these little yellow men, with their plump muscles" being given an opportunity "to show the world what they were made of."[9] It's hardly surprising Sherpas sometimes took offense. In 1998 Phu Tharkay, one of the last Sherpas still living from the 1950 Annapurna ascent, came to Paris and met Herzog, the man he had carried down Annapurna when Herzog was crippled with his horrific frostbite injuries. They had not met in nearly 50 years, but Herzog's meeting with his old comrade was brief. Afterward, Phu Tharkay told a French documentary maker: "Hillary is a hero in Nepal, but Herzog, I don't think so.… I carried this man on my back until I could taste the blood in my mouth, and today he has only five minutes for me. It's too bad for him."[10]

The final sentence is a typically Buddhist response. Phu Tharkay felt angry and humiliated, but still regarded Herzog as the real loser, because he was too self-absorbed. His comment also reveals how Sherpas felt toward prejudice. Those sahibs who shared discomfort and met the Sherpas on equal terms held a special place in their affection. Even though Bill Tilman was disliked by some, the fact that he carried heavy loads and performed acts of kindness for them more than compensated for his long silences and terse manner. And Tenzing thrived when he felt he was being treated as an equal. Trevor Braham recalled how Tenzing enjoyed for the first time that equality. "He had just experienced a fellowship with the Swiss which he had never experienced with any foreign climbers before, certainly not the British."

Tenzing had another, more practical reason to prefer the Swiss. In the 1930s, when Tenzing was first working as a porter, Ang Tharkay already held a privileged position among English climbers. And even if Ang Tharkay was unavailable, there were other sirdars whom the English knew well. Tenzing had earned the esteem of the Swiss and elevated his position through their expedition. He felt an emotional bond with them, a personal debt of loyalty.

Climbing Everest, most experts agreed in the 1950s, could be achieved only if a good supply line brought enough equipment, oxygen, and fuel to the highest camp for the two strongest climbers to use in reaching the summit. The key to that successful supply was the sirdar.

In 1950 Ang Tharkay seemed to be the odds-on favorite for that role. He was the sirdar on the famous French expedition to Annapurna and would organize the first serious reconnaissance of the southern Nepali approach to Everest, now slowly opening to foreigners. This expedition, led by Eric Shipton, would form the nucleus of the team members for the successful 1953 expedition.

Ed Hillary warmed to Ang Tharkay immediately when he met him in 1951, unlike fellow New Zealander Earle Riddiford. He preferred the sirdar who had worked for them on their recent expedition to the Garhwal Himal, Pasang Dawa Lama: "Earle was constantly singing Pasang's praises and even suggested he should be co-sirdar with Angtharkay, a suggestion that Eric [Shipton] ignored. Earle's praise for Pasang knew no end and he even suggested his technical climbing standard equalled that of my climbing mentor in New Zealand, the great Harry Ayres. This was too much for me and I told Earle so. In a rage he warned me that if I made another criticism of Pasang he would knock me down. I looked at the rather weedy Earle in astonishment and said in true schoolboy fashion, 'You and what army?' And that pretty much finished the discussion and the topic."[11]

While Ang Tharkay was enlarging an already considerable reputation on Annapurna and Everest, Tenzing spent the summer of 1950 on Bandarpunch, his third visit to the mountain with Jack Gibson. Thirteen years had passed since their first expedition, and Gibson's account of their climb is touched with nostalgia for their youthful attempt. This time he brought a young Indian teacher from the Doon School, Gurdial Singh, and his 16-year-old brother, Jagjit; Gen. Harold "Bill" Williams, engineer-in-chief of the Indian Army; and a warrant officer working at the Doon, Roy Greenwood. Gibson also says that Tenzing brought his brother to the Garhwal as one of two Sherpas and gives his name as Kinchok, Kenjan, and Kinchock, but adds that because they had trouble pronouncing it, they called him King John instead. Tenzing's two brothers were Kesang and Chingdu, but Tenzing's own account doesn't add much to this, except that he doesn't refer to him as his brother.

In 1950 Gibson made his attempt a month earlier than his previous expeditions, and the better weather allowed success. Tenzing and Kinchok reached the summit of Bandarpunch with Roy Greenwood on

June 20, apparently climbing all the way from Camp II at 18,000 feet to the summit at 20,720 feet. As for Gibson himself, he gave up this first attempt at the peak to bring Gurdial Singh down. Tenzing says this was because of altitude sickness, but Gibson's own diary makes it clear he didn't think the young man was sufficiently experienced and feared he would endanger the others on the descent. Either way, it was a selfless decision. While Tenzing was standing on top of the "Doon School" mountain, Gibson was still climbing back up to Camp III, at 19,000 feet.

Tenzing agreed to go back up to the summit with Gibson the following day. Unluckily for Gibson, it snowed heavily and they all retreated. Another attempt two days later, also with Tenzing, was called off for the same reason, and as a consolation Gibson opted to explore the western side of the peak:

"We woke at 4am and were off at 5.30am, having decided to try for the western or White Peak of Bandarpunch, height 20,020ft. I had thought of trying the summit ridge from the west, but Tenzing was all for an attack up the south face, so there we went, and all went well for a time. We climbed 3000 feet in the first four hours and then met vertical walls and ice-filled gullies. I fell off while leading up one of the former. A handhold I had tested gave and as I turned in the air I had a fine view of the valley thousands of feet below. Tenzing, who was directly below me on a broad ledge, fielded me cleanly, and both he and King John thought it a huge joke."[12] By mid-morning it started snowing again and they were forced to retreat. The monsoon was closing around the Garhwal, and it was clear climbing was finished for the season.

Bandarpunch was not an arduous climb, not compared with what Tenzing had already achieved, but in Krenek's 1950 log of porters it earned him particular credit: "He is a very good climber, well qualified to act as a 'guide.' His work on Bandarpunch in 1950 was highly praised. As he is the youngest [out of Tenzing, Ang Tharkay, and Pasang Dawa Lama] a great future is before him."[13]

Tenzing even had a portent of good fortune. On the walk-out from Bandarpunch, he fell asleep on the shore of Dodi Tal, his hat pulled over his eyes against the warm sunshine. "The next thing I knew I was half awake again, and with the strange feeling that the hat was somehow heavier than before. Reaching up, I felt to see why this was so. But it wasn't the hat I touched: it was something cool and slippery." A snake had curled around the crown of his hat while Tenzing slept and he threw both hat and snake away from him as far as he could. His Sherpa friends, seeing what had happened, caught the snake and killed it, but the local Garhwal porters thought this was a mistake; a snake sleeping on a man like that was good luck. "In fact," Tenzing recalled, "a man with a snake actually on his head is sure to become a king."[14]

Jamling Tenzing Norgay recalled a legend[15] he heard from villagers in Thame that a yak herder had once seen a cobra rear up over Tenzing's head, its hood flared open, its spine arched, a physical embodiment of the *naga* serpent spirits that appear in Buddhist and Hindu iconography as a shield for the deity beneath. But although cobras aren't found in Khumbu, there are plenty of snakes in Garhwal. Jack Gibson recalls that they infested the path leading to Dodi Tal and that he shot what he thought was a cobra as they descended back to Uttarkashi in 1950, so perhaps Tenzing's story at least is not apocryphal.

After the minor triumph on Bandarpunch, a low-key achievement compared with the international glory of Annapurna climbed two weeks earlier, Tenzing's next job started him on a pattern of tragedy that clouded the 18-month period leading up to his first expedition to the south side of Everest. In August he joined another British expedition planning to spend a year surveying and climbing west of the Karakoram in what was by now northern Pakistan. The three climbers were all in their mid-20s, and Tenzing had already guided Jim Thornley in the Kanchenjunga region north of Darjeeling. Fellow expedition member Dick Marsh called him "tall and wiry, the toughest and most determined man I have ever met." Marsh himself had been a lieutenant in the Bengal Engineers; Thornley and the third member, Bill Crace, were both ex-Gurkhas. Tenzing knew the British were planning a long and complex expedition, part of whose mission was to settle the exact location of the new Pakistani-Chinese border. All three men had been planning and saving for the trip for three years and couldn't wait to get started. That level of personal investment would cost them dearly.

Tenzing was also looking forward to it. "It was a prospect to stir the blood of an old wanderer like myself (what Ang Lhamu thought of it I will not go into), and in August of 1950, soon after my return from

Bandar Punch, I was on my way again."[16] As sirdar, Tenzing would choose the Sherpas to accompany him on what would be a very lucrative trip; a whole year's employment was worth chasing. He now had a kind of patronage and drew around him a crew whom he could rely on when he needed to supply an expedition with Sherpas. It made him someone of consequence, a social position to match his natural authority.

Allegiances were made and rivalries begun that were hidden from the Europeans who hired them. Most of them saw only the smiling, willing faces and missed the undercurrents, the strands of debt and familial loyalty, the favors given and returned, and sometimes not returned, that wove the community of Darjeeling Sherpas together. Like Ang Tharkay and Pasang Dawa Lama, Tenzing had men he trusted to do a job and men to whom he was obligated. Trevor Braham remembered climbing in Sikkim with a relative of Tenzing's, a man called Pasang Phutar,[17] who had been a popular jockey at the Lebong racecourse and had become Tenzing's protégé. Braham found him a bad character and almost had him sacked from his expedition: "As soon as I got back, Tenzing came and asked me, 'What did you think of Pasang Phutar?' And I told him: 'Not much.'" Expedition leaders didn't care how the Sherpas were related to one another as long as their sirdar kept supplies moving up the mountain, but if things didn't go well, a sirdar could look foolish in putting his friends' interests ahead of the expedition's, as Tenzing would discover on Everest in 1953.

He had a good crew ready when Dick Marsh arrived in Darjeeling in August 1950. Ajiba, Ang Tsering's younger brother and a cousin of Dawa Phuti, was one. Phu Tharkay, fresh from carrying Herzog down Annapurna, was another. The third Sherpa was Ang Temba, whom the others teased for his bearlike appearance. All three would go to Everest with Tenzing in 1952 and 1953. They crossed India and entered Pakistan, meeting Thornley and Crace in Rawalpindi before continuing to Peshawar. From there they flew to Gilgit; it was the first time any of the Sherpas had been in an aircraft: "I remember we were at first impatient at being tied into our seats by belts, and as soon as we could loosen them we began hurrying around and peering out of all the windows."[18] From Gilgit, Tenzing and Marsh trekked to the village of Shimshal, close to the borders of Afghanistan, Russia, and China. Both men became ill with diarrhea, and Tenzing found the landscape depressing and stark. They waited for more than a week for Thornley and Crace to catch them up, but one evening a telegram arrived: "UNDER ORDERS FROM PAKISTAN GOVERNMENT YOU ARE REQUIRED NOT TO PROCEED FARTHER." Their year-long expedition, planned with such care and anticipation, was effectively over.

Tenzing and Marsh trekked back to Gilgit, picking up Crace on the way. Thornley was already in Rawalpindi, arguing with the authorities, who gave no explanation for the cancellation of their permit. It isn't clear exactly why the Pakistanis changed their minds; possibly it had something to do with the deteriorating situation in Tibet. The Chinese didn't invade until October, but their intention to absorb Tibet into the motherland was increasingly clear. As the People's Liberation Army advanced swiftly across Chamdo Province, Zhou Enlai announced, "The PLA is determined to march westward to liberate the Tibetan people and defend the frontiers of China." Those frontiers included the region the three Britons were interested in exploring. Perhaps the Pakistanis feared antagonizing the Soviet Union.

Thornley stayed in Rawalpindi to continue the fight. Crace, Marsh, and the Sherpas returned to Gilgit, ostensibly to collect their equipment. Having spent more than £2,000, all the money they had, on the expedition, and having planned it for so long, they weren't prepared to go home without trying to climb something. In Rawalpindi the three hit on the idea of attempting Nanga Parbat. "No one had ever tried to climb any peak within a thousand miles of Nanga during the winter months," Marsh wrote, and for good reason.[19] Equipment in 1950 was barely capable of coping with climbing in summer. The French had suffered terrible frostbite on Annapurna and climbing on an 8,000-meter peak in winter would be inviting catastrophe.

They didn't tell the Sherpas of their change of plan. Nanga Parbat lay south of the Indus close to the Karakoram Highway and their route back to Rawalpindi. Thornley told the Pakistani authorities that he was off to Gilgit to help bring the equipment back and started walking, covering 165 miles in six days in the clothes he was wearing. Tenzing had in the meantime discovered what Crace and Marsh were planning and had some bad news for them: "Tenzing came over to us. He had an open, honest face, and this morning he was looking very troubled. 'Sahibs,' he said, 'I am sorry. Ang Temba, Ajiba and Phu Tharkay do not want to come above Camp One. It is too dangerous. They have families and the risk will be great. If they had realised you were really going to climb on Nanga Parbat, they would not have come. I am sorry, sahibs.' We sat stunned. Tenzing stood away downcast, miserable that he had let us down. There was no point in arguing. We realised that their decision was partly due to the stories they had been hearing from the local villages."[20]

They had a lot more reasons than that. Ajiba's older brother had almost been killed on Nanga Parbat. Their old friend Dawa Thondup had been a lucky survivor of an avalanche that killed nine other Sherpas. They also knew stories of obsessed, careless sahibs pushing on regardless of conditions. George Mallory had once written: "The party must keep a margin of safety. It is not to be a mad enterprise rashly pushed on regardless of danger. The ill-considered acceptance of any and every risk has no part in the essence of persevering courage."[21] At Fairy Meadows, the base camp chosen by the Germans for their attempt on the Rakhiot Face of Nanga Parbat, Tenzing and the other Sherpas saw the stone memorial to the 15 Sherpas who had died on the mountain in the two expeditions of 1934 and 1937. And those had taken place during the summer.

Tenzing himself was caught in a quandary. His instincts told him that it would be foolish to go on. His responsibility to his employer put him under pressure to continue. At least they could all work together as far as the first camp, and Tenzing was impressed by the load carrying of the sahibs. Thornley took 120 pounds up to their Base Camp at 11,500 feet. "With all the trouble and finally, tragedy that we had, this was one great thing about the expedition," Tenzing said. "There was no distinction at all between climbers and porters. We did the same work, shared the same burdens, everyone helping everyone else when help was needed. We were not like employers and employees, but like brothers."[22] The Englishmen relied on Tenzing's experience of big mountains, and he had never seen conditions this bad before. On November 10, Thornley and Marsh started up Nanga Parbat's lower slopes, the huge Rakhiot Face towering more than two miles above them. Their first objective was a hill of moraine at about 15,000 feet. Standing at its base, Marsh thought it would take perhaps an hour to climb the 1,400 feet to its summit in snow a foot deep. It was a gross miscalculation. "The snow was mainly waist deep, and the climb took four and a half hours. Tired and rather shaken, we turned back to camp. Conditions looked like being much worse than we had hoped when we decided to make the attempt."[23]

Over the next few days Tenzing helped carry loads up to Camp I, but he could see the attempt was hopeless. All of them were suffering from the cold. "Our teeth chattered incessantly," Marsh wrote of the morning of November 12, "and our fingers were so stiff that we struggled stupidly to get into our skis and to rope up." Even with their mountaineering skis, the climbers sank up to their waists as they found a complex route through the crevasses above Camp I. That afternoon Tenzing arrived at Camp I with Bill Crace. He had made his decision. "Bill poked his head out of the tent," Marsh wrote, "and said: 'Hallo, boys, I've some bad news for you. Tenzing won't come with us. He thinks it's too cold.' If the earlier withdrawal of the three Sherpas had dampened our spirits, this completely dashed them." If they chose to carry on, they would have to carry even more loads between camps than before. "But, perhaps most important, we would be without the advice and experience of Tenzing."[24]

Why the climbers decided to persist is uncertain; it probably was to them as well. Conditions were atrocious. They fell into crevasses, and Marsh suffered from cold feet. Struggling with 65-pound loads, far heavier than the packs Sherpas would carry on Everest, they were continually threatened by enormous avalanches thundering down the Rakhiot Face above them. On the days when the sun didn't shine, they found their tents and sleeping bags damp and chill. It's astonishing they kept going as long they did. At night they would read Shakespeare, each taking a part in *Richard II* or *Troilus and Cressida,* and talk about the food they would eat on their return. And they discussed what they should do. Thornley was the strongest of the three—Tenzing thought he was "the most powerful climber I have ever seen"—and he told Crace and Marsh that if they abandoned the attempt, he would go on alone. Crace wavered and then continued, but on November 18 Dick Marsh, whose feet were increasingly suffering in the cold, decided to descend. Phu Tharkay told him he had dreamed a few nights before that he would return, and dreamed again that Thornley and Crace would join them soon.

SIR EDMUND HILLARY/ROYAL GEOGRAPHICAL SOCIETY AND ALPINE CLUB

PREVIOUS PAGE: On May 29, 1953, Tenzing Norgay stands atop Mount Everest, becoming with Edmund Hillary the first to reach the Roof of the World. His face covered by his oxygen mask and goggles, Tenzing's anonymity made it easier for the image itself to be adopted as an icon of the triumph of the human spirit. ABOVE: Sherpa porters, both men and women, approach Base Camp at the end of the long approach to Everest. Those porters who went above Base Camp were considered the elite. RIGHT: Tenzing stands (fourth from the left) on the veranda of the Planters' Club in Darjeeling in 1935, waiting to discover if he will be taken to Everest. Eric Shipton sits on the right at the table.

LEFT: Tenzing and Annelies Lohner relax at base camp in the western Garhwal in 1947. She described Tenzing as "an absolute gem. Neat and full of initiative, he spoilt me dreadfully." ABOVE: Ang Lhamu and Tenzing are entertained by Maria Feuz and Raymond Lambert after Everest in 1953. Lambert's truncated boots, made to fit his badly frostbitten feet, are clearly visible.

ED DOUGLAS

ABOVE LEFT: Tenzing, in Darjeeling in 1972, is flanked by daughter Pem Pem (left), Daku, and daugher Nima (far right), holding her son Palden. Norbu stands in coat and tie with Jamling and Deki on his right and his hands on Dhamey's shoulders. BELOW LEFT: Ang Lhamu stands between Nehru and Indira Gandhi. Tenzing's daughters Nima and Pema are seated with friends in the foreground. ABOVE: Above the Kama Valley east of Everest lies the sacred lake of Tshechu, the likely birthplace of Tenzing. The Buddha Rock emerges from the cloud to the right of the screes.

ABOVE: Hillary and Tenzing celebrate their success on Everest. Asked about their historic climb, Tenzing replied: "Very excited, not too tired, very pleased." BELOW: The conquering pair pause on their descent at Camp IV, where the expedition party first learned of the happy news; Tenzing and Hillary had carried no radios.

They didn't. Over the course of the next ten days Tenzing watched from the top of the moraine hill through binoculars as the two men slowly moved their tent up Nanga Parbat. Despite the heavy snow that fell at the end of November, they carried on. Ajiba and Phu Tharkay caught a glimpse of them pitching a new camp at 18,000 feet, still more than 8,000 feet short of the summit. "They are certainly making a stout and persistent effort," Marsh wrote in his diary, wildly understating the situation. On December 1 it snowed heavily and then the weather turned cold but clear. There was no sign of them. They continued watching the tent at 18,000 feet through the binoculars, but nothing stirred for three more days. That night it snowed again, and Tenzing dreamed he saw the two men coming toward him dressed in new clothes and surrounded by other men with no faces. The meaning of the dream was clear. In the morning the tent high above them had disappeared.

Marsh decided to mount a rescue, and both Tenzing and Ajiba agreed to help. "It was a brave gesture, for during the fortnight I had been back with them, I had often watched each of them by himself silently and apprehensively staring up at the mountain."[25] Tenzing might have thought them foolish to go up there, but he remembered the way Maurice Wilson, a man who was genuinely deluded, had been abandoned by his porters. He could not live with the thought that he had behaved in the same way. Even though conditions were much worse than on the East Rongbuk Glacier in summer, they had at least to make an effort.

Climbing back up to Camp I, they discovered all their tracks obliterated, and without skis found themselves floundering in deep snow. Tenzing pulled Marsh out of crevasses on three occasions, and it was dark before they regained the platform they had dug out in mid-November. "Tenzing cooked and I admired the dexterity in those cramped quarters as he produced a quick hot meal." They squashed together for warmth. In the night an avalanche swept down the slopes only a hundred yards away. Tenzing shook Marsh awake, but all they could do was hold each other and pray they would be safe. Conditions were even worse in the morning as they carried on through a series of icefalls, the slopes above them loaded with fresh snow. Marsh asked Tenzing what their chances were: "'I think we might reach them in three or four days, provided that the snow is no worse higher up and so long as we remain as strong as we are now. But the avalanches are very dangerous, sahib.'

"What about frostbite?'

"'Well, sahib, I think we will get it today–certainly tomorrow. And by the time we get back I think we will lose our feet.'"[26]

Marsh knew it was over. His friends had been missing for almost two weeks, and he recognized that the Sherpas could be crippled for life if he persevered with a futile rescue attempt. They returned to Base Camp and spent another ten days waiting forlornly. Phu Tharkay and Ajiba built a memorial cairn while Marsh and Tenzing watched the mountain. On Christmas Day 1950 Marsh taped some sticking plaster to a pine cross, wrote the names of Thornley and Crace and fixed it to the Sherpas' cairn. One of the Sherpas, probably Tenzing, fired a couple of shots over their heads. Three years later, Nanga Parbat was climbed for the first time, days after Tenzing reached the summit of Everest, by Hermann Buhl, one of the greatest mountaineers in history. No 8,000-meter peak was climbed in winter before 1980, and Nanga Parbat, which is battered by more snow and worse weather than most of the Himalayan giants, never has been.

IN *TIGER OF THE SNOWS*, Tenzing explained that for Sherpas, a man's late 30s were the critical period of his life. Many Western men, caught in a midlife crisis, might share that view; George Mallory was almost 38 when he disappeared on Everest, a man in a hurry to make his mark. For the Sherpas and Bhotias in Darjeeling, the press of time was more immediate. Many of Tenzing's contemporaries were dead already, either on mountains or from illnesses and accidents below the snow line. The sense that opportunities were slipping through his fingers added a keener edge to Tenzing's ambition. With the new decade came a new impetus to Himalayan climbing. In the summer of 1951 Ang Tharkay was hired by Eric Shipton for a reconnaissance of Everest's southern approach, a precursor to a full attempt, presumably in the following year. The ascent of Annapurna in 1950, for which Ang Tharkay had been sirdar, made celebrities of the climbers in their native France, but was also a powerful advertisement for the Sherpas, not just in their effort climbing the mountain but in their selfless work to help evacuate the injured Herzog and Lachenal. "Their stories made me wish that I too had been part of that great adventure," Tenzing said.[27] He stayed on good terms with Ang Tharkay, who still lived in Bhotia Busti, a little way from Tenzing's home in Toong Soong. Their rivalry was not personal. But both men were highly competitive, and although Tenzing suggests he would have liked to have gone with Shipton and Ang Tharkay, he was not a spear carrier. Tenzing liked to be in charge.

Buoyed by the success of Herzog's team, a wave of interest in Himalayan climbing swept across France, and another major expedition quickly gathered momentum. Annapurna was a hard act to follow, and this new group of climbers, largely from Lyons and led by Roger Duplat, looked for a significant objective to match Herzog's. When they applied to the Pakistani government for permission to climb K2 or Nanga Parbat, they were refused and so fell back on the more accessible option of Nanda Devi. The main summit had been climbed in 1936, but the mountain also has an elegant eastern summit that had been climbed in 1939 by the first Polish expedition to the Himalaya. Now the French proposed to climb the former and traverse the length of the two-mile ridge separating the summits before descending Nanda Devi East.

It was an ambitious plan. Nanda Devi did not quite reach the magical altitude of 8,000 meters but was high enough to challenge even the strongest climbers. Good logistics and real determination would be required, and that put pressure on the leader. Duplat was slight, even scrawny, an impression underlined by his habit of smoking a large pipe, but despite his size he was a dynamo of energy; "*brûlante*," his climbing companion Jean-Jacques Languepin called him—"burning." He had learned to climb before the war and had been admitted to the elite Groupe de Haute Montagne in 1947 alongside Louis Lachenal. The rest of the team were younger, several of them still in their early 20s, such as the brilliant rock climber Gilbert Vignes, who was just 23, and they had experienced nothing like a Himalayan expedition before. Every twist and turn of traveling and climbing in India was fresh, each frustration a monstrous hurdle to be overcome. By contrast, Tenzing, now 37, was a veteran, a steadfast voice of competence at the heart of the expedition to match Duplat's passion and determination. While Duplat agonized over finding enough porters and getting supplies to Base Camp, *"notre sirdar,"* Languepin wrote, *"se révèle homme de resources*—He listens, reflects, suggests and executes with total enthusiasm."[28] Local porters constantly caused them problems as the expedition approached the Nanda Devi Sanctuary, something Tenzing anticipated after his experiences there in the 1930s. The Sherpas were relaxed about it, knowing how the game of bluff and double-bluff worked, but the situation drove the French crazy. Hardly had the expedition got under way after the last argument than loads were put down again and a fresh twist was added. *"Toujours l'argent,"* Languepin complained as another rupee was added to the deal. "Always money."

Under these circumstances it's hardly surprising that the French developed a close relationship with the Sherpas, who were playful, friendly, and helpful. "I love Panzi," Languepin wrote of one of Tenzing's team. "For him things are so simple: profitable, or not profitable, restful or tiring, good or not good—but never bad."[29]

Ultimately, the French were in too much of a hurry. "Duplat," Tenzing said, "seemed almost to think that the whole thing could be done in a few days."[30] They reached the Sanctuary on June 18 and quickly established three camps on the route taken by the Anglo-American expedition of 1936. On June 28, just ten days after reaching Base Camp, Duplat and Vignes moved through to Camp II to start their attempt on the traverse of Nanda Devi. Carrying a tent, stove, fuel, and food, they wanted to bivouac as high as they could the following day. Tenzing and Da Namgyal, later one of the strongest Sherpas on Everest, carried loads for them. Duplat was suffering from a headache, and they still had to climb another 8,000 feet to the summit. Soon he had another one. Tenzing asked him if he could go with him and Vignes to the summit and do the traverse with them:

"'No possible, no possible,' Duplat replied, not knowing how to explain to the eager sirdar that no one could pay another man to share such a risky venture. Most of the reasons that drew him up high were so personal, so intimate that he felt unable to translate them into a rational argument. The enthusiasm in Tenzing's eyes was dulled. He got up and gave a namaste in farewell to Duplat and Vignes, who in return held out their hands to shake his.

"'Good luck, sahib.'

"He forced a smile. Already Da Namgyal had started on the route down, and he followed in his steps, pausing to turn around once more and wave goodbye."[31]

No other Sherpa then alive would have approached the French in this way and asked to go to the summit. No other Sherpa would have wanted it. But for all Duplat's rationalizations about why Tenzing should not risk his life, the simple truth was they didn't want him there. He and Vignes had planned on a two-man attempt, and suddenly changing their plan would have required a level of flexibility the situation did not allow.

As events turned out, Tenzing might have kept him alive.

Duplat and Vignes were last seen just below the summit of Nanda Devi two days later, before the clouds shrouded them from view forever. In their last note, sent down with Ang Dawa and Da Norbu, who carried loads up to Camp III on June 29, Duplat told his team to clear the camps below them, before adding, "Gil and I have terrible headaches, but apart from that we're fine." No one knows how and when they died, but the scale of their undertaking was vast. No one has yet completed the traverse of Nanda Devi.

Ullman had little information from which to construct Tenzing's account of the expedition—Languepin's book *Himalaya, Passion Cruelle* wasn't published until 1955—and as a consequence some of the events are garbled and dates quoted in error. Duplat had ordered the route below them cleared, but the team members ignored him and remained in Camp III in case they returned. Meanwhile, below the eastern summit of Nanda Devi, Louis Dubost and the doctor, Louis Payan, were busy putting a camp on the Longstaff Col, at the base of the ridge leading to the summit. Tenzing came down from the main peak and met Sarki and Gyalzen, who had been sent down to Base Camp by Dubost to fetch supplies. Tenzing now opted to climb back up with the other Sherpas. The ridge above was heavily corniced, fat curls of wind-blown snow from which the climbers veered like ships from hidden reefs. They didn't go far. It was a clear day and they could see the whole length of the south ridge leading from the summit of Nanda Devi and the ridge separating the two peaks. Dubost could see men moving around at Camp III and wondered if Duplat had delayed his ascent. Then they went down to the Longstaff Col at 20,000 feet. "When we got back to camp where Payan had remained we didn't know what to do," Dubost wrote.[32] "But you think of the summit, and how I had wanted to reach it. If Roger was on the ridge, either going for it, or if he hadn't done the traverse, then either way we were better off on the ridge. Payan agreed but we did a head-count and realised we were lacking a tent. I was done in and half undressed, but Tenzing did not want to go down until the following morning. I don't know what came over me, but I was in a strange mood. Moving quickly, I got dressed again and with Payan, we left for the col."

Dubost and Payan didn't reach the Col until after dark, and then they spent the next day in heavy fog. The Sherpas didn't get away from camp until late in the afternoon. In the meantime they heard from one of the climbers that something had gone wrong. When Dubost and Payan heard this, they resolved to continue to the summit and hopefully get a good view along the ridge separating the two peaks.

On July 4, Payan, climbing with Gyalzen and Tenzing, and Dubost with Sarki, reascended the corniced ridge to a band of ice cliffs at 21,650 feet and there made another camp. Sarki and Gyalzen went no farther, settling in to wait for the others to return, but Tenzing climbed on with the two Frenchmen, the wind "cutting us in two," as Dubost recalled. The doctor's feet, in light boots, grew colder and colder. That night they camped at over 23,000 feet. The wind was tearing at the tent so much that Dubost had to climb outside in the night to tie it down more firmly, while inside Payan complained about his thirst and cold feet.

In the morning the sun warmed them a little, and they had a clear view along the ridge leading to the main summit: "But we never saw a thing."[33] Payan did a rope length with Tenzing and Dubost, but despite rubbing his feet before leaving, he couldn't feel his toes and went back to the tent to wait for their return. Then Dubost and Tenzing climbed a difficult section of rock, the snow blown off it by the icy wind. After-ward, when Dubost lost a crampon, he hesitated. Their hands and feet were frozen, and the threat of frostbite put doubt in their minds. Dubost was full of praise for Tenzing, describing him as the stronger and more cheerful. They kept a constant watch on the ridge where Duplat and Vignes had gone missing, but they saw no one. Buffeted by strong winds, they tacked away from the cornices of the ridge leading up to the summit at 24,391 feet.

It was the first significant peak Tenzing had climbed, and later he would say it was more difficult than Everest itself. He and Dubost peered toward Nanda Devi's main summit and then looked to the east, at the summits of Annapurna and Dhaulagiri, emerging from the heavy cloud cover. Vignes and Duplat had last been seen a week ago, and any hope of their survival was gone. Ten feet below the summit, out of the wind, they shook hands. Dubost believed the traverse possible in good conditions, "but with the wind, *ça doit être l'enfer*—it would be hell."[34] Five days later, the French turned their backs on Nanda Devi, and the Sherpas headed home to Darjeeling.

That autumn another climb resulted in yet another death, this time in front of Tenzing's eyes. An experienced Swiss mountaineer named George Frey, a 29-year-old assistant trade commissioner working in Bombay, hired Tenzing as sirdar on a journey exploring the Kanchenjunga region north of Darjeeling. Until the accident the expedition was fun, certainly not the kind of adventure that involved a high level of risk. Then, on the small, subsidiary Koktang Peak, only 19,900 feet, Frey slipped and fell to his death. In *Tiger of the Snows,* Tenzing explains that just beforehand he had told Frey that he was stopping to strap on his crampons, but Frey replied he wouldn't bother. Frey then slipped and fell past Tenzing, catching his outstretched hand and breaking a finger before falling the length of the slope.

Tenzing gave another, fuller account of the accident that was reported in the *Himalayan Journal,* and this version shows how close Tenzing himself came to disaster:

On the morning of 29th October 1951 we began the ascent. Phu Tharkay stayed in Camp II while Ang Dawa and I went with Mr Frey. We followed a steep gully, partly snow covered, partly consisting of rocks with a thin coating of ice. The upper part of the gully led to a very steep ridge and Mr Frey led; I followed ten steps behind with Ang Dawa ten steps below me. Not more than forty steps above the gully Mr Frey suddenly slipped and fell towards me. I tried to stop him but in vain, and began to fall myself. Fortunately I did not lose my ice ax as Mr Frey lost his and I tried to check the fall but failed. While sliding down I hit Ang Dawa and all three of us continued to fall towards the gully. Just before the steepest part I succeeded in stopping my fall but Ang Dawa continued to shoot down towards me. With great luck I was able to stop him. We then roped up and descended very carefully.[35]

Shouting down to Phu Tharkay to look for Frey, Tenzing and Ang Dawa reached the body after him. Frey had fallen more than 1,400 feet and was clearly dead. The three Sherpas carried the body to the end of the glacier and buried it there, near a huge block of stone. Tenzing had been on too many searches for lost relatives not to make sure that Frey's remains could be found again easily. Then they built a cairn above the grave and placed his ice ax on top of it.

Tenzing recalled that, just as on Nanga Parbat, he had dreamed of catastrophe the night before the accident. This time it unfolded in front of his eyes, Frey's body cartwheeling and bouncing, his camera torn from around his neck, and then, later, the dark shape lying at the foot of the slope, and all of it finished within a matter of seconds. The shock of this experience, seared into his memory, could not have failed to impress itself on Tenzing. For him and his fellow Bhotias and Sherpas the common occurrence of premature death might have made them more fatalistic. Even so, Tenzing, poised unwittingly on the brink of fame, must have felt the shadows closing around him. The critical years were upon him.

CHAPTER EIGHT

I HAVE BROUGHT A BEAR

The reader should know that the Swiss,
like ourselves, had to face difficulties with their Sherpas
over conditions of employment.
They were more fortunate in being financially more free to solve them.
—JOHN HUNT, 1955

SOUTH OF LAC LÉMAN and east of the Arve River is the Genèvois district of Contamines, a grid of quiet leafy streets and apartment buildings a mile from the city. Annette Lambert, now in her 70s, lives in a smart apartment, surrounded by souvenirs of her life. She was born in Sumatra and over the years traveled the world, but you sense that her most precious possessions are the photographs of her husband, Raymond. She showed me one of him in later life, a cigarette in his hand. "He smoked too much as he got older," she said, "but he took pleasure from it. I wasn't going to stop him."

The face in the photograph is far from refined: a blunt nose, a broad forehead enlarged by early baldness. It's his smile that holds your attention and his broad shoulders, a big amiable man you would instinctively trust. Tenzing certainly thought so. "Look," René Dittert told Tenzing, introducing him to Lambert, "I have brought a bear along." Lambert would quickly become, Tenzing said, "my companion of the heights and the closest and dearest of my friends."[1]

This was no exaggeration. In April 1954, as James Ramsey Ullman was preparing to start work ghosting Tenzing's autobiography, Tenzing wrote to urge him to interview "my best mountain friend."[2] In Annette Lambert's home in Geneva, among the mementos of a long career in the mountains, is a nondescript red scarf, laid around the neck of a wooden Buddha, that illustrates how much the friendship meant to both of them. Lambert, at the end of their second attempt to climb Everest together in the autumn of 1952, gave Tenzing the scarf as a token of friendship. Tenzing wore it when he climbed to the summit the following summer and then returned it to Lambert. Tenzing made no secret of the fact that he would have liked to have climbed Everest with the Swiss, and with Lambert in particular. After their attempts in 1952 ended, in which they climbed within a thousand feet of the summit, the two of them discussed the possibility that the British would ask Tenzing to go to Everest with them the following year. Tenzing was against the idea; he was too tired to think about Everest again, and anyway, he would rather wait until the next Swiss expedition, planned for 1956. Lambert wouldn't allow this: "Take the chance," he said. "It doesn't matter who it is with."

How did these two men become such lifelong friends so quickly? They could hardly communicate verbally: Lambert's English was almost nonexistent, and Tenzing had only a few phrases of French. And yet they could see things in each other that they recognized and understood. Much of this empathy had to do with mountains and mountain culture. Lambert, an exact contemporary of Tenzing, had been a dedicated climber since the age of 14, part of an elite climbing club in Geneva called the Androsace—an alpine flower—whose maximum number was fixed at 40. A legendary mountaineer, he climbed the famous Croz Spur on the Grandes Jorasses, one of the toughest routes in the Alps, in his early 20s. At the age of only 23 he qualified top of his class as a mountain guide, a city boy who outperformed the best of those who had grown up with the Alps on their doorstep. "The mountains were everything," Annette Lambert said, and she meant it.

In February 1938 Raymond and others from Geneva tried to climb a long, difficult ridge in the French Alps called the Aiguilles du Diable, a series of rock towers that from a distance look like devil's horns. The weather turned unexpectedly, and Lambert and his friends were trapped at over 13,000 feet in an Alpine winter storm. Taking shelter at the bottom of a crevasse to escape the bitter wind and wait for a break in the weather, they found themselves trapped in it for five long days. *"L'hôtel de la mort lente*,"[3] the climbers called it, as they waited for rescue or the end. When the storm ended, with all of them on the edge of exhaustion, only Lambert was strong enough to climb out of the crevasse and locate the rescue team searching for them. All survived, but Lambert paid a high price. He lost the tips of four fingers. His feet, clad in the old-fashioned leather boots of the 1930s, were frozen solid. When the surgeons finished, Lambert was left with half-feet. This didn't stop him from climbing again, or working as a guide, however. He had special boots made, bizarrely cropped. These fascinated the Sherpas as the expedition trekked toward Everest, the big *balu* and his tiny paws. After the ascent of Everest, Lambert would donate his strange footwear to the Himalayan Mountaineering Institute at Darjeeling, where they remain on display in its museum.

Raymond Lambert lived in the mountains, and as a guide he understood intimately the risks the Sherpas took to earn their living. There was something blue-collar about him, down-to-earth and practical, that the Sherpas liked. For the British, the Himalaya was often a vast, wild place, the antithesis of the gentle, green hills of England. For Lambert the mountains were home, just as they were for the Sherpas. It is no accident that the Swiss quickly developed such a close relationship with the Nepalese people when the country opened to the West in the 1950s. They recognized all the similarities they shared.

Tenzing's friendship with Lambert had a more personal cause as well. Throughout his life, Tenzing looked to men he felt had insight into the things he did not understand and from whom he could learn. He didn't just adopt ideas; after Everest he would dress in the manner of those he admired, as a Swiss guide or in the suits that Nehru gave him. The Tibetan idea of a zhindak explains this in part, the need for a patron to advance your cause, but Tenzing had evolved beyond a conventional Tibetan identity in the melting pot of Darjeeling. "Tibet is the home of my spirit, but as a living man I am a stranger there," he explained. In Lambert he found a role model who was more relevant to the man Tenzing had become. After he climbed Everest, Sherpas in Darjeeling would tell Tenzing he had been lucky, that he'd just been in the right place at the right time. That was true, of course, just as it was for Ed Hillary. But very few Sherpas understood what conquering the summit meant, and few of those were prepared to do what was necessary to reach it. Tenzing was lucky to find himself in the right situation, but he had the right mentality to exploit that chance. He saw an opportunity and took it, the perfect illustration of character being fate.

Lambert was as big-hearted as he looked, and by accepting Tenzing on his own terms, he gave the sirdar immense self-confidence. There is a photograph that captures this perfectly, taken by the Swiss-born American Norman Dhyrenfurth on the second Swiss attempt in the autumn of 1952, when Tenzing was made a full climbing member. Lambert, sitting on a granite block, has his left arm around Tenzing's shoulders, his right resting on his knee, a cigarette between his fingers, trimmed after the frostbite on the Aiguilles du Diable. He is smiling from under his Tibetan-style hat, his eyes narrowed to slits against the dazzling white ice. Tenzing is sitting on Lambert's left with his right arm hooked around Lambert's knee. Tenzing has taken off his sunglasses and is holding them folded in his left hand. Both men are looking directly into the camera. They look comfortable together, equals at home in their chosen environment. "They treated him like a brother," Trevor Braham said of Tenzing's experience of the Swiss.

If Lambert proved a good friend on Everest, Tenzing made another important connection in Darjeeling with a Bengali tea planter and newspaper publisher named Rabindrinath Mitra. If Lambert showed Tenzing how it could be in the mountains, Mitra guided Tenzing through the complexities of modern Indian life and the political maelstrom that would soon engulf him after his success on Everest. Mitra was a couple of years younger than Tenzing, born in Calcutta but into a Darjeeling family. After growing up in the Bengali capital, Mitra returned to the hill station in 1944 to take over a failing tea plantation, where he grew green tea for the Kashmiri market and quickly established a good reputation. He found himself charmed by the Nepalese population in the town, finding them to be more approachable and courteous than Bengalis. He became interested in Nepalese culture, teaching himself the language and translating Nepalese poetry. Mitra was also politically shrewd. There was no newspaper for Nepalese in Darjeeling, so he started a not-for-profit weekly he called *Saathi*, or "Friend." Mitra believed in individuals standing up for themselves, and when he came across the Sherpas, he gave them publicity in *Saathi*. "I became aware that there were all these Sherpas going on expeditions but who had never got publicity; only expedition members got publicity. So I contacted him and he came to my place."

Their friendship grew, and Mitra impressed on Tenzing that the Sherpas should organize themselves and not rely on the Himalayan Club to broker their employment conditions. It was an awkward situation for Tenzing because at the time the local secretary of the club, Jill Henderson, was perhaps the best champion the Sherpas had ever had. Those in Darjeeling at the time remember her with great fondness. "She was," Braham recalled, "the finest, most human honorary secretary we had in Darjeeling. She came to be loved by the Sherpas, literally loved. She was like a mother to them. If they had any problems, they went to Jill and she would help them."

That kind of reliance on the Himalayan Club was coming to an end. Soon the Sherpas would run their own businesses and make their living from mountain tourism. Not surprisingly, Mitra's sharp intellect and political robustness put him on a collision course with the Himalayan Club. "[They] didn't like the fact that I went to the Sherpas. And they were annoyed with me, that I was giving propaganda to them. They told the Sherpas: 'Don't allow that Bengali to come to your place, they're dangerous people.'" Mitra published an article in the Bombay paper *Saturday News* that suggested that Tenzing was so strong at altitude because he had three lungs. Mitra donated his fee from such articles into a benevolent fund for the Sherpas, but that didn't stop some of them from viewing him as a troublemaker. What was he trying to gain? And his suggestion that "a coolie" might one day stand on the summit of Everest was ridiculous as far as some less astute members of the Himalayan Club were concerned.

The political mixture within Darjeeling was complex and pressurized. The fading vestiges of colonialism were being swept aside by a growing sense of Nepalese identity, driven by the emergence of a freer, more open regime in Kathmandu. Nehru's government in Delhi was in the process of securing India's national integrity and defending her postcolonial borders in anticipation of the first Indian general election in 1952. The state government of West Bengal had its own agenda, moving Bengalis to Darjeeling to take up administrative posts previously held by Nepalese. To the north, the Tibetan border was closed after the Chinese invasion of October 1950. South and Central Asia were changing quickly.

Mitra understood this, and as Tenzing's public profile grew, he was well placed to offer him advice. He grew to admire Ang Lhamu too. "She was a very intelligent lady and gave him good advice. And they were very open with me; they treated me like a family member." His political beliefs also struck a chord with Tenzing's sensitivity to prejudice. "After Everest, Tenzing said that before, they had to eat *tsampa* [the Tibetan staple], and now they had the same food as the climbers. [Norman] Dhyrenfurth wrote to him that the Sherpas got the same food as the Swiss on Everest but they never said thank you. So I said to Tenzing: 'Bring the Sherpas and tell them that next time they've got to say thank you.'" Because of his illiteracy Tenzing relied heavily on educated men around him to read his correspondence and advise him on how to deal with the demands of the politically charged world in which he began to find himself. Mitra's self-assurance might have irritated colonial sensibilities, and it's a moot point whether his influence liberated Tenzing's attitudes or steered him on a more political course, but he was genuinely fond of Tenzing and genuinely principled: "There was an element of greatness about Tenzing. He was unique among the Sherpas. He developed the knack of picking up the good manners of each nationality he climbed with; he did that deliberately. That was something other Sherpas didn't do."

Tenzing's deputy on Everest in 1953, Dawa or Da Tenzing, was an interesting contrast. Whereas Tenzing cut his hair and dressed in plaid shirts and knickerbockers, Da Tenzing proudly kept his braids and pigtail and wore a traditional turquoise earring. He was a highly successful sirdar in his own right, going with the British to Kanchenjunga for its first ascent in 1955 and on a host of other significant expeditions. He enjoyed traveling, as Tenzing did, but wasn't wildly impressed by the technologies of the West. John Jackson, one of the Kanchenjunga expedition members, asked Da Tenzing what he had thought of London: "I don't think much of it. In that village no one has time to stop and talk to anyone else."[4] The only thing he wanted to take home with him from Britain was a cow, to improve the herds in Khumbu.

POLITICAL UPHEAVAL AFTER THE WAR changed the rules for attempts on Everest. After the chaos and misery of Partition in 1947, most of the

Himalaya was in turmoil. The Dalai Lama, threatened by the Chinese, drew up a horoscope that suggested that his country was in greater danger from foreigners than ever. Eric Shipton had written to the Alpine Club within weeks of the end of hostilities in Europe suggesting a renewal of the Everest campaign, but there were far bigger considerations in Asia than mountain climbing. When the Chinese occupied Tibet in 1950, any chances of returning to the north side of the mountain disappeared completely. That approach to Everest would remain closed to climbers for 30 years.

Nepal, on the other hand, began to open up. Since the Treaty of Sagauli in 1816 ended hostilities between the East India Company and Nepal, the Hindu kingdom had remained largely out-of-bounds to Europeans. Jang Bahadur had seized power in 1846 in the bloody Kot massacre, taking the title Rana and declaring himself maharajah. For the next hundred years, the Ranas treated Nepal as a private fiefdom with the kings of Nepal mere figureheads. The country remained almost medieval, with no roads, little health care, no education system, and—even in Kathmandu—almost no sanitation. The British were indifferent as long as Nepal continued to provide men for the Indian Army's Gurkha regiments.

When Nehru came to power, Nepal's fledgling political movement made great strides. The Rana family's friends in India were replaced by their enemies. The situation in Kathmandu became fluid and remained so for more than a decade. In November 1950 King Tribhuvan slipped his escort and sought asylum in the Indian Embassy. A few months later he returned and the Rana regime collapsed, starting Nepal on an unstable path of short-term governments. In all this change and confusion, a few explorers and scientists were allowed into Nepal. All parties understood that isolationism would no longer work. In 1949 Bill Tilman explored the Langtang Himal northeast of Kathmandu with Tenzing, and in 1950 he trekked into Khumbu with a small group of friends, becoming the first Westerners to visit the glacier that flowed south from Everest. Few in Kathmandu had any concept of the scale of natural riches found within Nepal's boundaries. The country wasn't just opening up to the world, it was getting to know itself.

In this spirit of geographical inquiry, the British launched a reconnaissance of the southern approaches to Everest, instigated by a young doctor named Michael Ward and led by Eric Shipton. While Tenzing explored Nanda Devi with the French, Ang Tharkay was appointed sirdar by his old friend Shipton. Places were also found, at the last moment, for two New Zealanders who were already in India, Ed Hillary and Earle Riddiford.

Shipton and the rest of his team followed Tilman's route to Khumbu from the Indian railhead at Jogbani, but whereas in 1950 Tilman had been trekking in the post-monsoon season, the reconnaissance started earlier, while the rains were still falling. Swollen rivers, leeches, and muddy trails hampered the approach. Porters were hard to find. Unlike in 1921 when they explored the northern side of Everest, Shipton's team had a good idea of where Everest was—at the head of the Khumbu Glacier—but they had little idea about how difficult it would be to climb up its Icefall into the long glacial valley George Mallory had called the Western Cwm. Mallory himself thought it horrendous, and Shipton, while acknowledging that it could be climbed, was worried about the Sherpas. Carrying loads every day through that kind of terrain brought terrible risks. Ed Hillary, who greatly admired Shipton, was more determined. "In my heart, I knew the only way to attempt this mountain was to modify the old standards of safety and justifiable risk and to meet the dangers as they came; to drive through regardless. Care and caution would never make a route through the icefall. If we didn't attack it that May, someone else would. The competitive standards of alpine mountaineering were coming to the Himalaya."[5]

As it turned out, the decision was made for him. When Shipton and Hillary returned to Kathmandu, they discovered that permission to climb Everest in 1952 had gone not to the British but the Swiss. The Swiss Foundation for Alpine Research, founded in 1939 to promote mountain science and exploration, was a well-funded organization with connections to government. It had supported René Dittert and André Roch in the Garhwal in 1947 when Tenzing had become sirdar. In 1949 Dittert and Edouard Wyss-Dunant approached them again on behalf of their friends in the Androsace to seek funding for another Himalayan expedition, this time to Nepal, perhaps even to Cho Oyu, one of the fourteen 8,000-meter peaks. The foundation, they learned, had applied for permission to try Everest. Would they be interested? The new regime in Kathmandu had none of the allegiances to the British the Ranas had.

Because the Swiss had asked first, they would make the first attempt on Everest from the Nepalese side.

In Darjeeling, Tenzing got a letter from Wyss-Dunant, the expedition's leader, inviting him to be sirdar. "'Would I go?' the letters asked. And they might as well have asked if I would eat or breathe. The way I behaved about the house for a few days, Ang Lhamu and the girls must have thought I was possessed by devils." It was an exquisite moment for Tenzing. He knew the British would be planning an expedition after their reconnaissance in 1951, and he could expect that Ang Tharkay would be put in charge of the Sherpas. Now it was his friends, the Swiss, who had been granted the permit. He had left Khumbu 20 years before as an impoverished Khamba with no social standing at all. Now he was coming back as a "big man," someone of consequence who was respected by Sherpas and climbers alike. Best of all, he would be climbing again on Everest.

The Swiss asked Tenzing to bring 13 Sherpas with him from Darjeeling—they would hire another 10 in Khumbu—but he struggled to find enough men. Tenzing claimed they were angry at being treated unfairly by the British on the 1951 reconnaissance expedition. "Many of the Nepalese porters who had been on the expedition claimed they had not received their full wages; there had been difficulties about a lost, or perhaps stolen, camera; and no baksheesh had been given out at the end of the climb."[6] Such differences were hardly new. Most large expeditions had problems; they were expected and even to be exploited as far as the Sherpas were concerned. The real reasons lay elsewhere, as Tenzing suggested: "Everest was too big, too dangerous; it was impossible to climb by the southern route. Even the great Tiger Angtharkay, who had been the 1951 sirdar, was not going back this time."[7] He bet Tenzing 20 rupees that the Swiss—"like Shipton's men"—wouldn't get across the huge crevasse at the top of the Icefall.

Tenzing was being unfair. Ang Tharkay wasn't going back to Everest because he would be working as sirdar on the British expedition to Cho Oyu, and several of his old crew would naturally go with him. As for the "huge crevasse," it was a challenge, but a technical one. The Swiss and the British wouldn't be competing so keenly to get back there if they thought it would stop them completely. But even if Ang Tharkay had been available to go to Everest, it's unlikely he would have. He was a proud man, like Tenzing, and wouldn't have welcomed handing over the role of sirdar after so many years.

As for the other Sherpas, concern about working in the Icefall hadn't been confined to Eric Shipton. The Sherpas had also experienced the ice shifting and creaking as it flowed inexorably down the mountain, and watched the sudden collapse of ice cliffs and pinnacles. They were always attuned to the dangers of avalanche or bad weather on a mountain, and without the impulse to reach the summit they were much less enthusiastic about risking their lives. Ang Tharkay's bet with Tenzing was not about reaching the Western Cwm, but persuading the Sherpas to carry loads through it. In 1952 the Swiss nicknamed one section "Suicide Alley"; in 1953 the British would call sections of the Icefall "Hillary's Horror," "Hellfire Alley," and "Atom Bomb." They also found the route substantially altered from that faced a year before by the Swiss, as crevasses closed or widened and ice cliffs disintegrated. No wonder the Sherpas were anxious.

Despite their reluctance, Tenzing got his 13 Sherpas, and they were largely a good team. Ajiba, his first wife's cousin, went on his first Everest expedition in 1933 with Ruttledge and accompanied Tenzing in the Garhwal in 1947. Tenzing had known Dawa Thondup as a boy. Pasang Phutar was the "Jockey," Tenzing's protégé. Pansi had been on Nanda Devi with Tenzing in 1951, and Aïla had climbed with the Swiss in 1949 when Tenzing had been exploring with Tilman in Nepal. Others had been on Annapurna with the French, such as Sarki, who had carried to the top camp. Da Namgyal and Phu Tharkay had been to Nanga Parbat on the fatal expedition of 1950. In early March they left Darjeeling to meet the Swiss in Kathmandu. The Nepalese had opened an airport, and for the first time an Everest expedition would start from the capital.

Since the 1970s, Everest expeditions have flown into Lukla or Shyangboche above the village of Namche Bazar. In 1952 it took 16 days' trekking to reach the same point. This had its positive aspects; trekking is good for the soul and gets climbers fit and acclimatized. But the logistical complexity of an Everest expedition in the 1950s cannot be overestimated. Equipment, food, oxygen, and fuel in the right amounts had to be delivered to Base Camp and camps higher on the mountain by porters who required their own equipment and supplies. At the heart of this operation was Tenzing, organizing loads, making sure that everything arrived where and when it was due, keeping porters from becoming discontented, and negotiating problems as they arose. That he could manage to do all this in his head without writing any of it down shows how capable he was as a manager. While the climbers enjoyed the scenery and prepared themselves for the climb, Tenzing worked from dawn until night in keeping things on track. It's not surprising that the dual roles of climber and sirdar began to weigh on him.

It was, despite all the pressures, a happy time. Dittert made the Sherpas laugh with his constant activity. They nicknamed him *kishigpa*, Tibetan for flea, because he couldn't sit still. When Ernst Hofstetter complained about his balding head, the Sherpas told him to smear his head with yak fat, which stank horribly. Part of the reason for the contentment the expedition experienced was that the mountaineers had climbed together for years. André Roch, Jean-Jacques Asper, and Raymond Lambert were among the best climbers in Europe.

On April 13 they reached Namche Bazar, and Tenzing was reunited with his mother. It was the first time he'd seen her since his father's death. Kinzom was now 80 and had been staying in Thame, where her younger daughter, Sonam Doma, was then living. A woman in Kharta recalls how her husband, Sonam, accompanied Tenzing's mother over the Nangpa La to Thame so she could see her son again. Tenzing rewarded Sonam for his efforts with a piece of jewelry that his widow still has. Jennifer Bourdillon, widow of Everest climber Tom Bourdillon, recalled meeting Kinzom at Thame while her son was climbing on Everest: "One old lady sat a little to one side. She did not join in the poking or hair-pulling and she was much calmer and more composed than the others, though she too had a very ready smile."[8] There is a stillness about this memory of Kinzom that seems wholly appropriate to her character, and it is easy to imagine a similar moment in the dusty streets of Namche as Tenzing caught sight of his mother. *"Ama la,"* he told her, "here I am at last."[9]

All the Sherpas were reunited with their extended families, and they had several years of gossip to get through. There was food and chang, dancing, and talking. Eyes would meet across a smoky living room and new relationships begun. Several of the Sherpas acquired girlfriends who, along with seemingly half the Sherpas of Khumbu, were hired to carry loads up to Base Camp. Among the porters were Tenzing's younger sister, Sonam Doma, and his brother Kesang's daughter Phu Lhamu. (Tenzing refers to his deceased brothers; both Chingdu and Kesang were now dead.) The festivities continued as the expedition left Namche for the gompa at Tengboche, where Lambert endeared himself still further to the Sherpas by gulping down all the salt tea left by his teammates to save them the embarrassment of refusing. The young abbot at Tengboche, Ngawang Tenzin Zangbu, blessed the expedition, and Tenzing organized the porters for the final stages to Base Camp below the Icefall of the Khumbu Glacier.

On April 26, Dittert, Gabriel Chevalley, Lambert, and René Aubert started the long process of finding a route through the maze of crevasses and ice cliffs that led into the Western Cwm. Tenzing said that it "went slowly" in the Icefall, but in fact the Swiss made excellent progress. In just four days they had found a route through the 2,000-foot-high mess and arrived at the huge crevasse that had so unnerved the Sherpas. In the modern era, Sherpas are paid specifically to manage and maintain the Icefall as hundreds of climbers, guides, and porters move through it in the course of an expedition. In the early days it was a place they dreaded. Sherpas would say their prayers as they stepped beneath the precarious tons of ice that could topple without warning. By 1986 the Icefall had killed 18 climbers; since then the death rate has dropped considerably, partly because of Sherpa expertise. But in 1952 the huge crevasse that stretched from the Southwest Face of Everest to the wall of Nuptse on the other side of the Western Cwm must have seemed like the jaws of hell.

Asper made short work of it, although at 19,000 feet it was not the place for the kind of gymnastics he would have relished in the Alps. Lowering himself on a doubled rope with a third safety rope above him, he tried swinging across the gap, but it was too far and he kept swinging back into the crevasse wall. Instead, Roch pointed at an ice bridge 60 feet down. Asper's friends lowered him deeper into the green darkness. Once on the bridge he was able to climb out the other side. After tying off the ropes, Leon Flory was able to cross, followed by Ajiba, who hesitated briefly, muttered a few mantras, and then crawled across the ropes as quickly as he could. They had passed through the Icefall in four days and could start supplying the upper section of the glacier. "What looked like an impossible crossing was the easiest sort of operation for both men and loads," Tenzing said.[10]

Back in Geneva, the Swiss had discussed placing their Camp III at the top of the Icefall and then making carries all the way up the Western Cwm and the Lhotse Face and placing Camp IV on the South Col. The scale of Everest now mocked their plans. It was another six miles to the South Col, and another six thousand feet in altitude. The Swiss preferred the name "Valley of Silence" to Mallory's "Western Cwm," but it could be an oppressive silence. The heat of the sun bouncing off the glacier, the huge walls soaring above them, and the gossamer trail stretching up toward the steep slopes leading to the South Col: This was their world for the next three weeks as the expedition labored to bring two and a half tons of supplies and equipment up the mountain. All of it was new: a new route, new weather patterns to judge, new dangers to assess. A fourth camp was placed halfway up the Western Cwm, a fifth at the bottom of the Lhotse Face. Now they had to choose the right approach to reach the South Col.

The obvious alternatives were up the glacier to the right, which was easier angled but more out of the way, or straight ahead up a steep snow and ice slope split by the rocks of what became known as the Geneva Spur. This was the line they chose. Ultimately, it proved a mistake—it was more dangerous and there was nowhere to place an intermediate camp—but the Swiss set to work, fixing ropes and leveling a ledge halfway up where they could dump loads to be moved up to the South Col at a later stage. The Swiss made a point of climbing with the Sherpas; Tenzing had already struck a rapport with Lambert, Leon Flory shared a rope with Dawa Thondup, and André Roch climbed with Pasang. But the Sherpas weren't happy. Sarki was suffering from malaria, and relations with the others were sometimes strained, as Dittert acknowledged in early May. "At nine o'clock the Sherpas arrived from below. No chatter this time and no smiles. They had an angry look and were muttering and grumbling. There was a storm brewing. The journey from Camp II to Camp III [through the Icefall] had not pleased them at all. I saw their point of view, but it was the best and the only way. The real reason was something else; they had fed badly at Camp I. There had been no yak and not enough tsampa; Pansi was not there. They declared that they wished to go down to the base camp, then, changing their opinion, they wished to stay with me."[11] Dittert was heartened, but knew he had to do something quickly to improve morale. He reminded them of Ang Tharkay's warning that none of them would be able to carry through the Icefall and yet look how much they had achieved already! They smiled even more broadly when Dittert promised any man who carried to the South Col another 20 rupees.

Despite these minor disagreements, the Swiss made steady progress. Then, in the third week of May, the climbers were pinned down by a storm at the head of the Western Cwm. For two days the wind thumped against their tents as they listened to the gale screaming across the South Col above them. René Dittert wrote that the winds were "the sole master of space" as the climbers lay trapped in camp, wondering what it would be like getting caught by such ferocity on the South Col itself. In the back of their minds they also feared that the monsoon was settling already around the mountain. Would they get their chance at all? At the height of the storm, Dittert was forced out of his tent to reinforce its wooden poles: "The fresh dusty snow was flying in uninterrupted whirlwinds and the dark storm clouds, coming from the south-west, were racing madly across the sky. I could hear them roaring as they broke more than 3,000 feet above against the rugged bastions of Everest, then invisible in the fog. Like a fear-stricken beast I went back to hide."[12]

If this really was an early warning of the approaching monsoon, they had to act swiftly. The Swiss moved with a new urgency to bring the expedition to its climax. They had, however, made a serious tactical error. By climbing directly up the Geneva Spur to the South Col in one push, they had given the Sherpas too much work to do. No one could carry a load all the way to the South Col from the Western Cwm in one day. When they made a final push to reach the summit, they would find themselves without the necessary supplies to mount a successful attempt.

One critical problem was already outside their control. Oxygen equipment brought with them from Switzerland seemed to work only when they were lying down. While carrying the heavy apparatus on their backs, they used so much effort drawing gas through the valve that the system offered no benefit at all. When oxygen was really needed, on the summit slopes of Everest, it would let them down badly.

By May 24 they were ready to try for the top, conscious that time might be running out. The first assault party included Lambert and Tenzing, Flory, Aubert, and six more Sherpas. Tenzing had climbed a great deal with Lambert so far, and it was clear they made a good team. Dittert told Gabriel Chevalley that Tenzing's leadership would be essential to get the Sherpas to the South Col: "He'll have to go with them, there's no question about it. And even if there was, I would leave him with Lambert. They understand one another and they make a fine pair for the assault."[13] Lambert was utterly relaxed about the decision; Dittert describes his "serenity" as being a calming influence on the whole team. They would carry enough supplies to the South Col to mount a serious attempt on the ridge above.

If Lambert had seemed confident when Dittert was selecting the assault team, by that morning of May 24 Tenzing's partner wasn't so sure. Perhaps it was the storm that had pinned them down for two days, but as they started up the 45-degree slope toward the South Col, he watched anxiously as clouds gathered in the sky overhead. "The thought of being involved in the unknown region of the South Col, where no one had yet been even in good weather, frightened us. The prospect of being blocked there, and of being frozen where we stood, or carried off by avalanches on the return, filled us all with fear. The flanks of Everest are one of the places of the Earth where one is not ashamed of occasional fear."[14] Dittert was not impressed and told Lambert so: "One day lost and we haven't too many. You will have to begin again tomorrow and push on to the end." The next morning they did exactly that, but low down Ajiba announced he was turning around. He'd been suffering from malaria and wasn't recovered sufficiently to climb. Bathed in sweat and shivering violently, he had no choice. His load was divided and the party went on, leaving Ajiba to descend alone.

Around midday they reached the dump of gear left halfway to the South Col, and the Sherpas picked up as much of it as they could carry: tents, food, fuel, and oxygen cylinders. Climbing without bottled oxygen, they continued slowly toward the South Col, but by four in the afternoon they still hadn't reached the end of the long slope. Two of the remaining Sherpas, Ang Norbu and Mingma Dorje, were exhausted and frightened; it was late and their feet were cold. They wanted to go down. Tenzing started to cajole them, but Lambert intervened: "How could we prevent them? Had we the right to do so?"[15]

Now they had lost three of the seven Sherpas and once again had to divide up the abandoned loads. Then, while they were sorting through the gear, Aubert's sleeping bag was caught by a gust of wind and blew away. Despite this they went on, for three more hours, grinding up the endless slope, desperate to reach the flat ground of the South Col and start putting up the tent. When they were close to 26,000 feet, their lungs hauling on the dry air, their throats raw and bloody, they had to stop. Darkness was falling, and they had no choice but to dig out platforms for the tents they were carrying. They scraped off the snow as fast as their leaden arms would allow. When they had dug ledges big enough, they put up the tents and the Sherpas crawled into one, the three Swiss into another. Tenzing kept going, melting snow for soup and bringing a pan over to the sahibs' tent. After that they rested as best they could: "The night was endless," Lambert complained. "We endured, we waited in patience, we breathed deeply in order to control our hearts, and we suffered the cold which at first froze our skins and then penetrated slowly to take up its abode in our flesh."[16] When the long night ended, they heard Tenzing call out: "Fine day, sahibs!" He was at their tent door, bringing them hot chocolate.

At ten o'clock they reached the shoulder a little way above the South Col. Tenzing took off his rucksack for Lambert to take down to where they would camp, and then he started down to fetch equipment left at their last night's campsite, where the remaining three Sherpas were supposed to be waiting. Phu Tharkay and Da Namgyal had already climbed down to the ledge below, where gear had been cached the day before, and had returned to the tents, but Pasang Phutar hadn't moved at all. "I'm sick," he told Tenzing, "I'm sick and I'm going to die." The sirdar wouldn't stand for it. He had committed completely to the climb and wouldn't allow his friend any weakness. Tenzing says they argued, and he swore at Pasang Phutar, "slapping and kicking him to prove to him he wasn't dead."[17] In *Tiger of the Snows* he explains he was worried that the sahibs above might die without the tents and equipment the Sherpas were bringing, but it was more than this. Tenzing wouldn't let the attempt fail because Pasang Phutar wouldn't move. There was too much at stake.

When the Sherpas reached the South Col, Lambert was moved by their poor condition. "Pasang declared that he wished to die where he was; Phu Tharkay zigzagged like a drunken man; Da Namgyal was suffering from migraine and held his head in his hands. They were out of action."[18] The contrast with Tenzing is startling. "He was in extraordinary condition," Lambert wrote. "Twice more he was to return to the bivouac site and reascend with loads." This was Tenzing at the height of his powers, doing things on a big mountain that very few modern climbers, with the best equipment and training, could match. Ambition, courage, and supreme physical ability drove him on. The other Sherpas, however, had had enough and in the morning, despite the night's rest, they wanted only to descend. "That's another trump card gone," Flory reflected.[19]

The Swiss now faced a difficult decision. If the monsoon was coming, did they have time to retreat, rest, bring up more supplies, and start again? Should they gamble on more time, or push on for the summit? They chose the latter. Crossing to the eastern side of the South Col, they explored the ground ahead, climbing up a snow couloir that pushed like a white boil into the black rocks of the summit pyramid. It was a reconnaissance, but they were moving well and Tenzing had slipped a tent into his rucksack. Occasionally, they would stop and suck on their oxygen tanks, "like a liqueur," as Lambert described it, but for much of the time the heavy load was dead, useless weight on their backs. In the afternoon they came out onto the Southeast Ridge itself, and for the first time they could look down beyond the East Face of Everest to the Kharta Valley. Lambert reckoned they had reached 27,500 feet, but it was a little lower than that, 27,265 feet—such differences are meaningful at that altitude—and Tenzing pointed to his rucksack in which he had put a tent. "Sahib, we ought to stay here tonight," he indicated, and Lambert agreed with a smile. Leon Flory and René Aubert were slightly behind them, but both men still felt strong. The problem was, there were four of them and one two-man tent. Who would stay and who would turn back?

Aubert had been one of the men who had rescued Lambert and his friends from the Combe Maudite when Lambert had lost the ends of his feet to frostbite. They were all three friends. But no one seems to have even debated that Lambert and Tenzing should take the tent and attempt the summit the next day. They embraced, and then the two watched

Aubert and Flory becoming smaller and smaller as they hurried down to the South Col before turning to put up their shelter.

Stupefied by lack of oxygen, they prepared for a night at altitudes no one had endured before, fumbling with the tent, reluctant to remove their gloves and expose themselves to the risk of frostbite. They finished before the sun disappeared behind the wall of Nuptse and then sat for a moment outside the tent, watching the light leave Kanchenjunga to the east. There was little each could say to the other that would be understood, but before crawling inside the tent, Tenzing pointed out a gathering mass of clouds to the west. Then darkness crept over the summit of Everest, and the long, grueling wait for dawn began.

Without sleeping bags it was too dangerous to sleep; they feared they might never wake up. And without a stove to melt snow they couldn't rehydrate their bodies, parched by the effects of altitude. "We were overtaken by a consuming thirst," Lambert recalled, "which we could not appease. There was nothing to drink."[20] Tenzing found an end of a candle and an empty tin and melted some ice in it, but they needed liters of water, not mouthfuls. They pummelled each other to keep warm, Lambert indicating his missing toes and encouraging Tenzing to hang onto his own. The tent snapped and rattled constantly, like prayer flags, Lambert thought, as the minutes crawled past. Black eventually turned to gray, and as he watched Tenzing's shape, curled into a ball on the tent floor, slowly hardening against the first light, Lambert knew the wait was over. "In a state of semi-hallucination the entire expedition seemed to me to be a stretched bow and ourselves the arrow. A poor blunted arrow at least."

Outside the tent, they looked in disappointment at the blanket of cloud shrouding the neighboring giants of Lhotse and Nuptse, although to the north the skies were clear. Should they go on? Lambert jerked his thumb at the ridge above and winked. Tenzing grinned at him. "We had gone too far to give up," he recalled. "We must make our try."[21]

They made a brave effort, but even in good weather they would have found themselves extended. Tenzing had already made a superhuman effort bringing abandoned loads to the South Col. More crucially, their oxygen sets were hardly worth carrying. As they climbed, the stiffness of the valves stopped them from sucking in the precious gas, and they had to halt every 20 yards to recover. Occasionally the clouds parted to reveal the lesser peaks now far below them, but the wind strengthened and the fog returned. Cut off from their friends below, climbing in the chill grasp of the mist, they made slow progress. After five hours Lambert reckoned they had gained little more than 650 feet in height. Tenzing rested his head on his ice ax, waiting for the dizziness he was suffering to ease. They were still 650 feet below the South Summit. And who knew how long that was from the summit itself? Lambert was revisited with the unreal euphoria of his last bivouac in the crevasse that had almost been his tomb; and he knew they were getting close to the point of no return. There was nothing to be done but go down.

They reached the South Col that afternoon, abandoning their tent at 27,250 feet for the next assault party. As he approached camp, Tenzing staggered and sank to his knees on the gentle slope. Flory and Aubert dragged him into a tent where he collapsed into sleep, exhausted by the days and night of continual effort at the limits of survival. Tenzing had worked harder than any of them to reach the summit, and now he paid the price. At noon the following day, Dittert met the first assault party struggling down from the South Col as he, Asper, and Roch, together with five Sherpas, started for their attempt. He wasn't prepared for what he saw: "I noticed with terror the havoc that had been wrought by altitude and effort. These men were at the limit of their resistance. Tensing was moving with extreme difficulty and had to be assisted. Aubert's eyes were sunk in their sockets and he seemed extenuated. All of them were lined, emaciated, consumed by fatigue to an unrecognisable state. It was a pathetic meeting."[22]

Dittert and the others would make a second attempt, but bad weather pinned them down at the South Col for three nights, and without Tenzing to motivate them, the Sherpas were disconsolate and reluctant to work. Only Sarki and Mingma Dorje offered to stay with the three Swiss to assist their climb, and Lambert's parting words to Dittert, that only a well-supported party on the South Col would have any chance of success, must have chipped away at his resolve as the hours passed. After two big efforts to reach the top, the expedition was effectively over.

At Base Camp, now recovered from their ordeal, Tenzing and Lambert were garlanded, not with flowers, which weren't available, but with strings of sausages. After the privations of altitude, the climbers and Sherpas were looking forward to an extended party. At Namche Bazar, as they started the long trek home, the Sherpas celebrated another expedition safely completed. No one had died on Everest since Maurice Wilson's pathetic and lonely death in 1934. Tenzing was reunited with his mother and sisters. "It was difficult to say," Dittert wrote, "whether it was the monsoon or alcohol that drowned that village."

At Namche, Dittert and the other climbers met Ed Hillary, back from the British attempt on Cho Oyu, a training expedition for Everest should the Swiss not succeed. As they swapped stories, Dittert happily shared information and the reasons for their failure, impressing on Hillary the need to properly supply the South Col and have oxygen equipment that worked. The Swiss had made other mistakes too, an inevitable consequence of being the first to attempt the south side of the mountain. They had, as it turned out, gone too early for the summit. The window of calm weather just before the monsoon which modern expeditions now rely on didn't arrive until they had returned to Namche Bazar. More crucially, they had persevered with the Geneva Spur, where they could not place an intermediate camp between the Western Cwm and the South Col. Some of the climbers, André Roch in particular, had advised that the line up the Lhotse Face to the right was more amenable, but Dittert, as climbing leader, had prevailed.

At least they had another chance in the autumn before the British came in 1953, but in the meantime Tenzing, still weary from the attempt on the summit, had to get the expedition home. While the sahibs could unwind from the privations of the mountain, their sirdar had to manage the porters along the trail. Not surprisingly, when he got back to Darjeeling in June, Ang Lhamu told him it was foolish for him to return so soon to Everest. No one had ever attempted the mountain after the monsoon, and he had barely two months to recover his strength. Who knew what problems he would encounter? Why not let someone else go?

There were plenty of reasons why not. First, Lambert would be returning for another try, one of only two from the original team to make the trip that autumn. Tenzing had cemented a lasting friendship with Lambert and felt he owed him. As Tenzing's nephew Nawang Gombu put it, Lambert showed Tenzing just how far he could go. He had been given a chance by the Swiss and he had taken it. Now he knew he could reach the summit and wanted it more than anything. In addition to his affection for Lambert, Tenzing would return not just as sirdar but to the team itself as a full climbing member. He would be getting 300 rupees a month, a hundred more than Ang Tharkay was paid as sirdar on Annapurna. The honor gave him even more reason to work for the expedition's success.

As it worked out, the Swiss left for their autumn attempt too late by two or three weeks and were stopped in their tracks by the onset of winter. They reached the end of the Western Cwm in late October but instead of moving right onto the Lhotse Face, the new leader, Gabriel Chevalley, first reconnoitered the Geneva Spur despite acknowledging that the Lhotse Face was the better alternative. Altitude bred a kind of indecision, a mistake that would have unforeseen, tragic consequences. Most of the Sherpas who had gone with Tenzing that spring had come back with him for the autumn attempt, including Mingma Dorje. On October 31 he was carrying a load under the Geneva Spur when some ice, breaking off from high above, crashed down around him. Other Sherpas were injured, among them Tenzing's own nephew Topgay, but a shard of ice seems to have penetrated Mingma Dorje's lungs and he collapsed and died before anything could be done for him. He was the first Sherpa to die on Everest since 1922. Tenzing dug the grave and heaped the stones over Mingma's body, saying a prayer as he and the other Sherpas wept. And Tenzing argued with the Sherpas when they told him they'd had enough and wanted to go home. (To their great credit, the Swiss had left it up to the Sherpas to make the decision.)

At least the tragedy gave Chevalley the impetus to switch routes, but the delay meant they could not move up to the South Col until the third week of November. The Swiss were simply far too late. When Everest was finally climbed in the post-monsoon period in 1973, a Japanese team reached the top a month earlier, in late October. Chris Bonington's successful post-monsoon expedition to the Southwest Face summitted in late September. When the Swiss reached the South Col on November 19, the bitter wind and cold would burn itself into Tenzing's memory, never to be forgotten: "For what seemed like hours more we staggered around, trying to set up our camp near the still-visible remains of the spring one;

and when at last two tents were up, the seven Sherpas piled into them and disappeared."[23] Once they'd got their own tents up, Lambert examined his thermometer: It was −30°C (−22°F), and the wind was gusting up to 60 miles an hour. Typically, Tenzing managed to provide the others with a drink of hot chocolate, hunched over his stove as the fabric of their double-skinned tent filled the air with sparks of static electricity.

Tenzing again put more effort into the attempt than anyone else on the team. He cut steps up the Lhotse Face with a 45-pound load and no oxygen. He pushed the route out and then raced down the mountain to keep the Sherpas moving, and as a consequence did twice as much climbing as anyone else. He put up tents, cooked meals, prepared drinks, and even extracted an infected tooth from Ang Norbu's mouth. Again the supply line wasn't up to the task, and again Tenzing picked up the slack. His dual role of sirdar and expedition member was taking its toll, not least in his relationship with the men he was leading. Tenzing may have been infected with the sahibs' ambition to reach the summit whatever the cost, but the Sherpas were there for the money and weren't about to lose toes or worse just to humor him.

The Swiss, on the other hand, were full of admiration. In an article for *Harper's* magazine, expedition member Norman Dhyrenfurth described how Tenzing came to his aid at 23,000 feet as the American lay stricken with laryngitis and fever in a collapsed tent:

> *Owing to my weakened condition, I was unable to get out of my tent to fix the pegs and guy ropes. I tried to call for help to some of my Swiss friends in the neighbouring tents, but because of my laryngitis and the storm they could not hear me. As I lay there in the dark, holding on to the flapping tent and trying to keep it away from my face to avoid suffocation, I was really desperate, thinking that I would have to hold on to the tent like that for the rest of the long night.*
>
> *All of a sudden I heard the noise of a tent's zipper opening, and Tensing's voice just outside of my tent coming through the storm: "I arrange, Sahib." How he did it I'll never know, since it usually takes two men even in calm weather to set up a tent, but he managed it despite the storm, and soon everything was back*

*to normal again, I could breathe again, and the terrible feeling
of claustrophobia passed. I tried to shout my heartfelt thanks to
Tensing, but managed only a whisper, lost in the noise of the wind.
Tensing said, "Okay, Sahib," and returned to his tent.*

When Lambert gave Tenzing his red scarf at the end of the expedition and told him to go with the British if they asked him, he was acknowledging just how much Tenzing had invested in Everest. He had been on six expeditions to the mountain, four of them serious attempts, but it was in 1952 that his relationship with the mountain deepened to something more akin to obsession.

On the way home, the months of effort extracted their price. Faced once again with the task of keeping the expedition moving, Tenzing's health began to unravel. At Namche he saw his 16-year-old nephew Gombu, who asked his uncle for a job next spring. "You'll have to work hard, Gombu," Tenzing warned him. He was drinking heavily as the expedition trekked toward Kathmandu, taking the edge off his exhaustion. His relationship with some of the Sherpas had deteriorated and one night he had a confrontation with Ajiba that ruptured their friendship. Old scores existed between Tenzing and Ajiba's family, going back two decades to his relationship with Dawa Phuti. Since that time Tenzing had become a "big man," and back in Darjeeling poor boys called him "Au"—or uncle—begging to do odd jobs for him, ingratiating themselves to get a place on a future expedition. This respect for someone who had started with nothing was too much for some of his older companions. Tenzing was finding out that success breeds jealousy. Ajiba, and several others, wouldn't be returning in 1953.

Soon after his fight with Ajiba, Tenzing's health broke. The weather had been wet and cold, and Tenzing had sprained an ankle, which forced him to hobble with ski poles. Now he also developed a fever. Whether or not it was a recurrence of malaria, as he thought, exhaustion made his condition much worse. When they reached Kathmandu, the expedition had an audience with King Tribhuvan. Tenzing, a Bhotia born in a yak herder's tent, who spent his childhood as a rich man's servant, was awarded the Nepal Pratap Bradhak medal for his contribution to the Swiss expedition and the honor he had brought Nepal. He was almost too delirious to accept.

CHAPTER NINE

A TALL WHITE DREAM
IN THE SKY

Such a scene as I've imagined but never believed could come true —
Everest was climbed yesterday by Ed and Tenzing, at 11.30 am.
We'd made it, exactly according to plan.
We had crowned the efforts of all our illustrious predecessors.
We had stood at the apex of this pyramid of hard-won experience and endeavour.
What a tale to tell the waiting world!
—JOHN HUNT, TO JOY, HIS WIFE, JUNE 1, 1953

TENZING WAS EXHAUSTED. He had lost 20 pounds and looked gaunt and close to collapse. Gabriel Chevalley and the other Swiss climbers were so concerned about Tenzing's condition that they flew him to Patna and had him admitted to the missionary Holy Family Hospital. Tenzing spent ten days there until he was strong enough to return to Darjeeling. While his wife and his teenage daughters fussed around him, their patient contemplated the contents of a letter that had arrived while he'd been in hospital. It was an invitation, sent by Maj. Charles Wylie of the Himalayan Committee, for Tenzing to join the British expedition of 1953 as sirdar.

Tenzing knew Wylie. In the winter of 1948 he had met the Gurkha officer in Kashmir while working as an outdoor instructor for the Indian Army, a job that had emerged from Jack Gibson's extensive network of contacts. One of the consequences of the enormous publicity that followed the successful ascent of Everest, inevitably dominated by Tenzing and Hillary and the expedition's leader John Hunt, is that the role of other members of the expedition faded into the background. The role played by Charles Wylie, like that by the physiologist Griffith Pugh, solved one of the key failings of the Swiss attempt in 1952—supply. Wylie had an intimate knowledge of Nepal. His grandfather had been the British resident in Kathmandu in the 1890s, hitting golf balls off his verandah for relaxation, and his father had been a Gurkha officer as well. Wylie spoke Nepali fluently, like all Gurkhas, and in some senses he was more Nepalese than English. He loved the country and understood those Nepalese social conventions too complex and subtle for most Western climbers. During the war he had suffered the brutality of a Japanese prisoner-of-war camp for three years, but the horrors he had endured there, which many of his climbing friends knew little about, had not undermined an essentially generous nature.

Wylie worked selflessly for the success the British achieved on Everest. It would be his job to organize the transport and liaise with Tenzing over the organization of the Sherpas—unglamorous perhaps, but the logistical support for the climb was staggering. Hundreds of loads had to be ferried from Kathmandu to the depot at Tengboche, all of which had to be carried on people's backs. The expedition would, at one stage or other, be underpinned by almost a thousand porters, Sherpas, cooks, and mail runners. The management of these men and women would be a critical ingredient in reaching the summit.

Unlike Wylie, the Himalayan Committee—which had inherited the functions of the Mount Everest Committee—was a new proposition to Tenzing. Nor did he know Col. John Hunt, the leader of the expedition. The fact that he knew none of the climbers made him hesitate. Wylie had also written to Jill Henderson, asking her to persuade Tenzing to accept the British offer, and armed with tins of Ovaltine and endless patience, she mounted a sustained campaign to win him over. Still weak and underweight, as well as mentally exhausted, Tenzing equivocated.

Ang Lhamu was determined not to let him throw his life away on some obsession with a mountain. After Tenzing's success she gave an interview, which appeared in Lord Beaverbrook's *Daily Express*, explaining her objections to Tenzing's going back: "The ice is slippery, and if there is any accident to you, what will happen to me and the children?" Tenzing, she says, told her: "I can't stop until I have climbed Everest. I would rather die on Everest than die in your hut."

Tenzing, through Ullman, spends a long time explaining his reasons for his indecision in accepting Wylie's invitation. Partly, this was to answer as honestly as he could media speculation after the climb about his relationship with the British. He acknowledges that he preferred the Swiss to the British, whom he finds "more reserved and formal than the men of most other countries I have known; and especially is this so, I think, with people not of their own race." John Hunt himself recognized this problem in a review of Tenzing's book: "This reserve of ours is proverbial. It has nothing to do with the background of our rule in India, but it is certainly a handicap. It naturally contrasts with the convivial temperament of the Sherpas, who find themselves in this respect more akin to certain others, in particular the Latin peoples."[1] But characterizing people purely on the basis of nationality was clumsy, and unfair to a group of climbers who respected him.[2] Tenzing did share tents with the British, and most of the other Sherpas had a warm relationship with the British. His teammate Wilfrid Noyce wrote, "All honour to him; he regarded himself most seriously as a climber, a representative of the Sherpas who should go to the top, and only secondly as a *sirdar*. And a fine climber he was, or he could never have been chosen."[3]

Tenzing had long experience with the British colonial establishment and made the assumption that this expedition would involve more of the same attitudes. The comments Tenzing made on the British character reflected more his personal objection to being treated as anything less than an equal. Trevor Braham said, "He was afraid that he'd join this army officer John Hunt and he would be treated like a servant again. He was thinking: 'I don't want to be treated like a servant anymore.'" To put it more bluntly, the Swiss had treated him as an equal, so why should he go and work for people who would treat him as an inferior?

His friends, however, pressed him to take the job. Tenzing might have wanted to climb the mountain with Raymond Lambert, but Lambert himself knew that Everest would probably be climbed in 1953 or 1954, certainly before the Swiss could get back there, and he encouraged

Tenzing to take the chance. Rabi Mitra also insisted that he go. "I told him: 'Tenzing, if you miss this chance and the British climb Everest, you'll be hitting your head against the wall with frustration.' After that he changed his mind." What Lambert and Mitra knew, and Tenzing had to accept, was that if he didn't go, then alternative plans were in place. "Hunt said that if you can't get Tenzing then you must get Ang Tharkay," Trevor Braham recalled. Despite his weakened state, despite his ambivalence for the British, he had no choice. At 39, time was running out for him anyway. One morning he went to Jill Henderson's house and accepted the offer. He took the chance. "There was that element of greatness about him," Mitra told me. "And God helps those who help themselves."

Once the decision had been made, Tenzing became driven by the challenge, avoiding cigarettes and alcohol, and training to recover his strength by hiking with a rucksack filled with stones. He told Mitra that this time "he would do or die."

In agreeing to go back to Everest for the third time in a little over a year, Tenzing set definite conditions that he wanted his employers to meet. He wanted to be treated as a full climbing member, just as he had by the Swiss. John Hunt was more than happy to oblige, but Tenzing remained suspicious that the British expedition would be a quasi-military affair in which Sherpas were treated merely as the hired help. Hunt—"A terrific Thruster," according to the secretary of the Himalayan Committee—had been brought in as leader precisely because of his military experience, replacing Eric Shipton in a scandalously underhanded and shoddy piece of realpolitik which appalled Hunt as much as anyone. The difference between the two leaders was neatly put by Ingrid Caufield, who got to know both men well in the 1960s. "To Hunt," she wrote, "an 'assault' on the mountain merely meant a concerted, military-style operation: whereas to Shipton 'assault' sounded more like a criminal offence." The Himalayan Committee was making a deliberate decision to put an able administrator in charge of climbing Everest. It lacked romance, but as John Hunt told his initially suspicious team of climbers, "This was going to be no ordinary climb."[4] The technical, dull but crucial details of oxygen and supply would be hammered out. The Himalayan Committee had turned their backs on Shipton's freewheeling approach for a pragmatist: "Everyone had accepted the importance of aiming single-mindedly for the summit."[5]

If the British were constructing a well-oiled machine, then the Sherpas were the oil. Tenzing's role would be critical. As sirdar he would be a key figure in executing the logistical plan drawn up in the expedition's offices in London. If the Sherpas didn't work well, then neither would the expedition. A brief comparison of the weight of supplies carried to the South Col in the spring of 1952 and 1953 offers a bald illustration of how, behind the heroism and excitement of the summit climb, was a logistical framework on which the glory hung. For Lambert and Tenzing's attempt, only four Sherpas, including Tenzing, reached the South Col, with three Swiss. In 1953, thirteen Sherpas reached the South Col, six of them twice, delivering 750 pounds of supplies at 26,000 feet for the two assault teams to draw on. "If there is one thing that I would like to come out," Charles Wylie told me, "is just how important the role of the Sherpas was in our success on Everest."

On March 1, Tenzing said good-bye to his family. His daughters remember the house was filled with well-wishers, drinking tea and offering him katas, ceremonial scarves given in welcome or farewell. Nima wanted her father to put on the summit a red-and-blue pencil she took from her school satchel. Rabi Mitra gave him a small Indian flag to "put in the right place," as Mitra called the summit.

Most of the expedition members arrived in Kathmandu on March 8 and found the Sherpas and advance party, Tenzing included, in the garden of the British Embassy sorting out loads for the long march to Base Camp. All the climbers apart from Charles Wylie were meeting him for the first time, and their first impressions build a composite both of Tenzing and, indirectly, of themselves. Hunt was generous and polite: "Tenzing's simplicity and gaiety quite charmed us, and we were quickly impressed by his authority in the role of sirdar."[6] Ed Hillary, in his first autobiography, was perfunctory, but in his third allowed more detail: "It was impossible not to be warmed by his flashing smile and charming manner, though I didn't really become a very close friend of Tenzing until the last few years of his life, when I was in India."[7] More fulsome descriptions were given by some of the less well-known members of the expedition. Michael Ward, the doctor, gives a characteristically precise and cool assessment:

He was of average height and moved very well, with a natural grace and ease which is so characteristic of those who spend their lives travelling in mountainous country. It seemed as if he were on oiled wheels. When stripped I noticed that his arms were much more muscular than those of the normal Sherpa whose upper limbs are not usually so well developed.

His whole body was finely but not grossly muscular, and seemed to be more like that of a young man in his twenties rather than one ten years older.... Tenzing usually wore a wide-brimmed sloppy hat and was always clean and neatly dressed. He had gracious, unforced good manners. His charming smile went well with the considerable authority he had over the other Sherpas. He was very experienced at high altitude, though not nearly so technically competent as any of the Europeans with whom he climbed. Unusually he wanted to get to the top of Everest, an ambition extremely uncommon amongst Sherpas, although they possessed the physical capacity.

Wilfrid Noyce, a poet, author, and schoolmaster who would die tragically in 1962 in an avalanche in the Pamirs, caught the different levels of Tenzing's relationship with his employers: "Tenzing is tall for a Sherpa (he is really a Bhutia) and heavy, weighing over ten stone. He appeared before us with the energetic air of an efficient climber; his every garment, and the axe that Raymond Lambert had given him, reminded you that he had served with expeditions. He knew his way about.... It struck me from the first that the dark eyes under the jet-black hair brushed straight back became thoughtful when summits were mentioned. This characteristic distinguished Tenzing, as I see it, from any other of his race that I know, Angtharkay included."[8]

Noyce also saw how well Tenzing understood the need to dress the part he was playing. Although the other Sherpas wore whatever they had been given on earlier expeditions—a French woollen hat, a pair of English plus-fours—Tenzing was dressed in "military-style shorts and puttees, topped by a green beret, giving him a more commanding appearance."[9] Despite his antipathy for military hierarchies, Tenzing knew how to command. The younger Sherpas tiptoed around him with respect, even fear.

He had presence, a calm, authoritative figure at the heart of an efficient organization. Wherever he went, he made things happen.

Hunt had asked for Tenzing to bring 20 Sherpas with him from Darjeeling who would be used as high-altitude porters, specialists who had been tried and tested. Another 18 were hired in Khumbu. His deputy was Da Tenzing, the pig-tailed, austere patriarch from Khumjung whose connection with his homeland contrasted with Tenzing's ability to absorb practices from outside his own culture. What they had in common was the air of natural authority they both carried. Da Tenzing was seven years older than Tenzing, but still immensely strong, carrying twice to the South Col in 1953 and later working as sirdar on the successful 1955 expedition to Kanchenjunga. He had brought his son Mingma with him for his first job on an expedition, the son who years later would be killed climbing, tipping Da Tenzing's wife into suicidal grief.

John Hunt had also asked specifically for Dawa Thondup. He had known him from an expedition to the Karakoram before the war, and Da Thondup also knew Charles Wylie. Now in his late 40s, he was the oldest Sherpa on the expedition and enjoyed a drink or three, although this didn't stop him making two carries to the South Col despite joining the expedition late while he recovered from illness.

At the other end of the scale was Gombu, Tenzing's 17-year-old nephew, who was, Wilfrid Noyce observed, the only Sherpa he ever met who asked a sahib to walk more slowly. Gombu, who had given up his studies at Rongbuk to join his uncle, would become one of the strongest Sherpas in history, meeting President Kennedy after climbing Everest with the Americans in 1963 and becoming the first man to climb the mountain twice in 1965 with an Indian team. "When I was at the monastery, the monks used to say that there was a golden calf on the summit and that's why the foreigners climbed," he told me. As a boy, Gombu wasn't overawed by climbing with the sahibs, and he asked Hunt as they climbed slowly up the Western Cwm why Hunt was carrying only one oxygen bottle when he had two. When they reached camp, Hunt told Tenzing about Gombu's remark. Hunt thought it funny, but his uncle wasn't pleased. "*Kina?*—Why?"[10] Lhatoo believes that Tenzing didn't give Gombu the credit he deserved, keeping his protégé in his shadow. Gombu himself recalled Tenzing asking him what the point was of climbing Everest twice.

Tenzing also hired his other nephew, Nawang Topgay, who had carried to the South Col the previous spring and survived the fall of ice that had killed Mingma Dorje. In 1953 he was 22, but Charles Wylie remembered him looking five years younger. His mother had recently arrived from Tibet after the death of Topgay's father and was living in Nauche.

Ang Nima was another veteran of the Swiss expeditions, a chainsmoker who required his own special ration of cigarettes. Sherpas call cigarettes Sherpa oxygen, which might explain why he was able to carry to the top camp used by Tenzing and Hillary—Camp IX on the Southeast Ridge—one of only three Sherpas to go higher than the South Col. The other two were Tenzing himself and Da Namgyal, a shy man whose slight frostbite, sustained carrying a load to 27,500 feet, was the only injury suffered by anyone on the expedition.

The British were seduced by the smiles and good humor of these men, and the women too who carried loads as heavy as the men and flirted and laughed all the way to Base Camp. Dressed in their high-altitude motley, they were a strange new hybrid of East and West and as fascinating to the climbers as they were to the crowds who gathered to watch the expedition. James Morris, later Jan Morris,[11] the *Times* correspondent who joined the expedition at Tengboche, described encountering Sen Tensing—the Sherpa Tilman had dubbed "The Foreign Sportsman"—who trekked with him to Khumbu: "On his head was a brown woollen Balaclava helmet with a peak, like the hats the Russian Army used to wear. His grey sports shirt had polished major's crowns on its epaulettes. Over long woollen pants he wore a voluminous pair of blue shorts, and on his feet were elderly gym shoes. A confused variety of beads, tokens and Tibetan charms dangled around his neck, and a bracelet hung upon his wrist. In one hand he flourished an ice axe, in the other a fly-whisk."

The high-altitude porters had a correspondingly strong impact on the local Nepalese. The tiny, wealthy elite thought it peculiar that these ignorant and unimportant Bhotias were the object of so much respect and affection. For those at the bottom of the heap, those carrying loads not for cash but for food, they must have seemed like movie stars. These differences of perspective are important because right from the start of the expedition, hierarchies and money dominated the mood of the Sherpas in general and Tenzing in particular.

None of the accounts of the British record the outrage Tenzing says the Sherpas felt when they were billeted in a stable block in the British Embassy compound, or that the Sherpas urinated in the street outside to protest their treatment. Tenzing says he is just being honest and laying the facts out as he saw them. The British were exploiting them, slipping back into the role of colonial masters. Yet for other Sherpas, being housed in a garage wasn't a problem, as Gombu acknowledged. They had all slept in far worse, and where else were they going to piss than the road outside?

The Sherpas were far more interested in the equipment the British were going to give them. This formed a substantial part of their wages. Livelihoods had been made by the income generated selling this equipment. The Swiss, generally better off than the British and less aloof, had been generous with these perks. The signs were not so good with the British. The climb would be more tightly controlled, and their kit wouldn't even be handed out until the expedition reached Tengboche. (The Sherpas took this as a slight as well until one of them pointed out that at least that meant someone else would have to carry the stuff to Base Camp.)

As far as Hunt was concerned, he was treating the Sherpas as fairly as he could. It hadn't been his decision to put the Sherpas in a stable. That was a decision taken by the British Embassy. The situation was complicated because the embassy officials were enraged by the Sherpas' behavior, which most climbers found quite funny. How the British were perceived nagged at the ambassador, Christopher Summerhayes, who was irritated by any negative coverage that undermined national prestige. When the *Daily Mail*'s correspondent Ralph Izzard filed a story suggesting that Tenzing had been happier working for the Swiss, Summerhayes was furious, telling the Foreign Office in London: "[Izzard] behaved badly by sending that unpleasant report about Tensing preferring to climb with the French or Swiss. This is infuriating in a place where other nationalities have cut in, mainly by paying lavishly and spoiling very happy relations."[12]

Influenced by Summerhayes, Hunt decided to give Tenzing's men a formal reprimand, a tactical error because Sherpas hate being bossed around, and the tension quickly became an issue for the expedition as a whole. If Hunt had laughed off the episode and encouraged them not to do it again, the Sherpas might have taken the formal, military atmosphere Hunt was creating less seriously. As for the terms of their employment, Hunt couldn't see what the Sherpas had to complain about. The British were matching what the Swiss had paid and had actually doubled the life insurance offered from 1,000 to 2,000 rupees. In modern values that equates to about $3,000, which is not far off what Sherpas receive now. Tenzing was earning 300 rupees a month, a premium rate in 1953. With tips and bonuses, this would also come close to what a sirdar makes in the modern era. These are paltry sums in comparison with Western wages, but in the context of Nepal are still—for the immediate future—worthwhile for men determined to change their circumstances.

In most ways the grumbling, tension, and even confrontation that marked the early part of the 1953 expedition were no worse than the difficulties faced by other expeditions of all nationalities. The Sherpas were shrewd and had long experience of improving their working conditions. The 1953 expedition was an exceptional chapter in the history of exploration, but that doesn't mean its problems were exceptional. Although Tenzing didn't know any of the climbers, other Sherpas did, and they remained good friends with many of the British and New Zealanders after it was over. When Da Tenzing was discovered to be living in near penury in Khumbu, his British friends organized a "pension" for him. Tenzing himself maintained good relations with the British, especially Charles Wylie. Whatever bitterness there was did not run that deep.

Pasang Phutar—the Jockey—did try to make political capital by accusing the British of being exploitative, but then the Swiss had found his attitude a problem too. Charles Wylie believed he was part of the communist movement in Darjeeling, and some have suggested that his comrades had persuaded him to derail the British attempt as a blow against colonialism. Pasang Phutar may have been a communist—Lhatoo remembers he liked to describe himself as all kinds of things—but this was no politically inspired revolution, just agitation for more than the British were prepared to give. When his agitation became detrimental to the expedition, Hunt, Wylie, and Tenzing held a kind of tribunal, which sacked Pasang Phutar from the expedition at Tengboche in early April. "He had given trouble before because of his laziness," Noyce wrote, "and seemed to understand the cause of his dismissal. He asked to be reinstated, but the resignation was insisted upon. Tenzing marched him into the big tent, rather like a sergeant-major before his colonel. John handed him his money. He gave back his clothes and went."[13] Tenzing had felt a debt of loyalty to Pasang Phutar that is difficult to explain. He had appointed him deputy sirdar, even though he knew there were better men for the post, but in sharing in the decision to sack him he reasserted his control over the Sherpas. In any case, almost all the difficulties between the British and the Sherpas evaporated when they started climbing Everest. With their girlfriends gone, the supply of chang reduced and their anxieties about pay and baksheesh settled, they simply got on with the job.

Tenzing, however, was in a different position. As both a climbing member and head of the Sherpas, he had to present the Sherpas' case in any disputes and keep the supplies moving up the mountain, yet he no longer shared the Sherpas' prime motivation—to make money. Getting to the summit had become much more important than his pay. His personal ambition had turned him into an innovator for his people, a trailblazer for future generations. "Come on!" he recalls telling his Sherpas, "Stop fussing about all these little things. We have a mountain to climb!"[14]

Balancing these often conflicting demands, coupled with his sensitivity, left Tenzing vulnerable to overreacting. His account of the early days of the 1953 expedition drips with the frustration that he is being overlooked. Hillary recalled a large party of Sherpas bringing the first loads through the Icefall with Tenzing among them:

> *It was Tenzing's first trip above Base Camp for the year and I didn't think he seemed very happy. With the Swiss he had been one of the lead climbers but John Hunt had felt that at this stage his influence and experience would be more valuable organising the other Sherpas and their loads up the icefall. I had considerable respect for Tenzing's reputation but it never entered my mind that we needed his help in tackling the difficult ice problems which I accepted we were quite capable of dealing with ourselves. No wonder Tenzing always had a warmer affection for the Swiss than he ever did for us.[15]*

Hunt, a sensitive man himself—he was a compassionate social reformer who believed India should have achieved independence before the war—was a capable leader. Although he had been born in Simla and was very much an army officer, he was not mired in a colonial ethos. He was anxious to see a Sherpa stand on the summit of Everest and knew that Tenzing was the man to do it. Hunt could have made this plainer, but Tenzing's anxiety about being shunted aside was largely unjustified. Most of the British performed supporting roles, and while they were disappointed not to be included in the summit teams, they were content that the team as a whole had been successful. Hunt knew that in the early stages it was in the expedition's interests for Tenzing to organize the Sherpas and kept him at the back, even though Tenzing was very reluctant to do so. Hillary remembered how, at the top of the Icefall, Hunt asked Tenzing to go down to sort out a logistical problem while he and others continued exploring the route. "Tenzing was quite indignant," Hillary recalled. "He was being sent down to do an important job but he wasn't gathered into the group of us who crossed the bridge and went on up. It wasn't the fancy job, but it was important. The year before, he was constantly with Lambert and they built up a very close relationship."

Hunt knew that a good supply line was essential for success. He wrote to his wife, Joy, on June 1, just after the ascent: "Some terribly difficult decisions had to be made, but somehow they have each and all turned out alright. I've felt very sure of the rightness of each one, as of the final outcome, all along, as though guided along a pre-destined track."[16]

Tenzing's impatience to be up at the front was shared by Ed Hillary, who wasn't inclined as Tenzing was to keep his own counsel. Making a summit attempt was also in Hillary's mind, and he made no secret of his confidence in being one of those selected. George Band, then only 23 to Hillary's 34, was impressed at how quickly the New Zealander positioned himself as a front-runner. Hillary wanted to go to the summit with the other New Zealander, George Lowe, but knew that Hunt wouldn't allow the old friends to team up in this way: "I always felt that [John Hunt] was nervous of us New Zealanders hijacking his expedition with our energy and our snow and ice skills."[17] Instead, he would have to form another partnership that would be more acceptable.

On April 26, two days after Hillary encountered Tenzing leading the first big team of Sherpas through the Icefall, the two of them tied into a rope for the first time. They planned to move the route up to where the British were planning to site their Advance Base, the Swiss Camp IV, and perhaps carry some supplies up. While Hunt and Charles Evans were on another rope, Hillary and Tenzing quickly showed how strong they were at altitude, making a diversion to rummage through the Swiss Camp III, then catching and overtaking the other two. "I was feeling particularly fit and pushed on hard," Hillary recalled. Tenzing made sure he did some leading too, wading through the deep snow of the Western Cwm, the sun searing down on the four tiny figures crawling up the white glacier, the glare reflecting off the steep white walls that boxed them in.

At the Swiss Camp IV, Hillary and Tenzing discovered a cache of abandoned food—biscuits, cheese, jam, porridge, and bacon—a welcome change from the dull military rations the British had brought. Then they turned their attention to the Lhotse Face. Standing halfway between the top of the Icefall and the steep slopes below the South Col, Hunt reckoned it would take only two or three more days to push the route up to 8,000 meters. Evans and Hillary were much less optimistic, figuring on a week. No one records if Tenzing said anything, but he could have warned them it would take much longer than that. They finally reached the South Col more than three weeks later. Hillary was in an optimistic mood, though, boosted by his strong performance that day. At the top of the Icefall he met George Lowe settling in at Camp II. As they left for Base Camp, Hillary told Lowe that he would radio up from Base Camp by five that afternoon, leaving himself an hour to get down. "That'll be the day," Lowe challenged him. Hillary set off at a jog with Tenzing running behind him. In the "Atom Bomb" area he jumped a crevasse only for its overhanging lip to collapse. In the split second he had to think, Hillary realized he might be trapped by the huge block his weight had broken off as it tumbled into the black slot of the crevasse with him. He threw himself away from the tumbling ice, and Tenzing, reacting quickly, held him on the rope, whipping the slack around his ax, which he drove into the snow. It snapped tight, and Hillary quickly scrambled out, chopping steps into the ice with his ax and jamming his back against the crevasse's facing wall while Tenzing pulled in the rope to protect and assist him.

Hillary's account of this incident—over in a minute but potentially catastrophic for both of them—mellowed over the years. In *High Adventure,* published in 1955, he depicts a young man determined to show that he was always in control, and the rope comes tight just as he catches himself on the walls of the crevasse. In his most recent autobiography, *View From the Summit,* the story has a wry, more human tone and gives Tenzing the credit: "I had time to start realising if the rope didn't come tight pretty soon I was going to come to a very sticky end at the bottom of the crevasse." In Tenzing's account of the same incident, he pulled Hillary out of the crevasse "with slow hauling and pulling," an almost impossible feat for an unaided individual, as most climbers know. Judging by the dialogue Ullman uses, this version was based on the interview Tenzing gave to United Press after the expedition, an account that the agency's sub-editors would have made as dramatic as they could. More recently, Jamling Norgay Tenzing's version of his father's accident emphasizes Tenzing's role even more: "My father, after positioning himself to gain some leverage, was able to gradually haul Hillary up to the edge of the crevasse, with some help from Hillary's single cramponed foot. He had lost his ice axe and a crampon in the fall."[18]

On any other expedition this would have been a minor incident that would have given both men a good story. Protecting each other on a glacier is just what climbers do, part of the responsibility that comes with tying into a rope, and not that big a deal. If both men had told slightly different versions over a beer or a cup of chang, then so what? Everest in 1953, however, was no ordinary expedition, and the interaction between Hillary and Tenzing has been picked over in minute detail, especially by those with a political or personal agenda of their own. This shading has been most prominent in accounts of the climb to the summit on May 29, but the crevasse incident touches on the same issues.

Hillary fell into the crevasse partly because he was in such a rush to get to Base Camp within an hour of radioing George Lowe. He was proving a point: that he was fit and strong and should be in the running for a place on the summit team. It's a common fault. Climbing judgment is often impaired by such motives, and Tenzing was just as prone to this.

The upshot of Hillary's near-miss was to persuade the New Zealander that Tenzing was the man with whom he should go to the top. "I had found Tenzing an admirable companion—capable, willing, and extremely pleasant," Hillary wrote in *High Adventure*. "His rope-work was first class as my near-catastrophe had shown. Although not perhaps technically outstanding in ice-craft, he was very strong and determined and an excellent acclimatiser. Best of all, as far as I was concerned, he was prepared to go fast and hard."[19] In *View From the Summit,* the older and wiser Hillary adds: "For the first time an idea entered my mind—it seemed very unlikely that John Hunt would let George Lowe and me climb together—you couldn't have two New Zealanders getting to the top—but what about Tenzing and me? It seemed a good idea and I decided to encourage it."[20]

The names Tenzing and Hillary are now so thoroughly interlinked that it is impossible to imagine one without the other, like Gilbert and Sullivan or Rodgers and Hammerstein. Yet they weren't particularly good friends and didn't even know each other well, at least not until late in Tenzing's life. The nature of the big, prestigious expeditions in the 1950s meant that some unlikely combinations were inevitable. Had the British expedition failed and had the French reached the summit the following year, or had Charles Evans and Tom Bourdillon reached the summit ahead of them, Hillary's partnership with Tenzing would have been a footnote, not a headline.

On the surface, they were very different. "An oddly assorted pair," James Morris wrote, the tall New Zealander who "moved with an incongruous grace, rather like a giraffe," alongside the sharply dressed Bhotia—"a Himalayan fashion model," Morris called him—whose luminous smile and eagerness to help endeared him so quickly to the climbers who employed him. Although Tenzing's people had been rooted in the landscape and culture of Everest for a thousand years, the New Zealander came from a nation that was in the process of creating itself. "Though it was a remote and raw colonial society," Hillary wrote, "it yet had many liberal characteristics. It was the first country in the world to give women the vote. Life was certainly tough in those days—a constant battle for survival—but it produced pioneer people who were both hard-working and amazingly creative."[21]

In terms of their personality, however, Hillary and Tenzing had much more in common than it appeared. Both men felt there was a bigger and

brighter world on the outside of their narrow societies that could offer
them the opportunity to fulfill their dreams. "Even in those early days,
I was a great dreamer," Hillary wrote, echoing Tenzing's own childhood.
"I used to go for long walks about the area, or cut across the paddocks,
jumping over the fences with my mind far away, just thinking about
adventures and exciting things to do. I'd have a stick in my hand and
imagine it was a sword and that I was fighting great battles."[22]

Hillary appeared tough, but was more emotional than he seemed.
Tenzing, to Western climbers at least, appeared eager to please but was
shrewder and harder than his appearance allowed. Both of them disliked
British diffidence and for the same reason: They saw it as a superior attitude. Hillary's childhood was marked by an often-abrasive relationship
with his father, a journalist turned beekeeper, and a shortage of money.
His grandfather had lost a small fortune betting on horses, and his grandmother raised his father with a mixture of moral conservatism and rigid
independence. In Hillary this background translated as a sensitivity to
perceived slight coupled with the kind of character that would get you
to the top of Everest. Circumstance had made Hillary and Tenzing burn
with ambition.

The two men also had something else in common; the nature of their
mountaineering background was similar. Hillary had learned to climb in
New Zealand, as remote and tough if not as high as the Himalaya, where
the ability to keep going and suffer hardship was as valuable as the ability to cut steps or finesse an awkward pitch of rock climbing. Tenzing's
acts of prodigious strength in ferrying loads high on Everest in 1952 came
from the same well of stamina, a mixture of physical strength and
psychological desire, that drove Hillary.

Throughout the early part of May 1953, Tenzing and Hillary climbed
together. Hillary hit on the idea of showing Hunt how fit they both were
by climbing from Base Camp to Advanced Base—Camp IV at over 21,000
feet—and back again in a day. "It probably served only one purpose—to
show how fit a team Tenzing and I were."[23] As a display, it was persuasive.
Hunt's most awkward decision as leader was to select the climbers who
would try for the summit. He spent the evening of May 6 in his tent, "his
typewriter tapping away," as Hillary recalled it, finalizing plans for the
next stage of the expedition. The selection was complicated by the job

being only half done. He still had to put the expedition onto the South Col with sufficient strength to reach the top. His climbers, on the other hand, were thinking about the summit already, and there was the danger of the team as a whole losing its focus. He had to plan to keep the summit teams fresh and those opening the route to the South Col motivated.

The following morning the expedition gathered at Base Camp to hear his decision. Inside the mess tent there was an atmosphere of intense excitement. Sitting in the corner taking notes was the journalist James Morris, quietly trying to figure out code words so that every possible catastrophe that might befall them would remain exclusive to the *Times*. "Tenzing sat there inscrutably," Morris wrote, "graceful and attentive, like a demi-god on parade before Zeus."[24] When the teams were announced—first Evans and Bourdillon, next Hillary and Tenzing—Morris thought he saw "the slightest flicker of satisfaction cross Tenzing's face, though in fact (we learnt later) he considered a Sherpa should have been in both parties; Hillary looked as if he had just been picked for the First XI, and was thinking about oiling his bat." (What Tenzing really said, in a private comment to John Hunt, was that there should have been a Sherpa in the first party. What he really meant was that he should have been in the first attempt; no other Sherpas were agitating for a try at the summit.) Michael Ward had a more immediate objection to Hunt's plan. He thought that Hunt had set himself too demanding a role in going high on the mountain in support, in effect leading from the front. Ward, as doctor, was being kept low, and as an experienced climber he resented it. Both Alf Gregory and Ward thought the first assault team of Charles Evans and Tom Bourdillon had no chance of success and served no useful purpose.

Hunt's plan for this first attempt on the summit has provoked a lot of speculation among Everest historians. Just how serious an attempt was it? Evans and Bourdillon would be starting from the South Col at almost 8,000 meters and using a different kind of oxygen system, a "closed" apparatus that recycled the climbers' exhalations through a "rebreather." Theoretically this got rid of the need for so many oxygen bottles and made supply more straightforward. The closed-circuit sets were very heavy, but they gave a far higher flow of oxygen, up to eight liters a minute. They required a spare canister of soda-lime, but otherwise were self-contained enough to allow climbers a realistic attempt from the South

Col without the need for resupply. If the system worked, then the climbers had a chance to rush the summit. But there were faults with the apparatus, which Bourdillon himself had worked on developing. When the canisters were changed in low temperatures, the system's valves froze solid. Hunt knew this, and some historians, following Ward and Gregory's view, believe the more logical approach to give Evans and Bourdillon a real chance was to place a camp on the Southeast Ridge 1,500 feet above the South Col first, and then start the attempts on the summit with an "open" system. Hillary certainly believed that the first attempt had the South Summit as its real objective, a kind of reconnaissance in force with the option of going on only if conditions were perfect.

Ward and Gregory were proved correct, at least as far as the result was concerned. On May 26 Bourdillon and Evans were delayed from starting their summit attempt by more than an hour because they had to fix a problem with the oxygen set Evans was using, and when they changed canisters on The Balcony at 27,600 feet later in the day, his system failed again. Until that point, however, they had made superb progress, climbing the first 1,300 feet in only an hour and a half. Despite poor weather, bad snow conditions, and then difficulties with the oxygen system that slowed them down, they still reached the South Summit from the South Col at one o'clock *having set off at 7:30.* Most climbers attempting Everest from what is now called Camp IV start at around midnight, a full seven and a half hours before Evans and Bourdillon left, and one o'clock is still often cited as the critical point at which climbers should turn around, successful or not. Had Charles Evans enjoyed the same reliable flow of oxygen that Bourdillon had, Everest would have been climbed on May 26, three days before Hillary and Tenzing's attempt. The Sherpas at the South Col thought for a short while that Everest itself *had* been climbed, believing that the South Summit was the true summit. Ang Nima, arriving at the Col with a load, told John Hunt: "*Everest khatam ho gya, Sahib—Everest has had it.*"

Tenzing was bitterly disappointed. Approaching the South Col, he and Hillary watched the two tiny figures of Evans and Bourdillon approaching the South Summit. "The Sherpas," Hillary wrote, "fully convinced that the two men were going to reach the top, were in a cheerful and noisy frame of mind, but Tenzing, in reply to my enthusiastic comments, seemed strangely silent."[25] That night Hillary discovered the reason Tenzing had been "so morose": "He desperately wanted a Sherpa to be in the first summit team, and he was as always confident that he himself was the right Sherpa for this task."[26] Hunt, lying exhausted in his tent after carrying a load onto the ridge for Hillary and Tenzing's attempt, wondered aloud if the news of a successful ascent could reach Britain in time for the coronation of Queen Elizabeth. As he waited for Evans and Bourdillon to return, Tenzing took this as proof that Hunt wanted Englishmen to reach the summit first. Later he would strenuously deny his resentment. "There is no 'first' or 'second,' and Hunt has just now almost killed himself carrying up supplies for Hillary and me."[27] But there was a "first" and a "second," and when Evans and Bourdillon returned coated in ice and close to collapse without the prize, both Hillary and Tenzing were a little relieved that the "first" was still there. Hillary wrote: "I greatly admired what Charles and Tom had done but I had a regrettable feeling of satisfaction as well. They hadn't got to the top—there was still a job to be done."[28]

It depends on your view of human nature whether the ambition and drive of Tenzing and Hillary put them on top of the heap, or whether out of a group of very strong and dedicated individuals they were the two who got the breaks. In any case, since someone had to climb Everest it would be difficult to imagine a much better outcome than Hillary and Tenzing having a chance. More than that, if anyone deserved the summit, it was Tenzing. Success in 1953 stemmed from a concerted effort, depending on good preparation and teamwork, and the linchpin for much of that effort was Tenzing himself.

For much of May the expedition's effort had hovered on the brink of collapse. The lead climbers spent 12 days stalled on the Lhotse Face, trying to push the route up to the South Col and opening the way for the summit teams to attempt the upper reaches of the Southeast Ridge. The slow progress wasn't through lack of effort. George Lowe spent 11 days above 23,000 feet trying to get things moving, but other expedition members were handicapped with illness, and the Sherpas did not manage to deliver the supplies needed for a final push toward the summit.

Hunt decided to send two groups of Sherpas, one led by Wilf Noyce and the other by Charles Wylie, to push on before the route to the Col was completed, while Lowe came down for a well-earned rest. On May 21, the climbers watched anxiously for signs of movement at Camp VII, high on the Lhotse Face. Outside the tents, Noyce and Annullu tried to motivate the other seven Sherpas to carry to the South Col. "Groans resounded from the tents. Some had dragged themselves out; one or two were looking at the loads with an eye which could only be called 'wan.' I asked who was well enough to come on up, and [one] stocky figure came forward."[29]

At Camp IV, Hunt watched with frustration as only two figures left Camp VII toward the South Col at around ten in the morning. There would be no big lift to the South Col that day after all. Noyce and Annullu were going on alone to break trail to the Col. With radio contact to Camp VII lost, Hunt had little idea of exactly what was happening, but Charles Wylie was due to arrive at Camp VII that afternoon with another eight Sherpas. As things stood, it would be down to Wylie to lead his Sherpas and any of Noyce's who were still fit to the South Col the following day. The expedition had reached its critical moment. Hunt realized that the situation was teetering on the brink of collapse.

At this moment Hillary attempted to intervene. "I'm not very good at begging, but I went over to John Hunt's tent and literally pleaded with him to let me and Tenzing go up to Camp VII and spur on the major lift the next day. I was absolutely sure that Tenzing and I could go to the South Col and return and still be fit for our assault on the summit."[30] To his credit, Hunt agreed, despite the risk of exhaustion his decision posed to his fittest climbers. Just as had happened on Everest in 1952, Tenzing's intervention in motivating the other Sherpas proved critical. "Some of them had headaches and sore throats, and all of course were tired, but no one was really sick, and it had mostly been fear of the mountain that had kept them from going on."[31] Some of the Sherpas were strong and had been going well. Ang Nima, the chain-smoker, had worked hard with Lowe on the Lhotse Face. Annullu, who went with Noyce to the col, was Dawa Tenzing's younger brother. Noyce wrote: "He must have shared the cigarette record with Ang Nima, and yet these were probably our best two Sherpas. There was about the amount that he smoked and drank, as well as the general reserve of the puckered eyes, a veneer of westernism contrasting strongly with his rugged brother. At the same time there was also in the smooth round face, when it smiled, something that gave confidence."[32]

Noyce wrote a great deal about many of the Sherpas in his account of the expedition, *South Col*, always respectfully and with a great deal of curiosity. While Tenzing and Hillary were climbing to the summit on May 29, he was climbing with three Sherpas to the South Col without bottled oxygen in support. Besides noticing that he was climbing better without oxygen than he had with it the week before, he paid close attention to the men alongside him. Pasang Phutar,[33] Ang Dorje, and Phu Dorje were all strong climbers, particularly Phu Dorje (who went on to climb Everest himself in 1965 with an Indian expedition but was tragically killed in the Icefall in October 1969 when a snow bridge collapsed). On May 29, Phu Dorje was nearing the South Col for the second time when Noyce asked him to take Ang Dorje, who had sat down in the snow and showed little sign of wanting to continue, back to Camp VII:

"Phu Dorje, tall and piratical of appearance, with orange balaclava and perpetually dirty face, was one of the most reliable. He was well set for the Col, and could have reached it easily. But he took the order without hesitation. A trained Sherpa, he was doing his job, obeying the sahib's instructions and going down. That, I think, is the attitude of these men. They have come to climbing through load-carrying. Load-carrying is the job and mountaineering a higher-paid carrying job than most. To be among the mountains, yes. That is their life, their work. To be on the snow is a different matter, hard work and dangerous at times. Sherpas have been killed on Everest. Therefore Phu Dorje went down, and I do not think he regretted it, for I later gave him the recommendation of a man who had reached the South Col twice. With Tenzing it would have been different."[34]

When Tenzing reached Camp VII on the afternoon of May 21, after a rapid four-and-a-half-hour ascent from Camp IV, he set about restoring the morale of his men. His loyalty to the expedition and his own personal ambition gave his words an irresistible force. He wasn't going to let the expedition founder because the Sherpas wouldn't get out of their tent in the morning. If Tenzing hadn't persuaded the Sherpas to move again, then no one could have. Charles Wylie, who was at Camp VII that evening with Tenzing, remembers how much the sirdar did in restoring confidence to the team. "They really did have such respect for him," he said, "that when he arrived it made all the difference." In the morning Tenzing got the stove going at six, producing a drink for all the men despite the overcrowding at Camp VII. A few of the Sherpas added Grape-Nuts to their tea, but most of them had nothing to eat all day. Charles Wylie turned out his pockets for the last boiled sweet and despite their weakness and fatigue, they all kept going. Tenzing's presence, urging them forward, had solved the crisis.

Using oxygen to climb to the Col, Hillary and Tenzing led the way, carving a trail in the snow and adding a load of oxygen to their own when one of the Sherpas—who weren't using bottled gas—turned around. A few of the Sherpas would spend a third night at Camp VII, struggling back to their tent as darkness fell. Others, like Dawa Thondup, put in an extra effort and raced all the way down to the security and warmth of Advance Base at 21,000 feet. Hillary and Tenzing, having climbed 5,000 feet to the South Col in 24 hours, now turned around and hurried back to Advance Base as well, passing Bourdillon and Evans on the way up for the first summit attempt. The expedition was back on track. Hillary and Tenzing recovered from their effort within a couple of days. The gamble had paid off.

TOM BOURDILLON WAS A BIG MAN, "built like a second-row rugby player," according to John Hunt, and strong. He was also one of the most talented alpine climbers in Britain in the post-war period, admittedly in an age when the Alpine Club was at an ebb and the working-class heroes of the mid-1950s had yet to emerge. When he and Charles Evans reached the South Summit on May 26, Bourdillon pressed on a little farther, still determined, climbing down to the start of the final summit ridge as though unable to accept that their climb was over. "Tom," Charles Evans warned him, "if you do that, you'll never see Jennifer again."

By that afternoon he was as weak as a baby, staggering awkwardly across the South Col under the weight of their oxygen sets. Hillary, moved almost to tears by their achievement and their suffering, crossed the South Col to help them. They were coated in ice, smothered in it. It hung from their beards and eyebrows, coated the rope in an extra icy sheath, formed icicles from their oxygen sets. They had to stop every couple of steps to rest. Hillary had never seen men this tired. And the following day it would be his turn.

Tenzing says that after they helped the two men back into camp and plied them with quarts of hot lemon, Evans and Bourdillon gave them as much information as they could. Evans did most of the talking, since Bourdillon was too exhausted. Evans, Tenzing says, told him that he thought they would do it, as long as their top camp was positioned high enough. Hillary remembers their comments as being more pessimistic, particularly when describing the summit ridge that Bourdillon had started along. Altitude suppresses emotion, but that night, as they settled in the tents crowded with climbers and Sherpas either going up or planning to retreat, the turmoil of anticipation, fear, and hope would have kept them awake, even without the problems of hypoxia and the ever-present wind.

The wind was what Tenzing recalled most clearly of those nights on the South Col. His daughter Pem Pem pronounces the word "terrible" with the same attention to every syllable that Tenzing used, capturing the true character of a primal force that inspires terror. Hillary remembered him saying that the wind roared like a thousand tigers, and on the night of May 26 that is what it did, battering their tents. "One of the worst nights I have ever experienced," Hillary wrote in his diary.[35] Nor did it let up as the purple light of dawn revealed the gigantic peaks around them. They soon realized that climbing higher that day was out of the question. At noon conditions improved, and the first assault team prepared to go back down, taking one of the assault party's three Sherpas with them. Bourdillon fell to his knees as they crossed the Col, still shattered from the previous day's effort. Hunt wrote in a letter to his wife that he had thought Bourdillon was dying. He himself was close to exhaustion after three nights at Camp VIII. Before he left, Hunt gripped Hillary's arm and told him, "The most important thing is for you chaps to come back safely. Remember that. But get up if you can."[36]

Left on the Col with Tenzing and Hillary was New Zealander George Lowe and Alf Gregory with the Sherpas Ang Nima and Pemba. Hillary and Lowe spent the afternoon sorting through the oxygen bottles, checking how much gas was available. They reckoned that they could use a little that night to help them sleep. Then the six men settled down for another night at Camp VIII. If the weather didn't improve the notion of a second attempt would start to unravel. Tenzing lay in his tent, caught between sleep and consciousness, turning over in his mind the possibilities of the next few hours. He breathed in a slow trickle of oxygen to ease the long hours of the night and warm his body inside his thick sleeping bag. "After that I was not thinking at all any more, but dreaming. I dreamt of yaks playing about in a pasture, and then of a big white horse. It is a Sherpa belief that to dream of animals is good. And that is what I dreamed of. Somewhere behind the yaks and the horse was another dream. A tall white dream in the sky … "[37]

The wind was still blowing before dawn, but it died away as the sun rose and lit the top of the peak. Hillary and Tenzing looked at each other in hope. The ascent was on. The bad news was that Pemba was sick. The climbers would have to rely on one Sherpa instead of the planned three. Lowe, Gregory, and Nima would carry loads, but Hillary and Tenzing had planned to conserve themselves. Now, with the shortage of porters, they picked up the abandoned gear instead. Setting off an hour after the first group at ten that morning, they followed Lowe's steps in the couloir above the South Col. The climbers converged again at the point where John Hunt and Da Namgyal had dumped a tent, food and kerosene, a candle and some matches, as well as their half-consumed oxygen bottles, about 27,395 feet,[38] a short distance above Tenzing and Lambert's campsite from 1952.

Evans and Bourdillon had warned them this was too low for Camp IX; they had to keep going. Hillary handed a 20-pound oxygen bottle to Gregory, taking in return the cooker and food he was carrying, along with the 14-pound tent. All of them besides Ang Nima were now carrying more than 50 pounds at over 27,000 feet. Hillary had more than 60 pounds. Lowe took the lead for much of the time, swinging his ax to cut steps where required while the others staggered after him. With such heavy loads progress slowed, and as the afternoon wore on, they began to look with increasing concern for somewhere to put the tent for the night. They were even forced to start using the oxygen put aside for next day's summit attempt.

They were now almost as high as Tenzing and Lambert had reached, and Hillary thought Tenzing would remember little from the year before. But Tenzing remembered the terrain clearly. As they climbed the snowed-up rocks of the Southeast Ridge, he thought there was a possible site over to their left. He traversed out toward it, pushing through deeper snow, but it wasn't big enough for the tent. Lowe climbed a little higher, finally discovering a narrow shelf below a small outcrop below and to the right of the easier ground of The Balcony. Only 1,410 feet from the summit, they had reached the highest campsite in history.

While the others dropped their loads and quickly descended to the South Col, Hillary and Tenzing began leveling a platform. The time melted away as they scraped and shoveled the snow with their ice axes. Not until five o'clock did they clear enough level space to pitch the tent, and even then the arrangement wasn't ideal. They were forced to use two separate tiers, one six inches above the other. Tying guy ropes to oxygen bottles buried in the snow, Hillary made up for their lack of pitons by shoving tent pegs into cracks in the rock. Then they settled in for the night. Tenzing spread his air mattress on the lower level, overhanging the vast South Face of Everest, while Hillary shoved his long legs across the tent, bracing it against the strong gusts of wind that snapped the cotton fabric and roared above their heads against the ridge so loudly that they caught each other's eye with apprehension.

In 1952 Tenzing had struggled to melt a little ice in an old sardine tin over a stub of candle. Now they had a primus gas stove that he set between his feet as he made a succession of drinks, chicken soup, and the heavily sweetened hot lemon that Hillary loved. They drank it, Tenzing recalled, "like camels" coming out of the desert. Despite the deadening influence of altitude on appetite they managed to eat, starting with sardines and biscuits, a tin of apricots thawed over the stove, dates, and then more biscuits with jam.

All this they managed without using their precious oxygen supply. Hillary checked the bottles and reckoned that by cutting their ration from four liters a minute to three on the climb to the summit, they could afford a little gas to help them sleep through the night, laying the shared bottle between them. They dozed for a while, but hypoxia twisted their dreams. "I tried to sleep but I could not," Tenzing said. "I felt uneasy and restless and my whole body was aching. I felt as though someone was choking me and I was gasping for breath."[39] At eleven o'clock, the bottle ran out and Hillary woke, suddenly cold and uncomfortable. He noticed that Tenzing wasn't happy either and suggested they light the stove to warm up and melt more snow for hot lemon. (One of the most impressive features of their ascent was Hillary's need to urinate near the summit, a sure sign that they had kept their bodies in top shape.)

At one in the morning on May 29 they started using oxygen again and drifted back into sleep. Hillary napped upright, his back against the tent wall. The wind had lost its edge, and the temperature inside the tent was not as low as they had experienced on the South Col two nights before. "God is good to us," Tenzing thought as he listened only to the sound of their breathing. "Chomolungma is good to us."[40]

Tenzing was still wearing his reindeer boots, given to him by the Swiss the year before. Hillary was wearing the high-altitude boots designed specifically for the expedition. They were light and comfortable, but he took them off and propped them under the end of his sleeping bag. They promptly froze. When the sleeping oxygen ran out at 3 a.m. and they started preparing to leave for the top, Hillary had to wait while he held his boots over the stove, scorching the leather and cursing his luck.

Through the tent doors, peering over Hillary's shoulder, Tenzing saw the monastery of Tengboche 15,000 feet below them catch the first light of morning. Then he busied himself making hot lemon and they both ate a little more. Hillary checked his camera, and then they left the tent. It was 6:30 a.m.

Still concerned about warming his cold feet, Hillary waved Tenzing into the lead. It was below –25°C (-13°F), and the cold seeped into their bones. Their brains were dull and slow with hypoxia. Under his windproof hood, Tenzing wore Earl Denman's balaclava. His socks had been knitted by Ang Lhamu, and his sweater was a gift from Jill Henderson. Around his neck was the scarf Raymond Lambert had given him, and in his pocket were the small gifts Nima had told him to leave on the summit. The weather was perfect, all the jagged summits around them free from clouds. Hillary followed Tenzing to the snowy shoulder above them at 28,000 feet, trying to find his rhythm, slowly warming to the job at hand, locked into the slow, wearying process of putting one foot in front of the other. All thoughts were immersed in the overwhelming drive of extreme effort.

Once on The Balcony, Hillary moved into the lead, and for a while things went smoothly. They picked up two one-third-full oxygen bottles abandoned by Evans and Bourdillon, and Hillary checked their pressure. Inside them was left another hour's oxygen, enough to get them from where they were back to the South Col. That meant they needed only the oxygen they were carrying to get them to the summit and back to The Balcony. Above rose a steep slope leading to the South Summit, now only 400 feet above them. On its left were broken rocks and snow that the first pair had taken, "the rock-climbing Britons," as Hillary called them. He opted for the snow, the slope disappearing between their legs over the East Face for 10,000 feet to the Kangshung Glacier.

The going was treacherous. Taking the lead, Tenzing broke through a thin crust after only a few steps into the deep, loose snow up to his hips. When Hillary took over a while later, he was terrified to see chunks of this crust breaking off and skittering down the mountain. It wouldn't take much to start a slide that could take them with it. "My whole training told me that the slope was exceedingly dangerous, but at the same time I was saying to myself: 'Ed, my boy, this is Everest—you've to push it a bit harder!'" Gripped with fear, he struggled on a bit farther and then stopped for a rest and for Tenzing to catch him up.

"What do you think of it, Tenzing?" Hillary asked.

"Very bad, very dangerous," Tenzing told him.

Hillary asked him whether he thought they should go on, and Tenzing, his ambition warring with the fear of the loose snow around him, equivocated: "As you like."

Hillary waved him back into the lead, and they carried on, looking for a belay on the rocks to the left but finding them blank. Finally they moved onto solid snow where the rocks disappeared. Soon after, they reached the South Summit. It was still only nine o'clock, and any doubts were left behind on the slope below. Hillary, in changing their oxygen bottles, was pleased to notice that even without his mask, he could do the mental arithmetic to calculate the flow rate required to get them up and off the summit.

The ridge ahead looked imposing, just as Evans described, with huge drops on either side, but Hillary felt confident. He followed the ridge down from the South Summit and then started cutting steps up it, bringing

Tenzing across when he'd finished the rope length. This was how they would climb, moving one at a time across the exposed length of the ridge, watching each other all the time. At the end of one pitch, when Hillary descended a little to avoid cornices hanging over the East Face, he noticed Tenzing moving slowly and gasping heavily. Checking his oxygen set, Hillary realized the thin rubber tube to his tank was blocked with ice. They worked to clear it.

In *Tiger of the Snows*, Tenzing took exception to Hillary's account of this final section of their climb. "I must say in all honesty that I do not think Hillary is quite fair in the story he later told, indicating that I had more trouble than he with breathing and that without his help I might have suffocated. In my opinion our difficulties were about the same— and luckily never too great—and we each helped and were helped by the other in equal measure."[41]

Tenzing was particularly hurt by Hillary's description of the most awkward part of the ascent, a step in the ridge that is now known as the Hillary Step. Hillary wasn't sure he could climb this section, a chimney created by a rocky outcrop and a frozen bank of snow that eased away from it, overhanging the Kangshung face. He took a photograph to prove their highpoint should he fail, "a surge of competitive pride," he wrote, "which unfortunately afflicts even mountaineers," and then set to work. Tenzing had a good belay, Hillary recalled, and the protection he offered, both physical and psychological, was valuable as he kicked and struggled his way up the chimney. They were, in that sense, a meaningful climbing partnership, in contrast to the loose assemblage of individuals that converge on the summit in the modern era.

Their stories contradict each other in some of the details. Tenzing thought the step 15 feet high, Hillary said 40 and described the rope going tight as he reached the top. But what hurt Tenzing most was Hillary's description of him giving the Sherpa a tight rope, effectively helping him up the difficulties before Tenzing "finally collapsed exhausted at the top, like a giant fish when it has just been hauled from the sea after a terrible struggle."

"It is the plain truth," Tenzing said, "that no one pulled or hauled me up the gap. I climbed it myself, just as Hillary had done; and if he was protecting me with the rope while I was doing it, this was no more than I had done for him."[42] Hillary quickly regretted the image: "There was one thing that I regretted," he said later, "describing Tenzing coming up on the rope like a giant fish." The simile, published in the expedition's official account, was noticed and caused offense. Hillary didn't use it in any of his autobiographies.

These few minutes on Everest still generate controversy almost 50 years after the climb. Tenzing's son Jamling Tenzing Norgay wrote that older Sherpas had told him that they had another name for the Hillary Step—Tenzing's Back. According to their story, Hillary stood on Tenzing's back to get over a difficult move at the start of the crack. There is no evidence in either man's account that this occurred. The story is more an apocryphal way of illustrating that Sherpas worked hard toward the success of climbing expeditions.

Tenzing suffered further insults to his reputation as a mountaineer. When Hunt lost his cool at a press conference in Kathmandu after the ascent and made a lukewarm assessment of Tenzing's climbing abilities, he took it very hard. Objectively, Hunt was correct. Tenzing wasn't a technically proficient mountaineer compared with the British and New Zealanders, but then there was no reason anyone would expect him to be. He'd picked up what he could during expeditions he worked. The true source of his resentment was the implication that he had somehow been dragged along for the ride.

Tenzing's own sensitivity was partly to blame. Having an iced-up oxygen set and being helped with it was hardly an accusation of incompetence by Hillary. Elsewhere in his account in *High Adventure* he went out of his way to praise his partner's contribution and strength. But both men were vulnerable to casual slights. Hillary's accounts of the climb altered subtly over the years as his own character matured. Those who knew him in the 1950s say that he could appear austere, even blunt, and crisp assessments were just the kind of thing to upset a man like Tenzing. Conversely, in the febrile atmosphere that surrounded their arrival in Kathmandu, there was much talk of how Tenzing had led Hillary to the summit, and the New Zealander's contribution was overlooked to some extent.

The influence of colonialism was reflected in the controversy over who reached the summit first. On the mountain, to climbers, the argument was meaningless. On the final section of ridge leading to the summit, Hillary was in the lead cutting steps. Tenzing says that he held coils of their rope—he describes it as 30 feet long—and followed six feet behind him. "I did not say to myself, 'There is a golden apple up there, I will push Hillary aside and run for it.' We went on slowly, steadily. And then we were there."[43] It was around 11:30 a.m. and they had been climbing for just five hours. Rabi Mitra recalled that Tenzing later cracked a joke: "If I'd known all the fuss it was going to cause, I *would* have pushed him out the way and run for it."

Although journalists focused on the small differences between Hillary and Tenzing, trying to suggest that one had been more important than the other, the broader picture was that several factors had allowed them success. Seven full-scale attempts on the mountain and the various reconnaissances over the previous 30 years, particularly those of the Swiss in 1952, had preceded this one. Hunt would tell them, "To you, a good half of the glory." Also, the understanding of high-altitude physiology that Griffith Pugh and Michael Ward contributed underpinned Hunt's detailed plan. And the logistical efficiency, executed by Charles Wylie, Tenzing, and the Sherpas, had allowed the British to make two serious attempts when the Swiss could barely manage one. The names of Hillary and Tenzing are globally famous, that of Hunt still honored. But climbing Everest was a consequence of cooperation.

Tenzing took the keepsakes his daughter had given him, the little red-and-blue pencil and some small offerings of biscuits and candy for the deity Miyolangsangma, and scraped away a hollow in the snow in which to place them. He posed for Hillary's camera, holding aloft his ice ax with the flags he had carried with him of the United Nations, Britain, Nepal, and India. Even so, these larger-scale issues were minor in comparison with his thoughts of his family and his god. "All I can say is that on Everest," he said, "I was not thinking about politics." At his feet was his past: to the east the Kharta and Kama Valleys, where he had been born and spent the first years of his life; to the south Khumbu, where as a teenager he had worked as a Khamba servant, dreaming of escape and a better life; to the north Rongbuk, where he had taken his first steps as a climber, on the slopes of the North Col. He could see the monasteries and the farms, the rivers and forests of his youth. No wonder a mere handshake with Hillary wasn't nearly enough.

Tenzing would spend the rest of his life finding ways to deal with his extraordinary success, but for the next few hours, as the two climbers picked their way across the summit ridge and started on the long descent, the glory of reaching the summit was their secret, and neither man had any conception of the impact revealing it would have. They reached Camp IX at two, and Tenzing got the stove going while Hillary checked their oxygen and discarded the empties. Then they carried on, still in control, tired but not on the edge of exhaustion. George Lowe was the first to meet them. He had walked across the South Col with soup and some spare gas. Hillary felt a surge of affection for his friend.

"Well, we knocked the bastard off," Hillary told him.

"Thought you must have," Lowe replied.

At the tents, Wilf Noyce was waiting with Pasang Phutar. He'd brewed tea, a drink Hillary wouldn't touch, but Tenzing took some and Noyce felt childishly happy about it. The summit stayed with this small group of men for another few hours. Noyce had laid out sleeping bags in a prearranged signal, but no one at Advance Base saw it. Noyce and Lowe listened to Hillary tell for the first time the story he would be telling for the rest of his life. Tenzing settled in the tent next door, talking to Pasang Phutar. Tenzing recalled: "I lay still, with my 'night oxygen,' and tried to sleep. I felt *ah chah*—O.K. But tired. It was hard to think or feel anything. 'The real happiness,' I thought, 'will come later.'"[44]

Afterward, Noyce wrote: "We talked of Tenzing. What a good thing he had made of it. Good to have a Sherpa on top. John sent him, in the first place, because he had proved his fitness with Lambert, and this year too was 'going like a bomb', in climbing parlance, with Ed. But he was sent also, a far more important reason as it seemed to me, as a Sherpa to represent all the Sherpas who had worked, and in some cases died, upon Everest."[45]

Early next morning, Tenzing called across to their tent, asking for the stove, and Noyce handed it over without either of them having to leave their tent. Shortly after, Pasang Phutar appeared with tea, and the long day began. Though they hadn't anticipated that anyone would still be at Camp VII, Charles Wylie had stayed behind and was delighted at their news. Slowly the trickle of joy coming down the mountain was building to a flood. At first the climbers waiting at Camp IV saw the weary climbers approaching and mistook exhaustion for defeat. Then Hillary weakly raised his ice ax in the air as a gesture of success. At that moment Tenzing slipped and almost lost his footing in the snow but stopped himself and then flashed his smile. Suddenly everything was clear. The climbers rushed as fast they could to embrace the heroes, a blur of smiles and shaking hands and embraces. Hunt, the "reserved and formal" English army officer, laughed and cried both at the same time, embracing the climbers. The response of the Sherpas to Tenzing's success, on the other hand, was almost reverent, as James Morris noticed in particular:

"Above the camp most of the Sherpas were waiting in an excited smiling group. As the greatest of their little race approached them they stepped out, one by one, to congratulate him. Tenzing received them like a modest prince. Some bent their bodies forward, their hands clasped as if in prayer. Some shook hands lightly and delicately, the fingers scarcely touching. One old veteran, his black twisted pigtail flowing behind him, bowed gravely to touch Tenzing's hand with his forehead."[46]

The "old veteran" was most probably Da Tenzing, who had been managing the Sherpas while Tenzing was away climbing the mountain with Hillary. This is an image loaded with meaning, the traditional Sherpa with his jewelery and braids touching the hand of what was, effectively, the future of his people. Griffith Pugh took the opportunity to examine them as they sat on packing cases. They weren't at all dehydrated, despite four nights at or above the South Col, although their blood pressure was low. Then they sat down in the mess tent and ate an omelette while Morris took down their story for his dispatch to the *Times*. What did you feel, he asked, on the summit? Relief, the climbers told him. Relief that there was no more "up," that the effort had come to an end. It wasn't a good answer for a journalist hungry for copy and he asked the question again:

"This time Tenzing paused in his eating and thought hard about his reply. 'Very excited,' he said judicially, 'not too tired, very pleased.'"[47]

THERE ARE SEVERAL WAYS OF HOLDING the memory of Tenzing's moment of success. There is the summit itself, his leg planted firmly against the slope, his image caught forever in the world's eye. Or the moment that he returned to the other Sherpas and a pigtailed old man put Tenzing's hand to his lowered forehead. There is the picture of Hunt, the English army officer, laughing and crying both at the same time, embracing him as he descended.

None of these moments captures the true length of Tenzing's journey. Perhaps a better image is one James Morris had, out for a walk at Lobuje having delivered the news to his paper. Catching sight of a figure hurrying down the Khumbu Glacier and fearing that some rival was attempting to scoop the *Times,* he returned to intercept him. (Tenzing understood very well that he had the power to scoop James. But, as he told Ullman: "I could have sent the news right away to Namche with a Sherpa. But I worked for the British. I eat their salt. So why should I? I tell the Sherpas not to break the news.")

"As I watched the approaching figure I realised that this was no ordinary Sherpa, moving so swiftly and gracefully down the valley, swinging and buoyant, like some unspoilt mountain creature. A wide-brimmed hat! High reindeer boots! A smile that illuminated the glacier! An outstretched hand of greeting! Tenzing!

"'Good gracious me, Tenzing! Haven't you walked far enough? Where in heaven's name are you off to now, like a bat out of hell?'"

"He took off his big hat, smiling still, and sat down upon a rock, while my excited Sherpas crowded round. He was going to the neighbouring village of Thamey, he said, to see his aged mother, who lived there."

It was the morning of June 1, less than three days since he had reached the summit of the world. All Tenzing wanted was to visit his mother, who he had left behind 20 years before, and let her know her only living son was safe.

CHAPTER TEN

THE JACKALS OF FAME

Tenzing, his hat pushed back on his head,
his face permanently wreathed and crinkled with smiles,
laughed and nodded and ate his omelette,
while the worshipping Sherpas at the door gazed at him
like apostates before the Pope. Indeed, he was a fine sight,
sitting there in his moment of triumph,
before the jackals of fame closed in upon him.

—JAMES MORRIS, *Coronation Everest*

DHARMA RAJ THAPA IS AN OLD MAN NOW, living in an apartment near Swayambhunath to the west of Kathmandu. His voice is a little tremulous, but sitting cross-legged on the floor he manages a few bars of a song that was on everybody's lips in the summer of 1953. *"Hamro Tenzing Sherpa le,"* he begins. "Our Tenzing Sherpa." Like any fond parent, Dharma Raj Thapa is more than happy to talk about a favorite child, and the song that he wrote about Tenzing's ascent of Everest proved one of his most successful. Anyone over the age of 60 in Kathmandu can sing at least the first few lines and for a while, until Tenzing committed to living in India, it was taught to Nepalese schoolchildren: "Tenzing, the warm heart of the cold Himalayan peak / Tenzing, the jewel of the world / Tenzing, born in the vast Himalaya / He must have quenched his thirst by the source of Sun Kosi / Must have guided Hillary through the confusing trails." Thapa's lyric was broadcast first as a poem; later he traveled to Calcutta and recorded it to music. The song did several things for Tenzing. It crystallized his popular support, and more controversially, it repeated the idea that Tenzing had led Hillary to the summit. It also fixed in Nepalese minds that his name was Tenzing Sherpa, whereas in Darjeeling he had been known for two decades as Tenzing Bhotia, a name that even the *Times* of London was still using. "My own name has changed often," he would say.[1]

When the news of Tenzing's success came through on All India Radio, the ambitious young songwriter was sitting in what is now Glenary's Restaurant in Darjeeling with Rabindrinath Mitra. Both men immediately understood the significance of what had happened. Mitra had pictures of Tenzing printed that were put up all over town and soon were selling well as souvenirs. Thapa set to work on some lyrics. This would be much more than a pop song to celebrate a new hero. As Nepal emerged from the era of the Ranas, a new sense of national identity was developing and alongside it a new cultural confidence. Nepalese folk music was given a contemporary spin, and Dharma Raj Thapa, as a producer for Nepalese radio, was at the heart of this renaissance. Said publisher and writer Kamal Mani Dixit, a student in 1953 recalled, "Wherever Nepalese were, they were singing this song. Nepalese songs on 78 rpm records were new. The idea of Nepalese nationality was new. A lot was happening."

Tenzing's resonance as a national hero went far beyond being a famous Nepalese. Thapa drew on Nepalese touchstones like the *danphe*, Nepal's national bird, and the life-giving Sun Kosi, in effect tying Tenzing into the Nepalese ideal. In 1953 Nepalese hardly knew their own country. Nepal's beauty and cultural diversity were unknown to subjects starved of education. There were no books, and no one outside the educated elite could read them anyway. And then, from the fringes of the kingdom, from a group of people on the fringes of society, came a hero who seemed to embody all the hope and optimism ordinary Nepalese held for the future of their changing nation. They might not have had a firm grasp on where exactly Everest was, and they might have thought mountaineering odd, but they knew success when they saw it.

Tenzing was a role model for ordinary people, someone of humble birth who had made headlines around the world. (And yet he was also worshiped as a god, because there must be something godlike about someone who could rise so far so quickly. The paradox makes perfect sense in South Asia.) "For those of poor birth," Kamal Dixit said, "Tenzing's success was a big impetus. At one time he was more popular than King Tribhuvan." Nepal was in a period of political flux, enduring a succession of governments that would ultimately lead in the late 1950s to a failed attempt at multiparty democracy.

Tribhuvan, once no more than a puppet, had relied on Nehru's assistance and the support of the Nepalese Congress Party to wrest power away from the Ranas. But the old order wasn't prepared to give up its interests too readily, and the King saw advantage in renewing his relationship with Nepal's former ruling family. Reform was good as long as it didn't interfere with his position as divine monarch. Democracy would have to wait, much to the irritation of Nehru. So when an Indian newspaper reporting the ascent of Everest ran the headline "Himalayan Hero Will Outshine the Ranas!" you could almost hear the sound of breakfast trays crashing to the floor in the neo-Georgian piles the Ranas called home. This man would need taking down a peg or two.

Nepal's relationship with India was also in a period of flux. Nepal's gigantic southern neighbor was on one hand regarded as a beacon of reform and democratic change, a nation with political vision whose leader, Jawaharlal Nehru, had close links with the Nepalese Congress. Nehru had brokered the deal that brought Tribhuvan back to Kathmandu in 1951 and began the process of reform. If India had thrown off her colonial oppressors, couldn't Nepal step out into the light as well? But at the same time ordinary Nepalese feared India's interference. They wanted to stand alone and maintain their identity. India has had the habit of treating its tiny Himalayan neighbors as minor irritations to be scratched occasionally and Nepalese were sensitive to this treatment.

Tenzing and the rest of the 1953 expedition had little idea of the maelstrom of political upheaval and popular frenzy waiting for them at the end of their two-week trek from Khumbu to Kathmandu. The response in Britain more captured their immediate attention. The expedition had tuned in to the BBC on June 2 and heard the news of their ascent reported alongside details of Elizabeth II's coronation. "Somehow hearing it officially over the radio from half the world away made the climb sound far more important and real," Hillary wrote. At Tengboche a cable was waiting from the prime minister, Sir Winston Churchill, congratulating Tenzing, and from then on the trickle of messages and telegrams became a flood. Hunt, with Alf Gregory and Tom Bourdillon, decided to go on ahead of the expedition to Kathmandu to prepare for the main party's arrival while the others followed at a leisurely pace. One afternoon, halfway to Kathmandu, George Lowe and Ed Hillary met a mail runner—the second that day—coming along the trail. Lowe took the stack of mail and sorted through it. With a broad grin he handed Hillary a letter addressed to Sir Edmund Hillary KBE. The conqueror of Everest had been given a knighthood. Hillary was not pleased: "It was a tremendous honour, of course, but I had never really approved of titles and couldn't imagine myself possessing one."[2] He would, he decided, have to buy a new pair of overalls. But what about his partner? How had the Queen of England rewarded him?

Tenzing was given the George Medal. Though Britain's second-highest civilian award for bravery after the George Cross, it was hardly a match for a knighthood. The response was obvious. Why hadn't Tenzing been honored in the same way as Hillary and Hunt? The implication was that Tenzing's contribution was considered less significant by either the British government or the expedition, or both. Hillary himself thought the disparity was unfair: "Some people claimed at the time that Indian and Nepalese citizens were not permitted to accept foreign titles, but I don't believe this is completely true. If Tenzing had received the KBE I consider it would have been universally applauded in India and Nepal."[3] The prime minister of Nepal, Matrika Prasad Koirala, thought the George Medal "an insult" and in Britain the announcement of his award was heavily criticized. In a leader of June 17, the *Guardian* questioned the justice of the decision:

"The knighthoods conferred on Colonel Hunt himself, and on Sir Edmund Hillary were announced with commendable promptitude on June 7. The position of Tenzing remains embarrassingly obscure. It is true that he is not a British subject. It is necessary to consult his own Government before a British honour can be bestowed on him.

"But it was obvious from the start to anyone with the least knowledge of mountaineering that he was quite likely to be a member of the assault party in view of his fine performance with Lambert in the Swiss expedition of 1952, and soundings could surely have been taken in decent time."

The leader concluded: "The George Medal is given in recognition of such acts of gallantry as the arrest by police officers of armed criminals. It seems hardly appropriate to Tenzing's feat.

"Would it not be wiser, since Sir Edmund Hillary and he stood on the summit side by side to honour them in the same way? Honorary knighthoods conferred on foreigners are rare but not unknown."

Annoyance at the injustice of Tenzing's award was not confined to left-wing journalists. The Conservative member of Parliament for Solihull, Martin Lindsay, raised the issue with the prime pinister on the floor of the House of Commons: "Is the Prime Minister aware of the general disappointment that it has not been thought appropriate to offer the Indian subject Tenzing an award comparable to that made to the New Zealander, Hillary?" Churchill's reply seems obscure: "That does not entirely rest with the British Government."

What Churchill was hinting at was that the decision to deny Tenzing a knighthood wasn't necessarily his. Any award to a foreign national had to be cleared with the individual's government. This had been done in the case of Hillary, and in fact the New Zealand prime minister had accepted on his behalf, making it impossible for Hillary to refuse without causing great embarrassment. Tenzing's position was complicated because his nationality was uncertain. But it seems likely that the British government, through its embassy in Kathmandu, approached the Nepalese administration. It is worth asking how those Ranas who still had influence in the Nepalese government would have felt about a Bhotia being termed "Sir." As for Tenzing himself, he claimed indifference to the controversy. "Would a title give me wings?" he asked.

Tenzing was anxious to see his family and had, with Charles Wylie's help, sent a cable to Ang Lhamu in Darjeeling telling her to meet him in Kathmandu but for some reason, it never arrived. Of course, Ang Lhamu knew that her husband had climbed Everest. As soon as Rabi Mitra heard the broadcast on All India Radio, he sent word to Tenzing's home. "I remember a tall fellow arriving at the door of our house in Toong Soong," Pem Pem recalled. "He was named Natmal and Ravi Babu had sent him. Natmal said, 'Mrs Tenzing, I have good news for you. Tenzing has climbed Everest.'"[4] Ang Lhamu's small home was overwhelmed by visitors rushing to share in the good news. Sherpanis rallied around to make tea while the deputy commisioner of Darjeeling and other dignitaries dropped by to pay their respects. (When the deputy commissioner arrived, Ang Lhamu thought it was bad news. "Look cheerful," he told her. "Tenzing has conquered Everest.") "I cannot say how happy I was," Ang Lhamu said afterward. "In my joy I could think of nothing properly. I will tell you, I was afraid too much joy might bring me heart failure. The letters and telegrams started coming in the whole day and night. They were all good and kind. But no letter from my Tenzing. My anxiety was about [his] safe descent."[5] Apart from the missing telegram, Tenzing had also dictated a letter and signed it with his characteristic signature, the only word he could write. This arrived in Darjeeling on June 10. "Myself and one sahib have been successful at Everest. Don't worry about me. Take good care of your health."

Ang Lhamu's main concern was getting her husband back. "I was so relieved. From June 2 to June 12 I could take no meals. I had to face a stream of visitors." She was also in a quandary over what she should do. Her instinct was to take the girls with her to Kathmandu, but she hesitated. It was an expensive journey, and Tenzing had not sent for her. Rabi Mitra intervened and told her she must go. He gave her a hundred rupees, Jill Henderson chipped in another 400, and they quickly left for Nepal. "Now I am very happy," she said. "We will have a new home of our own, and we hope to settle down to a life of rest."

While Ang Lhamu, Pem Pem, and Nima rushed to Kathmandu, Tenzing found himself enduring a bewildering new danger he had never had to face in the mountains—fame. The expedition's relationship with the media was complicated. They had signed an exclusive deal with the *Times* of London, which had sent its journalist James Morris to send back dispatches.[6] Tenzing, however, had not signed a contract. This made him an obvious target for reporters who couldn't get a story out of the other expedition members. Later, when John Hunt realized the media were exploiting this contractual oversight, Tenzing was asked to join the others in signing. He was even offered a salary of 500 rupees a month for eight months, but by then it was too late. Tenzing had already been approached and now understood just how much he could make from his story: "For the first time in my life I was in a position to make a considerable sum of money, and I could not see why it was not right and proper for me to do so."[7] He was absolutely correct.

The trek home was largely pleasurable for Tenzing. His sister—and Gombu's mother—Lhamu Kipa, her husband, Nawang, and their daughters decided to come with him to live in Darjeeling, so he was surrounded by relatives. He had the grind of organizing the huge number of porters, but others could share that burden and Tenzing was able to bask in his success for a while. Wilfrid Noyce wrote: "Tenzing would come into camp red with *holi* dust and garlanded from some local celebration, to lie in his tent and be ministered to by his two nieces. The interior of this tent reminded the visitor more of an Eastern potentate's than of a Sherpa dwelling: a handsome rug on the floor, tea vessels, two women busily going in and out. By contrast the other Sherpas looked as if nothing had ever happened to them."[8] He had stepped through a door that had closed forever behind him.

On June 19, the expedition passed through the village of Dhaulaghat, still a day's march from Kathmandu. A few Indian journalists were waiting for interviews, and photographers took shots of Hillary washing in the river. A reporter for a British paper sidled up to Hillary and offered him £10,000 for an exclusive, but Hillary, who was "a little prone to violence in those days," shaped to punch him and the journalist backed off. Tenzing wasn't so lucky. A group of Nepalese journalists and political activists—men who were left-wing, anti-British, and nationalistic—more or less kidnapped the sirdar and pumped him about the climb. They made no pretense of showing an interest in either the man or what he had done. This was the emotional hunger of a mob, not reasoned inquiry. All that was required was a confirmation that Tenzing was Nepalese and had reached the summit first.

What Tenzing actually told them hardly matters. Whatever he said about the climb would have been twisted out of shape. His appearances in print had so far been limited to a few generous remarks in climbing books and Rabi Mitra's puff pieces for the Indian press. He had no idea how he could be used by those with a political agenda. The mob surrounding Tenzing harassed him into signing a statement that claimed Tenzing had stepped on the summit first, a statement Tenzing couldn't even read.

This was bizarre territory for a mountaineering expedition. Tenzing himself said that he was used to arriving back in civilization without anyone paying the slightest attention. As expeditions go, it had been a very happy one. Other Himalayan expeditions in this period were far more rancorous. After the Italian expedition to K2 in 1954 one of the summit climbers, Achille Compagnoni, sued the Italian Alpine Club (CAI) for the frostbite injuries he suffered. Another climber sued for libel. The 1953 climb had some tensions, but at altitude, under pressure to succeed and with the threat of avalanche or illness, it's not surprising that climbers occasionally fell out.

At Hukse, John Hunt arrived with his wife, Joy, to join the expedition for one more night before accompanying his team into Kathmandu. He had met the Nepalese rushing back from Dhaulaghat with their "statement" from Tenzing that he had reached the summit first and warned Hillary of the atmosphere awaiting them in Kathmandu. Tenzing, meanwhile, was interviewed by *Life* magazine's New Delhi correspondent, James Burke, who transcribed verbatim Tenzing speaking in English and his joy at reaching the summit. It makes an interesting contrast to the fluid lyricism of *Tiger of the Snows:*

"On top I no think anything at first. Then I look at Hillary. He hold out hand for shake. I shake then throw arms around him and we hit other on back. Very happy. I look every side. Good day, no much wind. All hills below look like Buddha gods. I can see very far. North in Tibet I see Rongbuk *gompa* and North Col where old expeditions come. That way look very hard. In west I see Tengboche and I think lamas praying there. I put little offering in snow. I feel very good. I have make worship close to Buddha god like think when I am boy on ridge above Nangpa La."

Tenzing was also met by another American journalist, John Hlavacek, working for the United Press Association,[9] and he made Tenzing an offer. Although nothing was signed, Tenzing was now fully aware of the impact his climb had made.

Tenzing was to face an ordeal strewn with hidden pitfalls. On the morning of June 20, the expedition climbed the long hill to the roadhead at Banepa on the edge of the Kathmandu Valley. Ang Lhamu and the girls were waiting to greet Tenzing, but he was soon dragged away by the huge crowds. Dressed in Nepalese clothes, with a Nepalese flag thrust in his hand, Tenzing was led to a waiting jeep. Hunt and Hillary were crammed in the back, seated so low that they peered up at Tenzing, who held himself upright on a crossbar. A second vehicle, full of young Nepalese, followed behind. The rest of the expedition were forced to hitch lifts from the press corps and soon overtook the parade. Noyce recalled meeting trucks filled with people all asking the same thing: Where is Tenzing?

Along the route to Kathmandu crowds waited to greet him, showering the jeep with vermilion and rice and even coins. As the convoy passed, the young Nepalese passengers would shout out: *"Shri Tenzing!"* *"Zindabad!"* ("Honored Tenzing!" "Live Long!") the crowd roared back. After months on Everest looking at the same faces every day, Tenzing was confronted with thousands of strangers all edging closer toward him, offering garlands and shouting his name as he pressed his hands together in the Hindu greeting. *Namaste!* Waves of noise broke over his head. The smells, dust, and heat of the valley rushed to meet him as the jeep bounced along the rutted track. "Hymns were being sung to a god," Noyce observed, "not to a mortal man."[10]

Banners had been stretched across the road into town. "Hail Tenzing!— The Glory of Nepal," one proclaimed near the King of Nepal's palace. "Welcome Tenzing first man to conquer Everest!" Others showed a figure on the summit of a mountain with a Nepalese flag and a rope leading down to a second figure lying on its back. The point wasn't lost on Hillary, who started off laughing but found the banners increasingly irritating as the day wore on. The reception for Hunt and for Hillary in particular was most frosty on the edge of the valley where political feeling ran most strongly. Hillary recalled that after he spoke at one gathering he heard only the sound of his own steps as he left the dais, the faces of the crowd hostile and silent. While they were riding in the jeep, one overeager young man leaped on board. The disgruntled conqueror of Everest gave him a shove in the chest, and he was sent sprawling back into the road.

When they reached Kathmandu proper, the mood of the crowd was less charged and more welcoming to Hunt and Hillary. Speeches were made, Tenzing first, then Hunt, who addressed the crowd in Hindi. Hillary spoke briefly in English, still smarting from the hostility he had encountered. Loudspeakers blared out music, and flowers were thrown in the air as the crowd surged toward the balcony where they were speaking. Then the expedition, unwashed and in the clothes they had worn on the long trip home, moved off to the palace to attend a reception given by King Tribhuvan. Still dressed in the graying pyjamas he wore for trekking, Griffith Pugh settled into a chair beneath the chandeliers opposite government ministers dressed in frock coats and tight white trousers. Still coated in vermilion, Tenzing was awarded the first of many medals, the Nepal Tara, the highest decoration that a Nepalese who is not a member of the royal or Rana families can receive. Hunt and Hillary were also decorated, with lesser awards, and then the King gave a short speech, mentioning that Tenzing had told him he had reached the summit first, which stung Hillary. Everyone shook the King's hand, photographs were taken, and then the expedition retired to the British Embassy for the night.

The wild excitement didn't diminish over the five days Tenzing remained in Kathmandu. The heightened emotions led to offenses given and taken, many of which now seem trivial but at the time left a deep impression. Wilfrid Noyce recalled a series of speeches given to a large crowd gathered at Ratna Park. In one of them a Buddhist lama explained to the crowd that Nepal had produced two great men in history, Gautama Buddha and Tenzing. The other Sherpas who had sweated alongside him on Everest, his own friends and relatives, were introduced to him as though they were strangers. It was a topsy-turvy world. "As I thought of the last carefree stages of our walk," Noyce wrote, "a link seemed to have snapped. A man of simple life, but of determination and ambition, a friend and happy companion, was borne suddenly into this world strange to him as the planet Mars."[11]

Most of the expedition party were kept busy sorting out equipment for the return journey and attending receptions and parties. Tenzing, however, was kept under intense pressure from reporters asking questions, and their constant presence made sure that any rift within the team would be broadcast and then amplified by the mood in Kathmandu. It was, James Morris wrote in the *Times*, "a cross between a circus and a hustings." Tenzing turned down an invitation to attend a reception at the British Embassy. Given the way he and the Sherpas had been treated by the embassy staff, this was understandable, but it was grist to the rumor mill. He also equivocated over whether to accept Hunt's invitation to come to London to share in the celebrations there. Tenzing wanted to take his family with him, but Hunt was concerned about the extra expense. Ang

Lhamu made it clear, sitting with Hunt in the British Embassy gardens, that Tenzing wouldn't be going anywhere without them. Summerhayes took the opportunity to prejudice opinion in London against Tenzing and his wife, describing Ang Lhamu in a report to the Foreign Office as "forceful and grasping"[12] in sticking up for her husband. The behavior of the Sherpas in March clearly hadn't been forgiven.

The secretary of the Sherpa Association in Darjeeling, Lhakpa Tsering, had also arrived in Kathmandu and, quickly installing himself as Tenzing's adviser, wanted to go to London too. Although Ang Lhamu was supporting her husband, who was under terrific pressure from several sides, Lhakpa Tsering's interest was more self-serving. The High Commission in Delhi warned the Commonwealth Relations Office in London that Tenzing's new secretary was stirring up trouble. "This man has a bad reputation in European circles in Calcutta and Darjeeling and many attempts have been made in the last week to detach him from Tenzing's side. He is certainly a cleverer man than Tenzing, but whether he is more concerned with feathering his own nest than with protecting Tenzing's interests (which are now considerable in financial terms) is a matter of doubt. Over one point, however, there can be no doubt—that Tenzing was adamant, in the face of pressure from both the Indian and Nepalese sides, in refusing to visit England unaccompanied by the man he thought most likely to look after and support him and his family in a strange land."[13] Lhakpa Tsering wasn't more intelligent than Tenzing, but he could read. In the end, his advantage would cost Tenzing dearly.

The High Commission also warned London that elements in Kathmandu were presenting Tenzing's success as "a racial triumph of Asian over European." This was just the sort of emotional wildness that would irritate John Hunt, and he proved vulnerable to crass attempts by reporters intent on wringing a comment from the expedition leader that would build Tenzing's reputation even higher. Eventually, he cracked, replying icily to an Indian journalist, "Tenzing was a competent climber within the limits of his experience." This was true but hardly diplomatic. Hunt wanted the world to understand that the expedition had been a team effort, but in the febrile atmosphere the climb had generated his remarks sounded petulant. Tenzing was hurt by Hunt's remarks— quite reasonably, given that his contribution had been so great—and acknowledged that as a consequence of Hunt's halfhearted praise he "made a few statements that I later regretted." Their relationship in particular remained strained, if only for the next few days as the expedition prepared to return to Britain.

James Burke summarized the heightened atmosphere in *Life:* "To the distress and the half-resentful bewilderment of Colonel Hunt and his British climbers, these first wild welcomings carried a clear implication that, in Asia, the real hero of Everest was Tenzing alone. The conquest of Everest, a product of selfless teamwork between Asian and European, was being twisted into an ugly look of Asian nationalism, inflamed further by the normal British habit of treating the hired Tenzing like a hired man."

Two issues drove most of the controversy: who was first on the summit, and what nationality Tenzing was, Indian or Nepalese. To a climber, the first problem was nonsensical. A few feet of rope separating partners on a 29,000-foot mountain meant nothing, especially when a team of climbers and Sherpas had supported them. Those desperate to use Tenzing's celebrity, however, were not interested in logic, and so after two days of speculation, Hunt, Hillary, and Tenzing gathered in M. P. Koirala's office to lay the issue to rest. A statement claiming that they reached the summit "almost together" was drawn up and signed. Koirala, stung by reports that the Nepalese had given a hostile reception to the British, issued his own statement, which read like an Oscar acceptance speech. Going out of his way to praise India's weather forecasts, he explained: "The Nepalese nation is of course proud of Tenzing but no less are we proud of brave New Zealander, Mr Edmund Hillary, who was Tenzing's companion in attaining the topmost point of the globe. We are equally proud of the expedition's leader Colonel John Hunt but for whose wonderful organisation and attention to little detail the expedition might not have been the great success it is. Nor can we forget all other members of the expedition. As well as the brave and sturdy Sherpas."

This outpouring of global fellowship wasn't acceptable to those making political mileage out of Tenzing—"almost together" could mean anything—but Tenzing refused to play along in claiming the summit. He was offered substantial sums of money to change his mind, and when that didn't work he received death threats instead. One night he collapsed into tears in front of Ang Lhamu and his daughters, overwhelmed by the antagonism and pressure he had endured. Ultimately the argument was settled by Tenzing himself in *Tiger of the Snows:* "The rope that joined us was thirty feet long, but I held most of it in loops in my hand, so that there was only about six feet between us.... Hillary stepped on top first. And I stepped up after him."[14] To a climber, it was the rope that counted. Not Hillary *or* Tenzing, but Hillary *and* Tenzing. The controversy resurfaces regularly, but as far as history is concerned, Tenzing ended it categorically, and to his great credit.

The question of Tenzing's nationality was much more complex. Nepalese and Indians saw his success on Everest as a symbol of Asia's growing confidence and the collapse of colonialism. Tenzing's life was an outstanding example to ordinary Asians of how they could lift themselves out of poverty. Nehru grasped that immediately. Some in India also used him to fire a few parting shots at the British. One Indian police officer called S. K. Goswami even published a book in 1954 claiming that the ascent of Everest had been fabricated. He told Indian journalists: "The alleged news of the conquest of Everest is a sinister attempt to re-establish tottering, self-styled British supremacy once again." Tenzing, Goswami claimed, "was virtually kidnapped by a band of designing and conspiring British journalists and was indocrinated or tempted with money or prospects."

Another book about Tenzing, by the French journalist Yves Malartic, was fashioned from a brief interview with Tenzing as he passed through Switzerland that summer. (Malartic claimed their meeting lasted two hours; Tenzing responded that he had given a 15-minute interview at a cocktail party in Bern to a group of journalists, Malartic among them.) Malartic was equally hostile to the British, particularly Hunt. Most of the book was drawn from a mixture of published accounts, newspaper cuttings, gossip, and guesswork and rushed out in France and the United States before Tenzing's authorized autobiography could appear. Malartic also claimed that Tenzing had been taken to London "practically as a hostage" and exaggerated the Sherpas' differences with the British. When the book was published in the autumn of 1954, Tenzing issued a statement denouncing the account as inaccurate. "Several pages are devoted to my adventures on an expedition in which I did not even take part.

There is much misinformation about my home and family life. He twists the facts of the conquest of Everest, which relate to me, to suit his own political purpose."[15]

Tenzing's use as a symbol of anticolonialism was short-lived. Mountain climbing is not, in the scheme of things, of much importance politically and it didn't require a genius to realize that Tenzing had done rather well out of his association with the British. This was no victim. His real difficulty lay closer to home. In his interviews with John Hlavacek of UPA, given in Calcutta later that week, Tenzing hit on the elegant, even poetic explanation that he had been born in the womb of Nepal and raised in the lap of India. This should have allowed him a neat escape, but in the end he was forced to make a choice. Too much had been invested in him for Tenzing to get away that lightly.

At a reception given by Koirala the night before the expedition left Kathmandu, Tenzing learned that a public subscription in Nepal on his behalf had raised the equivalent of £500. He had already been offered a house and a pension if he decided to return to Nepal permanently. The *Statesman* newspaper in Calcutta, on the other hand, had also held a public subscription which Tenzing would collect the following day, and no doubt new opportunities in India awaited Tenzing as well. Nepal was a small country whose development had been arrested by an oppressive political system. As Dorje Lhatoo put it, "They were still throwing shit out of the windows in 1953." Tenzing was used to the comparative sophistication of India. Soon he would come under the aegis of Nehru, and the Indian prime minister's patronage and vision for Tenzing would open all kinds of doors. He had lived in India for more than 20 years, and most of his family resided there. Why shouldn't he stay?

His decision caused bitter resentment in Nepal, where some felt their welcome had been thrown back in their faces, not least the royal family. Tenzing left Kathmandu in King Tribhuvan's own personal aircraft—a Dakota. (Hunt and Hillary followed five hours later on a commercial flight, much to Tenzing's embarrassment and the manufactured outrage of several British journalists.) "People felt very let down," Kamal Dixit recalled. "After two years, when it was clear he wasn't coming back, popular opinion for him fell very sharply." When Tenzing next returned to Kathmandu, in the late 1950s, his reception was much cooler, and he rarely visited the capital after that. "It was unfortunate that ... the government of Nepal had neglected to pay much attention to my father after his Everest ascent in 1953," his son Jamling wrote.[16]

Disappointment in Nepal was predictable, but it is difficult to see what else Tenzing could have done. While journalists asked him again and again what nationality he considered himself to be, Tenzing himself was confused. No one in Kathmandu knew he had been born in Tibet and had come to Khumbu only as a boy or that he had spent merely a fraction of his life in Nepal. At the same time, paradoxically, this was the moment when he began to use the word Sherpa after his name. Until this point he had been known universally as Tenzing Bhotia[17] but if the people of Nepal were singing a song about "hamro Tenzing Sherpa," then wasn't it expected of him? Calling himself Sherpa was acknowledging what he had become, and would keep him out of further difficulty. Dorje Lhatoo said his mother used to scold him if he forgot that the name Tenzing Bhotia was defunct. He also told me that Tibetans in Darjeeling felt that Tenzing had betrayed *them*. For instance, Tenzing's sister Thakchey—known as Ani Choë—still termed herself a Bhotia, as did her son Lobsang, who tragically died on Everest in 1993. Part of the reason for the change of names was that the past embarrassed him. "He was very ashamed to say that he carried loads for such and such people," Dorje Lhatoo said, speaking of Tenzing's days as a teenager working for families in Khumjung. [Although, according to Pem Pem, he was proud to have carried on expeditions.] "He would say to us: 'I was on the lowest level and came up very slowly.' After 1953, he shot sky-high, as though he was catapulted."

"I suppose he was pulled in different directions," Trevor Braham said. "Maybe he felt he had to state some kind of Nepalese allegiance. He was very mixed up after Everest, very mixed up. He didn't know what he was. It was a whole new world for him. I know that once the Himalayan Mountaineering Institute was founded and he was asked to run it, he decided to cut off his relations with Nepal. He saw his future in India. He didn't feel the same attachment to Nepal that a [Khumbu-born] Sherpa might feel."

The disappointment ordinary Nepalese felt was matched by some Sherpas in Khumbu. This was largely resentment at another man's success, particularly a man who was Tibetan-born and not from one of the better established Sherpa families. Snobbery wasn't confined to the English. Tenzing was now a "big man" recognized by monarchs and prime ministers around the world. For a Khamba whose father had been reduced to nothing, this was an astonishing achievement and it bred envy. There was, however, an element of Nepalese nationalism among the Sherpas too, that part of them that drew back from identifying completely with Tibet. "I feel it was unfair for some Nepalese, and a handful of Sherpas, to say that Tenzing betrayed his Sherpa homeland," Jamling Tenzing Norgay wrote. "My father and other Khumbu Sherpas of his generation did not emigrate to Darjeeling for political reasons. Their move was strictly economic."[18] This was true, but their economic circumstances were defined by politics. The poorest Sherpas and Khambas worked for climbing expeditions, just as they do now. Later, as Chinese control tightened on Tibet, Khumbu Sherpas felt an even greater need to express their Nepalese identity. China claimed Khumbu as part of its sovereign territory for a while, and the Sherpas were anxious to avoid the fate of those living on the other side of the Nangpa La. Jamling Tenzing Norgay discovered to his cost how sensitive these issues are when he reached the summit of Everest in 1996: "I was the first Sherpa or Tibetan to fly a Tibetan flag from Everest's summit, and it was that flag that brought me the most criticism— ironically, from Khumbu Sherpas. They are Nepalese citizens, and Nepal doesn't acknowledge Tibet as distinct from China. They felt that I had turned my back on them in a way, because Nepal would be officially displeased if they were to fly the Tibetan flag."[19]

India was free of these difficulties. It was a place where a man like Tenzing could reinvent himself. India, Dorje Lhatoo says, was "our land of opportunity." On June 25, the *Times* reported Tenzing's arrival at Dum Dum Airport in Calcutta. "Tenzing, tired and garlanded, was hustled from the aircraft through the flashing cameras and the mob, but there were one or two reminders that he is, or was, a simple man of the mountains." Life was anything but simple. People were saying that Tenzing was an avatar of Shiva, a god incarnate, while a movie producer in Bombay wanted to put him and Ang Lhamu in his next film. (Ang Lhamu thought this was a great idea.) Tenzing was put up at Government House for the three days he spent in the Bengali capital. On the personal side, he was reunited with Rabi, and Tenzing asked him to send the scarf he had been wearing on the summit to Raymond Lambert. It was as if he was reconnecting to a world he understood. He needed a friend.

At another reception the *Statesman* presented him with the proceeds of their public subscription, equivalent to $17,000 today. Lhakpa Tsering negotiated Tenzing's deal with UPA in a rush, signing over 50 percent of any serialization rights to the news agency and a 10 percent cut of any book or film deal. James Burke, *Life*'s correspondent, was disappointed that Lhakpa Tsering had signed before his own organization could come back with a better offer. Tenzing had liked him, but Lhakpa Tsering was too eager to get a deal. "If you and Mr L. T. Sherpa had contacted me before you signed and could have delayed things two or three days, it might have been better," Burke wrote to Tenzing.[20]

If Ang Lhamu's hopes for a new house and financial security were looking brighter, Tenzing had been bruised by his experiences in Kathmandu, and continuing doubts about his trip to Europe left him anxious. Calcutta was sweltering in the pre-monsoon heat, and constant attention from huge crowds was taking its toll. Hunt wanted to bring both Hillary and Tenzing to Britain to share in the celebrations, but Tenzing was still adamant that his family and Lhakpa Tsering would have to come too. Hunt, under pressure from the Himalayan Committee, said there was not enough money in the expedition's funds to allow this. Meanwhile the *Daily Express*, which had bought the rights to Tenzing's UPA interviews that he was giving to John Hlavacek in Calcutta, offered him an all-expenses-paid tour. It would solve the problem of getting his family to Britain, but Tenzing was reluctant to appear in any more media circuses and turned it down.

If Calcutta was a hothouse, the reception the expedition received in Delhi was more intense still. A crowd of tens of thousands was waiting to greet them at the airport. "When we walked down the aircraft steps," Ed Hillary recalled, "they all saw Tenzing and the crowd broke the barriers and rushed towards us screaming 'Tenzing!' I have never seen a greater look of terror than in Tenzing's eyes and we were glad to slip through the crowd and leave him to his fate."[21] Tenzing became separated from Ang Lhamu and Nima, and then he lost his grip on Pem Pem's hand. She called out for her father as she was swallowed up by the mass of people. Finally the police intervened and his daughter was restored to him. Shaken, the family were taken to the Nepalese Embassy.

In the evening they attended a reception given by Pandit Jawaharlal Nehru. Tenzing, like so many, found Nehru a brilliant, compelling figure. A product of Harrow and Trinity College, Cambridge, Nehru was 64 in 1953, and at the height of his powers as the first prime minister of modern India. As a Kashmiri, mountains were in his blood, and he was thrilled by stories of exploration and discovery. He understood the significance of the ascent of Everest, and how it would be perceived in Britain. As in the West, mountaineering and exploration for Nehru were metaphors for the scientific and industrial progress India was striving toward under his leadership. Nehru, the architect of nonalignment, would help Tenzing pick his way through the minefield of instant celebrity.

"From the very first, Panditji was like a father to me," Tenzing said. "He was warm and kind, and, unlike so many others, was not thinking of what use he could make of me, but only of how he could help me and make me happy."[22] Tenzing shows his naïveté here; Nehru was just considerably more subtle and capable in his response than anyone else Tenzing had met. Still, Nehru didn't want to exploit Tenzing. He liked him and recognized a talented and intelligent man who had achieved greatness through his own efforts. It was a model that India needed to uphold. In Nehru, Tenzing discovered a friend who could solve problems with a word while at the same time being approachable and, most important, never patronizing.

The day after the reception, Nehru invited Tenzing to his office. There he advised Tenzing to go to London. "You should know," the high commissioner told the Foreign Office in London, "that Tensing's decision to fly to London with British members of the expedition is the result of considerable pressure not only from Nepalese Ambassador here but also from leading Indians including [Education Minister] Maulana Asad and Nehru himself. From the point of view of opinion here it is therefore much to be hoped that he will be treated in England on all public occasions in the same way as other members of the expedition and in particular that he will not be left out on any important occasion."[23] The Foreign Office replied icily that they wouldn't have considered otherwise, and paid for Tenzing and his family to fly to London.

Nehru, meanwhile, soothed Tenzing's anxieties, restoring his self-confidence and composure. Both men, they discovered, were the same size. Nehru opened his wardrobe and gave Tenzing suits of his own clothes. Tenzing's dress sense reached its apotheosis with Nehru's suits; he looks superb in them, like a well-tailored force of nature. Rashtrapati Bhavan, Nehru's residence, became Tenzing's home in Delhi. His daughter Nima remembered the informality of their visits. "Nehru said: 'You're not going to stay anywhere but here.' We'd play with Rajiv Ghandi, and we got to know Indira well." Nehru brushed aside Tenzing's quandary over what nationality he was. He must of course travel on *two* passports, Nepalese *and* Indian. And all the time Nehru was reasonable and supportive, Tenzing was developing a sense of mission within himself to help his adopted country. "If Nehru had told me *I* was Indian," Ed Hillary said, "I would have believed him."

Even before he stepped on the plane to London, much of the tensions Tenzing had been feeling had melted away. The Indians had welcomed all the expedition members on an equal basis, both in the press and in government. The president of India, Rajendra Prasad, gave a speech at the official reception in Delhi which was the epitome of good manners and generous praise: "Here is an example of team work which goes to show that with organisation, with experience, with fearlessness and courage, there is nothing which the human mind and the human body and soul cannot achieve."[24] No wonder the High Commission in Delhi reported happily that the expedition's stay in India had been "a thorough success." The petty nationalism that had dominated the week before had been replaced in the Indian press by the attitude that here was a triumph for all mankind.[25] It was only ten days since Tenzing had arrived back in Kathmandu, but it had seemed like ten years.

All political pressure on Tenzing effectively ended when he stepped on board the flight to London. With him were Ang Lhamu, Pem Pem, and Nima, as well as Lhakpa Tsering. All the climbers were delighted to have Tenzing's wife and daughters. The BOAC flight stopped at several points on the way to Europe. At Karachi more crowds came to greet them. As they approached Cairo, Charles Wylie started to give Pem Pem a brief history of the Suez Canal—before she explained she had studied it in school. The expedition was delayed for a night in Rome with engine trouble, then left next morning on the final legs to Geneva and then London.

On the way Tenzing noticed that Hunt was upset. He had been handed the first serializations of the interview Tenzing had given in Calcutta. They touched on some of the difficulties the expedition had experienced, and Hunt felt Tenzing had presented a poor image of them. (In fact, the articles were fairly tame and did nothing to undermine anyone's contribution.) Hunt moved down the aircraft and sat with Tenzing and the two men resolved many of their differences. For Hunt, awaiting them was the immediate promise of "the most longed-for welcome of all: that of our own people here at home."[26] This time it was Hunt, emerging first on the aircraft steps, who received the acclamation of the crowds.

Tenzing spent 16 days in Britain. For much of that time Pem Pem was ill and even hospitalized at one point, and so he was restricted to staying in London, as a guest of the India Services Club. For the first few days, most of the expedition dispersed to see their families and Tenzing was left alone, and his time was filled with interviews and appearances. They were taken on shopping trips, which delighted Ang Lhamu, although Tenzing exhibited his consistent reluctance to accept gifts. "People were all the time offering us presents, but, though I appreciated their kindness, I did not think we should accept too many. 'Why not?' Ang Lhamu and Nima would say. 'Because it's not right,' I would tell them. And there would be a family argument." At a photography store, where he was offered any camera he wanted, Nima picked out a Rolleiflex. Tenzing insisted she take a cheaper one.

Dressed in their traditional *bakus*, the girls and Ang Lhamu were an exotic hit with British press photographers, while Tenzing's dazzling smile and happy enthusiasm charmed the media. He was interviewed for television before he had ever seen one. The newspapers loved the angle of the simple man from the mountains who was so taken with the idea of wristwatches that he wore one on each arm. But their coverage of Tenzing was not restricted to his novelty. This was a new, post-war Britain where a working man like Tenzing, concerned about buying his family a new house and earning a decent wage, symbolized what ordinary Britons were thinking. The *News Chronicle*, for example, viewed the line drawn between Asians and Europeans to be as artificial as the social divisions that had plagued British society. It was, the paper argued, the same mentality that had required professionals and gentleman to use different gates when entering the field of play at a cricket match.[27] "Better times are dawning for Tensing," the paper announced. Tenzing himself was touched by his reception from ordinary people. "Their welcome to me, a stranger from a far country, was every bit as warm as that to their own climbers, and I could not help comparing this with the rather indifferent reception the British had had from the crowds in Nepal."[28] Tenzing put on Western clothes to walk around London, always alert to new experiences. It was his first trip to a Western city, and yet he was already developing a taste for travel.

After visiting Paris to celebrate the ascent of Annapurna, Ang Tharkay was content to stay at home. (Jill Henderson had visited him when he got back to Darjeeling, and the first thing Ang Tharkay took out of his suitcase was a program for the *Folies Bergères*.) Not so Tenzing. For much of the rest of his life he would make trips abroad every year. In London he went sightseeing and attended the theater. Tenzing took Ang Lhamu on a roller coaster, where she got so frightened she started pummelling him. "What are you trying to do, kill me?" During a reception at Gloucester House, Pem Pem and Nima watched through a balustrade as glamorous women floated by, mesmerized by their jewelry and gowns, and greeted their father, handsome and slim in the suit given to him by Nehru.

The main event of their stay in London was a garden party with the Queen at Buckingham Palace when Hillary and Hunt were knighted and Tenzing was presented with his George Medal. (Ang Lhamu and the girls gasped when they saw the Queen's sword poised above their heads.) The Queen gave them a short tour of the palace, and the girls were amazed at the playroom Prince Charles and Princess Anne shared. Pem Pem asked if she could see a portrait of Henry VIII—she had studied the Tudors at school in Darjeeling—and when one was produced asked if there were pictures of his wives as well. Ang Lhamu was typically shy and self-effacing. The Queen asked her what she had done when she had heard the news of Tenzing's success.

"I brought him a present."

The Queen was curious to know what she had bought him. Ang Lhamu, Charles Wylie recalled, giggled and blushed before whispering a reply.

"A tin of condensed milk."

CHAPTER ELEVEN

TIGER OF THE SNOWS

Sometimes the crowds around me have been so thick,
the pressures so great, that I have thought gloomily
that a normal life is no longer possible;
that my only chance for happiness
is to go off with my family to some solitary place
where we can live in peace.
—TENZING NORGAY, *Man of Everest*

TENZING ENCOUNTERED MANY OLD FRIENDS while he was in Europe, seeing them for the first time in the context of their lives rather than as sahibs descending as though visitors from another planet to Darjeeling. He saw Hugh Ruttledge, who had led the 1936 expedition and was now in his late 60s. He met Nugent Jekyll again, who had cared for Dawa Phuti when she was dying in Chitral. Jekyll had driven the length of Britain to see Tenzing, and the Sherpa insisted on his staying to examine Pem Pem. Eric Shipton, who had chosen Tenzing as a late addition to the 1935 reconnaissance, had come to London to greet them off the aircraft. Despite being so cruelly sacked from the leadership of the Everest climb, when Shipton heard the news of its success he wrote to a friend: "I'm really delighted that it was Ed Hillary who pulled it off—he is a grand mountaineer and a delightful person: he is one of the few I know who has the strength of character to withstand the avalanche of public acclamation that is coming to him. And *nothing* could have been more fitting than that Tenzing should have been there to represent the Sherpas."[1]

The other Sherpas, of course, had not come to London. The expedition had waved them good-bye in Kathmandu, where, unfêted and unknown, they had made the now familiar journey back to their homes in Darjeeling or Khumbu. They had been presented with no medals nor given any receptions with prime ministers and monarchs. Even Koirala's fulsome tribute made at the height of the public hysteria in Kathmandu over Tenzing's success had acknowledged them only as an afterthought. It is not difficult even now to find older Sherpas who are bitter about what Tenzing did, or more accurately, didn't do for them after Everest. It was, they say, Ed Hillary who helped Khumbu Sherpas by establishing the Himalayan Trust and building them schools and clinics and later helping underpin Khumbu's fragile environment.

In later years, when Tenzing visited Khumbu, he received a warm welcome from relatives and friends. But there were some who felt aggrieved by him. In the mid-1970s, Tenzing was in Nauche, the center of Khumbu commercial life. Hillary was also in Solu Khumbu, at a time when the Himalayan Trust was particularly active, constructing amenities for the Sherpas. Tenzing made a disparaging remark about Hillary, the kind of offhand comment that has only momentary significance. When Tenzing later approached the village of Phortse, some villagers, angered by gossip they had heard about the incident, came out and threw stones at him. It was an isolated incident, but it upset Tenzing deeply. In one version of the story he canceled his trek and immediately went home.

It was also unfair. Hillary has been widely and quite properly honored for his efforts in helping the Sherpas in Solu Khumbu. Yet what Tenzing did was just as useful. For a start, he gave the Sherpas a name that they could use to generate wealth. Sherpas are the most famous mountain tribe in the world, with an immediate advantage over other ethnic groups in Nepal and across the Himalaya as a whole. Until recently all kinds of tribes adjacent to the Sherpas would adopt the name "Sherpa" to boost their prospects of employment. Even for his Sherpa friends who went home barely acknowledged by the wider world, their participation in the first ascent of Everest gave each of them a cachet they were able to exploit on future expeditions. In effect, he put the word "Sherpa" into the global lexicon. Brand managers have turned to the word again and again, for every kind of product from sunscreen to delivery trucks.

Nor did Tenzing capitalize heavily on his fame, exploiting his success with endorsements and sponsorships. Dorje Lhatoo said, "India is a nation of hero-worshippers," and in the 1950s, Tenzing's celebrity matched the colossal fame of a modern Indian hero like the cricketer Sachin Tendulkar. Wherever he went in 1953 and 1954 he drew vast crowds. In the city of Madras, 50,000 people came to see him, and Tenzing asked Rabi Mitra to teach him a few phrases of Tamil so he could thank them in their own language. In a March 1954 letter to a member of the Himlayan Club, P. V. Patanakar, about a proposed visit to Bombay, Tenzing apologized for not having been in touch, but pleaded for forgiveness on the grounds that his life was still in turmoil, almost a year after going to Everest: "The burden, at times, seems too heavy for me. I am now surrounded with so many problems that I sometimes get lost altogether."[2] He promised that he would come to Bombay, asking that his visit coincide with a screening of *The Conquest of Everest,* the film shot by Tom Stobart. Tenzing did make it down to Bombay that spring, but collapsed during a heat wave and was too weak to go on. B. C. Roy, the chief minister of West Bengal, ordered Tenzing home to rest, but later that summer, staying with Nehru at Rashtrapati Bhavan after a trip to Punjab, he was once more overwhelmed by heat and exhaustion. Ang Lhamu was attempting to cool him with wet towels when Nehru and his daughter, Indira, looked into his room. Seeing that Tenzing's bed was some distance from the ceiling fan, he and Indira helped Ang Lhamu drag his bed underneath it to cool him further.

The effort Tenzing made to reach out to others was considerable and made for motives no more complicated than a desire to share his success with as many people as he could. "I do not think myself any biggish man," Tenzing told Patanakar. "I am the same old Tenzing Sherpa. By honouring me, my countrymen and people all over the world have honoured an ordinary toiler who by dint of courage and enduring patience has been able to do something which they admire."[3] This was no pose; Tenzing's modesty was genuine. Kaye Weatherall, whose husband, Micky, had grown up in Darjeeling, knew Tenzing well. Her sister-in-law Marigold had been secretary of the Planters' Club in Darjeeling, where Tenzing had queued to be interviewed for work in 1935, and which is now run for wealthy

Indians. Kaye would see Tenzing there and at his new home. "I remember the last time I met him in the early 1970s, at Losar [the Tibetan New Year], in his best clothes. He was such a distinguished looking man and didn't remotely look his age. He was so modest and retiring; not remotely big-headed. I thought he carried off his fame very graciously." Jack Gibson agreed. When they met for lunch in Delhi in 1961, Gibson hadn't seen his friend since his success on Everest eight years before: "He was quite unchanged and unspoiled and said the right thing when he exclaimed that I wasn't looking at all like an old man."[4] By contrast, Sachin Tendulkar (a cricketer) is a millionaire whose image is used to sell almost anything to modern consumerist India. Tenzing's celebrity was used in a different way, one that perhaps seems old-fashioned now and would ultimately penalize him, but one that had a vision and purpose behind it that ranged far beyond mere consumerism and celebrity.

WHEN TENZING LEFT LONDON, he flew to Switzerland to visit his friends from the 1947 expedition to Garhwal and Everest the year before. He had already seen Annelies Lohner—now Sutter—and Raymond Lambert when the expedition had stopped in Geneva on their way to London, but now he spent a fortnight there, starting in Zürich. The visit had been organized by the Swiss Foundation for Alpine Research, and its secretary, Ernst Feuz, who knew Tenzing from the Garhwal, and his wife, Maria, arranged an itinerary for Tenzing's stay. He spent much of his time in Geneva with Raymond Lambert— eventually Lambert's appartment would become a home away from home for Tenzing. After arriving in Zürich, Tenzing spent several days at a mountaineering school in Rosenlaui in the Bernese Oberland run by the guide Arnold Glatthard. In a stint of climbing, Tenzing made the short ascent to the summit of the Jungfrau with Lambert from the Jungfraujoch mountain railway station. "As we stood on top, looking out over the earth," *Tiger of the Snows* relates, "I think perhaps the same thought was in both our minds: that with a little better weather, a little better luck, we could have done this together a year before— on the top of the world."[5]

Later, back in Zürich, the Swiss Foundation for Alpine Research gave Tenzing a reception to which they invited the chief minister of West Bengal, Dr. B. C. Roy, who was in Switzerland for eye surgery. At the reception, Ernst Feuz and the wealthy founder of the foundation, Carl Weber, discussed with Roy and Tenzing the idea of a mountaineering school based in Darjeeling. The original idea had come from Tenzing's friend Rabi Mitra, who had written to Roy immediately after the Everest climb. Alert to the value of Tenzing's new fame, Mitra had in mind something more than a technical climbing school. He wanted to introduce Indians to their own mountains, not just as abodes for the gods but as geographical, cultural, and sporting entities. He wanted to broaden the curriculum of the proposed school—to be called the Himalayan Mountaineering Institute— to include study of medicinal plants, geology, and so on. Nehru was keen on the idea. "Now you will make a thousand Tenzings," he said, seeing the institute as a way of capitalizing on Tenzing's high profile, a new hero for a new nation. "Nehru," Mitra said, "wrote to all the district heads and said that wherever Tenzing went he should be treated as a national hero." The new institute would employ the euphoria and excitement of the climb for use by future generations. Dorje Lhatoo, who would eventually become deputy director of field training, said: "It was based around Tenzing to a great extent but the administration of an institute like that could not be left to an illiterate person." The Himalayan Mountaineering Institute (HMI) would be brought within the aegis of India's bureaucracy, its board composed of officers from the national and state departments of education and the ministry of defense. "In effect, he was working for the army," Lhatoo said. Tenzing would not be the principal, but director of field training. "Tenzing was really the number two but he wasn't seen as that. He was the star. He could talk to the prime minister directly and when Nehru came to Darjeeling he wanted to speak to Tenzing. In the early days Nehru gave the institute his personal attention. He was keen to come and see what was happening."

Privately, Nehru was not convinced that the institute would attract enough students to sustain it, but plans continued to be laid, and Roy set about energetically raising the two million rupees—$420,000 in 1954—from government and industry to build and launch HMI. Nehru was criticized for spending so much on what was perceived as a Western sport when so much basic development work needed to be done, but he understood the value of symbols to a new nation. At the institute's opening ceremony, he said: "The lure of the Himalaya is spreading now all over India among our young people, and that is a sign and a symbol of the new life and the new spirit that is coursing through India's veins."

Roy invited Nandu Jayal, Tenzing's companion from the Doon School expedition to Bandarpunch in 1950, to become the first principal. Although an army officer, Nandu Jayal was a philosophical mountaineer, having more in common with his hero Leslie Stephen, the elegant climbing writer and founding editor of the *Dictionary of National Biography*, than his later successors, who saw the sport as an expression of nationalism. Climbing, for Jayal, had been a saving grace.His headmaster, Arthur Foot, described him as "as scruffy a small boy as could be imagined." Too restless for an academic career, Jayal found true fulfillment in the mountains. "The Himalaya," Foot wrote, "had completed his education into a stature of enduring nobility."[6] Tenzing is now honored as the founding father of the HMI, but Jayal's love for the mountains gave the school the kind of depth that would mark its earlier years as a highly successful operation.

In the fall of 1953, Arnold Glatthard traveled to India, and with Nandu Jayal and Tenzing explored the mountains east of Kanchenjunga for a suitable location for the school's field operations. They settled on Ratong and Kabru, technically straightforward peaks, but at 21,000 and 24,000 feet considerably bigger than anything Europe had to offer. A site for Base Camp was found at a point they named Kabur Saddle near the village of Dzongri in Sikkim, located below an area suitable for rock climbing. Other base camps for ascents of Ratong, the mountain for intermediate students, and Kabru, the most advanced, were also chosen. Glatthard wanted to build a hut at Kabur Saddle, but Tenzing preferred to use tents. Much of the instructing he had done for the Indian Army had been about "camp craft," traveling and surviving in the mountains, rather than technical climbing, and he felt that managing a tent camp was an important skill. This kind of approach, addressing the practicalities of life in a harsh land, would characterize the courses at the new institute.

In June 1954 Tenzing and Jayal went to Europe, again as guests of the Swiss Foundation for Alpine Research, to take the course at Champex.

Most of the 50 or so candidates for the guide's course were experienced alpine climbers with a much higher technical standard than Tenzing. Now 40 years old, with two decades' experience of the harshest conditions on Earth, Tenzing was forced to start at the beginning again, and it was not always a comfortable experience. He acknowledged his lack of rock-climbing expertise, but didn't enjoy being treated as a novice. Afterward, they moved on to Rosenlaui, where Glatthard would train them and six other Sherpas as instructors. The six chosen to accompany Tenzing and Jayal were among the best of the Sherpas: Da Namgyal and Ang Temba from Everest the year before; two highly experienced sirdars, Ang Tharkay and Gyalzen Mikcha; and Tenzing's nephews Nawang Gombu and Nawang Topgay. Glatthard later said that the Sherpas struggled to see the point of deliberately picking a harder route to the summit of a mountain: "They thought it was a childish waste of time."[7]

Tenzing was now in a position of considerable patronage. Working as an instructor at HMI was a much easier life than working on expeditions. The job offered year-round employment for a start, plus the promise of a pension and housing, the full panoply of benefits offered by the juggernaut of Indian bureaucracy. Ang Tharkay would not last long as an instructor, perhaps inevitably. Both he and Tenzing were proud, and until very recently the older man had been the more widely respected. Now he was in effect in an inferior position, and within only a few years he left to take up a new career in business.

Gombu and Topgay were both excellent Sherpas, but there were others not selected by HMI over the years who felt they were denied a chance by Tenzing's relatives. One of Ang Tsering's sons told of the resentment at the way Tenzing favored his family members. Lhatoo, who married Tenzing's niece Sonam Doma in 1962, was in the Indian Army earning 60 rupees a month before his wedding. "Once I was a member of the family," he said, "it was easy for me to get employment [at HMI]." Yet nepotism played only a partial role in the selection process. Gombu was a strong mountaineer who taught himself to read and write and was independent-minded. Tenzing liked to think that Gombu owed a lot to him, but his nephew, as Tenzing had, made the most of his opportunities. Likewise, Lhatoo was one of the strongest mountaineers India ever produced, reaching the summit of Everest in 1984. If Tenzing promoted his relatives, he was only behaving as any other Sherpa would have, and he didn't use men who weren't up to the job.

Like most Sherpas before him, Lhatoo was not prepared to take only what he was given. Being gathered into the family firm didn't stop him from demanding improved pay and conditions. "The original Sherpas were happy with what they'd got. Tenzing would say: 'Don't complain, you've got far more than your fathers had.' But we had learned to complain. We were trouble." Tenzing now found himself in the position of his erstwhile employers. The irony wasn't lost on Lhatoo.

After he climbed Everest, Tenzing gave some of the money raised for him by the *Statesman* to the Sherpa Buddhist Association, now renamed the Sherpa Climbers Association, established to help impoverished retired porters. He also tried to set up what was effectively a cooperative travel agency in competition with the Himalayan Club, offering Sherpas better rates of pay than they had enjoyed until then. It was another practical example of the ways Tenzing used his success for the benefit of Sherpas. Ultimately his plan didn't get off the ground, and not until the 1970s did former Gurkha officers such as Jimmy Roberts and Mike Cheney start trekking agencies that allowed the Sherpas to take control of their own futures. The Sherpa Buddhist Association, however, its main center now transferred to Kathmandu, still looks after old Sherpas and arranges funding for their funeral rites when necessary. It also offers support for the poorest Sherpa families irrespective of their involvement in mountaineering.

As the Himalayan Mountaineering Institute became more established and Tenzing got older, he became impatient with those like Lhatoo who wanted more. Hadn't he done enough for them? He took it personally, as though they were criticizing his life's work. "I tolerated him so much and no more," Lhatoo said. "I fought back. I was always thinking of better conditions for my family and at the time I was angry, even harsh. As I've got older, I realize I should have tolerated him more." Relations grew so strained that they stopped speaking to each other and were no longer able to work on the same courses at HMI. Gombu, tough and straight-talking but also devoted to his uncle, eventually persuaded Lhatoo to make peace. Together they walked around to Ghang La, Tenzing's big new house on Tonga Road, with Lhatoo carrying a kata to offer as a traditional token of conciliation. When Tenzing answered the door and bent his head slightly to accept the scarf, Lhatoo froze, unable to overcome his pride. Instead Tenzing took the scarf from him, put it around his neck, and embraced his niece's troublesome husband. Relations were restored.

Offices for the Himalayan Mountaineering Institute were planned for a site on Birch Hill, close to Darjeeling's zoo with its Siberian tigers— a gift to Nehru from Nikita Khrushchev—and Himalayan bears. Meanwhile, Jayal, Tenzing, and their staff started work in temporary accommodations. The Swiss Foundation donated the necessary equipment: 25 sets of crampons, 25 ice axes, 25 of everything. The enterprise started on schedule in November 1954 with just 18 students. Nehru himself, the founder-president, came to cut the ribbon, and Tenzing welcomed him at the gate to Ghang La in his knickerbockers and argyle socks.

Ultimately, Tenzing would leave the institute a bitter and frustrated man, but during his 23 years as director of field training over four and a half thousand students completed courses under his tutelage. "Especially I would like," he said in *Tiger of the Snows,* "to help and teach young people with their lives before him. What I can teach is not from books, to be sure, but what I have learned from living my own life." That in itself was a great deal. Seven of Tenzing's students would go on to reach the summit of Everest in 1965 as part of the first successful Indian expedition, and many others had successes throughout the Himalaya. "It was, under Tenzing's leadership, a very special place," Dorje Lhatoo said. In the final analysis, Nehru's faith in Tenzing was realized.

Nehru became, for Tenzing, the ultimate zhindak, a patron who could unlock every door. To Nehru, Tenzing was a breath of fresh mountain air, a man of action outside the manipulative and subtle world of Indian politics. Nehru understood exactly how the system could trample over someone like Tenzing. "When I was with Tenzing in Pandi Nehru's house," Rabi Mitra recalled, "Nehru gave Tenzing a personal letter to the Chief Minister of West Bengal. Nehru told Roy that Tenzing must have a house of his own; it must be bought from the public fund so Tenzing would have that sense of belonging. It must not be a gift from the government. His daughters must be taught in English-medium schools. I handed the letter to Dr. Roy and all the bureaucrats said: 'No, they must be taught in Nepalese schools, in their own culture.' But these men were themselves sending their own children to English-medium schools. Roy said it was a direct order from Nehru and the matter was settled."

On the same occasion, Nehru's secretary offered Tenzing Indira Gandhi's car to drive down to Agra and do some sightseeing. Rabi Mitra was all for it; he had never seen the Taj Mahal and was excited by the prospect. Tenzing said he would rather not. He didn't want people to think that he was using the prime minister's car for something so frivolous when people were so obviously hard at work. Nehru could be thoughtful himself, on one occasion asking a secretary to check the time of Tenzing's arrival into Delhi so he could send a car to collect him. But he was also shrewd enough to understand Tenzing's independence and pride. Nehru suggested that Tenzing not use the money subscribed by the public to build himself a new house. "I am not a beggar," Tenzing would say. Materials for renovation were donated and some of the money from the *Statesman* did go toward the purchase of Ghang La, but the balance went to the Sherpa Buddhist Association. All told, according to Mitra, Tenzing earned from his deal with United Press, the climb, and various subscriptions about 60,000 rupees, in today's terms more than $84,000. More would follow with the publication of *Tiger of the Snows*. For a Sherpa that was a colossal amount of money, more than many Nepalese even now would earn in ten lifetimes. But as Tenzing gradually discovered, it wasn't that much in the world he was now moving in. "Nehru had assured him," Ed Hillary said, "that he would never again be poor; that he would have a good standard of living. But the standard of living they paid him was for an averagely well-to-do person in Darjeeling. As Tenzing traveled around the world he realized that the amount of money he was getting was very little."

Ghang La was a substantial house on the other side of the hill from Toong Soong Busti and the one-room apartment he had shared with Ang Lhamu and the girls for so many years. It had an excellent view of Kanchenjunga and in the years before Darjeeling became overcrowded and heavily polluted, it was in a prime location. The "Ghang La" was, Tenzing explained, his clan name, although in reality it was the place where his father had grazed yaks in the summer, and the sight of the monastery nearby. The name expressed his connection to his family roots in Kharta. Inside, the house was decorated in a Tibetan style. There was a prayer room, with the rugs, *thangkas,* icons, and brassware found in all Tibetan houses, and what amounted to a trophy room. The windows were large and looked out over a veranda toward Kanchenjunga. On the wall opposite was a portrait of Gandhi, with those of Nehru, Queen Elizabeth, and the Duke of Edinburgh just below. The duke had sent Tenzing a Christmas card in 1953 and this was displayed too, alongside one from John Hunt and addressed simply to "Tenzing of Everest." Arranged around the room were ice axes and knives, a primus stove and other souvenirs, photos of Tenzing with Lambert on the Jungfrau, his various medals, a silver relief map of the Himalaya, and on the wall to the right the famous shot of him standing on the summit. Tenzing would show almost anyone who turned up around his new house, and Ang Lhamu never failed in her hospitality. Christopher Rand, writing a profile of Tenzing for the *New Yorker,* asked him why he was so welcoming. "'If I don't,' he answered, 'they say I am too big.' And he scratched his head and laughed nervously." By the time Rand visited Tenzing, Mitra was working full-time as Tenzing's secretary, managing his engagements and writing his correspondence. As Rand realized, access to Tenzing was everything. "Mitra is a warm, idealistic young man who seems to be devoted to Tenzing, but he is also an ardent Indian patriot and Bengali—Bengalis are traditionally impassioned—and he may contribute tension as well as advice to his employer." But Tenzing needed someone like Mitra to bridge the gap between the narrow world of the Sherpas and the global stage onto which he had stepped. If Mitra understood politics, he also understood the significance of Nehru's patronage and the importance of what Tenzing was doing. Rand also observed that Tenzing was no businessman. "In the ways of the world," Hillary said, "he was rather a simple soul. He liked the idea of being well-to-do but he didn't really know how to go about doing it."

Tenzing's openness to visitors could be a terrific strain. Rand describes an uncomfortable scene at Ghang La when an American tourist, with no real interest in mountaineering but certain that Tenzing was a celebrity worth meeting, paid a call. "[He] started by offering Tenzing a cigarette. Tenzing refused, saying he never smoked. The American began to light one himself, then stopped and asked if it was all right. 'Ooh, certainly,' said Tenzing, and eagerly brought forth an ashtray. There was a pause. The caller looked out the window. The day happened to be clear, and he could see the distant snows. He remarked on how splendid they were, and Tenzing agreed. 'Because one week ago weather not so good,' Tenzing said gropingly, 'but today quite good.' The caller asked if it would be clear right along now, with spring coming on. Tenzing thought this over and said it would. 'But Darjeeling also always September, October, November is the best season,' he added, and smiled his dazzling smile and laughed his nervous laugh."

Everyone came to Tenzing's door, from dignitaries like Nehru and Roy down to India's poorest, who venerated Tenzing as a god and prostrated themselves before him. Ang Lhamu, who was always pleased to welcome film stars such as Dilip Kumar and Shashi Kapoor, would cook for them all and line up for yet another family portrait. It's hard to imagine this kind of access to a modern celebrity, even one who liked nothing better than meeting the public, but even Tenzing eventually learned a few tricks for avoiding unwanted strangers. In later years he became an avid gardener and was often outside tending to his plants. "Family and friends," wrote Jamling Tenzing Norgay, "always got a chuckle to see Bengali tourists shout up to him from the street below when he was out gardening, 'Hey gardener! Where's Tenzing Sah'b? Is he in the house?' And my father would respond, 'No, I think he went into town.' When he did leave, he often took a secret route, up through the grove of mountain bamboo behind the house and onto the high road above."[8]

While Tenzing's new house was under construction by 1954, the book he had committed to provide for United Press became stalled. For a start, confirming Rand's view of Tenzing as an innocent in business, the deal was complicated. UPA, as Tenzing's agent, sold the world rights to the London publisher George C. Harrap, who in turn sold rights around the world, taking 25 percent of each deal, before UPA took 10 percent of whatever was left. Had Tenzing waited for a deal with *Life*, he might have done a lot better. Despite his contract, Tenzing was looked after, particularly by UPA's European business manager, George Pipal, who took a long-term interest in Tenzing and attempted to guide him away from the pitfalls. Unluckily for Tenzing, members of the Indian government now saw the Sherpa as public property, meaning his private affairs were a matter of national interest. Nehru appointed a lawyer, Anand Prakash, in Delhi to manage negotiations and thus influence Tenzing's decision making. He also wanted his niece Nayan Tara Saigal to ghost Tenzing's book. This wasn't acceptable to United Press or Tenzing's British editor, Walter Harrap, who wanted a Westerner, specifically an Englishman, to write it. Richard Marsh, Tenzing's companion from Nanga Parbat three years before, was commissioned to write the book but gave up as the project faltered. As far as the Indians were concerned, if Tenzing couldn't have an Indian writing his story, then he wasn't going to have an Englishman either. Then, in the fall of 1954, Malartic's creative intepretation of Tenzing's life appeared, diluting the impact Tenzing's own book might make. The delays undoubtedly affected Tenzing's chance at cashing in on his fame. Harrap told James Ramsey Ullman, after the manuscript of *Tiger of the Snows* was completed: "I should not be honest with you if I did not admit that we could in all probability have doubled, or even trebled subscription sales if Tenzing had not played the fool by procrastinating over the choice of collaborator."[9] It wasn't Tenzing's fault. By December 1954 George Pipal was telling Ullman that it was no use threatening Prakash, Tenzing's lawyer, to withhold payments to sort out a contractual problem because it was "clear that Tenzing had no liaison with or influence over Prakash." United Press, it turned out, had been representing the Indian government's wishes for Tenzing, not Tenzing himself.

Fate instead sent James Ramsey Ullman, a best-selling popular novelist with a great interest in mountaineering. Ullman had been in the offices of New York publishing house Putnam when Ted Purdy, who would edit the American edition of the book, discovered in a letter from Walter Harrap that Dick Marsh had abandoned the project. Ullman, who had regretted missing the chance to write Tenzing's book and had asked to contribute an introduction to any American edition, now took his chance. United Press cabled Anand Prakash in Delhi to ask if an American would be acceptable. George Pipal of UPA was especially pleased to recommend Ullman, who had agreed to take a 25 percent royalty, compared with the 50 percent Nehru's niece had been asking. Tenzing, mixing naïve enthusiasm with the feeling that he should be cautious, wrote to Ullman in early April 1954: "I have just received your letter. I have heard of you as an author of repute on mountains and mountaineering. My friends also speak highly in praise of you. I am feeling really very happy that my agent—the United Press of America—have ultimately been successful in getting you for me. Very warmly and heartily I welcome you."

Ullman flew to India to start work but was annoyed to discover that Tenzing was about to leave for Switzerland to take the guide's course with Nandu Jayal. Any plans for a book couldn't interfere with India's desire to open a mountaineering school. Instead B. C. Roy loaned Ullman his stenographer so he could at least make a start. With Mitra acting as interpreter, they set to work roughing out, as Ullman saw it, the most important chapter of all—the ascent of Everest. "By trial and error," Ullman explained to the *New York Times Book Review*, "we finally arrived at a method which involved four people—besides Tenzing and myself, Mr. Mitra, Tenzing's friend and assistant, and Mr. Gupta, the stenographer on loan from [Roy]."[10] Ullman said that he spent three weeks—"six days a week, eight hours a day"[11]—with Tenzing, and another week in Europe that spring. He was under time pressure. In the original contract United Press had wanted a book delivered by September 1953, and Harrap's was desperate to get the book out before interest in Everest waned. Ullman drew up his conversations with Tenzing into notes and used these as a basis for the narrative. He adopted a very deliberate style that was not apparent in Tenzing's speech but that captured what Ullman perceived to be Tenzing's character. Wherever Tenzing is quoted, it is with the refined gloss of James Ramsey Ullman.

After completing his first set of interviews, Ullman began writing, drawing in reports from other sources. In July he checked with the Royal Geographical Society in London on Tenzing's account of the climb. The exchange was reported to the Himalayan Committee. Its secretary, L. P. Kirwan, hurriedly wrote a letter to John Hunt to warn him that Tenzing had given Ullman a "mass of incorrect information," which gave "the impression of the terrific efforts that Tenzing had to make to stop the arrogant British from making complete fools of themselves but how he finally succeded in getting us to the top of the mountain."[12]

Of course, plenty of British climbers in the 1930s had felt that the Royal Geographical Society needed saving from itself to avoid looking foolish, so Kirwan's reaction seems rather extreme. Tenzing was proud and wanted people to know about his contribution. Several members of the expedition did the same, albeit with the sophistication of worldly, well-educated men. Ullman was shrewd enough not to allow Tenzing to appear churlish. He went out of his way to create an impression that Tenzing was stating his case and no more.

Tenzing couldn't wait to see the book. "I can't imagine what old photos of me you have dug up, but I trust you will have pity on me when the final selection is made. In the meantime I am waiting impatiently for that moment when you are going to sing to me about me. If it has a good marching tune to it, I shall learn it to spur me on when climbing."[13] By the end of October Ullman had sent the first 13 chapters to Tenzing for his comments. "So far it has been wonderful," Tenzing wrote to him, requesting very few changes and none at all in the remaining chapters that arrived later in the year. How thoroughly it was read to him remains a matter of conjecture. Inevitably, there were errors and gaps that Ullman was forced to paper over. The broad outline is true, but some of the details, particularly about his early life, are fudged, not least because Tenzing didn't want to have to explain too closely his origins and the poverty his family endured. Ullman wanted to visit Khumbu, but visa problems and lack of time prevented him. As a consequence the chapter devoted to the culture and history of the Sherpas is really an account of their lives in Darjeeling.

Ullman chose to use a very simple style which he felt matched Tenzing's lack of sophistication, but in doing so he missed undercurrents and complexities in Tenzing's life, which, had they been explained, would have shown the true scale of his achievement. Walter Harrap, however, was delighted with the book, praising Ullman for capturing "the simplicity of Tenzing." "Must mention that your book has it all over Hunt's *Everest* as real enjoyment," he wrote to Ullman in early 1955. "C___ and H_____ will be gnashing their teeth when you sell a 100,000 in a number of weeks." Although Harrap complained that bookshops were reluctant to take another story about Everest, orders were strong enough to reprint before publication and he expected the book to be a best-seller.

In April 1955 the book was heavily serialized in *Sports Illustrated*— "*Sports Illustrated* brings you everything but the snow!"—and in *Reader's Digest*. These deals alone netted Tenzing $25,000. In Britain, rights were sold to World Books for a book club print run of a quarter of a million.

When it was published in May, *Tiger of the Snows* made a big initial impact around the world, particularly in America, where it was reviewed most notably by William O. Douglas, Associate Justice of the U.S. Supreme Court. Douglas, who matched his principled defense of civil liberties with a passion for mountains and wilderness, was then at the height of his fame, having faced charges of impeachment over his stay of execution for the spies Julius and Ethel Rosenberg. Later, he would face further criticism for his opposition to American policy in Southeast Asia. Douglas actually met Tenzing during a visit to Darjeeling soon after the book was published, and he told him he thought it would be a bestseller. Ullman's portrait of Tenzing as the simple man of nature uncorrupted by the cynicism of the West appealed to Douglas, who reviewed it in the *New York Herald Tribune*. "The warm heart of a noble Asian comes through on every page," he wrote, touching on Rousseau's ideal of the noble savage. "He comes through in these pages a fine human being—tender in emotions, discriminating in his judgments, tolerant of people, dedicated to mountain life." Others, such as the mountaineer Charles Houston, writing in the *New York Times Book Review,* echoed Douglas's view: "This record has the fresh naïveté, the natural candor and the warmth of a simple man telling his story without act or pretense." Ullman's portrayal matched an ideal that resonated particularly with those who saw the appeal of nature as a moral force for good.

Other reviewers were suspicious of Ullman's role. The *New York Post*, with characteristic directness, said: "You'd think the stuff would come out sounding more Ullman than Tenzing, and this is exactly what happens." W. G. Rogers, in a review syndicated all over the United States thought it "silly" to call the book an autobiography when its author couldn't read. In Britain, where the book was published as *Man of Everest*, Tenzing's naturalness was deemed appealing, although perhaps in less lofty philosophical terms than Douglas or Houston had expressed. "Not having been to an English public school he is entirely without inhibitions," John Morris wrote in the *Observer*. "Only a man of outstanding character could have survived the adulation and honours that were later showered upon him, but this honest and sincere account shows him to be quite unspoilt." The *Sunday Times*, on the other hand, was suspicious of the book's simple tone. "The reader stops from time to time, at the apparent identity of the thoughts of this great Sherpa mountaineer with those of the not-too-sophisticated middle-Westerner to whom he has told his authentic and official life-story." The book attempted the simple prose of Ernest Hemingway. One reviewer—Hugh Popham, writing in *Time and Tide*—even suggested, "If Ernest Hemingway were ever to create a mountaineer, as he has created bullfighters and soldiers and the fisherman of the *Old Man and the Sea*, the emerging portrait might come very close to the Tenzing of *Man of Everest*."

The book sold well during the summer of 1955, reaching the eighth spot on the *New York Times* best-seller list, but it stayed there for only two weeks and then slipped back down, failing to catch fire in the way that other mountaineering books have done, before and since. It certainly appealed more to the public than Edmund Hillary's rather tight-lipped version, which was published in the same year. ("Sir Edmund Hillary," Elizabeth Cox wrote in the *Spectator*, "is not interested in Tenzing's feelings, or in any feelings, not even his own.") By mid-July, Putnam was telling Ullman that sales for June were a little over 15,000, less than they had anticipated, and that in the first week of July sales were only 900. The book would not make a fortune for either of them.

In one sense Ullman did succeed with *Tiger of the Snows*. Tenzing was a remarkable man, open, honest, and engaging, and this emerges in the book. John Hunt recognized the portrait as that of Tenzing. "Ullman," he wrote in an unpublished *Sunday Times* review, "has interpreted the real Tenzing whom I knew. He has revealed his frank, engaging manner, his quaint mode of expressing his thoughts, almost even his wide smile and the dancing humour in his eyes." Other friends of Tenzing were less persuaded. Charles Wylie and Trevor Braham both thought Ullman's style made Tenzing seem too simple, without giving credit to his intelligence and courage in overcoming his problems and without showing the subtlety and richness of Tibetan culture. That charge is true. Ullman didn't pass beyond the superficial, smiling image of the Sherpas to the more complex and less flattering world beneath. He understood his readers would prefer an idealized version of the truth. *Tiger of the Snows* fed the tradition of writing admiringly and uncritically of the Sherpas, a habit that encouraged in readers a false impression of an enchanted world. The reality has always been that life on the roof of the world was just as complex and messy as life below. Perhaps the shrewdest—and most kind—view came not from a critic but from the principal of St. Joseph's College in Darjeeling, Father M. Stanford, who wrote to *Sports Illustrated* following their serialization. "The passage about who got there first," he wrote, "belongs to the ages."

Tiger of the Snows was published at a difficult time for Tenzing. On the first day of June his elder sister, Lhamu Kipa, died. She was a strong connection to his early life, his sense of place in a changing world, and her loss had a heavy impact on Tenzing's morale, as he told John Hunt in a letter written a fortnight afterward. "During the long illness of my elder sister for the past few months I had to keep up wakeful nights at her bedside, and ultimately with her passing away, I too have suffered a great mental and spiritual setback. The physicians now advise me to take complete rest for some months to regain full health and stability. Naturally, therefore, I have had to cancel my U.S. visit."[14] Tenzing's letter to Hunt showed that their relationship had healed. Hunt had written a generous letter to Tenzing congratulating him on his book and tackling head-on the difficulties between them in Kathmandu.

"I was not at all angry," Hunt wrote, "at the press conference at Kathmandu when a question was put to me about your skill and standing as a mountaineer. What I actually said was that I considered you a very fine mountaineer but you had not yet had experience of some of the very high standard technical climbing to be experienced in the Alps. What I should have added was that Hillary was exactly in the same position." Hunt knew Hillary was technically the better climber, but he was anxious that Tenzing understood how much his contribution was valued. "I fully admit that it would have been much wiser for you and Hillary to have written the summit chapter of my book together."[15]

The final reference in Tenzing's reply to Hunt was his proposed visit to the United States. "I can think of few things I want more," he said, "than visit the United States."[16] He had turned down an invitation from the Explorers' Club in early 1954 because, he said, of commitments to the institute, although it is clear the Indian government wasn't happy about Tenzing disappearing while he was still doing engagements in India. Instead, the American ambassador, George V. Allen, traveled to Darjeeling to present Tenzing with the National Geographic Society's

Hubbard Medal. United Press had talked about organizing a series of lectures and lined up a top agency in New York. Tenzing understood very well the kind of impact he could make. He was delighted by the response to his book, and in July 1955 wrote to Ullman: "Almost every other day I am receiving letters of appreciation from the American readers of my biography."

Politics would once again impinge on Tenzing's life. He benefited a great deal from his friendship with Nehru, not least in his appointment to the Himalayan Mountaineering Institute, but there were those in Delhi who felt this gave them the right to interfere in his private business arrangements. In the spring of 1955, George Pipal of UPA met Krishna Menon, then leading the Indian delegation at the United Nations, at a party in London. "Menon," Pipal wrote to Ullman afterward, "who is as anti-American as any hothouse Russian, would dearly love to slit our collective throats, and he expressed his strong belief that neither J. R. Ullman or the United Press had a great deal to do with the book, although he did say he had confidence in Ullman." Menon threatened to tell Nehru not to let United Press sell the film rights to Tenzing's story; he also told Pipal that he didn't like the fact that Ullman had kept 25 percent of the copyright—as though it were any of his business in the first place—while conceding that the author was entitled to 25 percent of what he called "property rights." "I asked him what the difference was," Pipal continued, "and he said, one of prestige, which is very important to the Indian government. I told him I thought his objection was not only baseless, but rather ungrateful to a 'true friend of India' who accepted a twenty-five percent cut because he wanted to write the book more than he wanted to turn a quick rupee, 'like certain authors which the Indian Foreign Office tried to ram through at fifty percent.' It was all very dramatic."[17]

Tenzing was now seen by some in the Indian political elite as an emblem of Indian prestige. As an employee of the education ministry in West Bengal, Tenzing's activity could be monitored and even controlled. Tenzing himself felt adrift in this world. "If only people will leave me alone politically things will be all right."[18]

While the institute was still being established, Tenzing could afford the time to travel. He went to London in the autumn of 1955, taking in a visit to the dog show at Olympia to watch an Apso terrier he had given to Mrs. Henderson entered in best of breed. (Offspring of the parents acquired at Lhasa during the Tucci expedition in 1948, it was the *only* entry.) But getting permission to go on to America was proving difficult. At the end of May 1955, M. O. Mathai, a special assistant to Nehru, wrote to Pipal conceding that Tenzing might be able to go to America "for a short period" to give lectures and promote his book, but it seems the view of Tenzing as just a simple, uneducated man of the hills extended to Delhi. "We just do not understand how Tenzing is to go about delivering lectures. He cannot lecture." At that stage, however, it is doubtful whether any audience would have cared. "He sounds so nice," one British reviewer wrote, "that, reading the book, English people will regret that he does not like us more." Ullman had put Tenzing's human face on what appeared otherwise as a tough, remote feat of extreme endeavor, and everyone wanted to meet him. Tenzing was still talking about going to America, but the date was pushed back, to October 1958 and then February 1959. The truth was that it was no longer just his decision. While the rest of the Sherpas in Darjeeling carried on with their lives much as before, Tenzing had become, like Tennyson's Ulysses, a name, albeit one employed by the government of India. He would have to live with the burden of that for the rest of his life.

CHAPTER TWELVE

DAKU

I remember my youth and the feeling
that will never come back any more—the feeling that
I could last forever, outlast the sea, the earth, and all men;
the deceitful feeling that lures us on to joys, to perils, to love, to vain effort—
to death; the triumphant conviction of strength, the heat of life in the handful of dust,
the glow in the heart that with every year grows dim, grows cold, grows small,
and expires—and expires too soon, too soon—before life itself.
—JOSEPH CONRAD, *Youth*

THROUGHOUT THE WINTER AND SPRING of 1960 and 1961, Ed Hillary led a multifaceted expedition to Khumbu in Nepal that blended mountaineering, the construction of a school in Khumjung village, physiological research, and a hunt for the yeti, the one part of the enterprise, until Hillary fell ill, that attracted media attention. The "laboratory" for the high-altitude medical work was a shiny aluminum structure prefabricated in England and carried piecemeal to a high snowy col on the slopes of Ama Dablam, the stunning, precipitous mountain that guards the head of the Imja Khola Valley. Called "The Silver Hut," it housed for several months a team of researchers led by Griffith Pugh, the doctor whose work had contributed so much to the 1953 Everest expedition. After months of conducting the most important high-altitude physiological research done to that point, the expedition had a small problem: What should they do with the hut? It couldn't stay where it was, cluttering up the beautiful side valley, so Hillary wrote to the Himalayan Mountaineering Institute and asked them if they could find a use for it. The offer was accepted, and Tenzing was dispatched to go to Khumbu and arrange for porters to carry it down from the mountains and transport it back to Darjeeling.

Although much had been achieved over the nine months of his expedition, it had been personally traumatic for Ed Hillary. During an attempt on Makalu, the world's fifth highest mountain, in the spring of 1961, he had suffered what co-expeditioner Michael Ward diagnosed as a cerebral vascular accident, essentially a stroke, ending his high-altitude climbing career. Still weak from its effects, Hillary trekked slowly through the monsoon rains toward Kathmandu. Soon after crossing the Lamjura Pass, still several days from reaching the capital, Hillary met Tenzing walking in. "He had with him the most gorgeous-looking young lady that you'd ever seen in your living days," Hillary recalled, "and he introduced her as his niece. That was the first time I'd met Daku. We were all very impressed."

Daku was 21, and not only was she beautiful, she was vivacious and extroverted. In later life, she became deeply spiritual, but as a young woman, Daku was ambitious. The younger daughter of farmers in Chienyak, a small village above Thame, Daku—her full name was Dawa Phuti, like Tenzing's first wife—had come to Darjeeling to see the world beyond Khumbu. Like many young Sherpanis she found work with the institute carrying loads for the courses that trekked into Base Camp above Dzongri at Kabur Saddle. "In the beginning it was a love affair," Lhatoo said. "He was a father figure to these young girls who had come all the way from Solu Khumbu. Tenzing liked girls and he fell in love with Daku and soon she was carrying his child."

If there was an episode in Tenzing's life when he behaved with real selfishness, then this was it. The reasons were understandable enough. Tenzing was moving into his late 40s, and the attention of a beautiful woman made him feel vibrant and youthful. Ang Lhamu was a good friend, but their relationship was not sexual. She was a little older than Tenzing and by the early 1960s was not in good health. Tenzing's relationship with Daku was not the first outside his marriage. Tenzing liked the company of women; he was handsome, successful, and well-respected. But Daku's energy and youth were in another category altogether.

Just as pressing in Tenzing's mind was his desire to have a son. Ang Lhamu could not have children, and the memory of his little boy, Nima Dorje, haunted Tenzing. What good was all his success if he had no son to pass it on to? Tenzing knew that his affair caused Ang Lhamu pain, but in his second volume of autobiography, *After Everest*, Tenzing glossed over what happened. "There came a time when Ang Lhamu said that I must marry again so that I might have a son. And so, not only with her agreement, but urged by her to do so, I married Daku in 1961 and soon we did have a son, and later two more sons and a daughter."

"Not true," Pem Pem said. "He had to say that. Daku became pregnant with Norbu and my mother [Ang Lhamu] had no choice." Pem Pem was not happy about the prospect of her father marrying a woman who was a couple of years younger than she was, and she told her father that he was creating trouble for himself. She was also upset that her mother had been hurt, and this created tension between her and Daku. "It was the saddest part of Ang Lhamu's life but she had to accept the fact," Pem Pem said. "She could have been cruel, but she accepted and welcomed Daku for the sake of my father's happiness." Nima recalled, "She was hurt, but she tried to see things from a wider perspective. Ang Lhamu looked after Norbu when Daku traveled abroad."

Tenzing's relationship with Daku was further complicated because Norbu was not Tenzing's first child out of wedlock. In the late 1950s he had had an affair with a house servant at Ghang La who had become pregnant and given birth to a daughter. Had the child been a boy, the mother might well have stayed, but she returned quietly with her daughter to Solu Khumbu, well provided for with money. She later married a Tibetan. Among Sherpas back home, this kind of situation would have been dealt with maturely, focusing on the interests of the child, but Sherpa culture in Darjeeling was swayed more by Hindu attitudes, which were much less forgiving. Polygamy was routine in the mountains of Nepal or Tibet, but it was hardly acceptable in Hindu West Bengal. "It's a mixed-up place," Dorje Lhatoo told me. "There is an Indian morality that has been absorbed by the Sherpa community. Tenzing had much to lose and much to defend. He was a big man. People were looking at him all the time." (Eventually, in the 1970s, Tenzing's daughter returned to Darjeeling carrying her infant son. Her mother, Tenzing's lover, was ill and she had sent her daughter to ask for Tenzing's help. "Daddy wanted to adopt," Pem Pem said, "but Daku wouldn't let him.")

After this indiscretion, Ang Lhamu was anxious that Tenzing's reputation not suffer from any more gossip. The Sherpa community knew about his daughter, and he was under pressure to accept his responsibilities for this new child. He was also in love. Ang Lhamu had no choice but to move aside and allow her husband to take a second wife. Tenzing and Daku had four children: Norbu was born in 1962, Jamling in 1965, Deki, their daughter, in 1966, and Dhamey in 1969. In *Touching My Father's Soul*, Jamling Tenzing Norgay describes Tenzing, a father again in his 50s, as disciplined and tough. "My father understood hardship, and he wanted to show it to me and my siblings." Jamling resented his father's long absences, often for months at a time, and as a young man he felt the burden of growing up the son of a famous man. "'Do you your homework,' he'd say to us at home. 'Don't eat with your hands.' 'Sit there.' 'Get up and wash the dishes.' Offering to wash dishes was a custom he picked up in America, and he made us do it, too. We had live-in help, but he always said, 'There are no servants in this house.' On the mountain, when he gave orders, he would always jump in and help the other Sherpas with the work, such as pitching tents and carrying loads. A lightheartedness always accompanied my father's strictness."[1]

Although Ang Lhamu accepted her new position, the atmosphere at Ghang La changed and her final years were unhappy. In *Touching My Father's Soul*, Jamling Tenzing Norgay wrote that Ang Lhamu "didn't like to mix much socially." But this simply wasn't true. Ang Lhamu was self-effacing and modest, but she loved company and the house was always full of people. "She never got tired of entertaining guests," Pem Pem recalled. "Every day people used to come, from outside and our own relatives and community, and she would welcome them all."

She was compassionate too, and in practical ways, not just as a religious concept. In 1957 Gombu's wife Dawa Phuti gave birth to a daughter but tragically died after hemorrhaging during childbirth. Ang Lhamu, her daughters, and Gombu's sister Doma rushed to the house and found funeral rites being performed for Dawa Phuti and the baby fending for herself. Realizing that as a widower Gombu would find it difficult to look after a baby, Ang Lhamu took her to Planters' Hospital, where she was examined, then cared for. One of the nurses gave her the name Rita, and after six months Ang Lhamu took her back to Ghang La, where she spent the first few years of her life calling Ang Lhamu "mummy," just as Pem Pem and Nima had. Afterward, when Gombu remarried, the child returned to her father's house.

Similarly, when Tenzing's younger sister, Sonam Doma, died in 1956 of heatstroke near the town of Jaynagar and her husband, Namgyal, took to drink, Ang Lhamu and Tenzing absorbed their four daughters into their household. "They had dozens of people living there, up to sixty at one time," Lhatoo recalled. In his introduction to *Tiger of the Snows*, James Ramsey Ullman wrote in 1955: "His new home in Darjeeling hums with life. Presiding over it is his wife Ang Lhamu, a round and animated lady with a shrewd eye and a girlish giggle." By the early 1960s, things had changed. Pem Pem had married and was having her own children, the nieces were older and Nima too was grown up.

Tenzing had once complained if Ang Lhamu took the girls to the movies, but after Everest she welcomed these same Bombay movie stars into her own new home. It was a vibrant and exciting time, and Ang Lhamu reveled in it. "She was always there to help him," Pem Pem recalled, "and when he needed protection after Everest she was always there to protect him. She was a wonderful host; my father had a lot of pressure, mentally and physically. Sometimes my father would go wrong, make mistakes— and my mother would be there to put things right." With Daku's arrival at Ghang La, Ang Lhamu found her advice was no longer wanted.

In the mid-1960s Tenzing was doing even more traveling than he had in the ten years after Everest. Then most of his trips had been to Europe, but in 1963 he went all over the world, starting in the Soviet Union in the winter. He hoped, in vain, that his trip might act as leverage in extracting royalties from a pirated Russian edition of *Tiger of the Snows*. In the spring, he traveled to Australia and Singapore and then to Europe for the tenth anniversary celebrations of the first ascent. He recorded radio programs for the Gurkhas in Malaysia and shook Acker Bilk's hand—"You have climbed the highest mountain, and I have reached the highest note!" In Singapore he was paraded once again as the hero of Asia at functions where he sweltered in the heat and felt unappreciated and used. When he was offered the chance to take someone with him, he now took Daku. Ang Lhamu stayed at home with Tenzing's new son, a state of affairs she preferred anyway. She had, in effect, been put to one side, and many in Darjeeling felt it hastened her end. "She was human," Lhatoo said, "and she'd lost her husband."

In 1964 Ang Lhamu developed lung cancer and became seriously ill. Raymond and Annette Lambert visited Tenzing in Darjeeling that year but were uncertain about what they would find: "He had told us he was married again and we were a little bit anxious about how we would all get on. Ang Lhamu had a golden heart but she was in a very bad way in 1964. She was in the last stages of her life." Rabi Mitra also visited her. He had moved away from Darjeeling in the late 1950s. Tenzing's marriage to Daku had strained the relationship. Mitra never met Daku or her children, and felt Tenzing had lost his way. "Ang Lhamu was very ill at that time. Her friends came to see me and said she's very sick and he won't see her. So then I went and talked with him." In late 1964 Ang Lhamu was admitted several times to the hospital at the Planters' Club, but when it was clear that she had little time left, she came home to die. Pem Pem, who along with Nima had nursed Ang Lhamu through her illness, was pregnant with her third child. Tashi, a son, was born in the hospital at ten o'clock at night on November 30. The news of his birth was whispered to Ang Lhamu before she died just after midnight at Ghang La.

In the mid-1940s, when Tenzing was at his lowest ebb, Ang Lhamu had worked and supported his daughters and, in Nima's words, "shared my father's burden." In the heady days after Everest, when Tenzing became the focus for the aspirations of hundreds of millions of Asians, Ang Lhamu kept Tenzing centered as the pressures of fame threatened to swamp their lives. When age and disillusionment crept over him, the brilliance of those days would slip through his fingers without Tenzing ever really understanding how it happened. In the year he turned 50, Tenzing lost two of the people who had helped him most through those euphoric days. While Ang Lhamu was struggling against cancer in May 1964, Pandit Nehru, Tenzing's father figure, suffered a fatal hemorrhage. Just before he died, Nehru wrote out a few lines of Robert Frost's poem: "The woods are lovely, dark and deep, / But I have promises to keep, / And miles to go before I sleep. / And miles to go before I sleep."

Soon after Nehru's death, in July 1964, Tenzing traveled to the United States for the first time at the request of the Indian government as an ambassador for the Darjeeling tea industry at the World's Fair in New York. He was a star attraction, meeting U Thant, the secretary-general of the United Nations, and on the following day—designated "Tenzing Norgay Day" at the World's Fair—Charles Poletti, former governor of New York. He took the elevator to the top of the Empire State Building. "Somehow it seemed very different from looking down from the top of a mountain—everything looked quite remote."[2] Tenzing didn't much enjoy the disorienting noise and bustle of a modern city. He never developed much interest in technology, although he enjoyed owning a jeep. When traveling abroad, he preferred to see landscapes and discover different systems of farming. Mike Westmacott, from the 1953 expedition, remembered Tenzing staring nostalgically out of the car window as they drove across the bronze moors of West Penwith in Cornwall during a visit in the late 1950s. The country reminded him, Tenzing said, of the Tibetan plateau. In New York, during a visit to the zoo, he was surprised to find yaks inside one of the enclosures, and called to them in Tibetan. "They actually turned towards me with an eager look."[3] He opened a Boy Scout jamboree in Philadelphia and was invited to meet baseball star Mickey Mantle in front of the fans at the plate in Yankee Stadium. Tenzing had come a long way from a yak-skin tent in a remote corner of Tibet, and at times, like the yaks in the zoo, he found himself wondering what he meant to the people who came to stare. "I do not know," he wrote to James Ramsey Ullman, a familiar face in a crowd of strangers, "what we would have done without you."[4]

Tenzing had received a number of honors from America, apart from the National Geographic Society's Hubbard Medal. He had also been made an honorary member of the American Alpine Club, and at a reception at the club's headquarters in New York he met several of the first American team to climb Everest, including Jim Whittaker, the first American to reach the summit with Tenzing's nephew Gombu, and Lute Jerstad, Barry Bishop, and Tom Hornbein, who all reached the top in the following weeks of May 1963. (Tenzing had written to James Ramsey Ullman, who was commissioned to write an account of the expedition, recommending Gombu as sirdar.)

America's Everest heroes invited Tenzing and Daku to travel to Washington for a climb up Mount Rainier. They reached the summit, Daku's first, via the Nisqually Glacier, a more demanding climb than the ordinary approach. "I don't think she had ever climbed a mountain before," Tom Hornbein recalled. "Tenzing was warm, relaxed but seemingly with a slight British air of dignity that contrasted with us informal Americans. Daku was like a lovely, little sprite." The climbers left Camp Muir at midnight, climbing under a full moon. Whittaker led Tenzing and Daku, Jerstad, and Hornbein climbing together. "What I remember is traversing some steep stuff in moonlight, Tenzing cautiously cutting steps while Daku danced along on his heels, rope hanging in a large loop, asking why he was going so slow. By 12,000 feet in daylight all of us were slowing a bit, except Daku. It was a delightful trip."

Lute Jerstad in particular would become Tenzing's close friend. Between the mid-1960s until the early 1980s Tenzing would have the sort of close connection with America that he had once had with the Swiss. Jerstad was a mercurial figure, a drama teacher and mountain guide who took a doctorate in Asian culture, arts, and anthropology. In the early 1970s he ran a trekking company and climbing school for which Tenzing worked. He was also a committed conservationist who believed in the restorative influence of nature, impressing Tenzing with his course run for the mentally disabled.

Tenzing's relationship with Lute Jerstad included an event that is far more outlandish than almost any other in climbing history. Following his trip to the United States, Tenzing explains in *After Everest*, he spent the next five years "completely taken up with my work at the Institute."[5] This is surprising behavior for a man who enjoyed traveling so greatly. Perhaps part of the reason for his staying put seems to be locked in classified files at the Central Intelligence Agency.

In October 1964 China successfully detonated its first atomic bomb at the Lop Nor test site in Xinjiang Province. Lyndon Johnson ordered China's atomic program be assessed but the few satellites American intelligence had were in orbit over the Soviet Union. And so the CIA hit upon the unlikely plan of monitoring tests at Lop Nor with an atomic-powered device placed on the mountain frontier between India and Tibet. It selected Nanda Devi as the highest, most politically convenient peak close enough to the test site. All it needed was a team of mountaineers who could put the 125-pound spy station on top of Nanda Devi.

Fourteen climbers were chosen to undergo training, nine of whom would eventually operate in India on four separate missions. Four Indian mountaineers, working under the aegis of India's equivalent to the CIA, the Central Bureau of Investigation (CBI), joined the Americans, and later, in early 1968, mounted their own expedition to complete the task. The only substantial description of what took place on these expeditions was an article by investigative journalist Howard Kohn published by *Outside* magazine in 1978,[6] which shows the entire enterprise to have been dogged by accidents, poor planning, and strained relations between the Indians and Americans, not least because the Indian government neither knew about nor sanctioned the operation.

On the first expedition, in the fall of 1965, a SNAP atomic generator, filled with plutonium 238, was cached 2,000 feet below the summit ridge of Nanda Devi, only to be buried by an avalanche during the winter of 1966. Despite the efforts of subsequent expeditions to recover it, the generator remains in place, corroding gradually and presenting a potential health hazard to the hundreds of millions of people who live downstream of the rivers that issue from this region of the Himalaya. In 1967 a second listening device was installed on nearby Nanda Kot and functioned for more than a year before it was entombed in snow and ice. Eventually, the effort was superseded by a new spy satellite launched to watch the buildup of Chinese nuclear forces from the comparative safety of space.

Although neither government is prepared to acknowledge even the existence of these missions, they were common knowledge among top mountaineers of that generation. The climbers were well paid and, not surprisingly for men who enjoyed risky enterprises as a hobby, they were thrilled to be involved. Some even saw it as their patriotic duty. The identities of most of the team are known within the climbing community, including the four Indian climbers who, like some of their American counterparts, had been involved in expeditions to Everest in the early 1960s.

Whether or not either Lute Jerstad or Tenzing Norgay participated is a matter of conjecture. A close American friend of both men said that they had got to know each other well as a result of the missions. Jerstad was certainly in Darjeeling in February 1966, because Tenzing wrote to

James Ramsey Ullman telling him that Jerstad had been staying at Ghang La. And there is no question that Sherpas were involved in carrying loads on the mountain. Chris Bonington, who had discussed the missions in the early 1970s with some of the Americans involved, said that at least one of the Sherpas he hired for an expedition to Changabang in the same region of the Indian Himalaya had carried for the CIA-sponsored trips to Nanda Devi. Tenzing had worked for the Indian Army training in Kashmir and after more than a decade at the Himalayan Mountaineering Institute he had excellent contacts in the Indian military, the very people the CBI would have approached to seek assistance in mounting the enterprise. Furthermore, he was one of the few mountaineers still active to have reached a summit in the region, that of Nanda Devi East in 1947 with the French. He would have been consulted if not used, and at least one instructor at HMI participated, but it seems unlikely that Tenzing himself traveled to the Garhwal.

The late 1960s were a critical period for Tenzing as a whole. Although he had said he would never go back to climb Everest, he had been hurt that the three Indian expeditions that attempted the mountain from 1960 had left him behind. These large-scale, militaristic ventures were the culmination of the process Nehru had started with the foundation of the Himalayan Mountaineering Institute, a way for India to generate national prestige. The Indian climbing personnel was drawn almost exclusively from the armed forces and relied more heavily than Western expeditions on the Sherpas to prepare the ground for a successful ascent. India hadn't had the time to develop the depth of mountaineering experience that the Europeans or even the Americans could draw on. As for Tenzing, the organizers of these expeditions, which culminated in success in 1965 when Tenzing's nephew Gombu reached the summit for the second time, were reluctant to include a celebrity of his magnitude in case it diluted India's success.

More than ten years had passed since Tenzing's moment on the roof of the world, and although little had changed in Himalayan climbing, change was on the way. He had remained committed to HMI but increasingly felt he should move on to new challenges before he became stuck. In 1964 he wrote to George Pipal at what was now United Press International seeking his help in raising a substantial sum of money for an all-Sherpa expedition to Kanchenjunga led by Tenzing himself. "For many years, as you know, Sherpas have gone out with expeditions from many countries and helped them climb the world's biggest mountains," he wrote. "Now I think it is time that the Sherpas have an expedition of their own."[7] It was a visionary idea, even more so because the expedition would do without bottled oxygen. Pipal had to persuade Tenzing to lower his proposed budget to £10,000, still a substantial sum in 1964, but the expedition didn't get off the ground.

Nor did his idea for a sequel to *Tiger of the Snows*. Ullman's book had continued to sell slowly over the years, and in May 1962 Harrap held a balance of £1,672 (roughly $34,000 in today's U.S. dollars) for Tenzing. When he asked about a reprint two years later, after hearing complaints that the book was difficult to obtain, he was told that the book was still in print and there were no plans to print more copies. Pipal wrote to James Ramsey Ullman, angling for a bite of interest while acknowledging that Ullman would be too busy. "I doubt that the general public would shell out in anticipation," he concluded. In fact, Ullman did rough out a structure for a second volume of autobiography, but the project went no further.

Increasingly Tenzing looked for ways to escape the routine of HMI. With a growing family, he needed a regular income and couldn't jeopardize his position without having something concrete to replace it, but at the same time his salary did not keep pace with the level of inflation. In 1966 Tenzing and Daku's daughter Deki was born, and in November he wrote to Ullman telling him that he was thinking of resigning from the institute.[8] Tenzing wanted to ask Ullman's advice on what he could do instead to make a living. There is no record of a reply. "He had had offers," Lhatoo said, "but he didn't take them, partly because of Nehru's influence. He made Tenzing feel special, as though he was on a mission, part of a new country. Later, he felt it was too late. This was his home."

Tenzing's friendship with Lute Jerstad opened one important door for him. In the late 1960s Nepal refused permission to mountaineering expeditions, partly because of political turmoil across the border in Tibet. In the fall of 1969, however, Tenzing went to Khumbu at Jerstad's invitation, accompanying a trek arranged by Mountain Travel and led by Jerstad. The party included Stan Armington, who would soon become involved in Nepal's embryonic trekking industry and became a close friend of Tenzing's. Daku also came along with Norbu, who was put in a climbing belt by his father and kept on a lead to stop him running off the trail. It was a happy time for Tenzing, and the trek was a great success. When Jerstad set up his own travel company, Tenzing led treks for him and later for Mountain Travel, owned by Jim Edwards and based in Kathmandu. In 1972 Tenzing reached the statutory retirement age for Indian bureaucrats of 58, but he was hardly a typical government employee, and carried on as before. Combining his job at the institute, where his interest had largely waned, with trekking holidays to Nepal, Sikkim, and Bhutan kept him going. He and Daku started traveling to the United States again, visiting Jerstad's climbing school on Mount Hood and joining in summer camps for Girl Scouts. "He had a wonderful time," Armington said.

Then Tenzing's enemies pounced. Nehru had promised Tenzing that he would have a job for life, but India was now a very different country and Tenzing no longer had the patronage of Nehru's family to shield him. "It was not Indians as a whole," Lhatoo said. "He was worshipped by Indians, mobbed wherever he went. It was just a few individuals in the position to do him down." He had enemies, mostly in the bureaucracy that oversaw the Himalayan Mountaineering Institute, men such as H. C. Sarin of the Indian Civil Service in Delhi—"a tyrant of another kind," Lhatoo told me—and they now moved to get rid of him. Tenzing, they argued, was three years over the official retirement age. Under civil service rules, he would have to go. Tenzing had thought about leaving the institute for at least ten years, but being forced out was too much for his pride. Also at stake was the critical issue of his pension. Although other instructors were guaranteed an income, Tenzing had no such arrangement and with four children still at school, he panicked. How would he continue to put them through school, or pay for a college education, the advantages for which he had worked so hard?

He could have made much more money working elsewhere and Daku was already organizing treks in Sikkim and Nepal to help pay the bills. But Tenzing had given a commitment to Nehru. Now, as he saw it, a few manipulative bureaucrats were dismantling the self-respect he had built up in fulfilling that promise. "He realized he had stayed too long," Lhatoo said. "He should have got out of it years before but he needed money. He was a hero living in a big house. His salary was not commensurate with his position."

The struggle left Tenzing bitter. The institute had been built around him, as a way of carrying forward the impetus of his success on Everest. By the 1970s it had become mired in procedure and bureaucracy and lost its edge. "While Tenzing Norgay was there," Lhatoo said, "the training was very good and Gombu tried to maintain that. But after Tenzing died, things slowly began to fall away. It had been a special place, but then it became like any other." Eventually, partly as a result of public outrage at the treatment of an Indian hero, the authorities relented and a compromise was reached. Tenzing would remain at the institute as a "special adviser" on his old salary, but his day-to-day involvement would cease. Very quickly, Tenzing's practical involvement in the institute that he had helped create was over.

The growing Himalayan travel industry seemed the likeliest arena in which he could capitalize on his fame. Jerstad's travel company, always a shoestring affair, went bankrupt by 1974, but other opportunities arose. At a party at Ghang La, Tenzing was introduced to Lars-Eric Lindblad, an American tour operator who was pioneering the whole concept of adventure travel. (They had met once before, in 1954, when Lindblad was starting out as a travel agent.) He asked, "How much do you get from the mountaineering institute?" Tenzing told him; it was by then 1,400 rupees a month. Lindblad replied, "Tenzing, you'd get that for shaking hands with an American."

Lindblad had created a successful business organizing exclusive holidays for wealthy clients to such remote, celebrated places as the Galapagos Islands and Antarctica, often on his ship, the *Lindblad Explorer*. He was a charming man with a strong interest in conservation who enjoyed meeting and befriending celebrities, men such as the ornithologist Roger Tory Peterson and Albert Schweitzer. In the 1970s areas like the Everest region or Sikkim were still thought of as inaccessible, and Lindblad was looking for ways to add adventure vacations to his brochure. Mountaineers such as Jimmy Roberts and Lute Jerstad had tried to capitalize on the growing interest in the Himalaya, but it took travel experts like Lindblad to make them profitable. Tenzing was set up in Darjeeling to provide logistics for these forays and also acted as a celebrity hook for Lindblad's wealthy clients. He went on cruises to Antarctica and led treks to Sikkim while Daku built up the business. Lindblad, for his part, helped put Norbu through college in the United States and later employed him there.

Liberation from the humdrum of regular courses and familiar routines rejuvenated Tenzing, and for a while he was happy, as though he had taken a new lease on life. The humiliation of his "retirement" from HMI was left behind as he spent more time with his Western friends and less time arguing with Indian bureaucrats. The world seemed a big place again.

Work also finally started on a second volume of autobiography, thanks to a contact of Ernst Feuz at the Swiss Foundation for Alpine Research. Malcolm Barnes was a partner at the London publishing house George Allen & Unwin. Barnes had published a number of mountaineering books, including an English edition of the Swiss mountaineering journal *Mountain World*. After the 20th anniversary reunion of the Everest team in North Wales, where Daku impressed Mike Westmacott with her rock climbing, Tenzing stopped at Barnes's home in Surrey. The interviews started there and continued as Tenzing traveled with his new co-author to Switzerland for a vacation in Interlaken. Barnes did a number of interviews with Tenzing before he returned to Darjeeling and then bombarded him with letters in an attempt to cover any gaps. Tenzing dragooned his son Norbu and others to read and reply to his queries.

After Everest didn't meet with nearly the same success as *Tiger of the Snows*. There was no American edition, and George Allen & Unwin did not think it worthwhile putting out a paperback edition. The book has long been out of print. Tenzing himself noted that audiences for the lectures he still gave were aging as he did. Even Barnes, steeped in mountaineering, wondered, "Does anyone care now about Everest as we cared then—other than Tenzing's own generation everywhere, who shared the excitement, and that international body of mountaineers to whom the event will not fail to be significant?"[9] The book certainly has an elegiac feel of a golden world now lost to the gray face of modernity. Tenzing speaks with sadness of the mundane effects of tourism—garbage, deforestation, and social change—while at the same time, without irony, talking about his own part in the new adventure tourism industry. It is an account of reunions between aging climbers, of the years passing.

Perhaps the most touching incident in the book is the lecture he gave at the University of California at Los Angeles, where he was made an honorary citizen. Although Tenzing hated public speaking, he acknowledged the evening had gone well. The climax of the event was a showing of Tom Stobart's film, and by the end the audience was on its feet cheering. Stan Armington was one of them. "I felt good about that evening," he told me. "The audience, however," Tenzing wrote, "was a typically middle-aged one ... because few people of less than middle age can remember the climb at all. Most of the people at a university now were not even born when it took place."[10]

Tenzing was approaching 60, and despite his enduring fitness, his reaction to events like the lecture in Los Angeles showed that he was living more in the past than the future. The certainties of his world were crumbling around him. For a man who had built his legacy on discipline and ambition, the mood of the times seemed alien. "Hippies have been seen for some years past in the region of Tengboche monastery," he complained, as though travelers were an infection unconnected with the excitement his climb had generated. "Some of the trekkers, especially Americans, thoughtlessly give large tips to Sherpa guides and porters, which the men—who can blame them?—soon learn to accept as normal."[11] This from a Sherpa who had done as much as anyone to fight for a decent income. His complaints reflected nostalgia for the world of his youth more than the problems of the world as it had become. He had, after all, run away from Khumbu to make a new life. Now Sherpas were changing their world without needing to leave home.

Much of *After Everest* details his work at the Himalayan Mountaineering Institute, which is not interesting enough for the general reader, and a catalogue of travels insufficiently leavened by anecdotes. There are no thrilling ascents or hazardous exploration. Tenzing loved traveling, but he regularly comments that on these trips he never had enough time to go climbing. If he had wanted to badly enough, he could have made time, of course, but he effectively retired from climbing when he came down from Everest. This didn't stop him taking a swipe at the Indian mountaineering establishment for not inviting him on their expeditions. "Although I had no real wish to climb Everest a second or third time, nevertheless when three separate Indian expeditions were arranged to climb Everest, I was never invited to take part, for the simple reason, I am firmly convinced, that Indian climbers did not want me on their expeditions despite all I have done for Indian mountaineering and the twenty years I have spent on training their climbers."[12] The word "their" was a giveaway. After 40 years in India, Tenzing still felt like an outsider. It's true that some of the egos in Indian mountaineering would not have tolerated having a man of Tenzing's celebrity stealing any glory. But most Indian climbers would have jumped at a chance to climb with him. "To us novices in a sport new to India," Gurdial Singh, who went to Everest twice, told me, "he will forever remain a much-loved icon."

Older climbers will recognize the scenario of an aging hero wanting to move on but still needing to feel he can cut it. In *After Everest*, despite passing 60, he stated that he felt sure he could make another ascent. He still spent a great deal of time in the mountains, both in Darjeeling and traveling abroad. Tenzing preferred this to climbing anyway. He had never done it for recreation; it had always been his livelihood. But Tenzing retained a strong connection to the mountain landscapes of his childhood and was always superbly fit. Lhatoo recalled him trekking more comfortably in his early 50s than students half his age he was leading.

A sour note dominates *After Everest*, especially at its conclusion, when he describes how he came to leave the institute. His complaints seem clumsy and petulant. "I have never had free housing in all those twenty-two years. It is true that I have a house of my own, but they should have given me a housing allowance instead. It is due to me as a government servant; yet I never asked for it, nor was it offered me. Moreover, my pay today is the same as when we started! Even though the price of a chicken has in the same time gone up from two to eleven rupees."[13] Tenzing had wanted to name the men who he felt had betrayed the promises made to him by Nehru, but Barnes sensed they could face problems with libel. Instead the references are vague and a moody, incoherent discontent colors the end of the book. "If I had foreseen from the beginning what I now know," he said, "I doubt if I would have joined the Institute at all."[14] Tenzing sensed his enthusiasm and commitment had been betrayed by self-servers more interested in making what they could out of Nehru's vision. It was demeaning, but he couldn't find the right way to articulate it. "He was justified," Lhatoo said, "but he expressed it in the wrong way."

The same problem arose in how he discussed the demands his rise to fame placed on him by his own family "Because I was famous they thought I was rich. I was not, and I am not rich today. You do not make a lot of money by climbing a mountain, and I had rightly turned down a lot of commercial offers because of their difficult complications. Yet I was able to manage and I did what I thought was my duty. Most of these people were ungrateful. They never seemed satisfied, and I do not like them. Some are with me still. It was very difficult. It still is."[15]

"What relatives?" Lhatoo asked. Tenzing's own relatives, of course, were now mostly dead. In the mid-1970s only his sister, Thakchey, and her one son, Lobsang, were still alive. His mother, whom he had been so desperate to bring to Darjeeling, had finally died there in the late 1950s, well into her 80s. His beloved older sister, Lhamu Kipa, had died in the 1950s, and Sonam Doma also, leaving Tenzing to care for her daughters, Ang Nemi, Pem Phuti, Yangzi, and Ang Phuti. By the mid-1970s they were largely grown up and had anyway worked hard in Tenzing's household to earn their keep. Ang Lhamu had been more than happy to welcome people into her house, and when the Dalai Lama fled Tibet, they gave shelter to the family from Tsa, the relatives of Lhamu Kipa's husband Nawang. Daku's brothers had followed her to Darjeeling, and perhaps Tenzing's complaint was a way of letting off steam about his in-laws.

What really lay beneath his frustration was the thought that people were forgetting the trials he had gone through to reach the position he held. People still greeted him on the streets of Darjeeling with the kind of respect beyond the dreams of someone born in obscurity. Daku had been four years old when Tenzing's first wife Dawa Phuti died, leaving him alone to bring his family back to a one-room shack in Darjeeling. Perhaps the book was a way of reminding those around him of what they owed him.

Barnes seemed unwilling or unable to balance Tenzing's criticisms or put them in context. "The first book made him," Lhatoo told me, "the second book unmade him." That is an exaggeration. Most Indians weren't even aware of Tenzing's second book. Criticism of it was confined to those sensitive to India's image who felt Tenzing should have shown more gratitude. Others, such as Trevor Braham, are less critical of the book. Barnes does give a clear image of the older Tenzing in the introduction: "And Tenzing at sixty? The brilliant smile, the wonderfully expressive and mobile features, are still there; a leaner, harder face perhaps, and certainly more lined, but full of intelligence.... His delight in living is deep and infectious and vigorous; his interest in all things human and natural (as opposed to technical things like speed-boats and skyscrapers) is deep; his laughter is genuine and contagious."[16]

For a few years Tenzing's friendship with Jerstad and Lindblad reinvigorated this zest for life, but as the decade wore on his enthusiasm was dulled. Travel began to lose its appeal and Tenzing found being the celebrity hook on a package tour wearisome, surrounded all the time by new people who knew his name but not who he was. Even worse was the collapse in his relationship with Daku. "She was getting younger and younger," Lhatoo said simply, "he was getting older and older." "She was a formidable lady," Ed Hillary said, "strong and determined. While she was producing the kids, Tenzing was the force in that house, but as Tenzing got older she was much more dominant. It was she who got the trekking business going. She was determined to get her children a good education."

Daku was spending more and more time away from Darjeeling on treks, and Tenzing believed she was having affairs. He could be possessive and jealous and resented Daku's energy and initiative. She had her own friends, including the mistress of the former King of Bhutan, and liked to see them well away from Tenzing. Gossip about her behavior and Tenzing's depression spread from Darjeeling to Kathmandu, where Daku spent much of her time. Over the years he had added several new buildings to Ghang La, partly in the hope that his children might live near him. Once the place had been full to bursting with people, visitors dropping by every day. In the 1980s Norbu and Jamling moved to the United States to start their college education while Deki and Dhamey attended boarding school in Darjeeling. For weeks on end, Tenzing was on his own in the big house with nothing to do.

He confided in women like his niece Doma and his daughter Pem Pem, and he talked freely with his old friends in Europe about his problems, particularly Annette Lambert, whose English was always better than Raymond's. "To begin with we were quite friendly with Daku but when she started to treat him badly we couldn't accept this. We wouldn't say she couldn't come to stay, but Tenzing had this feeling and he didn't bring her again because we didn't want to be rude. He was very unhappy. He would say: 'She's always away.' He would complain that the beautiful rugs in his house were moth-eaten and unused."

Without the discipline of walking into the mountains to guide courses, his fitness began to slip away. In 1981 Ed Hillary, George Lowe, and Tenzing all found themselves in Lhasa without knowing that each was going to be there. Tenzing was killing time between tours for Lars-Eric Lindblad, and he complained that they hadn't given him the money to go home for the intervening period. He didn't want to be in Lhasa, was lonely and bored with attending receptions and greeting strangers, but he needed the money. It all seemed so effortless for Hillary and Lowe in comparison. "I tried to point out to him that although he didn't personally have vast sums of money, there were many people who supported him, like those in America who educated his children. He was regularly traveling to Europe for skiing holidays and so on." That was part of the problem. Tenzing was treated like a wealthy man but was in reality beholden to others to maintain that image. At least when he had been working at the institute he'd had a position of respect. With his wife away so much and his independence curtailed, Tenzing felt he was losing control of his own direction.

For much of his life he had been a very moderate drinker, but now he went through bouts of drinking heavily and his chiseled looks became puffy and blurred. He grew an Indian military-style handlebar moustache and took to wearing huge sunglasses that smothered his eyes, giving him the appearance of a reclusive film star. Trevor Braham caught up with Tenzing in Darjeeling in 1982. "Even then I thought he wasn't looking too well. We talked about the old days. He said: 'Things are so different now, I don't have much ambition or energy to do very much.' He sounded rather under the weather. He didn't seem to be as full of vitality as I would have expected him to be."

Tenzing had not had a drinking problem before. When Lhatoo started work at HMI in 1962, Tenzing had been teetotal, not as a principle but because he was fit, active, and absorbed in work. The following year on his tour of the Soviet Union, he had plenty of opportunities to get drunk with his hosts, especially when he reached the Caucasus: "The Georgians are gay and they drink a great deal—everything and anything alcoholic, vodka and wine in huge quantities. Too much for me, since at that time I did not touch any kind of strong drink, not even beer. Only soft drink."[17] Years before, John Hunt had warned him of the dangers of alcohol, he said, and warned him to leave it alone. "Once you start, he told me, it is difficult to stop." Like most Sherpas Tenzing had loved a good party and would join in the singing and dancing. After the expeditions to Khumbu in the 1950s there had been huge parties that extended over several days. But those had been a release of tension and a farewell to relatives and friends. Now he drank because he was lonely, bored, angry, and frustrated. He could feel his vitality and optimism for the future ebbing away.

He was not, however, self-destructive. Pem Pem recalls that he would drink a glass of water alongside the rakshi or other spirit he was taking to blunt its effect. He still got up early each morning and often started the day with a long walk over the hill from Ghang La to Pem Pem's house in Toong Soong Busti. Sometimes she would be woken up by his shouting: "Hey! Are you still in bed?" Pem Pem would see him every Tuesday, on her day off as matron at St. Paul's, and they would sit and talk. "He was so often on his own in Darjeeling. I was the only daughter around so he used to call me, and confide in me and tell me about his problems and share everything."

On other mornings he would walk up to St. Paul's and then back to Chowrasta, telling friends he met along the way the latest news of his children in America or at school. Then he'd walk through the woods along Birch Hill, now renamed Jawaharlal Parbat, to drink tea with Gombu and his friends at the institute. Only in the evening, when his daughter and his friends were with their own families, did he drink, alone in a big house with the souvenirs of his life on the wall. In his bleakest moments, in the early hours of the morning, he would call Pem Pem, fearful with depression and she would go to him to offer reassurance. "He craved company," Lhatoo said, but Daku stayed in Kathmandu when she wasn't working with trekking groups, effectively avoiding him. Tenzing began to talk about divorce, but separating would have caused a scandal and undermined his reputation. Pem Pem told him that he had made his decision 20 years before, and now it was too late.

In 1985 Tenzing's health collapsed, and he was admitted into hospital in Delhi suffering from pneumonia. His great-niece Rita was living in Delhi and Pem Pem's son Sonam was a student there; Daku and their children also visited. Even now, 32 years after Everest, ordinary people would prostrate themselves before him as he lay in a hospital bed and touch his feet. Ed Hillary had arrived in February as New Zealand's high commissioner to India, and he also visited Tenzing in hospital a number of times. Thanks to Tenzing's much improved English, they were able to talk about their experiences together and how their lives had unfolded. Hillary had heard that Tenzing had been drinking and was depressed: "He was really a rather sad person at that stage, even if he'd had a rather marvelous life. He'd traveled round the world and he'd been given tremendous respect and credit, as was his due, but he always had a considerable resentment about the Indian government not living up, he believed, to what they had promised." Again, as he had in Lhasa four years before, Tenzing regretted that he had not matched Hillary's humanitarian efforts in Khumbu, and again, Hillary attempted to reassure him. Money was also still a source of worry for him. "I did all I could to reassure him but he was now drinking a good deal and just didn't want to believe it."[18]

During his illness, Tenzing shed weight and now looked gaunt and haunted. He smiled far less now, and his eyes were dull and weary. What else did he have to offer anyone? In November 1985 he traveled to Switzerland for a vacation, visiting his old friends the Lamberts and Annelies Sutter. They were aghast at his decline, and when he visited Maria Feuz in Zürich she arranged for him to undergo tests. Having seen his weight loss, at the back of their minds they were worried he had cancer, but after a spell in hospital at Interlaken and a full examination he was given a clean bill of health. Tenzing's cancer was in his soul, not his body.

Annette Lambert always made sure that Tenzing's visits to the apartment in Geneva were private affairs where Tenzing would not be bothered with interviews or public engagements. His friendship with Raymond extended back to before Everest and a simpler world that he had understood, a place where he had flourished. Tenzing had grown up in a world of social cohesion. If you had relatives living, they would be around you in old age. Now, after a lifetime of striving and then world celebrity, he was reduced to a gaunt old man living on his own in a big house that he could barely afford, finding it impossible to let go of his grievances. Annette and Raymond Lambert urged him to make peace with the world. Annelies Sutter felt that he was preparing for death, that his unhappiness was wearing him down.

Back in Darjeeling, his friends and relatives felt that in the spring of 1986 Tenzing was more robust than he had been the year before. He continued his habit of taking long walks, kept up with his gardening, and on cold mornings would sit in the sunroom at Ghang La looking across at the mountains where he had spent all his life. Practically every day he went to HMI to see his old friends and drink tea with Gombu. Every week Pem Pem would go to Ghang La to sit with him. One Tuesday she had to call at the post office on the way down to the big house, and he wondered what had kept her. That day they ate *paratha,* the fried spicy potato pancakes that were Pem Pem's favorite.

"Do you like it?" he asked her.

"It's very tasty."

"I cooked it myself."

Rather than letting the house servant do it, as a special favor for his daughter he had worked in the kitchen that morning. They spent lunch talking about the past and future plans. In the weeks before his death Tenzing talked a great deal about his wish to visit the grave of his first wife Dawa Phuti in Chitral. Pem Pem had said she would go with them, but as Indian citizens visiting modern Pakistan the arrangements would take time. "It was very exciting for both of us."

That same afternoon Daku arrived back from Kathmandu after a two-month absence. Not for the first time, Pem Pem and Daku argued. His daughter was concerned about her father's mental state and insisted Daku stay in Darjeeling. His wife was reluctant to abandon her independence and career to look after an ailing man. Then Pem Pem said good-bye and told her father that if he needed her before the following Tuesday, he should call. He said nothing and just smiled.

It was the last time she saw her father alive. Early on the following Friday morning, around four o'clock on May 9, 1986, Pem Pem got a call at home from a servant at Ghang La. Her father had been taken ill, she was told, and she should come at once. By the time she arrived at the gate below the house, the doctor was just coming out. Pem Pem was too late. Tenzing was already dead. He had woken in the early morning to use the bathroom, and when he returned to bed he complained he was in pain. He had, Daku explained, suffered a fatal brain hemorrhage and died very quickly.

Despite years of depression and physical weakness, Tenzing's death still caused a surprise. "I thought he would live for another fifteen years,"

Pem Pem said. "It's still shocking for me, but I took everything for granted. He was healthy, he was quite OK. It's true he was depressed; he was a lonely man. But he was OK." Gombu was also stunned. "The day before he had come to HMI and when he left he said: 'I'll see you again tomorrow.' It was completely unexpected." Lhatoo said: "Two days before he'd been at our house, talking. Then we suddenly heard he was dead. But he was still full of life. He was a healthy, strong man and could have lived another ten or fifteen years."

His death called home his far-flung children. Dhamey was in Darjeeling, but Norbu was in New Hampshire, Jamling was at college in Wisconsin, and Deki was in Michigan. Pem Pem's sister, Nima, was living in Singapore with her journalist husband. On the same flight from Delhi to Bagdogra, the closest available airport to Darjeeling, were Sir Edmund Hillary and Tenzing and Daku's three children. The jeeps were delayed on the three-hour drive into the hills by political unrest. Ethnic Nepalese were calling for more autonomy for the hill regions of West Bengal, for the creation of "Gorkhaland," and a general strike had been called. To the throng Hillary's escort—an army captain—shouted, "Hillary sah'b" was coming to pay his respects to his old friend. The crowds parted at the mention of Tenzing's name, and his jeep continued.

Tenzing's body was lying in the beautiful prayer room at Ghang La. "I looked for the last time," Hillary recalled, "on the still, waxy face of my friend who had shared that great moment with me on Everest some thirty-three years before. He seemed so much smaller than the strong, vigorous person I had known."[19] The family had planned to cremate Tenzing in the vegetable garden at Ghang La, but the numbers wishing to pay their respects would make that impossible. Instead, a procession a mile long wound up through the streets of Darjeeling to the Himalayan Mountaineering Institute. Tenzing's body, carried on an army truck, was covered in a blizzard of marigolds thrown by the waiting crowds as he passed. His cremation site was on a small hillock above the institute, within view of Kanchenjunga, and his body was surrounded with juniper branches and logs, incense, and messages from relatives and friends.

"Norbu, the very handsome eldest son," Hillary wrote, "stood at his father's head throughout. There were many Buddhist monks present, marking the ceremony with a constant chanting of prayers and clashing of cymbals. In many ways it was a happy occasion with an almost picnic atmosphere of laughter and tea-drinking."[20] Rain started falling as the time came to light the pyre. The monks and family members paused as the rain became a downpour. Nevertheless, the monks poured ghee onto the pyre, and then Tenzing's three sons and his nephew Lobsang set the wood alight. For hours the ceremony continued, with monks chanting prayers and the crowd standing patiently in the rain. Then the moment they had been waiting for arrived. Tenzing's skull cracked, and his soul, the essence of his being, was released to begin the process of rebirth.

TOWARD THE END OF HIS LIFE, Tenzing saw his old friend Rabi Mitra, who had been living and working in Siliguri for some years. When they were together in the 1950s, the world had seemed almost limitless with possibilities. Now Tenzing seemed at the end of his tether. "Six months before he died he came to see me. He did not die a happy man. It's difficult in this life to have good friends. And he didn't have good friends around him." Many who saw Tenzing near the end of his life felt that somehow things had gone wrong for him, that the excitement and brilliance of those heady days in 1953 had been dissipated.

Ed Hillary tells the story of meeting Neil Armstrong on an extravagant adventure tour in the Arctic. Over dinner in a well-insulated hut on Ellesmere Island, he asked the first man to stand on the moon how it came to be him who was given the chance. "Luck!" Armstrong said. "Just luck!" Hillary thought there was rather more to it than that, just as there was in his own destiny of being, with Tenzing, the first to climb Everest. But in a way Armstrong touched on something much deeper. The opportunity to do something momentous and unique requires skill and determination just to be among the few contenders who might be the one. But ultimate success does carry an element of luck. Both Hillary and Tenzing, like others, offered themselves up to a lightning strike of fate. One of them could have gotten sick that day in May 1953, or Evans and Bourdillon could have succeeded before them. But none of the things that could have robbed Hillary and Tenzing of that moment intervened. The lightning did strike them and as a consequence they stepped into a world of fame from which there was no going back. The scale of that celebrity was gigantic, far bigger than anyone might have expected, and both men struggled to come to terms with it. Everest—Chomolungma—gave them both more than it took, but their lives changed in ways they could not have foreseen.

Tenzing's legacy is not just that he was the first man to climb the highest mountain on Earth, although that was inspirational enough, or that he made the Sherpas famous and trained a generation of Indian climbers. The story of his life is really about the choices one man makes, the opportunities he grasps to turn abject poverty and obscurity into a glorious success. He was not a complex man but he was honest and very loyal, sometimes more loyal than people deserved. He had a mixture of practical intelligence and brilliant intuition. Annette Lambert said that Tenzing could remember the shape of addresses or telephone numbers without knowing what the symbols meant. That acute observation of the world around him was just one of his qualities.

Perhaps his greatest strength—and his greatest lesson to us—was his courage, his indomitable spirit. Consistency, sticking power if you like, is not considered a glamorous attribute in the modern era, but Tenzing was a man who never gave up. Against the longest odds and in the face of personal tragedy he kept going and finally achieved a position not even he could have imagined as a young boy watching his father's yaks on the grassy pastures close to Everest.

Many people offered me their assessment of Tenzing. When I asked the songwriter and musician Dharma Raj Thapa, the man who had immortalized Tenzing's name for the Nepalese people, what he thought of Tenzing he was silent for what seemed like minutes as he thought. Then he looked up and said one word: "*Pani*—Water." Tenzing was like water, he explained, because he ran easily through every channel, changing direction as necessary. There is truth in this. Tenzing could adapt his behavior, his dress, his habits, to fit in with the world he wanted to join. This was what Thapa meant. But water also cuts its own path, wearing down the hardest rocks over time, like the rivers of Tenzing's youth slicing through the Himalaya to the plains below. Even the highest mountains of all cannot resist the passage of water. This was the true meaning of Tenzing's life. His last years were characterized by unhappiness and depression, but he did not lose sight of who he was. Nor did he lose his natural grace and modesty. His friend Stan Armington said, "It didn't go to his head; he was still a real person." He was not a perfect man but he paid for his mistakes, and looking back from an age of manufactured heroes, it is hard not to conclude that Tenzing was the real thing.

ENDNOTES

CHAPTER ONE

[1] Quoted from *Modern Literary Nepali,* edited and translated by Michael J. Hutt (Oxford University Press, 1997), pp. 125–26. The final stanza is also apposite: "Beneath this super-human mountain-hero's snow peak, / The conqueror of nature, sweat on his brow, / Is rich with pearls, / Above there is only the lid of night, / Studded with stars. / In this night he is rich with sleep."

[2] "Himalayan Porters," *Himalayan Journal* 16 (1950), pp. 121–33.

[3] This low figure, only 29, illustrates the impact of the war and the political upheaval that followed it. Simply put, there were hardly any expeditions to service.

[4] There is a wide variety of spellings for Dawa Thondup's name; this seems to be the most regularly used and one that more readers will recognize, but the "p" is silent and "Tundu" would do just as well.

[5] For a fuller history of how Darjeeling first became known to the British, see pp. 19–21 of *Darjeeling,* by L. S. S. O'Malley (Logos Press, 1985), a reprint of the original *Bengal District Gazetteer (Depôt, 1907).*

[6] Ibid., p.186.

[7] Ibid., p. 185 for a synopsis of census information.

[8] Ibid., p. 188.

[9] Tenzing/Ullman, 1955, Chapter 3.

[10] O'Malley, 1907, pp. 45–46.

[11] *After Everest: The Experiences of a Mountaineer and Medical Missionary,* by T. Howard Somervell (Hodder & Stoughton, 1936), Chapter 18.

[12] Ibid., Chapter 13.

[13] "Nanda Devi and the Sources of the Ganges," by H. W. Tilman, *Himalayan Journal* 8 (1936), pp. 1–26.

[14] *George Mallory,* by David Robertson (Faber & Faber, 1969), Chapter 7.

[15] Written by Norman Collie, *Alpine Journal* 34 (1921), pp. 145–47.

[16] The two men came very close to climbing Kabru, an outstanding achievement even though it was Monrad Aas's first climbing trip. Rubenson says of the Sherpas: "The natives whom we found most plucky were Nepalese Tibetans, the so-called Sherpahs [*sic*]. If they are properly taught the use of ice axe and rope I believe that they will prove of more use out here than European guides, as they are guides and coolies in one, and don't require any special attention. My opinion is that if they get attached to you they will do anything for you." "Kabru in 1907," by C. W. Rubenson, *Alpine Journal*

24 November 1908), pp. 310–21.

[17] Howard-Bury, et al., 1922, p. 49. In fact, Howard-Bury had altered his opinion on this. While negotiating the first ever Everest permit with Charles Bell, who stood between the Royal Geographical Society and the Tibetan government, Howard-Bury sent this assessment to Francis Younghusband, chairman of the Mount Everest Committee: "Sherpa Bhootias [sic] would seem to be the best for high mountain work; they are less independent than Tibetans."

[18] Ibid., p. 198.

[19] Bauer, who in 1929 observed that the Sherpas were happier working at high altitudes than the Bhotias, seems to have been bemused by the Sherpas' attitudes: "T by something like four hundred of them, men like Walung, Khams, Amdo and Lhasa as well as from Sikkim ... the Sherpas stood to one side round their sirdar. They believed that they had had cause to be dissatisfied with their treatment by an earlier expedition. It caused them to demand that I should hire only Sherpas, threatening that unless I did so no Sherpas would go at all."

[20] As Eric Shipton did, on the 1935 Everest reconnaissance, Tenzing's first expedition.

[21] Tenzing/Ullman, 1955, Chapter 10.

[22] For a much more detailed version of this appalling expedition, read *Tigers of the Snow: How One Fateful Climb Made the Sherpas Mountaineering Legends,* by Jonathan Neale (Thomas Dunne Books, 2002).

[23] Tenzing/Ullman, 1955, Chapter 3.

[24] *The Assault of Mount Everest 1922,* by Brig. Gen., the Hon. C. G. Bruce (Arnold, 1923), Chapter 2.

[25] *Through Tibet to Everest,* by Capt. J. B. L. Noel (Arnold, 1927), p. 195.

[26] From the autobiography of Dzatrul Rinpoche, quoted in *Everest: The Best Writing and Pictures From Seventy Years of Human Endeavour,* edited by Peter Gillman (Little, Brown, 1993), p. 33. This translation appeared in "The Lama and the General," by Alexander W. Macdonald, *Kailash, A Journal of Himalayan Studies* (1973).

[27] Somervell, 1936, Chapter 18.

[28] *Tenzing and the Sherpas of Everest,* by Judy Tenzing and Tashi Tenzing (HarperCollins, 2001), pp. 34–35.

[29] *Mount Everest 1938,* by H. W. Tilman (Cambridge University Press, 1954), Chapter 9.

[30] *Mémoires d'un Sherpa,* by Ang Tharkay (Amiot-Dumont, 1954), p. 83.

[31] "Himalayan Porters," 1950. For all his reputation as a misogynist, Tilman was one of the few climbing writers of this period to mention a Sherpa's family life, describing how Pasang Bhotia got married to a Tibetan woman while coming home from an expedition. Sadly, she died soon afterward, an illustration that the uncertainties of life weren't confined to the men, as the mortality rate from childbirth among Bhotias demonstrates.

[32] *Upon That Mountain,* by Eric Shipton (Hodder & Stoughton, 1943), Chapter 9.

[33] Ibid.

[34] *Everest: A Mountaineering History,* by Walt Unsworth (Oxford Illustrated Press, 1989), p. 222.

CHAPTER TWO

[1] *Tiger of the Snows: The Autobiography of Tenzing of Everest,* written in collaboration with James Ramsey Ullman (Putnam, 1955), Chapter 1.

[2] I was fortunate to hear a lecture at a meeting of the American Alpine Club in 2001 by the mountaineering space shuttle astronaut John Grunsfeld, whose perspective of the world's mountains from space was mesmerizing.

[3] Tenzing/Ullman, 1955, Chapter 2.

⁴ Much of my information on Khenbalung has been drawn from Gangla Tshechu, *Beyul Khenbalung: Pilgrimage to Hidden Valleys, Sacred Mountains and Springs of Life Water in Southern Tibet and Eastern Nepal*, by Hildegard Diemberger (Ethnographic Museum of the University of Zurich, 1993).

⁵ *Mount Everest, The Reconnaissance, 1921*, by Lt. Col. C. K. Howard-Bury and other members of the Mount Everest Expedition (Arnold, 1922), Chapter 7. Reprinted as *Everest Reconnaissance* (Hodder & Stoughton, 1991).

⁶ *Alpine Journal* (1987), pp. 287–88.

⁷ Howard-Bury et al., 1922, Chapter 4.

⁸ Tenzing/Ullman, 1955, Chapter 10.

⁹ Ibid., Chapter 2.

¹⁰ Kinzom's mother and Trulshik Rinpoche's father were half brother and sister—they shared the same mother—but although Kinzom was, according to Tenzing, born in 1870, Trulshik was born in 1924, a span of 54 years between grandchildren of the same grandmother.

¹¹ Tibetans and more usually Sherpas name their children after the day of the week they were born. Nima = Sunday, Dawa = Monday, Mingma = Tuesday, Lhakpa = Wednesday, Phurbu = Thursday, Pasang = Friday, Pemba = Saturday. Other names refer to deities or religious devotion, such as Lhamu or Tenzing. Names are also adapted to avoid confusion. "Ang," meaning "young," is used to differentiate between members of the same family sharing the same name.

¹² Mingma's house is now abandoned following some bad luck that has left it an unpropitious place to live. It is a ramshackle structure, not like the new house that stands behind it, just stacked stones and wooden roof poles. What this little collection of buildings on the north bank of the Kharta Chu is called is not absolutely clear. Tashi Tenzing, Tenzing's grandson, who has traveled to Kharta several times, refers to it as being part of the village of Moyü (this village is sometimes transcribed as Moyun or Moyey; the given transcription is how it sounded to me when spoken by people at Kharta, but the abbot at Tharbaling and others in the community referred to it as Dangsar while I was there. Since Moyü is only a very few hundred yards away, it's an academic point, because the house itself is not in dispute. A more important question is why Tenzing wasn't born inside its walls. And the answer to that lies at the heart of how Tenzing started his long journey to Darjeeling.

¹³ Diemberger, 1993, p. 64.

¹⁴ Tenzing/Ullman, 1955, Chapter 2.

¹⁵ Howard-Bury et al., 1922, Chapter 4.

¹⁶ Much of my information for adaptation at altitude was drawn from "The People," by Susan Niermeyer, Stacy Zamudio, and Lorna G. Moore, published in *High Altitude: An Exploration of Human Adaptation*, edited by Thomas F. Hornbein and Robert B. Schoene (Marcel Dekker, 2001).

¹⁷ Tenzing/Ullman, 1955, Chapter 2.

¹⁸ Howard-Bury et al., 1922, Chapter 6.

¹⁹ *Touching My Father's Soul: A Sherpa's Journey to the Top of Everest*, by Jamling Tenzing Norgay (HarperSanFrancisco, 2001), Chapter 1.

²⁰ Tenzing/Ullman, 1955, Chapter 9.

²¹ Ibid., Chapter 2.

²² *Life and Death on Mount Everest: Sherpas and Himalayan Mountaineering*, by Sherry. B. Ortner (Princeton University Press, 1999). Chapter 3 explores the biographies of Ang Tharkay and Tenzing.

²³ Ibid., p. 85.

²⁴ Howard-Bury, et al., 1922, Chapter 7.

²⁵ Tenzing/Ullman, 1955, Chapter 2.

²⁶ Ibid., Chapter 1.

27 One of a group of five minor deities who inhabit five separate peaks along the Tibetan-Nepalese border, she is depicted in murals at the monasteries of Rongbuk and Tengboche riding a tiger and holding both a bowl of tsampa flour and a mongoose spitting jewels. Her name translates literally, Bernbaum explains, as the "Unmoveable Goddess Who Is a Benefactress of Bulls"—and thus good for the local yak population. But there are other interpretations and it's worth pointing out that Chomolungma has had a local name far longer than there has been a monastery at Rongbuk.

28 Howard-Bury et al., 1922, Chapter 7.

29 Tenzing/Ullman, 1955, Chapter 1.

CHAPTER THREE

1 *Himalayan Traders: Life in Highland Nepal,* by Christoph von Fürer-Haimendorf (John Murray, 1975), p. 87n.

2 See Ortner, 1999, pp. 144–45.

3 Tenzing/Ullman, 1955, Chapter 2.

4 Howard-Bury et al., 1922, Chapter 11.

5 Ullman Archive, Princeton University.

6 *The Sherpas Transformed: Social Change in a Buddhist Society,* by Christoph von Fürer-Haimendorf (Sterling, 1984), pp. 156–57.

7 *The Sherpas of Nepal: Buddhist Highlanders,* by Christoph von Fürer-Haimendorf (John Murray, 1964), p. 32.

8 Ibid., p. 45.

9 Tenzing/Ullman, 1955, Chapter 2.

10 von Fürer-Haimendorf, 1984, p. 65.

11 The process is less formal in the modern era, with the ritual sodene frequently now omitted altogether. This is often cited as a weakening of Sherpa culture.

12 von Fürer-Haimendorf, 1964, p. 4.

13 Tenzing/Ullman, 1955, Chapter 3.

14 Ibid.

15 Ibid.

16 Ibid.

17 Ibid.

CHAPTER FOUR

1 Tenzing made 12 annas a day, or three-quarters of a rupee. Tenzing/Ullman, 1955, Chapter 4.

2 The lack of Sherpa surnames often causes confusion. There were, for example, four Ang Tserings on the Himalayan Club's books. "Himalayan Porters," 1950.

3 In fact it was 16. Shipton was probably not counting Karma Paul's personal servant.

4 *That Untravelled World,* by Eric Shipton (Hodder & Stoughton, 1969).

5 Tenzing/Ullman, 1955, Chapter 4.

6 Howard-Bury et al., 1922, Chapter 17.

7 Obituary of Hugh Ruttledge, by Jack Longland, *Alpine Journal* (1962).

8 The army officers E. St. J. Birnie and Hugh Boustead, under Birnie's direction and to the fury of Percy Wyn Harris, who was climbing with them, ordered porters to descend in reasonable weather a thousand feet short of Camp V, critically delaying the expedition's progress. "The fucking soldiery!" Wyn Harris complained after the retreat. The weather was perfect for the next three days and the British missed their chance.

[9] Shipton, 1969.

[10] Ang Tharkay, 1954, Chapter 5. Author's translation.

[11] Tilman, 1948.

[12] Ang Tharkay, 1954, Chapter 5.

[13] Ibid.

[14] Ibid.

[15] *New Zealanders and Everest*, by L. V. Bryan (Read, 1953).

[16] Ullman Archive, notes for manuscript of *Tiger of the Snows*, Princeton University.

[17] "Sahibs and Sherpas," by Michael Thompson, *Mountain* 68.

[18] Only Tewang Bhotia is listed by Krenek as having been with Wilson on Everest in 1934 but Ang Tharkay is most specific that the Rinzing and Tsering Wilson took were those listed by the Himalayan Club. Wilson had sold his plane for £500 and had plenty of money to persuade experienced porters to come with him.

[19] Unsworth, 1989, Chapter 11.

[20] After working on Everest for Hugh Ruttledge's expedition in 1936, Tsering fell in love with a Tibetan girl who wouldn't leave her village for Darjeeling. Soon after getting home, Tsering was in hospital, delirious, repeating the woman's name over and over again. "He lost all hope and the spark went out of his eyes. He died a month later." Ang Tharkay, 1954, p. 76.

[21] There are several inconsistencies in Tenzing's account of this story in *Tiger of the Snows*. He talks of meeting the three after the 1935 expedition in Darjeeling, when they had been with him all along. This is most likely a construction of Ullman's and not Tenzing's. Warren, in his diary, notes that Wilson was within hailing distance of Camp III, "where Tewang was supposed to have been waiting for him." He also speculates that Wilson's tent had been blown off him. It's possible that the Tibetans, frightened at the prospect of dealing with a dying man, simply didn't investigate and that Wilson was too weak to draw their attention. We will probably never know exactly what happened and how culpable the three were.

[22] Tenzing/Ullman, 1955, p. 61.

[23] Ibid., p. 94.

[24] "A 1935 Yeti on the Rongbuk?" by George Band, *Alpine Journal* 106 (2001), pp. 153–54.

[25] Unsworth, 1989, Chapter 8.

[26] According to Judy and Tashi Tenzing in *Tenzing and the Sherpas of Everest*, Pasang Phutar tied a village headman to a tree on the Manaslu trip while he negotiated access to the mountain (p. 31).

[27] Shipton in fact considered resigning his place because he wasn't sure he could face another large-scale trip to Everest. *Eric Shipton: Beyond Everest*, by Peter Steele (Constable, 1998), p. 70.

[28] Obituary of Tenzing Norgay, by Charles Warren, *Alpine Journal* (1987), p. 288.

[29] Unsworth, 1989.

[30] *Alpine Journal* 17 (1952), pp. 159–60.

[31] *Wildlife and Adventures in Indian Forests*, by B. B. Osmaston (1999). Appendix 6: Gordon Osmaston and Tenzing.

[32] Ibid.

[33] Tenzing/Ullman, 1955, Chapter 4. Shipton may not have been as sympathetic. In his paper to the Alpine Club on their surveying expedition, he mentioned how strong the local Lata tribesmen had been as porters. "They worked splendidly and with a little training would be as good as the Sherpas."

[34] Tenzing/Ullman, 1955, p. 68.

[35] Osmaston, 1999, details. Osmaston found marks left by a team of geologists 33 years earlier. The glacier had retreated 560 yards in that time.

[36] Osmaston, 1999, p. 285.

[37] Ibid. pp. 286–88.

38 *As I Saw It: Records of a Crowded Life in India 1937–1969,* by Jack Gibson (Mukul Prakashan, 1976), pp. 14–15.

39 Ibid., pp. 20–21.

40 Ibid., p. 21.

41 Tenzing/Ullman, 1955, Chapter 5.

42 Gibson, 1976, p. 23.

43 Tenzing/Ullman, 1955, Chapter 5.

44 Gibson, 1976, p. 28.

CHAPTER FIVE

1 From Tilman, Everest 1938, Appendix A and quoted in Unsworth, 1989, Chapter 9.

2 Ang Tharkay, 1954, p. 76.

3 *The Kangchenjunga Adventure,* by F. S. Smythe (Gallancz, 1932), p. 92. It was good advice. A number of Bruce's porters had been plagued by worms and suffered ill health that prevented them from working. Tilman's porters were clear, although one was suffering from boils, and Rinzing and Pasang were suffering from alcohol poisoning.

4 Tilman, 1948, Chapter 3.

5 Tenzing/Ullman, 1955, Chapter 5.

6 Ibid., p. 224.

7 Tilman, 1948.

8 Ang Tharkay, 1954, Chapter 5.

9 Tenzing/Ullman, 1955, Chapter 5.

10 Tilman, 1938, Chapter 7.

11 Ibid.

12 Ibid, Chapter 8.

13 Tenzing/Ullman, 1955, Chapter 5. In fact, the 1930s apparatus was marginally lighter than that used in 1953, just less efficient.

14 Tilman, 1948.

15 Tenzing/Ullman, 1955, Chapter 5.

16 Tilman, 1948, Chapter 8.

17 Ibid.

18 Steele, 1998.

19 Letter to Pamela Freston, quoted in Steele, 1998, p. 95.

20 Ang Tharkay, 1954, Chapter 5.

21 Tenzing/Ullman, 1955, Chapter 6.

22 Ibid.

23 *A Taste of the Hills,* by Miles Smeeton (Hart-Davis, 1961), p. 184. The Smeetons and Tilman later became good friends.

24 Ibid., p. 185.

25 Ibid., p. 187.

26 Ibid., p. 192.

27 Ibid., p. 195.

28 Ibid., p. 187.

29 Ibid., p. 187.

30 Ibid., p. 198.

31 Tenzing thought he was Scottish.

[32] Ibid, p. 206.

[33] Gibson, 1976, p. 115.

[34] Ibid., p. 122.

[35] Tenzing/Ullman, 1955, Chapter 6.

[36] Jekyll is incorrectly identified in Ullman as "N.D. Jacob." Jekyll, the nephew of the famous gardener and writer Gertrude Jekyll, was awarded the OBE for his work in Chitral.

CHAPTER SIX

[1] To dispel the rather gloomy impression created here, it's nice to report that one of them, Sen Tensing, lived for many years to come. "The Foreign Sportsman," as Tilman dubbed him, was encountered by Eric Shipton's biographer, Peter Steele, in Khumbu in 1969. He still had his logbook from the Himalayan Club and his old boots and climbing breeches. Lhakpa Tenzing, whom Tilman described as the "Apache," had returned to Tibet.

[2] Tenzing/Ullman, 1955, Chapter 3.

[3] Interview with Trulshik Rinpoche, Nepal, February 2002.

[4] Norgay, 2001, p. 111.

[5] Tenzing/Ullman, 1955, Chapter 8.

[6] Ibid., Chapter 7.

[7] Ibid.

[8] Gibson, 1976, pp. 214–15.

[9] Ibid, p. 389.

[10] The name is a misnomer; the lake has dried out.

[11] *Alone to Everest,* by Earl Denman (Collins, 1954), p. 23.

[12] Ibid., p. 23.

[13] Ibid., p. 16.

[14] Ibid., p. 145.

[15] Ibid., p. 141.

[16] Tenzing/Ullman, 1955, Chapter 8.

[17] Denman, 1954, p. 144.

[18] Denman refers to her as Ang Nima, the name she used as an ayah.

[19] Denman, 1954, p. 146.

[20] "Himalayan Porters," 1950. Krenek is possibly referring to Ang Tharkay on Annapurna.

[21] Denman, 1954, p. 234.

[22] Ibid.

[23] Ibid., p. 211.

[24] Ibid., p. 222.

[25] Ibid., p. 230.

[26] He was less generous in an article written by Krenek for *Mountain World* based on Tenzing's information.

[27] *The Valley of Flowers,* by F. S. Smythe (Hodder & Stoughton, 1938), pp. 8–9.

[28] Ibid., pp. 127–28.

[29] The history of the Sherpas in some ways shadows the earlier history of Alpine guides; Tenzing's own family has become something of a mountaineering dynasty with three of his nephews working on Everest and his grandson Tashi running a guiding company. As in the Alps, mountaineering offered a new economic dynamic to mountain cultures.

[30] Tenzing/Ullman, 1955, Chapter 8.

[31] "The Swiss Garhwhal Expedition of 1947" by Mme A. Lohner, Mm. A. Roch, A. Sutter, & Ernst Feuz, *Himalayan Journal* 15 (1949), pp. 27–28.

[32] Tenzing/Ullman, 1955, Chapter 8.

[33] Lohner et al., 1949, p. 31

[34] Ibid., p. 32.

[35] Tenzing/Ullman, 1955, Chapter 8.

[36] Ibid., Chapter 9.

[37] *Secret Tibet,* by Fosco Maraini (Harvill Press, 2000), p. 2.

[38] *To Lhasa and Beyond,* by Giuseppe Tucci (Snow Lion, 1983), p. 11.

CHAPTER SEVEN

[1] *Annapurna,* by Maurice Herzog (Editions Arthaud, 1951), Chapter 12.

[2] Ibid.

[3] Ang Tharkay, 1954, pp. 162–63.

[4] Herzog, 1952, Chapter 20.

[5] From the suppressed "Commentaires," appended to *Carnets du Vertige,* Louis Lachenal's auto-biography, and quoted in *True Summit: What Really Happened on Maurice Herzog's First Legendary Ascent of Annapurna,* by David Roberts (Constable, 2002).

[6] Ibid.

[7] *South Col: One Man's Adventure on the Ascent of Everest 1953,* by Wilfrid Noyce (Heinemann, 1954), pp. 32–33.

[8] Ang Tharkay, 1954, p. 182.

[9] Herzog, quoted in Roberts, 2001, p. 46.

[10] Ibid., p. 187.

[11] *View From the Summit,* by Sir Edmund Hillary (Doubleday, 1999), p. 82.

[12] Gibson, 1976, p. 328.

[13] "Himalayan Porters," 1950, p. 131.

[14] Tenzing/Ullman, 1955, Chapter 11.

[15] Norgay, 2001, p. 110.

[16] Tenzing/Ullman, 1955, Chapter 12.

[17] There were several Sherpas called Pasang Phutar. This was not the man who had lost his fingers on Masherbrum and who later became Tenzing's closest friend.

[18] Tenzing/Ullman, 1955, Chapter 12.

[19] "We Challenged the World's Cruellest Mountain," by Richard Marsh, *John Bull* (February 14, 1953), p. 8.

[20] Ibid., p. 9.

[21] Howard-Bury et al., 1922, Chapter 17.

[22] Tenzing/Ullman, 1955, Chapter 12.

[23] Marsh, 1953, p. 9.

[24] Ibid., p. 22.

[25] "I Came Back Alone From Nanga Parbat," by Richard Marsh, *John Bull* (February 21, 1953), p. 25.

[26] Ibid., p. 26.

[27] Tenzing/Ullman, 1955.

[28] *Himalaya, Passion Cruelle,* by Jean-Jaques Languepin (Flammarion, 1955), p. 74. Languepin's book is one of the great unsung classics of mountaineering literature.

[29] Ibid., p. 89.

[30] Tenzing/Ullman, 1955, Chapter 13.

[31] Languepin, 1955, p. 183.

[32] Ibid., p. 221.

[33] Ibid., p. 223.
[34] Ibid., p. 224.
[35] "George Frey, In Memorian," *Himalayan Journal* 17 (1952), p. 163.

CHAPTER EIGHT

[1] Tenzing/Ullman, 1955, Chapter 14.
[2] Ullman Archive, Princeton University.
[3] Literally, "the hotel of slow death."
[4] Quoted in Tenzing and Tenzing, 2001, p. 33.
[5] *High Adventure,* by Edmund Hillary (Hodder & Stoughton, 1955), Chapter 3.
[6] Ibid.
[7] Ibid.
[8] *Visit to the Sherpas,* by Jennifer Bourdillon (Collins, 1956), p. 153.
[9] Tenzing/Ullman, 1955, Chapter 14.
[10] Ibid.
[11] *Forerunners to Everest,* by René Dittert et al. (Allen & Unwin, 1954), p. 100.
[12] Ibid., p. 138.
[13] Ibid., p. 137.
[14] Ibid., p. 143.
[15] Ibid., p. 144.
[16] Ibid., p. 146.
[17] Tenzing/Ullman, 1955, Chapter 14.
[18] Dittert et al., 1954, pp.147–48.
[19] Ibid., p. 148.
[20] Ibid., p. 151.
[21] Tenzing/Ullman, 1955, Chapter 14.
[22] Dittert et al., 1954, p. 158.
[23] Tenzing/Ullman, 1955, Chapter 15.

CHAPTER NINE

[1] This review, contained in the Ullman Archive at Princeton, was written for the *Sunday Times,* but according to a note included by Hunt was not published because of a train strike. A shorter and more negative piece was run in its place.
[2] This image of the British has persisted among some Sherpas. Tenzing's son Jamling writes, half-quoting *Tiger of the Snows:* "The English are more reserved and formal than other foreigners. They are brave, just, and fair, and even good-humoured, but in my father's day they didn't fully treat outsiders as equals. I've detected this disposition myself in older Brits."
[3] Noyce, 1954, p. 33.
[4] *Life Is Meeting,* by John Hunt (Hodder & Stoughton, 1978), p. 114.
[5] Ibid., p. 114.
[6] *The Ascent of Everest,* by John Hunt (Hodder & Stoughton, 1953), p. 57.
[7] Hillary, 1999, p. 108.
[8] Noyce, 1954, p. 32.
[9] Ibid., p. 52.
[10] Tenzing and Tenzing, 2001, p. 152.
[11] James Morris completed a change of sexual role in 1972, and has since lived and worked as Jan Morris.

[12] FO 371/106879, Public Records Office, Kew.

[13] Noyce, 1954, p. 85.

[14] Tenzing/Ullman, 1955, Chapter 16.

[15] Hillary, 1999, p. 112.

[16] "Letters From Everest," by John Hunt, *Alpine Journal* 98 (1993), pp. 10–21

[17] Hillary, 1999, p. 108.

[18] Norgay, 2001, p. 93.

[19] Hillary, 1955, Chapter 8.

[20] Hillary, 1999, p. 114.

[21] Ibid., p. 37.

[22] Ibid., p. 40.

[23] Ibid., p. 114

[24] *Coronation Everest*, by James Morris (Faber & Faber, 1958), Chapter 5.

[25] Hillary, 1955, Chapter 8.

[26] Hillary, 1999, pp. 4–5.

[27] Tenzing/Ullman, 1955, Chapter 17.

[28] Hillary, 1999, p. 5.

[29] Noyce, 1954, p. 190.

[30] Hillary, 1999, p. 116.

[31] Tenzing/Ullman, 1955, Chapter 17.

[32] Noyce, 1954, p. 188.

[33] Not to be confused with the Jockey, or with the Pasang Phutar who had lost the ends of his fingers on Masherbrum and was Tenzing's closest friend in later years, this was a third Pasang Phutar.

[34] Noyce, 1954, p. 221.

[35] *Nothing Venture, Nothing Win,* by Edmund Hillary (Hodder & Stoughton, 1975), Chapter 10.

[36] Hillary, 1955, Chapter 9.

[37] Tenzing/Ullman, 1955, Chapter 17.

[38] These heights were calculated by the American photographer and climber Bradford Washburn, after some controversy, following interviews with the relevant climbers. His conclusions are published in the *Alpine Journal* for 2003.

[39] Ullman Archive, Princeton University.

[40] Tenzing/Ullman, 1955, Chapter 18.

[41] Ibid.

[42] Ibid.

[43] Ibid.

[44] Ibid.

[45] Noyce, 1954, p. 238.

[46] Morris, 1958, Chapter 9.

[47] Ibid.

[48] Ullman Archive, Princeton University.

[49] Tenzing/Ullman, 1955, Chapter 10.

CHAPTER TEN

[1] Ullman Archive, Princeton University.

[2] Hillary, 1999, p. 23.

[3] Ibid., p. 29.

4 Tenzing and Tenzing, 2001, p. 91

5 Interview with United Press, published by the *Daily Express* on July 5, 1953.

6 All the money that the expedition generated has for 50 years provided grants to climbing expeditions through the Mount Everest Foundation.

7 Tenzing/Ullman, 1955, Chapter 19.

8 Noyce, 1954, p. 276.

9 The UPA would later merge with the Hearst organization International News Service to form UPI.

10 Noyce, 1954, p. 279.

11 Ibid., p. 284.

12 CAB 124/2924, Public Records Office, Kew.

13 Ibid.

14 Tenzing/Ullman, 1955, Chapter 18.

15 Ullman Archive, Princeton University.

16 Norgay, 2001, p. 28.

17 Tenzing was usually written as "Tensing" until 1953. He also started using the second part of his name, Norgay, sometimes spelled Norkey, around this time.

18 Norgay, 2001, p. 277.

19 Ibid., p. 276.

20 Ullman Archive, Princeton University.

21 Hillary, 1999, p. 25.

22 Tenzing/Ullman, 1955, Chapter 19.

23 FO 371/106880, Public Records Office, Kew.

24 CAB 124/2924, Public Records Office, Kew.

25 PREM 11/458, Public Records Office, Kew.

26 Hunt, 1953, p. 205.

27 "The Tensing Story," by Geoffrey Murray, *News Chronicle* (July 3-7, 1953).

28 Tenzing/Ullman, 1955, Chapter 19.

CHAPTER ELEVEN

1 Steele, 1998, p. 207.

2 *Himalayan Club Newsletter* 53, p. 54.

3 Ibid.

4 Gibson, 1976, p. 576.

5 Tenzing/Ullman, 1955, Chapter 19.

6 *Narendra Dhar Jayal 1926–1958*, by Arthur Foot, collected in *For Hills to Climb*, edited by Aamir Ali (The Doon School Old Boys' Society, 2001).

7 *Collier's*, (November 26, 1954).

8 Norgay, 2001, p. 286.

9 Letter to JRU from Walter G. Harrap, April 24, 1955, Ullman Archive, Princeton University.

10 Ullman Archive, Princeton University.

11 This seems unlikely, given the pressure Tenzing was under from other quarters, but it's clear Ullman spent a substantial period in Tenzing's company.

12 Royal Geographical Society, Everest Expedition Box 67, letter from L. P. Kirwan to John Hunt, July 12, 1954.

13 Letter from Tenzing to James Ramsey Ullman, August 7, 1954, Ullman Archive, Princeton University.

14 Letter from Tenzing to Sir John Hunt, June 14, 1954, Ullman Archive, Princeton University.

15 Letter from Sir John Hunt to Tenzing, June 8, 1954, Ullman Archive, Princeton University.

[16] Tenzing/Ullman, 1955, Chapter 20.

[17] Letter form George Pipal to James Ramsey Ullman, April 19, 1955, Princeton University.

[18] Tenzing/Ullman, 1955, Chapter 20.

CHAPTER TWELVE

[1] Norgay, 2001, pp. 85–86.

[2] *After Everest, An Autobiography of Tenzing Norgay,* as told to Malcolm Barnes (George Allen & Unwin, 1977), p. 128.

[3] Ibid.

[4] Letter from Tenzing to James Ramsey Ullman, August 3, 1964, Ullman Archive, Princeton University.

[5] Tenzing/Barnes, 1977, p. 133.

[6] "The Nanda Devi Caper," by Howard Kohn, *Outside* (May 1978).

[7] Undated prospectus sent to George Pipal in 1964, Ullman Archive, Princeton University.

[8] Letter from Tenzing to James Ramsey Ullman, November 11, 1966, Ullman Archive, Princeton University.

[9] Tenzing/Barnes, 1977, p. 13.

[10] Ibid., p. 146.

[11] Ibid., pp. 89–90.

[12] Ibid., pp. 79–80.

[13] Ibid., p. 177.

[14] Ibid., p. 178.

[15] Ibid., p. 40.

[16] Ibid., pp. 16–17.

[17] Ibid., p. 106.

[18] Hillary, 1999, p. 278.

[19] Ibid., p. 279.

[20] Ibid., p. 279.

Any unnoted quotations are from a series of interviews conducted by the author between January 2001 and October 2002, excepting quotes in Tenzing's own voice, which are from his biographies.

BIBLIOGRAPHY

THE BOOKS I DREW ON for the writing of *Tenzing: Hero of Everest* are listed below. The publisher cited is the first to have published the work in English, where available, as recorded in Jill Neate's bibliography *Mountaineering Literature*, an invaluable source for the literature of mountaineering in English. Apart from these sources, I relied heavily on the *Himalayan Journal* and the *Alpine Journal*. Individual articles in these and other journals are referenced in the notes, as are a number of useful magazine and newspaper articles.

Ali, Aamir, ed. *For Hills to Climb*. The Doon School Old Boys' Society, 2001.

Anderson, J. R. L. *High Mountains & Cold Seas: A Biography of H. W. Tilman*. Gollancz, 1980.

Ang Tharkay. *Mémoires d'un Sherpa*. Amiot-Dumont, 1954.

Aziz, Barbara Nimri. *Tibetan Frontier Families*. Vikas, 1978.

Babicz, Jan. *Peaks and Passes of the Garhwal Himalaya*. Alpinistyczny Klub Eksploracyjny, 1990.

Bernbaum, Edwin. *Sacred Mountains of the World*. University of California Press, 1997.

Bourdillon, Jennifer. *Visit to the Sherpas*. Collins, 1956.

Brower, Barbara. *Sherpa of Khumbu*. Oxford University Press, 1991.

Chan, Victor. *Tibet Handbook*. Moon Publications, 1994.

Clark, Miles. *High Endeavours: The Extraordinary Life and Adventures of Miles and Beryl Smeeton*. Prairies Books, 1991.

Coburn, Broughton. *Everest: Mountain Without Mercy*. National Geographic Society, 1996.

Coxall, Michelle, et al. *Indian Himalaya*. Lonely Planet, 1996.

Curran, Jim. *K2: The Story of the Savage Mountain*. Hodder & Stoughton, 1995.

Denman, Earl. *Alone to Everest*. Collins, 1954.

Dittert, René, et al. *Forerunners to Everest*. Allen & Unwin, 1954.

Finlay, Hugh, et al. *Nepal*. 3rd ed. Lonely Planet, 1996.

Fisher, James F. *Sherpas*. University of California Press, 1990.

von Fürer-Haimendorf, Christoph. *The Sherpas of Nepal: Buddhist Highlanders*. John Murray, 1964.

von Fürer-Haimendorf, Christoph. *Himalayan Traders*. John Murray, 1975.

von Fürer-Haimendorf, Christoph. *The Sherpas Transformed: Social Change in a*

Buddhist Society of Nepal. Sterling, 1984.

Gibson, Jack. *As I Saw It: Records of a Crowded Life in India.* Mukul Prakashan, 1976.

Gillman, Peter, ed. *Everest: The Best Writing and Pictures From Seventy Years of Human Endeavour.* Little, Brown, 1993.

Gillman, Peter, and Leni Gillman. *The Wildest Dream: Mallory, His Life and Conflicting Passions.* Headline, 2000.

Harrer, Heinrich. *Return to Tibet.* Weidenfeld & Nicolson, 1984.

Herligkoffer, Karl. *Nanga Parbat.* Elek, 1954.

Herzog, Maurice. *Annapurna.* Cape, 1952.

Hillary, Edmund. *High Adventure.* Hodder & Stoughton, 1955.

Hillary, Edmund. *Schoolhouse in the Clouds.* Hodder & Stoughton, 1964.

Hillary, Sir Edmund. *Nothing Venture, Nothing Win.* Hodder & Stoughton, 1975.

Hillary, Sir Edmund. *View From the Summit.* Doubleday, 1999.

Howard-Bury, Charles. *Mount Everest: The Reconnaissance, 1921.* Arnold, 1922.

Hunt, John. *The Ascent of Everest.* Hodder & Stoughton, 1953.

Hunt, John. *Life Is Meeting.* Hodder & Stoughton, 1978.

Hutt, Michael J., ed. and trans. *Modern Literary Nepali.* Oxford University Press, 1997.

Kapadia, Harish. *Meeting the Mountains.* Indus, 1998.

Kapadia, Harish. *Trekking and Cilmbing in the Indian Himalaya.* New Holland, 2001.

Keay, John. *The Great Arc.* HarperCollins, 2000.

Kielkowski, Jan. *Mount Everest Massif.* Explo, 1993.

Languepin, Jean-Jacques. *Himalaya, Passion Cruelle.* Flammarion, 1955.

Languepin, Jean-Jacques. *Nanda Devi: Troisième Expédition Française à l'Himalaya.* Arthaud, 1952.

Lindblad, Lars-Eric. *Passport to Anywhere.* Times Books, 1983.

Malartic, Yves. *Tenzing of Everest.* Crown, 1954.

Maraini, Fosco. *Secret Tibet.* 2nd ed. Harvill Press, 2000.

Morris, James. *Coronation Everest.* Faber & Faber, 1958.

Mason, Kenneth. *Abode of Snow.* Hart-Davis, 1955.

Mishra, Kiran. *B. P. Koirala.* Wishwa Prakashan, 1994.

Moran, Kerry. *Nepal Handbook.* 2nd ed. Moon Publications, 1996.

Murray, W. H. *The Story of Everest.* Dent, 1953.

Noel, John. *Through Tibet to Everest.* Arnold, 1927.

Norgay, Jamling Tenzing (and Broughton Coburn). *Touching My Father's Soul: A Sherpa's Journey to the Top of Everest.* HarperSanFrancisco, 2001. Published in London (with the subtitle *In the Footsteps of Tenzing Norgay*) by Ebury Press, 2002.

Noyce, Wilfrid. *South Col.* Heinemann, 1956.

O'Connor, Bill. *The Trekking Peaks of Nepal.* Crowood, 1989.

O'Malley, L. S. S. *Darjeeling, Bengal Secretariat Book.* Depôt, 1907.

Oppitz, Micahel. *Geschichte und Sozialordnung der Sherpa.* Universitäts Verlag Wagner. 1968.

Ortner, Sherry B. *Sherpas Through Their Rituals.* Cambridge University Press, 1978.

Ortner, Sherry B. *High Religion: A Cultural and Political History of Sherpa Buddhism.* Princeton University Press, 1989.

Ortner, Sherry B. *Life and Death on Mt. Everest: Sherpas and Himalayan Mountaineering.* Princeton University Press, 1999.

Osmaston, B. B. *Wild Life and Adventures in Indian Forests.* 2nd ed. Henry Osmaston, 1999.

Roberts, David. *True Summit.* Simon & Schuster, 2000.

Ruttledge, Hugh. *Everest 1933.* Hodder & Stoughton, 1934.

Ruttledge, Hugh. *Everest: The Unfinished Adventure.* Hodder & Stoughton, 1937.

Shakya, Tsering. *The Dragon in the Land of Snows: A History of Modern Tibet Since 1947.* Pimlico, 1999.

Shipton, Eric Earle. *Nanda Devi.* Hodder & Stoughton, 1936.

Shipton, Eric Earle. *Blank on the Map.* Hodder & Stoughton, 1938.

Shipton, Eric Earle. *The Mount Everest Reconnaissance 1951.* Hodder & Stoughton, 1952.

Shipton, Eric Earle. *The Six Mountain-Travel Books.* Diadem, 1985.

Shipton, Eric Earle, and H. W. Tilman. *Tilman, Nanda Devi, Exploration and Ascent.* Bâton Wicks, 1999.

Smeeton, Miles. *A Taste of the Hills.* Hart-Davis, 1961.

Smythe, F. S. *The Valley of Flowers.* Hodder & Stoughton, 1938.

Smythe, Frank. *The Six Alpine/Himalayan Climbing Books.* Bâton Wicks, 2000.

Somervell, T. Howard. *After Everest: The Experiences of a Mountaineer and Medical Missionary.* Hodder & Stoughton, 1936.

Steele, Peter. *Eric Shipton: Beyond Everest.* Constable, 1998.

Stevens, Stanley F. *Claiming the High Ground: Sherpas, Subsistence and Environmental Change in the Highest Himalaya.* University of California Press, 1993.

Stobart, Tom. *Adventurer's Eye.* Odhams Press, 1958.

Tenzing, Judy, and Tashi Tenzing. *Tenzing and the Sherpas of Everest.* HarperCollins, 2001.

Tenzing Norgay (in collaboration with James Ramsey Ullman). *Tiger of the Snows: The Autobiography of Tenzing of Everest.* Putnam, 1955. Published in London as *Man of Everest.* George Harrap, 1955.

Tenzing Norgay (as told to Malcolm Barnes). *After Everest: An Autobiography of Tenzing Norgay.* George Allen & Unwin, 1977.

Tilman, H. W. *The Ascent of Nanda Devi.* Cambridge University Press, 1937.

Tilman, H. W. *Nepal Himalaya.* Cambridge University Press, 1952.

Tilman, H. W. *Mount Everest 1938.* Cambridge University Press, 1952.

Tilman, H. W. *The Seven Mountain-Travel Books.* Diadem, 1983.

Tucci, Giuseppe. *To Lhasa and Beyond: Diary of the Expedition to Tibet in the Year 1948.* Newton Compton, 1980.

Unsworth, Walt. *Everest.* Oxford Illustrated Press, 1989. The heavily extended 3rd ed. was published by Bâton Wicks, 2000.

Unsworth, Walt. *Encyclopaedia of Mountaineering.* Hodder & Stoughton, 1992.

Unsworth, Walt. *Hold the Heights.* Hodder & Stoughton, 1993.

Ward, Michael, *In This Short Span.* Gollancz, 1972.

Webster, Ed. *Snow in the Kingdom.* Mountain Imagery, 2000.

INDEX

GLOSSARY

Ang Lhamu was Tenzing's second wife, a Sherpani born in Darjeeling to a family from Thamo in Khumbu.

Ang Tharkay was arguably the greatest sirdar of the early Sherpas and Bhotias who worked as mountain guides and porters. Born in Khumbu in 1909, poverty drove him to Darjeeling to seek his fortune. He worked extensively with the British in the 1930s, and later gained fame as the French sirdar on Annapurna in 1950.

Ang Tsering was a first cousin of Dawa Phuti, Tenzing's first wife. Born in 1904, he was on the 1924 expedition to Everest and worked for the Germans on Nanga Parbat in 1934. He died in 2002. His younger brother Ajiba worked with Tenzing on Everest in 1952.

Béyül Khenbalung is the sacred and mythical area in which Tenzing was born.

Bhotia is a catch-all term meaning a Tibetan, whether or not they were born within the geographical boundary of Tibet.

Busti is a slum, or shantytown.

Chingdu was Tenzing's older brother. After his death, his son Topkay was hired by the Swiss expedition of 1952. Chingdu's wife was, like Tenzing's mother, called Kinsum.

Da Tenzing was a Sherpa born in 1907 who worked on Everest in 1953 and was later sirdar for the British on Kangchenjunga in 1955. Unimpressed by modernity, he retained a strong traditional sense of his ethnicity. His wife committed suicide after hearing erroneously that both her husband and son had been killed in climbing accidents. His younger brother Anullu was also on Everest in 1953.

Daku, whose full name was Dawa Phuti, was Tenzing's third wife. Twenty-six years his junior, she was born in Chienyak near Thame in Khumbu. They had four children, Norbu, Jamling, Deki and Dhamey.

Dawa Phuti was Tenzing's first wife, born at Thame Og in Khumbu to wealthy parents. She eloped with Tenzing in the early 1930s. They had three children, a son Nima Dorje, who died in 1939, and two daughters, Pem Pem and Nima.

Dawa Thondup was born in Khumbu in 1907 but migrated from Khumbu at the same time as Tenzing. They worked on several expeditions together, including Gangotri in 1947 when Tenzing was made sirdar and Everest in 1952 and 1953.

Dolka Marpa was a house servant at the house at Tsa who cared for Mingmar during his final illness.

Dzatrul Rinpoche, whose name was Nawang Tenzing Norbu, was the great religious leader of the Dingri region whose catalysing influence saw a great resurgence in Buddhism in the Everest region.

Kama Valley is the sacred region below the east face of Everest where Tenzing's parents looked after their yaks during the summer.

Kasang was the oldest son of the family at Tsa, for whom Tenzing's parents worked in their latter years. He married Tsering Bhuti Dingsta who now lives in the exiled Tibetan community in Kathmandu.

Kesang was Tenzing's oldest brother. He died during the war.

Khamba is the term used by Sherpas for Tibetan immigrants to Khumbu.

Kharta is the valley to the east of Everest where Tenzing's parents had a small farm.

Kinzom was Tenzing's mother, born in Chongda in the valley immediately north of Kharta.

Kipa was Tenzing's oldest sister, the mother of Gombu, who married Nawang, the younger son of the landowner at Tsa.

Mingmar was Tenzing's father, a yak herder for a monastery in the Kharta region whose herds perished some time in the 1920s precipitating the family's migration.

Nangpa La is the high snowy pass at 18,753 feet between Khumbu and Tibet, often referred to by Kharta residents as the Khumbu La.

Nauche, also known as Namche Bazar, is the "capital" or market town of Khumbu and the Sherpas.

Pasang Phutar is another common Sherpa name. Tenzing's great friend Pasang Phutar was born in 1910 and after several successful expeditions including Kabru and Nanda Devi, lost his fingers on Masherbrum in 1938. Another Pasang Phutar was "the Jockey," who was also close to Tenzing but was dismissed from the British expedition for trouble-making.

Rinzing was a Tibetan mountain porter who went to Everest before the war with the British, particularly the self-fantasist Maurice Wilson in 1934, and worked with Tenzing in Chitral. He died in 1947.

Rongbuk is on the north side of Everest and is where Dzatrul Rinpoche established an important monastery. The base camp for expeditions is a short distance beyond it, near the snout of the Rongbuk Glacier.

Sherpas are an ethnically Tibetan tribe who have migrated over several centuries to several regions of Nepal, particularly in the region immediately south of Everest.

Sonam Doma, also Sona Doma, was Tenzing's younger sister. When she died in 1956 of heat stroke, Tenzing and Ang Lhamu took care of her four daughters.

Thakchey was Tenzing's older sister.

Trulshik Rinpoche was the second abbott of the monastery at Rongbuk established by Dzatrul Rinpoche, currently in exile at Junbesi in Nepal. He was related to Tenzing's mother.

Tsa is the village in the Dzakar Chu valley where several of Tenzing's immediate family lived and worked.

Tshechu is the holy lake located in Béyül Khenbalung. Tenzing was born on its shore in 1914.

Yueba is a substantial village in the Kharta Valley proximate to the dzongpen's house at Kharta Shikar.

ACKNOWLEDGMENTS

He has no written records for the writer to examine and exploit, no diaries, no letters
written with his own pen, no note of any kind of any event as it happened.
MALCOLM BARNES, *After Everest*

A LARGE NUMBER of people have given me a great deal of help in
the research and writing of this book. I owe a particular debt to
those members of Tenzing's family who gave me so much of their time
and advice, particularly Pem Pem Tshering in Darjeeling but also Nima
Tenzing Galang in Manila and Judy and Tashi Tenzing in Sydney. I am
also grateful for the advice and information provided by a number of
Sherpas in Darjeeling, including Tenzing's nephew Nawang Gombu, the
distinguished Indian mountaineer Dorje Lhatoo, Ang Tsering, who despite
his great age had clear memories of events up to 80 years before, his son
Da Temba who sadly passed away in 2001, his brother Tharchen Sherpa,
and many others in the Darjeeling Sherpa community. Ang Tsering himself died in 2002.

I was only able to piece together Tenzing's early life—to the extent
that I have—with the help of a number of older Tibetans in Kharta, particularly Dolka Marpa, Tenzing's family at Dangsar and elsewhere in the
Kharta Chu Valley, and the yak herders of the Kama Valley who shared
their experiences and knowledge of this beautiful and holy region. I was
very fortunate to be guided around the Kharta and Kama Valleys by
Kalsang Marpa. The first part of this book relies heavily on the advice,
introductions, and patient questioning Kalsang performed on my behalf.

As a yak herder who left Tibet for an education and the chance of work, he has lived a life that in some ways mirrored Tenzing's. I'm also grateful to my friend the photographer Ray Wood who spent some time in Tibet waiting for me to get on with it.

I am grateful to a number of authors and editors who have written or are in the process of writing or have edited articles and books that touch on the life of Tenzing and who offered their advice beyond what they had already published. Tony Astill, who is writing an account of the 1935 Everest Reconnaissance, gave me a great deal of help on this subject. The 1935 trip is probably the only expedition before about 1988 that didn't have a book written about it so his contribution plugs an important gap. Ed Webster, who spent time in Kharta and the Kama Valley during the 1988 Kangshung Face Everest expedition, was a regular correspondent who gave me a great deal of help. Trevor Braham, whose contributions to the *Himalayan Journal* were a valuable source, also gave me a crucial insight into the world of Darjeeling in the 1930s and 1950s. I am also grateful to Judy and Tashi Tenzing, authors of *Tenzing and the Sherpas of Everest*, and Peter Steele, author of *Eric Shipton*. Audrey Salkeld, who holds the largest private archive on Everest in the world and has been endlessly supportive over the years, has again helped me with this project.

A number of libraries gave me a lot of help, particularly the Alpine Club Library in London. The librarian there, Margaret Ecclestone, went far beyond meeting my requests in rooting out references she thought might interest me. I would also like to thank Margaret Sherry and her staff who made available the James Ramsey Ullman Archive held at the Firestone Library at Princeton, and the Royal Geographical Society, particularly Joanna Scadden in the picture library.

There are a number of others I would like to thank either for contributing directly to the book or for simply offering hospitality when I was a long way from home:

Stan Armington; George Band; Simon Bolton; Jennifer Bourdillon; Lisa Choegyal; Brot Coburn; Ingrid Cranfield; Wade Davis; Vishnu Prasad Dhital; Kamal Mani Dixit; Kanak Mani Dixit; Jim Edwards; Sir Charles Frossard; Noli Galang; Roy Greenwood; Heinrich Harrer; Liz Hawley; Donna Heeps; Sir Edmund Hillary; Tom Hornbein; Charles

Houston; the late Lord John Hunt; Michael Hutt; Katie Jacobs; Paul Knott; John Lagoe; Daniel Lak; Annette Lambert; George Lowe; Fosco Maraini; Kalden Norbu; Henry Osmaston; Myles Quin; Ang Rita; the late Jimmy Roberts; Gurdial Singh; Lt. Col. H.R.A. Streather; Salil Sumadra; Norbu Tenzing; Dharma Raj Thapa; Trulshik Rimpoche; the late Oliver Turnbull; Sonam Tshering; Stephen Venables; Kaye Weatherall; Sally Westmacott; Mike Westmacott; Ken Wilson; Charles Wylie; Ngawang Tenzin Zangbu.

I'd also like to thank my editor Kevin Mulroy, and Johnna Rizzo, also at National Geographic, for helping to make the writing of this book such a pleasurable experience.